Parent-Focused
Child Therapy

Parent-Focused Child Therapy

Attachment, Identification, and Reflective Functions

Edited by
Carol Wachs and Linda Jacobs

ROWMAN & LITTLEFIELD PUBLISHERS, INC.
Lanham • Boulder • New York • Toronto • Plymouth, UK

Published in the United States of America
by Jason Aronson
An imprint of Rowman & Littlefield Publishers, Inc.

A wholly owned subsidiary of
The Rowman & Littlefield Publishing Group, Inc.
4501 Forbes Boulevard, Suite 200, Lanham, Maryland 20706
www.rowmanlittlefield.com

Estover Road
Plymouth PL6 7PY
United Kingdom

British Library Cataloguing in Publication Information Available

Library of Congress Cataloging-in-Publication Data

Parent-focused child therapy : attachment, identification, and reflective functions /
edited by Linda Jacobs and Carol Wachs.
    p. cm.
  Includes bibliographical references and index.
  ISBN-13: 978-0-7657-0468-9 (cloth : alk. paper)
  ISBN-10: 0-7657-0468-4 (cloth : alk. paper)
  1. Child psychotherapy—Parent participation. 2. Parent and child. I. Jacobs,
Linda, Ph.D. II. Wachs, Carol.
RJ505.P38P37 2006
618.92'8914—dc22
2006004746

Printed in the United States of America

♾ ™The paper used in this publication meets the minimum requirements of
American National Standard for Information Sciences—Permanence of Paper for
Printed Library Materials, ANSI/NISO Z39.48-1992.

For Sophie, Laura, Luke, and Callie;
graced by their parents' reflective functioning.
— LJ

For Nadine and Isabelle and
for their real friends, Tiger and Moosey.
— CW

This collection of papers was compiled for the increasing number of clinicians who have pursued clinical work with parents despite the prevailing approaches that focus on work with children in individual child therapy or family therapy. It is often difficult to intervene directly with primary caregivers and to forego direct interventions with children. It is our hope that this volume will promote and facilitate parent-focused work. Over the years we have been contacted by many clinicians whose child therapy has focused on enhancing the parent-child relationship and who feel that their work has not received sufficient support and recognition. This volume was written for all child therapists who wish to engage in a dialogue with other clinicians working directly with parents.

—Linda Jacobs and Carol Wachs

Contents

1

Introduction

Carol Wachs and Linda Jacobs

Much recent literature on child therapy has pointed increasingly to the efficacy of working with parents; there is a developing appreciation for and
focus on the parent-child relationship, and therefore, greater numbers of clinicians are turning to work with parents as a primary modality in the amelioration of children's problems. The contributions of relational theory, infant
research, and attachment theory, over the past several decades, have done
much to create this paradigmatic shift—a shift that reasserts the centrality of
the parent-child relationship. The idea of the identified patient, used prominently in the family therapy literature, frequently represented the child as a
repository or reflector of unexpressed systemic conflicts. Although this model
tended to de-emphasize or even negate the contributions of individual personalities, it did influence a relational psychoanalytic model, which sees the
child as a participant in a complex behavioral matrix in which treatment
interventions can occur. Neuroscientific research has also furthered the growing awareness of the bidirectional regulatory processes that are continually
operating between caretaker and child; thus, the neurobiological and temperamental sensitivities the infant is born with engage the parent in specific
ways, exerting additional influence on parenting style, which then, in turn,
continue to contribute to the child's behavior.

In our book on parent therapy (2002), we proposed a shift in the treatment
of children that sought to circumvent some of the possible negative effects of
involving children directly in the treatment setting. Underlying this idea was
an attempt to avoid the potential disempowering of parents, which frequently occurs as a consequence of the therapist's replacing the parent as the
ultimate expert on the child and the parent's relinquishing the self-representation as the child's primary advocate. A predominant theme in our book on
parent consultation focused on the repercussions of child treatment on the
dynamics of family life: the stigmatization of the child and the potential for
unconscious vilification and exclusion of the parents. For future parental efficacy, we need to consider the implications of the therapist becoming a more
effective parent to the child. Moreover, attachment research has suggested

that the formation of character and the psychic life of the child are inextricably entwined with the relationship with the caregiver.

The essential concept underlying attachment theory rests on the idea that children rely on primary attachment figures to form a secure foundation from which to explore their environment. The security of the attachment thus has significant implications for the child's capacity to form other relationships and to engage in interpersonal experience in childhood and later on throughout life. Research has indicated that the freedom to explore, the capacity to modulate impulses and affective states, and the capacity for positive relationships are founded on a secure base with attachment figures (Stroufe 1996, 7).

Attachment theory as reflected in the work of John Bowlby (1969, 1973) focuses on the parent-child interactions as the basis of "internal working models"—internal structures that form the foundation for the intrapsychic and interpersonal life of the child. Underlying developmental attachment theory is the idea that the main source of emotional well-being and self-esteem, indeed, the very launching pad for the child's future endeavors, is a secure relationship with primary caretakers. Conversely, the main source of anxiety, and therefore a powerful motivational force for the child, is anything that intrudes on the stability of the bond with attachment figures. This seems to present credible support for the idea that much of children's behavior is shaped by the nature of the relationship to parental figures and the perceptions of parental values and expectations.

Mary Ainsworth's (Ainsworth et al. 1978) seminal research on attachment experience categorized children's attachment as *secure, avoidant,* or *ambivalent* in the face of brief separations from the caregiver. The *secure* child, though distressed by separation, was able to trustingly reengage upon reunion with the caregiver. The *avoidant* group did not seek contact or comfort but avoided the caregiver on the reunion after separation. The *ambivalent* group became extremely upset on separation, could not be consoled by the stranger, and was not consoled on reunion with the caregiver. This group tended to alternate between contact seeking and angry resistance. Mary Main (Main and Solomon 1986) added a fourth dimension in reviewing Ainsworth's work: the *disorganized* group. This group displayed contradictory behaviors in the presence of the caregiver; although they made attempts to approach, they did so with averted gaze or fearful affect. In general, what is understood from this research is that children's behaviors are integrally correlated with the quality of care-giving. The insecurely attached children had generally less reliably soothing care and were thus less trusting. The avoidant group had caregivers who tended to rebuff their children specifically at times when the children exhibited dependency needs. We can see from this research that it is difficult to separate the behaviors of children from the behaviors of their caregivers. Most importantly, these patterns, which develop in childhood through interactions with primary caretakers, were later correlated with relationship experience in adult life. Histories of secure attachment were found to be related to attributes such as autonomy and the capacity for positive relationships (Stroufe 1989, 1996). Main's amplification of Ainsworth's research introduced the idea that the capacity for positive adult relationships is correlated with the individual's early attachment experience. Her development of the Adult Attachment Interview shed new light on the influence, later in life, of the child's early attachments. Established from this work was the idea that secure attachments in childhood led to autonomous experience later on and thus lends further support for an emphasis on the predominance of the parent-child relationship, which continues to pervade relational life into adulthood. Main's Adult Attachment Interview provides clear evidence of the generational transmission of attachment experience. The Adult Attachment Interview explores adults' reconstructions of early relationships. A secure pattern of childhood attachment correlates with interviews that are characterized by positive and realistic recollections of childhood. The interview that is *dismissive* is marked by a denial and lack of recall of the specific effects of the actual interpersonal environment. More importantly, perhaps, is the fact that research has linked the security of the child's attachment to parental capacities for reflection. We have emphasized here the attachment experience in our focus on consulting with parents to ameliorate the difficulties that have traditionally placed the child in the consulting room. The enduring nature of the effects of the parent-child relationship is a concept supported by Fonagy and Target (1998), who note that this relationship can either facilitate or impair the reflective capacities that affect adult relational capacities, which include the child's future parenting capacities. In his discussion of relationship disturbances, Thomas Anders (1989) makes the assumption that it is a disturbed relationship that leads to disordered behavior in the infant. He suggests that it is unlikely that psychopathology can be sustained in an individual infant alone because most psychological and behavioral syndromes of infancy disturbance occur in the context of relationships.

According to Anders, relationships regulate behavior at many levels of organization. Any disruption in a regulatory function is associated with pathology, not in the individual alone, but rather in the relationship. He posits six patterns that can disturb the functional status of relationships. They include appropriate regulation, overregulation, underregulation, inappropriate regulation, irregular regulation, and chaotic regulation. Anders found that, in diagnosing a relationship, an evaluation of individuals and their relationship in three areas of assessment are required. These areas include the current state of the relationship and its history; an evaluation of each partner in the relationship as an individual; and the family's socioeconomic circumstances, current stresses, and social supports. An appropriately regulated relationship has dynamic properties, which include synchrony, reciprocity, engagement, and attunement. In an overregulated relationship, the caretaker is intrusive and insensitive, and the child is not given the opportunity to initiate or direct his or her own interactions. This may lead to infant behavior that is excessively clingy or actively avoidant. An underregulated relationship lacks inhibition and mutual involvement is low. When the caregiver is chronically inattentive, emotional avoidance, as well as withdrawal and isolation, become internalized, in some form, in the child. Inappropriate regulation also takes place when infants are given controls that are inappropriate to the age or developmental age, and this too can lead to negative interactions. According to Fonagy, these types of disruptions in the mutual regulation of interactions are most common when parents' reflective functions are impaired. We also see compromised interactions when temperamentally sensitive infants and children have negative effects on the capacities of the caregiver. Psychopathology is, under these conditions, a consequence of the neurobiological difficulties with which the infant is endowed and which then tax parental capacities and mutual regulatory processes. It is for this reason that the enhancement of parental reflective capacities may be the most effective approach for the amelioration of childhood problems.

In his analysis of a young child with profound separation fears, Anders, with a relational perspective in mind, does not focus on individual symptomatology but rather emphasizes the relational environment, even over generations, in which the child is embedded. He elucidates the inappropriate regulation in a mother's relationship with her son, which is characterized by struggles over the child's autonomy and the mother's independence. The child's clinging is correlated with the mother's own unresolved issues of separation. One of the critical points that Anders emphasizes is that the mother's relationship with her own mother was characterized by dependency and difficulty in separating and that, not coincidentally, she has developed the same type of relationship with her son. In other words, Anders finds evidence of inappropriate regulation, which began with the mother-daughter relationship and continues or is transmitted to the son through the mother's characteristic way of relating to others. Her son's dependency is a reflection of her own dependency because her internal model is one of dependency. One of the implications of Anders work is the idea that the child's internal life can be significantly affected by changes in the internal life of the parent.

This, of course, echoes Selma Fraiberg's (Fraiberg, Adelson, and Shapiro 1975) work, in which the transmission of parenting style from one generation to another has significant implications for the developmental life of the child. It supports the idea that the development of character is integrally related to the relational experience of the individual and focuses on the prominence of the intersubjective world of mother and child.

Stephen Seligman (2003) describes the "relational baby" as being alert to the outside world from the very beginning and also motivated from the beginning by social interests. He suggests that early development is continuous with later experience since it is the early relationships that organize adult experience. Thus, relational thinking shifted the assumptions about development; it is interpersonal processes that were understood as the primary organizers of self and object experience. Through this historical movement, the focus of attention shifted to the parent-child dyad. Furthermore, Seligman goes on to discuss the implications of this shift for analytic work. He states: "Applied to analytic clinical work, the image of the infant and parent as a dyadic mutual influence system supports the emerging relational-intersubjectivist conception of analysis as a fundamentally two-person process. . . . Interventions are mediated in the interpersonal-intersubjective process, rather than in the isolated mind" (483). Seligman's points are reflective of the seminal research in infant development that has elucidated the bi-directional, mutual influence between caretaker and child and, furthermore, has critical importance for our current thinking about therapeutic intervention with children.

The literature on reflective functions, conceptualized by Fonagy and Target (1996, 1998), further implicates the parent-child relationship in developing the psychological and cognitive capacities of the child. The capacity to both modulate and tolerate affect and to empathize with the experience of others is rooted, many believe, in the capacity to reflect on experience in general. From the earliest interpersonal interactions, the mother functions to transform events into meaningful experience by providing a sense of safety in the face of affectively charged events. By transforming moments of heightened affective arousal and anxiety into verbalized form, the mother creates an atmosphere in which the child can metabolize experience without becoming overwhelmed. Fonagy (2001) states that

> reflective function enables children to be able to conceive of others' beliefs, attitudes, feelings, desires, hopes, knowledge, imagination, pretense, plans, and so on. At the same time as making others' behavior meaningful and predictable, they are also able flexibly to activate from multiple sets of self-other representations the one most appropriate in a particular interpersonal context. Exploring the meaning of actions of others is crucially linked to the child's ability to label and find meaningful his or her own experience. (165)

Daniel Gensler has enumerated the many ways in which parents find the extrafamilial psychotherapy of their child to be disruptive to their sense of themselves as adequate, competent, and benign in their parenting. He points to the enormous range of ways in which direct work with parents benefits both them and, ultimately, their children. "This range of possibilities includes parent guidance and education, providing a model or mentoring parental behaviors." He suggests that in these ways parents can be helped to create a more facilitating environment or therapeutic milieu in the home. Underlying some of these points is Gensler's awareness that some parents who are encountering problems with their children were themselves never adequately cared for in "the way that the therapist would now have them take care of their child [and] may now be so envious of the child for getting what they never got" and for having the opportunity through the therapist to receive that kind of care. That many parent consultations result in extended therapy for the parents is also alluded to by Gensler, and he poignantly describes how the therapist must often focus empathically on the parents' needs first, which, in turn, can lead to greater empathic capacities on the part of parents toward their own child.

This book is compiled of chapters about child treatment approaches that are parent focused. Consulting with the parent and intervening at the level of the relationship that is both vital to the child and that is the most abiding in the child's life is an integral part of the work presented here. The chapters represent a variety of theoretical perspectives; many of them differ from our original relationally informed psychoanalytic conception. Some of the clinicians represented here include the child in parts of the treatment process. However, what binds them together is a conviction or an implicit acknowledgment that engaging the parent in therapeutic work with children is of the utmost importance and has the greatest potential for the amelioration of psychological difficulties.

Elizabeth Berger's discussion addresses both the subject of parenting in our culture and the issue of how the mental health field approaches the parents of troubled children. Her position focuses on the insufficient emphasis, in general, on the importance of the emotional ties between parent and child and the idea that our field does too little to strengthen, or even explore this most crucial of relationships. Berger's concern is that, rather than help parents think in a meaningful way about who their children are, little is done among child guidance professionals to promote attentiveness, curiosity, or even mindfulness about children by their parents; conversely, parents are seldom encouraged to think about the child's subjective, interior experience at all. She believes that parents are actually actively discouraged from thinking about their children's motivations, thoughts, and feelings. In a culture that emphasizes behavioral outcomes, children's behavior becomes a reflection of parental success or failure, so that exploration or interest in individuality and the subjectivity of the child's experience is often precluded. Berger contends that this often leads to the ubiquitous, unnecessarily severe adolescent rebellion. She suggests that, by virtue of inadequately developed intimacy between parents and children, true independence is disallowed by the push to develop premature independence in the early years.

In her chapter, Berger argues for a greater promotion of more meaningful, less behaviorally driven, independence, derived from a fuller, richer parent-child relationship in which the child admires and therefore emulates the parent. We have included this chapter in the book because of the eloquence with which Berger makes a plea for parents to be encouraged—allowed even—to reflect on and empathize with the inner meaning of their children's internal experience.

Ester Cohen's chapter "Parental Level of Awareness" offers therapists who engage directly with parents a perspective and framework with which to approach the parent consultation. In a sense, offering this schematic approach is akin to providing parents with a developmental sequence that can aid in the understanding of their children's issues and help their interactions achieve greater fluidity.

Cohen addresses the different developmental levels that parents have achieved and which are defined by their capacity to appreciate the subjectivity of their child and to foster genuine autonomy. She focuses on ways to help parents develop greater reflective functions and pays particular attention to the degree of impairment that the parent brings to bear on the parent-child relationship. According to this conceptual scheme, parenting capacities reflect four developmental levels: the narcissistic, in which parenting style derives primarily from the parent's own needs; the conventional, in which parenting style is determined by the desire to conform to social norms; the child centered, in which the parent attends exclusively to the perspective of the child even when this conflicts with the needs of others; and the mutual/relational, in which the child is seen as a separate person with independent thoughts and feelings, which are then integrated realistically into family life. By identifying the overarching themes in parents' attitudes toward their children, therapists are provided with a perspective about the level of impairment in parental reflective capacity and can thus develop ways in which to assist parents at their level. Approaching parents at their assessed developmental level allows the therapist to target interventions in such a way that can be best absorbed. This, in turn, can foster parents' appreciation of the developmental capacities of their children.

Parents are seen as being primarily at one level, with moments of greater- or less-developed capacities. Furthermore, Cohen highlights the ways in which the experience of heightened anxiety, for example, during difficult phases of development, medical illness, or financial stress, can cause parents to revert to less optimal parental functioning than is their norm. In these instances, which can result in a referral for parent consultation (or in treatment for the child), therapists help the parents to recalibrate their functioning to their previous higher functioning.

In his chapter on the transmission of trauma, Stephen Seligman provides a theoretical basis for the argument that interventions with the parent may prove to have the most far-reaching effect on the child's psychic experience. Seligman's description of a parent-infant interaction, in which a father forcefully ignores his baby's cues, conveys the immense power of the disavowed and projected experience of the father's feelings of helplessness and anxiety, which may come to be introjected by the infant over the course of many repetitions of similar interactions. Through extended psychotherapeutic work,

> this father became aware of how helpless he had been as a child, especially when he was beaten by his own father; how much having his own children reminded him of this; and how intolerable this feeling was for him. Thus, the father was inducing a feeling in his son that he was not able to tolerate in himself, intensified as the infant's presence evoked that feeling in him. (74)

In this vignette, we can see how, from earliest infancy, the parent who does not possess the reflective functions to hold the infant's experience in mind as separate from his own will then not be able to relate to the child empathically. The most obvious course of treatment intervention must be with the father himself if the child's object world is to be meaningfully affected by clinical intervention.

Susan Coates and Daniel Schechter, in their chapter, emphasize the ways in which a parent's capacity to contain a child's emotional reaction to traumatic events serves to provide a protective function against the possibly deleterious, even catastrophic, effects of traumatic incidents in the child's life. They point to the fact that parental avoidance, emotional numbness, or inability to engage in "remembering" proves to be the most problematic response to trauma and may perpetuate the child's posttraumatic stress. It is not simply the soothing presence of caretakers that offers this protection but also the parent's capacity to focus on the child's experience of the trauma empathically and, additionally, to help the child to imagine repair that offers this containing influence and mitigates more enduring anxiety. Coates suggests that the involvement of parents who can provide a sense of safety through the active reflection on the child's anxiety represents the most mitigating force with which to counter the effects of traumatizing experience. This can be achieved only when the parents do not become overwhelmed by their own anxieties as they attempt to facilitate the child's recovery process, which can be an immense challenge for a parent who is experiencing similar feelings. The therapist's task is seen largely as providing a containing function for the parent in order to offset the difficulties the parents may have in doing the same for their children.

Kerry Kelly Novick and Jack Novick make a lucid and convincing case for the initial evaluation phase, usually utilized primarily for information gathering, to serve, simultaneously, as an effective arena in which the therapeutic process can begin. They conceive the initial meetings as a way of establishing a collaborative approach in which the parents' own knowledge and motivation to help their child are mobilized and supported by the therapist in the service of the child. Underlying this collaborative process is the Novicks' conviction that parents' internal experience is intimately connected to their children's manifest behaviors, and that helping parents to clarify and modify their perceptions of their children's issues can serve to bring about changes in their child's experience. This, they believe, is achieved by means of enhancing the parents' reflective functions by assisting them in thinking about their children's subjective states. Many parents meet with a therapist with the intention of providing information that the therapist can use when they begin the therapeutic process with the child. The Novicks use the consultation as a way of jump-starting the therapeutic action and engaging the parents' curiosity, interest, and motivation to help their children.

The initial meeting is designed to reestablish the sense of parental competence in lieu of relinquishing their authority and parental role to the therapist. The Novicks conceive the collaborative effort of therapist and parents as a way of establishing transformations in parental experience that can change guilt into "usable concern," manifest explanations into internal meaning and motivations, and externalizations onto the child into attunement with the child. The Novicks make the argument that parent-focused work must begin at the outset, in the initial consultation, in order to achieve a therapeutic alliance that expands parental skills and bolsters parents' capacities to help their children.

The Novicks' approach, in many ways, more closely resembles the attitude put forth by many child therapists whose clinical work involves the child exclusively. We have included it in this book because it represents a shift in clinical approach from a theoretical perspective that attributes children's problems to their parents' psychopathology and therefore excludes the parent from the clinical work to an intervention that puts parents at the *center* of the therapeutic endeavor. In so doing, the Novicks have challenged other child therapists to confront the negative attributions about parents' motivations and behaviors and to convert these into a useable and productive therapeutic alliance through which parents can derive support, insight, and improved parental functioning.

Our previous book, *Parent Therapy: A Relational Alternative to Working with Children*, was based on the idea that parents should be seen in treatment exclusive of the child. However, under circumstances in which it is deemed necessary to see the child without doing a disservice to the relational life of the family, and to parental authority, the Novicks' work provides a useful guide to creating a working alliance and collaborative relationship with the parents.

Chapters 7 and 8 are on the preschool child. Both our contributors, Peter Deri and Ionas Sapountzis, suggest that effective therapeutic interventions at the earliest stages of development and into early childhood can be achieved through consultation with parents. Both therapists express concern over treatment approaches that focus exclusively on the neurobiological determinants of behavior or, conversely, exclusively on the psychogenic etiology of psychopathology. Both authors emphasize the importance of incorporating these two components of the child's experience and integrating the information into the other salient domain—the interpersonal world.

Deri explicates, in detail, the ways in which he has worked with parents to help them unravel the knot of temperament, behavior, and familial dynamics in their children's development. His approach is highly attuned to the nuances of the subtle but significant sensitivities in young children. These sensitivities, according to him, may be neurological in origin. However, the behaviors that accompany atypical brain-based anomalies of development often create unmanageable levels of anxiety and guilt in parents, and it is these feelings, as well as the child's own anxieties, which tend to exacerbate children's behavioral difficulties.

Sapountzis expresses similar concerns addressing the insufficient attention given to the parents' contribution to their children's problems. His clinical example focuses on the ways in which parental anxieties about their child's difficulties, in tandem with their own underlying anxieties about parenting, combine to exacerbate rather than ameliorate their son's discomfort and negative self-representations. Sapountzis attempts to clarify and resolve parental confusions and ambivalence when the parents' "own internal self-states interact with the child's temperamental sensitivities" (155). His work, like Deri's, attempts to facilitate in the parents an increased capacity for observation. That is, both authors strive to assist parents in seeing their children's issues with a more complex understanding of the ways in which temperament, interpersonal style, and familial contributions interact.

These two chapters elucidate the difficult task of holding multiple perspectives in mind when parents or school staff members are trying to resolve children's behavioral problems. What both clinicians ultimately strive for is to provide support for the parent, which then allows for the opportunity for a more realistic and less self-punitive perspective.

Chapters 9 and 10, on the treatment of adolescents, focus on different types of disturbances—children who internalize their problems and those who externalize or act out. James Lock, Ester Cohen, and Etan Lwow have concluded that direct intervention with parents tends to be the most effective approach with these youngsters. Traditionally, parents have been excluded from the psychotherapeutic treatment of their adolescent children because parental control has been implicated in the development of many adolescent disorders and because adolescents' need for privacy, when separating from the family, has been seen as essential to the treatment process. These authors, in contrast, view parental guilt and deferral of authority as counterproductive. Rather, they aim to empower the parents, reversing some of the difficulties that are inherent in the perception that parents are responsible for their child's disorder. They emphasize the idea that parental skills are essential to the child's recovery. Critical in these models is the conviction that only through strengthening the parents' confidence in their own ability to help their child can treatment be beneficial and effective. The overwhelming nature of the child's self-starvation or severe pathology leaves parents with varying degrees of emotional devastation and thus leaves them poorly equipped to assume the challenge of helping their child.

In "The Parent-Child Mutual Recognition Model," Cohen and Lwow circumvent the enormously difficult problem of engaging disturbed, acting-out adolescents in a therapeutic process. They conceptualize much of the difficulty experienced by these youngsters as the result of the surrender of parental authority. This helplessness on the part of the parents leaves these children without the provision of developmentally necessary guidance and support. In the treatment paradigm developed by Lwow, the clinicians engage parents in establishing boundaries; they model consistency and structure, which the parents can then incorporate into their interactions with their children. Lock, in contrast, does not purport to know the etiology of the eating disorders he treats, yet his clinical approach is similar. He helps parents to recover some of their lost esteem and also emphasizes the necessity of the parents' role in restoring their adolescents' optimal functioning.

The final chapters also focus on the therapist's role in enhancing parental capacities that, under stressful or problematic life events, are severely taxed. These capacities are, the authors believe, clearly implicated in the unfolding of children's behavioral difficulties and are therefore indispensable in the amelioration of those difficulties. In Sharon Kozberg's discussion of divorce, she points to the diminished capacities of parents whose lives are disrupted by the loss of a spouse, while Lock, and Cohen and Lwow refer to parents' failure to assume *ordinary* parental authority. These clinicians focus on assisting the parent, through empathic support, to develop greater ability to reflect on their own and their children's experience, and to consequently develop a more actively protective stance toward their troubled children.

Kozberg emphasizes the defensive behaviors that parents assume and attempts to relax these defenses through the therapist's empathy. The separation anxiety and emotional lability that accompany the rupture in the marital relationship significantly reduce parental efficacy. For the parent, the loss of the partner reactivates their own dependency need; they feel less protected and are therefore less capable of protective behavior toward their children. For Kozberg, an exploration of the parent's subjective experience has a dual purpose: it provides a holding environment for the parent, and it encourages the parent's reflection on the child's internal, affective life. She guides the parent in providing a containing environment by helping them to establish a predictable narrative of events and an understanding of the feelings that may accompany those events. This supports the idea that naming affective experience promotes a tolerance of one's feelings and transforms behavior into a digestible framework. Kozberg emphasizes the value of helping parents to imagine how their children will react to anticipated changes and uses this approach to encourage the parents' empathic stance.

Judith Harel et al. describe a model of child therapy that places primary emphasis on the parent-child relationship. Their work is based on a relational perspective and theoretical assumptions that view children's development and interpersonal experience as rooted in parental self-perceptions as well as parental perceptions of the child. Basing their clinical model on a trajectory that follows the work of Winnicott, Bion, and Fonagy (Winnicott 1965, 1971; Bion 1962; Fonagy 2001) and the relational-intersubjective approach of Stephen Mitchell (2000), they review, in this chapter, the significance of attachment and reflective functions for children's development. They begin with Fonagy's idea that the child identifies with the parent's representations of the child as a reflective self. Consultation and collaboration with parents is therefore seen as essential because of the "formative impact of parental character" (234) and perceptions, and the quality of attachment that exists between parent and child. The clinical work described here rests on the idea that the parent who is unable to reflect on their own mental processes or that of their child is not only failing to help the child develop reflective functioning but will also be less able to empathize with the child's affective experience. In consequence, they will be less able to "contain" the child's anxiety.

According to Bion, the mother transforms intolerable experience into manageable experience, thereby containing the child's anxiety. The mother's capacity to assign meaning to experience enables the baby to symbolize and internalize the capacity for mental processing. It is the failure of such processes that Harel et al. encounter in their practices and the enhancement of these functions that they attempt to foster through a therapeutic encounter that verbalizes feelings, intentions, and thoughts. Their model attempts to generate interest in the mental states of others by focusing on the parents' perception of the child's mental state. The idea here is that behavioral difficulties such as frustration intolerance, impulsivity, and the inability to modulate feelings stem, in large part, from the child's failure to have developed sufficient reflective capacities. However, these capacities are inextricably linked with the parental capacity to attend to the affective and mental life of the child.

Harel et al. make the case for working directly with parents because the potential negative therapeutic reaction when children are involved in the treatment setting is that the parents' curiosity about the child's mind is relinquished to the therapist, who, presumably, already has well-developed reflective capacities. In working with parents as the experts about their own children, the therapist is in a position to question the parents about what they think is in their child's mind. In this way the therapist creates a "shareable world of meanings" (228) with the parent, whose reflections and curiosity are further enhanced. Whereas direct work with children that excludes the parents may truncate their reflectivity, a consultation that consists of a joint endeavor between therapist and parent, and promotes the pursuit of curiosity about the child's thoughts and behaviors, can result in the parent's active and independent reflective functions. The emphasis on empowering parents underlies much of the new approach in the therapeutic models of child therapy.

Arietta Slade's chapter, which elucidates the link between attachment theory and significant aspects of the parent-child relationship, provides a clearly delineated example of the parent-focused approach to treatment. Although her work also includes individual work with the child (see Slade 1999), her treatment of a mother, whose child was experiencing severe separation anxiety, emphasizes the importance of the development of reflective functioning in the parent. Through the mother's reflection on her own separation anxieties and her own attachment history, she was, together with the therapist, able to address the child's difficulties in separating and developing relationships outside of the family. Slade provides a thoughtful explication of the ways in which the child's psychology was interdependent with the mother's and supports the theoretical basis for the fact that, in the absence of an intensive therapeutic intervention with the mother alone, the child's issues could not have been addressed as effectively. What is most deftly explored in this chapter is the power of the parent's self-representations and her representation of her child in forming a link with the *child's* developing self-representations. Slade's treatment of the mother helped her to reflect on her feelings and motivations that, in turn, enabled the development of mentalizing and symbolizing capacities in the child. These capacities then mitigated the child's separation fears. Slade considers the mother's capacity to make sense of her child's emotional experience the most important component in altering the mother-child relationship. Her theoretical perspective makes a compelling argument for the importance of parent-focused work. Her clinical descriptions are both nuanced and compassionately drawn, and provide a welcome alternative to approaches that underemphasize the parent's experience. Yosef Prinz and the Hadarim group have developed a parent- and teacher-focused program, which they have implemented in the school setting. Following a consultative paradigm, the program is designed to enhance parental capacities by developing greater reflective functioning. The unique feature of this program lies in the fact that the classroom teachers work directly with the parents of the children in their classes. In this way, the two groups with the most intimate knowledge and experience of the children collaborate in the service of those children. It not only establishes a venue for the parents to reflect on their children's subjective lives, but it also sensitizes teachers to the experience of parents. This collaboration creates an alliance between teachers and parents in the same way that the parent-therapy model binds therapist and parents in the pursuit of a common goal. The value of such an approach is that it diminishes the potential conflicts and negative transferences that can and often do exist between parents and teachers. Overall, it is designed to encourage, for both parties who work so intimately with children, a way of focusing on the positive attributes of the child. It helps them to draw upon the child's intrinsic motivations to participate in school and home life in optimal ways. Moreover, the involvement in the program provides a holding environment that produces a sense of empathic support for both teacher and parent; it develops specific parenting skills through mutual reflection on children's behaviors.

REFERENCES

Ainsworth, M. S., M. C. Blehar, E. Waters, and S. Wall. 1978. *Patterns of attachment: A psychological study of the strange situation.* Hillsdale, N.J.: Lawrence Erlbaum.

Anders, T. F. 1989. Clinical syndromes, relationship disturbances, and their assessment. In *Relationship disturbances in early childhood*, ed. A. J. Sameroff and R. N. Emde, 125–44. New York: Basic Books.

Bion, W. 1962. A theory of attachment. *International Journal of Psychoanalysis* 43:306–10.

Bowlby, J. 1969. *Attachment and loss. Vol. 1: Attachment.* New York: Basic Books.

———. 1973. *Attachment and loss. Vol 2: Separation, anxiety and anger.* New York: Basic Books.

Fonagy, P. 2001. *Attachment theory and psychoanalysis.* New York: Other Press.

Fonagy, P., and M. Target. 1996. Playing with reality. 1: Theory of mind and the normal development of psychic reality. *International Journal of Psychoanalysis* 77:217–33.

———. 1998. Mentalization and the changing aims of psychoanalysis. *Psychoanalytic Dialogues* 8(1):87–114.

Fraiberg, S., E. Adelson, and V. Shapiro. 1975. Ghosts in the nursery: A psychoanalytic approach to the problem of impaired mother-infant relationships. *Journal of the American Academy of Child Psychiatry* 14:378–421.

Gensler, D. 2002. "PsyBC" online discussion and conference on working with parents.

Jacobs, L., and C. Wachs. 2002. *Parent therapy : A relational alternative to working with children.* Northvale, N.J.: Jason Aronson.

Main, M. 1998. Adult attachment scoring and classification system. Unpublished manuscript. University of California, Berkeley.

Main, M., and J. Solomon. 1986. Discovery of an insecure-disorganized/disoriented attachment pattern. In *Affective development in infancy*, ed. T. B. Brazelton and M. W. Yogman, 95–124. Norwood N.J.: Ablex.

Mitchell, S. 2000. *Relationality: From attachment to intersubjectivity.* Hillsdale, N.J.: Analytic Press.

Seligman, S. 2003. The developmental perspective in relational psychoanalysis. *Contemporary Psychoanalysis* 39(3):477–508.

Slade, A. 1999. Representation, symbolization, and affect regulation in the concomitant treatment of a mother and child: Attachment theory and child psychotherapy. *Psychoanalytic Inquiry* 19:824–57.

Stroufe, L. A. 1989. Relationships, self and individual adaptation. In *Early childhood: A developmental approach*, ed. A. J. Sameroff and R. N. Emde, 70–94. New York: Basic Books.

———. 1996. *Emotional development: The organization of emotional life in the early years*. New York: Cambridge University Press.

Winnicott, D. W. 1965. *The maturational processes and the facilitating environment: Studies in the theory of emotional development*. New York: International Universities Press.

———. 1971. *Playing and reality*. New York: Basic Books.

I

PARENT-FOCUSED TREATMENT

2

Managing Childhood: Behavior Experts and the Eclipse of Intimacy

Elizabeth Berger

An emphasis on behavior and a mistrust of theory seem to characterize the parenting styles of most American parents today as well as the attitudes of many educators and clinicians who deal with children. This mistrust is the outcome perhaps of many forces—our overall cultural faith in pragmatic approaches and immediately observable results, a negative reaction to the lamentable tendency among previous generations of child psychologists and physicians to blame mothers for any and all of their offsprings' clinical difficulties, and a well-entrenched national skepticism of experts. The presumptive antitheoretical position embedded in the DSM-IV and its emphasis on observable behaviors has also contributed mightily to an avoidance of theory in child development and child guidance. We like things simple, and one of our favorite simplifications is to take the theory out of childhood and regard the management of childhood behavior as an end in itself—indeed, often the only end of parenting.

It is the premise of this chapter that this antitheoretical position and emphasis on behavior management so popular among parents and child experts is itself a theory—and like all theories, a perspective that emphasizes certain values and aspects of reality while obscuring others. This does not make the behavioral approach to children altogether bad, but it suggests that behaviorism may have covert and unintended limitations. I examine here in a highly speculative way some of the cultural origins and consequences of behavior management as the implicit goal of parenting. Consider the following vignettes, presented (with appropriate disguises to protect privacy) in the parents' words:

Case 1: Mother and father are professional people in their late twenties, with one daughter. Mother says,

Ashley is two and a half, and I'm having a terrible time with her behavior. I guess it's just the terrible two's, but I just don't know how to manage her. It's a lot harder than I thought. Every morning there's a scene when I get ready to leave—she clings and wails and screams. She was so good before, when she was younger, when I had to get ready. Now that she's older she's less independent somehow. I don't understand this backsliding. It's getting so I just dread being with her in the morning because I know what's going to happen when I head for the door. At the day care she's completely fine, so I know it isn't anything serious. Her behavior with me though is—I don't know—extreme. I know she just has to get over it. If I just don't give in eventually she'll settle down. And I can see the problems down the line if we give in—I mean, she just can't rule the roost here! But I'm getting to the end of my rope. I've just tried everything, and nothing works. What I really need is some new techniques.

Case 2: Jamie is nine, with twin sisters of four. Parents are concerned by the school's complaints of poor academic achievement and general immaturity in the classroom. The child tests intellectually in the average range with no specific learning or attention problems noted. Father says,

Jamie just wants to dawdle—he doesn't want to settle down and work. You tell him to do his homework or clean his room and he doesn't do it. That boy has no follow-through. I've seen this in him for a while now, but the teacher is seeing it now too. We tell him he can't go out until he's finished what he needs to do, and he just wastes the whole afternoon fiddling around. Last week he left his jacket on the school bus. We're making him earn back the money—otherwise he'll never bother to keep track of his things. We've been trying to crack down on him, but he doesn't seem to care. He just says he's finished his chores and then when you check up on him, he hasn't. How can I get him to take responsibility for himself?

Case 3: Jen is fifteen, and a good student. Her father divorced her mother and left the state when she was six. There is an older brother in college and a little brother of ten. Jen complains of depression; in fact, Jen has a secret: through a series of events in a complicated romantic triangle, she has been blackmailed by a classmate into providing oral sex to him—if she doesn't comply, he will reveal this to everyone. Jen confided this problem to her older brother, who advised her to tell their mother and to get professional help. But Jen is afraid to tell her mother, thinking, "My mother would kill me." Mother says,

I don't know what I'm going to do with Jen. She says she's depressed all the time and wants me to take her to a therapist. But I think she's just a typical angry adolescent. She's grounded now because she had a party in the house last week when she thought I was going to be at my sister's. I grounded her for a month. She's basically a good kid, but she never wants to help with anything. We have a lot of fights. She's got to learn that it's not all about her all the time.

She's got to think about other people too. The situation at home is hard on her, but it's hard on all of us.

These cases represent (one might argue fairly representative) typical parental concerns, couched in a very ordinary, everyday language probably well familiar to most working guidance counselors, social workers, family therapists, pediatricians, and other behavioral health clinicians. These are parents who are sane, concerned, well intentioned, reasonably observant, and troubled by their children's behavior. What is notable about these statements is that the parent sees himself (successfully or unsuccessfully) as the administrator of the child's behavior; the parent is concerned above all with what the child does or does not do. What is absent is the parent's assessment of what the child is experiencing, or what might be occurring within the human relationship between the parents and the child.

Why is this? It is my observation that these parents, and millions like them, are not unfeeling as human beings. They omit from their formulations both their suppositions regarding the child's presumptive experience and their understanding of the human relationship in the moment not because they are unable to conceptualize these abstractions, but because they do not perceive them as relevant to the matter at hand. This is their theory—that their job as parents is to manage their children's behavior in the here and now and that problematic behavior on the part of the child indicates a need for them to manage the child more effectively. This is a conceptual edifice of discipline and expectations, of tasks and consequences, of time frames and time-outs, of what is acceptable and not acceptable. This is the language of making rules, of being matter-of-fact and impersonal about enforcing limits. This is not a theory that concerns itself with how people feel inside or how they feel about each other. It is not a theory that concerns itself with long-term outcomes—such as the question of how children ultimately grow to be responsible, trustworthy, or caring human beings—it is a theory of making things happen right now.

Parents adhere to the administrative model of parenting because it is in the air, because it is a broadly based cultural assumption underlying popular advice that parents receive from every quarter—from public health directives, from schools, from the magazines, and from many clinical professionals. The fundamental assumption, borrowed from the principles of industrialization, is that administrators maximize the functioning of those under them through the imposition of reasonable discipline—clear directives that establish tasks, boundaries, time frames, and consequences for infractions. Who could argue with that? This is the rationale for enlightened management of the military, of educational institutions, of human resource departments, and bureaucracies everywhere. Yet there is a problem with defining parenting by this administrative approach—it is impersonal. Administration is by definition directed at generic categories of persons, not particular persons, and indeed, in order to be successful, administration is dependent upon the maintenance of strict impersonality to keep emotion and intimacy and all the psychological quirks that bedevil specific individuals completely out of the picture. But parenting isn't impersonal—quite the contrary. Being a parent is quite personal and intimate, and involves the deepest of human emotions. Parenting, like mature romantic love, calls upon our most fully realized individuality. Who would talk about romance in terms of time frames, expectations, and consequences? The very idea is laughable.

However, what one often sees clinically is that for many reasons parents are loathe to examine their own and their children's lives from an intimate angle, and one finds in the administrative parenting agenda a series of alternative preoccupations that—although these preoccupations generate their own perplexities—often act as a convenient resistance to the parent's coming to terms with emotion as it is embedded within his current life choices and relationships. The parent feels he has enough on his plate simply anticipating that the child must one day answer to the administrative demands of the world at large; concerned that the child be maximally prepared to soldier on effectively in this relentless world, the parent is in a hurry to demand that the child cope successfully with impersonal programs in the place of intimate attachments. Fears of babying, spoiling, or indulging children become thus ways of dismissing dependency as a human dynamic of any potential legitimacy within either the parent or the child; it is indeed often something of a muddle who it is that is in need of being independent, and from whom.

The mother in case 1 resembles many mothers poised at the door, briefcase in hand, uncertain how to "make the child more independent." This particular mother sought relief from a therapist who offered no techniques to achieve this as an immediate goal but rather explored in an open-ended way what the mother experienced at these times, how the mother imagined her little girl to feel, and what the mother was hoping to accomplish in the long run by making Ashley independent in this way and at this time. Through these questions, the mother recognized that she struggled with a deep sense of loss when she went to work each morning, and that her reluctance to identify this sadness was wrapped up in indirect and surprising ways with a recent pregnancy that had miscarried, with certain frustrations in her marriage, and with her own childhood—troubled by her father's withdrawal into alcoholism when she was about the age that her daughter Ashley had been at the time of consultation. This mother discovered that by holding her child at arms length, so to speak, she succeeded in protecting herself from acknowledging varied sources of her own distress. She had projected her own disavowed neediness onto the daughter—who was of course herself actually quite little and needy—and demanded that the child pull up her socks and get on with it. Without learning any special techniques in therapy, after a few months the mother found herself more alert to her daughter's emotional reactions and more responsive to them. At about this time, she became interested in reducing her position at her place of business from full time to part time, a change that allowed her to spend more time at home. This career choice meant that she was now considerably more dependent upon her husband and his salary—but she had (somehow in the midst of all this discussion) come to feel more certain that she was truly in love with her husband after all and that her marriage would last.

An administrative approach to motherhood avoids examining why children might protest and regress in the face of limited access to mother's time, attention, or (in primary process terms) the goodness and nurturance of her body. It defines as a given that there is a certain limited amount of mother to go around, and that regression is not acceptable. However, we note that the administrative approach is not the same thing as an honest admission of hardship. A financially strapped mother is likely to say as she leaves for work, "Look—I'd rather be with you too. It's just that I need this job, because we're struggling for money." The enemy is the reality, which imposes hardship from outside the relationship, and the mother and child are at least genuinely united in their regrets that a reality prevents them from arranging their lives in ways that would be happier for them both. This may dash the child's hopes of a morning together, but at least it reassures him that he and mother are on the same team, pitted against that hard reality. But the mother who chooses to work to fulfill herself, to hedge her bets against the odds of being divorced one day, or to provide more to an already financially secure household in the form of enhanced purchasing power cannot claim that she and the child are in the same boat against hardship. This mother may have a difficult time explaining to the child why it is that she is leaving; she may have a difficult time explaining this adequately to herself. The administrative approach evades legitimizing personal issues involved in the child's behavior, negating the mutuality of the interaction. The administrative approach performs an end run around the child's natural protest "Why are you leaving, Mommy?" and the feelings this protest might generate by defining the protest as irrelevant to the child's "job." His "job" is to let Mommy leave.

What the hurrying mother conveys to the needy child through the administrative model is that his need is hopelessly vast, that it is unacceptable, and that it is taboo. This sets up the child for trouble with his instinctual life insofar as it undermines his capacity to identify and master yearnings with regard to other people. He has been shown that his yearnings are illegitimate. It leaves the child with only regressive solutions, narcissistic and aggressive transformations of these yearnings, and negative images of both himself and others. The mother fears that the child is insatiable, and rather than trying to satisfy him or to validate his frustrations, she tries to stifle his urges before they have a chance to grow and assert themselves. Naturally the mother thus intent upon "making her child more independent" so that she does not feel eaten alive by his dependency often has an inkling that she is depriving the child of something of value, and experiences considerable guilt and ambivalence. But the destructive piece is not so much that the child is *left* but that he is led to understand that his rage and grief at being left have no meaning to other people. Mother is advised by the behavior experts to dismiss her ambivalence and her child's protests in the same brisk spirit. If the child is good, she will buy him something later as a reward.

The administrative approach to phasing out the child's babyish behavior becomes a matter of encouraging him to disavow the pressure of his own wishes, rather than encouraging him to understand them and master them through mutual dialogue, action, thought, or symbolic play. The parent typically experiences the most inner conflict, and the most overt conflict with the actual child, when the parent "doesn't have all day" to devote to the child and his ridiculous insistence that his socks do not feel right, or similar complaints. The child's fussing and carrying on is viewed as manipulation, insofar as mother has an intuition that this is not really about socks. It is part of an overall dance, in which the child approaches and the mother avoids. An administrative approach precludes examining the interaction from a perspective that might reveal this dimension or open it for negotiation; however, the child simply needs to get out the door to his playgroup.

It cannot be entirely accidental that a vocabulary of parenting that is relatively empty of human meaning, emotion, and attachment has come to dominate our popular approach to children at a time when the structure of society itself seems increasingly dominated by impersonal transitions. In an era of rapid displacements, the administrative model of parenthood is perhaps only one manifestation of an entire cultural pattern of emotional engagement that is time limited, partial, reward contingent, and episodic—a new spin on family life that is based on the likelihood of short-term arrangements and impermanent attachments. An administrative model of human affairs both inherits its metaphors from the industrial marketplace and reinforces its values in psychological life—emphasizing an unsentimental coping with stress and a relatively businesslike denial of the meaning of loss.

This is the new family so often encountered in advice-seeking contexts, where the claims of the workplace are embraced without much discussion and the timing and content of any intimacy must take shape in the margins lying about the relatively inflexible contours of the parents' employment. This used to be the domain of fathers ("Don't wake up Daddy—he needs to get up early!") but now is one of those prerogatives shared by both genders. Where does this leave the child? The child whines and clings, naturally, in a primitive effort to extract from his elders some time and attention—just what neither of them appear disposed to give willingly. Affect-hungry and irritable, the child experiments with one form of childishness after another in an attempt to coerce the evaporating parents into accessible form. But here enters the administrative agenda and vocabulary, which defines the child's behavior as unacceptable. The emotional significance of the clinging—that the child naively still clutches onto his silly hopes of intimate attachments— is not relevant to any of the participants. Instead, the parent (lest he or she be tempted to give in, to be inconsistent) is cowed by the assertion that it is the parent's *job* to make the child independent, that the child simply needs to get used to it, and indeed, that the child's immature fussing and ranting potentially stigmatizes the youngster as a poorly equipped competitor in the all-important race to achievement.

This dynamic tends to reinforce itself: the more clingy the child, the more the parent yearns to run to the office for relief. As family life becomes increasingly problematic, anxiety-ridden, and confusing for many adults, so their professional lives become correspondingly engrossing, enlivening, and validating. The child's early disappointment in love, so to speak, is a suitable preparation in the long run for his future role as an individual prepared to travel light in the sphere of human commitments, to accept solace in the form of shallow engagements and material things. What began as the child's affective hunger—his craving for the personal interest and intimate involvement with his parents as specific human beings—has become effectively transformed into a hunger for other things altogether. The child has become greedy not for people but for substitutions—commodities or stimulations available at the mall. It is somehow easier for parents today to deal with this material greed than with the original psychological neediness; the new greed is conceptualized in behavioral terms and dismissed with cynicism. As for his ambivalence about close human relationships and his difficulties with trust—why, the kid is a chip off the old block!

The father in case 2 confronts a situation seen with regularity in guidance offices and consulting rooms—a school-aged child who is not motivated to accomplish all the usual tasks in the classroom or at home, a puzzling affair to his father since the father has been busy applying the typical carrots and sticks to no avail. Here, the administrative model on the surface would appear to hold more promise as a way of understanding and responding to the latency-age child—latency being a most industrious period for most children, wherein the child is especially in love with mechanisms and rules, with order and discipline, and with regimented systems of all sorts. But in order for any child to make use of the opportunities afforded by school (or, in a broader context, to the varied apprenticeships to adult skills and techniques afforded by any culture to its latency-age children), the child must have consolidated within himself certain expectations about himself and the world of other people, developmental milestones in human relations and personal maturity.

The therapist learned that Jamie had been three when his mother became pregnant with twins, a pregnancy complicated by medical conditions requiring bed rest and a subsequent delivery of premature infants extracting enormous time, energy, and financial expenditures. At this very time, unfortunately, Jamie's father was threatened with a general layoff at work and had to take a position at reduced pay and reduced hours for which he considered himself overqualified. Thus, Jamie's mother was bringing in the larger salary, and Jason's father took on the majority of child-care responsibilities (including taking Jason for this consultation), a development for which he felt personally quite unprepared. A rather rigid man already, Jamie's father felt deeply humiliated and betrayed by an industry where he had worked for decades and was altogether depressed and overwhelmed by his circumstances. Jamie's twin sisters had a medically rocky beginning, further taxing his parents who needed to frequently take them to specialists in a nearby city. Jamie, a timid and dreamy boy, was often left to his own devices at three and four and five and, when he entered school, was passive and inept, quickly attaching himself to a single classroom friend—a large, belligerent girl who had failed a grade and bossed Jason mercilessly.

The therapist could see that Jamie had not had opportunity to identify with his parents as vigorous, effective human beings who provided personal encouragement to him, as a small person who would one day grow to be big and effective himself. Instead, Jamie had experienced his parents over a period of several years as remote, preoccupied, and overburdened, too busy to offer support and leadership in day-to-day ways. Furthermore, worried about Jamie's poor academic achievement and general inadequacies, in the last year his father had been quite pointed and sharp with Jamie about his son's shortcomings, attempting to criticize and correct his behavior by, as the father put it, "laying down the law" with specific rules and deprivations for each poor grade that the child received or each chore that he failed to complete. The father was dimly aware that this management plan was not working, but he knew no other approach to try.

The therapist evaluated Jamie's father for what emerged to be a moderate clinical depression and treated him with appropriate medication as well as ongoing sessions originally focused on the father's stated source of maximum distress—Jamie's poor performance in school. The therapist included Jamie and Jamie's mother (episodically, depending upon her ability to absent herself from work) in these sessions. This approach gradually succeeded in widening the discussion beyond the sore point of schoolwork onto other areas of potential family interaction such as an interest in sketching animals, which Jamie and his father were surprised to discover that they shared. What the therapist slowly accomplished was to lay the groundwork for a more companionable relationship between father and son, in which both of them felt more adequate and lively as human beings. Achieving this goal was considerably more complicated than suggesting that Jamie and his Dad throw a baseball around the back yard, because both parties needed quite a bit of help in discovering how to be intimate with each other. When Jamie's father felt less depressed and more aware of his son's thoughts and feelings, he experienced more confidence as a father and more enthusiastic about Jamie as a person; of course, this change in attitude helped the boy find in his father a strong personal support, someone he could admire as a model of commitment and responsibility. For the first time, Jamie began to get satisfaction out of applying himself in school and was astonished by his father's pride in his growth.

What is it, after all, that children need from their parents? Do they need an intimate, human relationship, or do they need behavioral administration? It is sometimes forgotten that the slogan "children need rules" emerged in the United States from public health concerns a century ago, where advice regarding adequate clothing, nutrition, school attendance, sleeping arrangements, and sanitation was desperately important to an urban population swollen with recent immigration of families from rural settings and from other countries. These public health directives were positive measures, and still are. The original advice for parents to make rules was not designed to produce a society of regimented clones; it was designed to bring some order into struggling households that were disorganized and chaotic. Likewise, the advice for parents to be matter of fact was not designed to erase the personal relationship between parent and child and substitute impersonal discipline. It was designed to encourage parents who were tempted to lose control of their emotions to embrace the goal of regaining control of themselves, and to explain themselves to their offspring with dignity rather than yelling at or hitting their children. It extolled the virtues of patience and calmness, and directed parents to aim to master themselves. This was all very wise, since it is the parent's own self-discipline that gives rise in time to self-discipline within the child through a process of idealization and identification.

What structures children in relation to morality is not rules or discipline but personal love, and no other thing can achieve it. The loved child, puttering under the eyes of the parent, is intimately supported in his exploration of the world. The world achieves significance to the child through the presence in the background of the loving adult. The adult controls the situation so that it is safe for the child; the wise adult minimizes as much as possible the need to control the child. In this fashion the child gains self-mastery and self-control. Adults do not need to make rules for the child—the rules are already there, embedded in reality: if you run you will fall; if you are unkind to people, they will not respect you. These are not the parent's personal edicts so much as aspects of the world to which we must all submit—universal laws of the physical and the moral universe. The adult helps the child gain insight into the rules that govern reality as part of the adult's overall inspiration and leadership. The parent's goal is that the child's insight into reality grows. This is, of course, a gradual process with many steps backward and forward. The adult has authority in the eyes of the child not because the adult is bigger (which only suggests that "might makes right") but because the child finds the adult admirable and trustworthy. Of course, because children have limited understanding, from time to time the adult must override the child's immediate intent in the interest of safety and common sense. But the more the parent's right to interfere is framed as an ongoing personal power struggle between the parent and child, the less the child can benefit from any guidance about reality. He's too busy resisting the parent. The world tends to get ignored.

These developmental considerations are negated by an administrative parenting agenda that asserts that the parents' main *job* overall is to *make rules* and to make them stick. This sets up parent and child for an endless battle. What began as a humble invocation for ill-informed parents to make rules—wear warm clothes in the snow, go to school every day, don't play in the street where you'll be run over—has been turned today into something entirely different. The parent has been installed as the policeman of the child's every experience, monitoring the child's every move, proscribing and constricting all aspects of the child's existence. In the course of half an hour at dinner, a child is instructed to wash your hands this way, to come to the table right now, to sit up instead of slouching, not to knock your feet against the chair, to eat all the broccoli on your plate, not to interrupt your little sister, not to tip the chair backward, to avoid putting on so much salt, not to talk with your mouth full, not to use the ungrammatical construction "felled down," not to pass your pot roast to the dog under the table, to listen when I'm talking to you, to put back that extra cookie, and to brush your teeth very carefully right after meals. The parent is working very hard at all of this, because he has been convinced that it is his job to do so, that the child's development requires endless instruction and effortful pushing and pulling in order to move forward. And sure enough, the child exposed to this litany gives plenty of evidence of resistance. You can see why. What we have here is not a child who shares a bed with three other people and has never heard of attending school—a child without rules; what we have here is a child who has heard the rules a thousand times and to whom they are a background noise. This is not a child whose aim is to be like the parent; his aim is to escape from the parent.

The issue is not whether brushing prevents tooth decay, or whether it is fair to interrupt your little sister, or whether "fall" is an irregular verb. The issue is the way that children internalize rules, whether these are the rules of preventive health, the rules of good manners, or the rules of grammar. The administrative parent feels that it is imperative to remind the child, since the child's error must mean that he has forgotten. The administrative parent is on a campaign to stamp out these errors. What is apparent to the observer is that the parent is struggling to control the child and that the child is struggling to be free of this control, and that this battle is the music of the relationship underlying its specific words. Moreover, this is a battle that interferes with the child's development, rather than facilitating it. The administrative approach to the parental relationship undermines the child's inclination to take an active role in preventing tooth decay or to be genuinely concerned with his sister's feelings. The parent presents rules as a series of administrative demands, as marching orders. The child's body is a captive audience, but his spirit alternates between apathy and resistance.

It is not part of the administrative approach to consider that a child has an inside, where his spirit dwells. The child's spirit grows as the child gradually learns to do things the "right" way, like the grown-ups do—not because someone makes you, but because you can do so "all by yourself." This is a path full of mistakes, which are always part of genuine growth. Wanting to do a good job, wanting to be a good person, aspiring to stand for something and to be someone—this vocabulary is the language of spiritual autonomy, of courage, and of personal responsibility. But this is exactly what the administrative vocabulary leaves out—and by omitting, invalidates and denies. School-age achievements depend upon the child's pride in ownership over his activities, his methods, and his goals. The child's fledgling sense of adequacy is sorely taxed by any learning situation, a setting that presents pervasive challenges in the form of all the many things that the child does not yet know and cannot yet do. To rise to these tasks, the child needs considerable bravery and confidence, yet courage and character is not formed by rewards and punishments but by intimate relationships. The administrative parent undermines his relationship with the child, not recognizing that by making the child perform he is paying a price in terms of the child's sense of self-worth and in terms of his bond with the child.

A major goal of the administrative modality is to move the task along. Now it is clear that a great deal of parenting involves moving the task along, and it is equally clear that this is arduous at best for every parent because children have a decided tendency not to be on task with the various activities that the adult considers important. The adult wants to get there, while the child wants to smell the flowers along the way. If the parent's job is to get out of the street in a hurry, because traffic is dangerous, the parent naturally moves the child along without negotiation. The adult might pick the child up, in fact. When danger presents itself, the adult simply takes charge without a second thought and restores safety. This is an example of adult authority, which is based on the adult's greater wisdom. The child doesn't have to respect the adult's authority, and the adult is certainly not in need of the child's respect. The parent just acts. In a very gradual way, the child comes to appreciate that the parent's actions are based on his devotion to the child's well-being, even if immediate dangers cause the parent to override the child's impulse from time to time. In the long run, the child respects the parent for keeping him safe, and internalizes this devoted relationship through self-respect and his desire to keep himself safe. This is the slow path of maturation.

These moments of danger are few. Tasks like doing homework, taking out the trash, brushing your teeth, and all the other jobs of childhood need to move along as well—but here the real question is not imminent danger but rather the slow process of the child taking on an increase in responsibility for himself. In this everyday arena, the administrative model reigns supreme for many parents and is certainly the dominant model upon which experts base their advice to parents who struggle with their children around these tasks. The administrative approach seeks a quick fix to the child's incomplete reliability (to his childishness, in other words, his inability to function as a miniature independent adult). By making the child do his homework, the parent may succeed in getting the homework done on a particular night—but the child can legitimately ask, "Whose homework is it, anyway?" Making the child do his homework and raising a child who wants to do his own homework is not the same agenda.

But the administrative parent, by putting punishments and rewards on the task of homework, has in so doing asserted eloquently that the task is not worth doing in itself and that the child is not worthy of wanting to do it for himself. The parent, by creating artificial contingencies to the child's on-task behavior alienates the child from genuine motivation, which comes from the child's authentic sense of himself as a human being in relation to others and in relation to his own future. The child's zest to work his hardest and to do his best rests above all upon the core of his identity and aspirations—psychological structures that have been put in place through enduring love relationships. The child is motivated not through artificial consequences but rather through the growth of trust, optimism, and commitment within the child's heart and soul. The child does his best not so much to please the parent directly, but because he deeply yearns to be like his beloved parents one day—capable, hardworking, devoted, and self-reliant. By doing his best, he feels gratified in the knowledge that he is working toward getting somewhere on the road to his own future, toward fulfilling his own dreams. Of course, since he is still a child, he is prone to regressions and digressions, and needs continuous actual ongoing support from his parents in the moment—not just high-minded encouragement from afar. The parents' support is often concrete, but equally often indirect and unconscious. Cajoling, nagging, reminding, and directing the child's behavior typically backfire because these interventions violate the child's dignity. The child thus impelled by his parents to go through the motions is likely to wonder, "Whose future is it?"—a question that renders him passive, discouraged, resentful, and lonely.

Management of children's behavior is in these ways covertly dehumanizing. All management, after all, assumes that the motives of the individual worker differ from the purposes of the institution. Few factory workers today long to be on time every day for the sake of the factory—that's why there are time clocks. The principle of human resource management indeed presupposes the recalcitrance of the worker and his basic resistance to the task. The genius of impersonal administrative management is that it succeeds in getting people to do things whether or not they are particularly interested in doing these things on a personal level; this is what discipline is—the very opposite of self-discipline. Discipline is what you apply when you have given up all hope that self-discipline can do the trick. With the application of discipline, you negate the idea of self-discipline and undermine all faith in it.

Many childhood tasks are important for parents to manage because the parent is on a time clock—getting the child dressed and out the door in the morning. These are issues not of the child's safety or education but rather of the parent's convenience or necessity. Administrative parenting is invoked as a means of making children independent in matters of getting dressed, collecting their belongings, brushing their teeth—various kinds of efficient "getting ready." The administrative model congratulates the parent for success in making the child independent as if these behaviors had something to do with the child's real independence of spirit or independence of mind. These behaviors may succeed in making the parent independent of the child—so that the parent is free at those moments to do something else—but they do not fortify the child's spiritual independence, which depends on his confidence in his self-worth and his judgment. If anything, this program of independence training convinces the child that the parent is more interested in his own schedule than the child's spirit.

There would be nothing wrong with a parent telling a child, "I am really suffering because I'm afraid I'll be late. You could help me out here if you would be good enough to hurry. I would really appreciate it." This statement is genuine, it is truthful, and it is respectful. When requests are put this way, children are often only too happy to help, proud of their ability to actually influence grown-up affairs. This kind of language defines the situation in terms of human beings and their feelings, and the mutuality of their effects upon one another. It appeals to the child's best nature and nourishes it. Similarly, a parent who loses his temper and lowers himself to a certain level of childishness might say angrily, "You're driving me nuts here, you silly slowpoke. Can't you hurry it up?" Although not a very mature remark, this is at least an honest one and an understandable reaction to frustration, a bit of childish temper that the parent can then regret having expressed. In this context, the child might also regret his pokiness—then the two could "kiss and make up." However, these responses emerge from a focus on the human relationship, not on the child's behavior. Behavior management is a perspective that defines the child's task as a success or failure for the child, while leaving the parent as a responsive human being out of the loop.

Indeed, all developmental expectations for children approached administratively have undergone a peculiar distortion, which has elements of industrialization on one hand and a certain reformatory spin on the other. In a simpler time, children were expected perhaps to work hard, to harvest the crops, to mind their manners, and to keep their private minor mischief within reasonable bounds. Today, parents expect a three-year-old to put away his toys. It's not that the child is expected to get the idea, more or less, that it is good to keep his playthings in order—but rather he's directed daily to put his things away, right now, as if it were an element in a training program. It is part of the parent's perceived job to make the child accountable for his toys. The proof that the parent has succeeded in this job is not that the child gradually becomes more reliable—more sensitive to the possibility that other people might not want to trip on his belongings or might prefer to sit on a couch free from pointed objects—the proof is that the child has been made to put his toys away today.

In a culture where models of adult commitment, empathy, and responsibility seem increasingly hard to find, the need to *make* children responsible in a tangible and immediate way seems to have become an all-absorbing mission. The administrative parent, like the head nurse, invokes the language of necessity: "You need to put your toys away right now." The child can see that this need is not the same as the need to get the harvest in. It is not a genuine need, built upon a profound interdependence in the face of tenuous survival; it is an administrative need. On a good day, the small child might be up to the challenge, might want to put his toys away as a novelty or to express a sudden rush of tenderness for the parent. But mostly he isn't up to the challenge. He is physically able to do it, but he is not emotionally able to do it reliably. He is too little to take it on as his job. Indeed, as acknowledged through the ages, a child under seven or eight is not much good at any job. The idea of a job is not relevant to children under that age, since their job is to play. Play is serious and consuming work for children. Of course, it is reasonable for the parent to enlist the child's help in putting the toys away, as a token of the child's good will—this partnership begins to lay down some of the idea that grown-ups put stuff away when they're done.

But so often the fact that the child is not big enough to be truly responsible for much of anything is manifested by the outcome—the child doesn't put away his toys. At least, the child doesn't put his toys away without the parent making a fuss about it, without consequences, limit setting, time-outs, and a general hullabaloo. Sensing a flaw somewhere (or merely exhausted), the parent may realize that he just doesn't have the heart to follow through with the consequences as stated. He caves in. The behavior expert informs the parent that he has failed to stick with the program and the parent's failure is laid at his feet as proof of the need to apply it with greater consistency. The parent may not see that the administrative mentality itself isn't suited to family life in general or to small children in particular. The parent may not see that the management ideology—so familiar to him from group discipline situations like school, the workplace, or the military and so very effective in those group situations—cannot be integrated into intimate relationships. The parent is brainwashed to think that he is simply a wimp, a weak administrator—to think that he is letting his intimate feelings for the child get in the way of his real job of imposing rules effectively.

Models change. There was a time in the earlier part of the twentieth century when a scientific approach to the child's digestive tract achieved an almost-unimaginable importance. What went into the child's mouth, and what emerged from his rectum, became the focus of studious attention and great anxiety. Infants were fed on regimented schedules, and regularity in bowel movements for children was enforced with daily laxatives and enemas. One hears much less about such struggles these days—making a child finish what is on his plate at every meal or making him evacuate on schedule. The huge literature of books, pamphlets, and magazine articles by experts in this arena, with its underlying metaphor of the child's body as a kind of factory or train station, seems quaintly dated to us now. Yet what has replaced the metaphor of the child's body as a mechanical mechanism is the metaphor of the child's spirit as a mechanical mechanism—a miniature employee, soldier, or inmate who must be pushed and pulled into submission against all his natural inclinations by the power of institutional demands. Otherwise he will never learn.

Although the machine-child of old had his food and feces subjected to regimentation, the rest of his time was his own. But today the child's every moment, every activity—his personality and soul—are being managed, subject to programming, specified activity, and structure. Parents are subject to a barrage of indoctrination that they are neglecting their *job* as parents to merely *be* with the child, to hang out in an unplanned, spontaneous, and intimate way. The parent is coached to transform this apparently empty and meaningless *being* with the child into something useful—a learning situation or stimulation of some dormant embryonic skill or preparation for some task or an encouragement of the child, endlessly, to be more independent. The parent is encouraged in these endeavors to make sure that the time with the child "pays," by making it productive. But is this what children really need from their parents? And how would we know this?

The mother in case 3 approached the school guidance counselor for advice. The counselor met with the mother and Jen, who was not very forthcoming about her personal problems with her mother in the room. Mother reviewed her laundry list of complaints about her daughter. The counselor made reference in a diplomatic way to Jen's excellent school record and pointed out that on balance the mother must have been doing a good job raising Jen despite her concerns. The counselor told them both kindly that the relationship between a mother and teenage daughter was bound to be a rocky one, since adolescents struggle with raging hormones that make them moody and angry at times. She said with a wink that it was a mother's job right now to set limits with all of her strength, just as it was a daughter's job to rebel against those limits with all of hers. Reassured, the mother did not bring her daughter for treatment, because the school had reassured her that the girl's behavior didn't warrant intervention. Indeed, Jen continued to earn good grades in school and to busy herself with typical teenage activities. Inwardly, she was bitterly miserable—when her brother home from college asked her why she still wanted professional help, she replied with a sad smile, "Because I hate everybody." Her mother succeeded in managing her behavior, as she considered this to be her aim. Jen lived out her period of grounding, as she lived out her adolescence, with an expressionless look on her face. She knew that her mother, a very decent and hardworking woman, was a good person; but she felt that there was no possible basis of genuine communication between them. Eventually, the boy who had tormented and abused her moved along to other things, and Jen threw herself into looking for college scholarships for a worthy and clever student, as far from home as she could possibly find.

What is troubling about this vignette can be approached from several perspectives. It is certainly a mistake to attempt to evaluate an adolescent's problems (or anyone's problems, of course) without meeting with the adolescent in a one-to-one fashion and making inquiry in a respectful way as to the individual's own perception of her situation. A failure on the part of the school counselor to set the stage for authentic listening, as a preliminary stage of problem solving, is notable—but of course, if one is chiefly concerned with behavior rather than what might be going on inside people's heads, there is no reason to concern oneself with what people might be thinking or feeling—their behavior speaks for itself. Jen was present at the meeting on a physical level and, shall we say, on an administrative one. The format precluded her participating on a level that included her as a full human being with personal, private, intimate experiences that had any relevance to the proceedings.

Furthermore, the guidance counselor invoked a model of adolescent development that is immensely popular, persuasive, and supportive of behavior management as the key concern of parents. This is the model of teenage rebellion. The guidance counselor interpreted as normal and inevitable— indeed, she wryly invoked as human nature—the battle between parents who set limits on their teenager's behavior and the adolescents whose days and nights are devoted to resenting, testing, and flouting these limits. As a behavioral description, this construction sums up fairly well what we see in many families—unhappy angry teenagers either flirting with or deeply committed to a variety of self-destructive activities. The myth of normal rebellion accepts these lamentable behaviors as seductive traps that adolescents (driven by their hormones) lack the brains to resist, a vast area of peer-pressured quicksand that only a powerful application of parental rules and vigilance will prevent from engulfing the adolescent.

The finding of "normal teenage rebellion" is omnipresent because it is the outcome of establishing behavior management as the goal of parenting, as is so common today. The product of this approach to child rearing is an adolescent with a constellation of developmental weaknesses—impairments regarding a clear sense of identity, a language for understanding emotion, a capacity to relate on an intimate level with other people, and a deep trust in both their own judgment and in their parents as personalities who can provide safety, guidance, leadership, and inspiration. Children who have been raised with the modalities of management borrowed from the assembly line or penal institutional—with a behavioral focus on tasks, jobs, and consequences—eventually become big enough to rebel against the supervisor or the warden, a goal that they have inwardly tendered all along. Alas, however, these children have not had the intimate relationships with their parents that are needed to prepare them for genuine independence; these youngsters lack the strong character and self-discipline to take over the role of parental judgment when the parents are not physically present. Their parents, busy with imposing discipline (and often too busy to do anything but this) have not interested themselves in the children's insides. The child's body is now big—but his emotional life and ability to manage decisions for himself are extremely immature. For these adolescents, this emptiness in their spirits—a lack of direction, goals, ideals, and values—makes them perpetual prey to the lure of impulsive foolishness and excitement. Their disappointment in their parents impels such teens to provoke them; these adolescents reveal their true lack of independence in their resentful fixation on their parents and their parents' shortcomings—rather than a constructive focus upon the real world and their own role as the new movers and shakers within that world.

This does not mean that adolescents do not need parents; indeed, they need their parents as intimate sources of strength more than ever and in more compelling ways than smaller children. Jen was in desperate need of a mother. Her mother did not understand that Jen yearned for a relationship where she could share her problems openly, where she could be listened to with respect, and where she could experience trust. Her mother was a sensitive person, and recognized and indeed even regretted that Jen did not share her intimate feelings with her; however, under the influence of guidance from child behavioral experts, the mother had been encouraged to anticipate that teenagers normally feel alienated—after all, she didn't aspire to be her children's pal. That, mother had been advised, would interfere with her job as limit setter.

What one sees here is the parent faced with an apparent forced choice between the kind of relatedness that occurs among peers and the relatedness that occurs between a group of peers and its administrator. The experts warn parents "not to be your child's friend." The parent is encouraged thereby to write off as inevitable the frustration that the adolescent expresses when the parent adopts the managerial stance. What this model leaves out is the fact that administrators can pretty well succeed in knowing whether they have met production quotas or realized a certain capital return, because the industrial proof is in the pudding. The life of an adolescent, however, never has this kind of transparency to the parent. On the contrary—teenagers have endless opportunities to act behind their parent's back—and are so often involved in countless activities that are not shared with the parent because the parent has not fostered the kind of rapport with his offspring that encourages intimate communication. When adolescents back off from genuine emotional connection with their parents, indeed, the administrative parent is often relieved. The emotional drain, the potential for ambivalence, confusion, and raw new sensations stirred up by authentic interactions with teenagers is evaded through embarrassed distancing on the parent's part. Rules only make sense when they can be enforced. No parent can enforce rules on a teenager, if only because the parent never can have complete information. All the parent has to go on is what the adolescent chooses to reveal. This is a function not of the parent aspiring to be his teen's peer or pal, of course, but of being a trusted and devoted mentor, leader, and resourceful advisor.

Parents lean on the advice of child experts not only in specific instances of trouble but also in regard to how the overall mission of parenthood is conceptualized. And following the lead of child experts, today most parents seem convinced that their job is a hard one, the task of confronting, shaping, limiting, and managing their children's behavior. The language of task administration that underlies this job is invisible to many parents and professionals alike, so saturated is our vocabulary for family life with metaphors from industry and commerce. But what is eclipsed is a language of personal intimacy and meaning. Setting out to *make* children independent, hardworking, and responsible through managing their behavior is impossible; children become independent, hardworking, and responsible through their deep love for people who themselves manifest these character qualities in their daily intimacy with the child. We can insist on children imitating conscience behaviors, but going through these motions will never instill a sense of conscience. Children grow to develop respect and concern for others only through the abiding respect and concern that they have experienced from people who are devoted to them. It is in these areas that families often need our help. Parents often struggle with painful questions of who they are, and where they are going—issues of intimacy, trust, and communication with their children that call for sensitivity to human needs and expression. A child's behavior can be modified in the short term, but its message may be lost and driven underground. Parents often crave understanding of the child's message when its significance is validated, but this cannot happen if our experts turn a deaf ear.

As a final note, one cannot escape the observation that administrative advice is relatively easy to dole out, whereas helping people learn to trust, communicate, and experience deep empathy with one another is a long and arduous path. Behavioral interventions sound good as clinical recommendations, especially because they promise to work for any child and any parent—evading disagreeable and time-consuming entanglements such as a genuine recognition of who these people might be as individuals. The expert who deals with behavior is wonderfully free from bothering with difficult intimacies that make persons unique, and can proceed briskly and efficiently from one family to another. Suggesting activity plans is an easier undertaking that helping parents to gain understanding, sensitivity, and self-awareness. Reimbursement schemes would like clinicians to deal with problem behavior and its administration, through observable end points, with checklists and graded scores. Thus it is that the economic realities shaping our patients' lives, our cultural metaphors, and our own fiscal situation as professionals have led child experts to bypass understanding and proceed directly to management techniques. Dispensing impersonal administrative advice has all but replaced the hard work of helping parents listen to themselves and to their child. But what gets lost here is a respect for the role of emotional relatedness in child development. We have abandoned a claim to expertise in the arena of feeling, to the degree that behavior has dominated our stock-in-trade as clinicians. It is forgotten that the vicissitudes of family life and the psychological development of children are not about management protocols—they're about deeply passionate emotions. They're about love and all of the problems that love can involve. And if we as child experts don't reclaim this human truth through our leadership and expertise, who will?

3

"Parental Level of Awareness": An Organizing Scheme of Parents' Belief Systems as a Guide in Parent Therapy

Esther Cohen

Ample research evidence from the field of developmental psychology is available today, confirming that children's psychological well-being is deeply affected by their relationship with parents, the behavior of parents, and the environment of the homes in which they live. Evaluations of early intervention projects for high-risk parents demonstrate that the quality of a parent's care-giving can be improved, but that it is not easy to do so (Shonkoff and Phillips 2000).

The use of focused work with parents as a main clinical intervention to alleviate children's problems is recently being similarly recognized in the field of clinical psychology as an important and effective therapeutic approach, deserving of the title "parent therapy." This recognition represents an innovation in the psychodynamic tradition (Jacobs and Wachs 2002; Frick 2000; Cramer 2000; Pantone 2000), and a change in focus in the family therapy tradition, from an emphasis on the general system to the parental subsystem (Zimmerman and Protinsky 1991; Pallazoli et al. 1998; Diamond, Diamond, and Liddle 2000).

The complex nature of working with parents around child-related complaints, both from the perspective of the therapist as well as from the perspective of the parents, needs to be better acknowledged and understood, in order to improve parent therapy. Although many parents aspire to be able to function as the change agent for their children, they often seem especially vulnerable when issues related to their functioning as parents are being examined. The moral, social, and emotional implications of the sense of failure as parents, perceived to be implied by such an examination, are likely to produce much anxiety, guilt, and defensive reactions of anger and rejection.

39

Pantone (2000) points out that although most parents earnestly want to help their children, they may nevertheless resist participating in the process because it involves exploring issues that they have avoided for years.

These sensitivities require therapists to pay much attention to the nature of their relationships with the parents, who are both their children's helpers and those being helped. Therefore, parent therapy requires the flexible integration of a consultative, collaborative, and therapeutic stance (Jacobs and Wachs 2002). This may present a challenge to many therapists. Mental health professionals, especially child therapists and social workers, may be inclined to assume a protective role toward children, and thus run the risk of unconsciously provoking critical or patronizing relationships with the parents. Conversely, therapists working with individual adults, or couples, may run the risk of identifying with the adults, who are often the complainers or the "customers" of the therapy, and focus on their needs, thus neglecting to keep in mind the needs of the children.

An additional difficulty often emerges in situations in which parents directly ask for guidance for managing children's problems. Therapists may quickly respond by offering advice and practical suggestions, unaware of the risks involved in their sometimes-naive expectation that parents readily espouse their worldview about child rearing and will be able to adopt their recommendations. Thinking in the field of parenting, based on research, has changed in recent years, replacing succinct formulas for good parenting with an appreciation for the many complex ways in which parents adjust what they do in response to the needs and characteristics of their children, their inner resources, and the circumstances of their lives (Shonkoff and Phillips 2000).

Some of these issues have been approached, although in a limited way, in the literature dealing with therapeutic work with parents and children, especially in the psychodynamic tradition (Fraiberg 1980; Orenstein and Orenstein 1985; Horne 2000; Green 2000). The reluctance in the field of family therapy regarding the use of such psychoanalytical concepts as "transference" and "countertransference" has obscured the discussion of some of these issues until recently, except for some attempts at integrating parent and family therapy (Tymchuck 1979). Carr (1997) claims that countertransference reactions to families where child abuse has occurred are inevitable and points out that these feelings are experienced not only by individual therapists but also by teams. They tend to be expressed in various acts of rescue and persecution directed at different family members. He posits that the acceptance of the inevitability of these reactions, and their open discussion in a team, may neutralize their effect on therapeutic functioning. Boyd-Franklin and Bry (2000) similarly deal with the issue of the therapist's reactions to parents' expressions of criticism, rejection, or anger at their children by stressing the importance of supervision and self-examination in these cases. In addition, they follow Henggeler et al. (1998) in trying to mitigate these feelings by identifying positive parenting practices, and challenging parents through the therapist's trust in their untapped abilities, rather than through negative confrontations. Wachtel (1994) tackles some of these issues by making a case for an integrative approach that takes into account parental feelings and attitudes, before a child-directed intervention can be planned. Celano and Kaslow (2000) further emphasize the need for adapting therapy and its goals to the family's cultural context, especially around issues of child rearing.

It is suggested that further advancement of our understanding of the complexities involved in the process of change in parenting can be gained from the remarkable body in research, pointing out how quality of parenting and parenting risks are determined by multiple systemic and individual variables (Belsky 1984, 1993). Of particular interest in this chapter is the research examining the role of parental beliefs and parental perceptions (Newberger 1980; Bornstein 1991; Smetana 1994; McGillicuddy-De-Lisi and Sigel 1995; Garcia Coll, Meyer, and Brillon 1995). Both explicit and implicit parental beliefs have been consistently found to be predictive of present and future parental behavior toward their children, in areas such as managing sibling conflicts, the use of prohibitive actions and harsh practices, autonomy granting, and teaching styles. These parental behaviors affect the child's development and adjustment (Sameroff and Feil 1985; Kochanska 1990; Perozynski and Kramer 1999; Sigel 1998).

Recently, a number of authors have shown that the types of attributions parents make about the cause (or causes) of their child's behavior, and their perceived control over his or her behavior (or their parenting self-efficacy), relate to the emotional and behavioral responses of parents toward the child. Such attributions are predictive of the quality of the parent-child relationship and the child's development in general. In parents of children diagnosed with attention-deficit/hyperactivity disorder, they appear to be related to treatment outcome and to the severity of the child's behavior disorders (Hoza et al. 2000; Harrison and Sofronoff 2002). Moreover, parental beliefs and perceptions seem to play an important role in the transmission of intergenerational parenting risk. Findings show that a major characteristic differentiating maltreating caretakers from adequate caretakers is their lack of understanding of the complexity of social relationships, especially of caretaking, and their limited ability to reflect on thoughts and feelings related to interpersonal relationships (Newberger and Cook 1983; Pianta, Egeland, and Erickson 1985; Crouch and Behl 2001). Consistently, parental beliefs related to corporal punishment, as well as parents' insensitive attributions and inappropriate expectations of their children, appear to be related to child abuse potential (Newberger and White 1989; Peterson et al. 1997; Stern and Azar 1998; Gara et al. 2000).

These data are suggestive of the involvement of limitations in the mentaliza-tion capacity (i.e., the ability to reflect upon others', as well as one's own, mental states, and the meaning of behavior) in adults as a major risk factor for their parenting ability (Fonagy 1996; Jacobs and Wachs 2002). They point to a need to place a greater emphasis on the individual parent in the system, and to address systems of inner meaning related to the subjective experience of parenting, influenced both by personal history and cultural context (Demick, Bursik, and DiBiase 1993; Garcia Coll, Meyer, and Brillon 1995). Additionally, these findings imply that addressing individual conceptual structures related to parenting by relating to content, that is, providing information or advice, is an insufficient practice. Rather, what is imperative is changing the structural organization of cognitions (Bromwich 1981; Strike and Posner 1985; Mass 1995; Thomas 1996) by increasing the ability to espouse multiple perspectives in interpreting situations, improving the ability to reflect on interpersonal rela-tions and situations, and by deepening the ability for self-reflection. The development of such abilities in parenting has become a central focus of inquiry within the framework of attachment research dealing with the quality and nature of internal representations. The research points to links between adult attachment representations, parental representations of the child, parental behavior, and child attachment security (Slade et al. 1999). While belief systems are usually conscious mental constructs, internal representa-tions constitute unconscious structures. Belief systems may therefore be a less anxiety-provoking "entry port" for parent therapy.

In this chapter I address the challenge of helping parents make these metacognitive changes through the clinical use of an empirically derived conceptualization of adult cognitive development, related to parenting belief systems (Newberger 1980). This framework, referred to as "parental awareness," offers a useful guide for forming an alliance with diverse par-ents and for dialoguing with them in a sensitive yet challenging manner, in order to expand their current structure-organization of parenting, and make it more differentiated and flexible. The systematic consideration of the par-ents' style of thinking and interpreting, within a developmental framework, may also be useful in helping therapists overcome possible negative coun-tertransferential feelings toward parents, evoked by evidencing objection-able parental handling of their children. This scheme can be used in conjunction with other individual and systemic considerations in an inte-grative practice.

The concept of "parental awareness" (Newberger 1977, 1980; Newberger and White 1989) refers to the typical way in which parents tend to think about their children and understand their behavior, as well as the way par-ents tend to think about their role and function as parents. These tendencies are associated with systems of knowledge, beliefs, and thought patterns that are activated when the parent needs to make a decision related to the child.

Newberger's (1980) emphasis is on the complexity of the parent's decision-making process and on the kinds of perspectives and considerations taken into account, regardless of the nature of the decision that is being made. Adopting this emphasis in clinical practice allows the therapist to be accepting of a wide range of individual and cultural parenting practices.

Newberger's structural-developmental scheme is based on an analysis of extensive interviews with nonclinic parents and comprises four orientations arranged as "levels of parental awareness." Each successive level includes both the preceding levels and a new, qualitatively different, set of considerations. It progresses from self-centered considerations to conventionally oriented ones, reflecting prevalent explanations and norms. Further progression is indicated by considerations based on recognizing each child as a unique and complex individual. The most elaborate level encompasses a simultaneous consideration of the components of the parent's and the child's unique relational system and ecology. Each parent can be characterized as typically employing one of the four orientations, since most of the individual responses to parental awareness questionnaires are found to reflect one level of awareness, and occasionally the adjacent levels (Newberger 1977).

Since Newberger's (1977) questionnaires were developed for research purposes, I found it necessary to replace them, for clinical use, with questions that are more integral to a clinical interview, or a therapy session, with parents. The analysis of each parent's responses, however, employs Newberger's definitions and criteria. Examples of questions that I use routinely in parents' interviews to identify the level of parental behavior are as follows: "Did you enroll your child in after-school activities this year? If so, which ones and how was this decided?" "Does the child have a fixed bedtime? If so, how was it established and why?" "Are you involved with the child's homework? If so, why and in what way?" In addition, spontaneous descriptions by parents during sessions related to either their own or the child's action are routinely followed up by questions inviting them to explicate their reasoning, such as "How do you understand this?" "Why?" and "What else?"

The four levels of parental awareness (Newberger 1977, 1980) are to be briefly defined and clarified by using examples of typical responses of parents to one of these interview questions, regarding the choice of after-school activities. The names for the different levels were also somewhat modified from Newberger's original ones (termed egoistic, conventional, subjective, and analytic) for clarity purposes.

EGOCENTRIC LEVEL

Parents at this level understand their child primarily in terms of their own experiences, and their parental role is organized around their own needs and wishes. Thus, they might choose to enroll their child in a particular class or activity that they had desired as children, or that they find gratifying now (e.g., "I always wanted to be a ballet dancer"; "I feel special because my son is the only one taking Chinese"). They might also choose to enroll their child in a specific class because it is convenient for them, that is, allows them some leisure time. Reaching a decision not to enroll the child is similarly based on considerations related to their own unpleasant experiences with such classes or with their being currently inconvenienced by it.

CONVENTIONAL LEVEL

Parents at this level understand their child in terms of rather stereotyped, external explanations and definitions provided by tradition, culture, or authority. The parental role is organized around socially defined conventions of correct practices and responsibilities. A parent at this level may argue that he or she drives the child to a computer skills class because "everybody says it is important to develop these skills early in life." Alternatively, a parent may argue that nobody in their community sends children to classes at such a young age.

CHILD-CENTERED LEVEL

Parents at this level perceive the child as a unique individual who can be understood via the intimate parent-child relationship, rather than through external definitions. They amass a great deal of specific knowledge into their child's external behaviors and try to gain insight into the child's internal psychological dynamics. Such parents perceive the parental role as the identification and fulfillment of their child's specific needs. Thus, they would tend to choose their child's after-school activities on the basis of their intimate knowledge of their child's interests and talents, and spare no effort in their attempt to find the most suitable classes for their child. Alternatively, they may also present detailed evidence as to why the child would be better off to engage in self-guided activities at home, rather than in organized group activities.

RELATIONAL-SYSTEMIC LEVEL

Parents at this level understand their child as a complex and changing psychological system and recognize that both parent and child grow through their respective roles in the parent-child relationship. The parents know that their role is to continuously attempt to find a responsible balance between the competing needs of the parents, the family, and the child. Thus, the parents are likely to decide on after-school activities for the child on the basis of the child's own interests and needs, and balance those with the needs of other members of the family, as well as their own needs, while also taking into account present and future possibilities. If a family is under financial constraints, for instance, parents at this level may offer their child recorder lessons, rather than the more expensive piano lessons the child has requested, while planning to fulfill the child's request at a future, more appropriate time, if he or she proves to be talented and dedicated to this choice.

Research supports the idea that level of awareness in interaction with stress may be related to actual parental behavior and especially to abusive behavior; high level of awareness serves as a protective factor against child abuse in stressful familial circumstances (Newberger 1977, 1980; Newberger and Cook 1983; Pianta, Egeland, and Erickson 1985; Thomas 1996). Newberger presented some evidence to support the idea that the scheme of parental awareness may meet criteria for a cognitive-developmental stage sequence by showing that progression to higher levels is associated with age and experience in child rearing. However, she did not explicate how different parents start their progressive development at different initial levels, or what may influence a halt in this development. It is suggested that the level of parental awareness may reflect two aspects of parental development and functioning: the first aspect is related to the parents' enduring internal representations and the connected reflective capacity, while the second aspect is related to processes of coping with the unique experiences of actual parenting (Slade et al. 1999). The capacity for mentalization (Fonagy et al. 2003) should be viewed as a continuum of relational capabilities, rather than a dichotomy of "mindblindness" (Baron-Cohen 1995), namely, the inability to see others' minds, and "mindsight" (Siegel 1999), the ability to perceive the mental state of another. Research suggests that individual differences in this reflective capacity in parenting may be construed as originating in both neurology and developmental experience, and their mutual interactions. Siegel (1999) points out that, in fact, in addition to the more severe impairments of the autistic spectrum disorders, there appear to be mild degrees of impairment in mindsight that have neurologically constitutional underpinnings. Attachment studies (Fonagy and Target 1998) support the notion that interpersonal experiences within early child-parent relationships can facilitate or impair the development of such reflective capacity, and their impact may be carried forward into adult relational capacity and parenting capacities.

The level of parental awareness evidenced at a specific point in time may, however, also reflect a setback or regression in the use of existing capabilities, since such factors as anxiety, stress, and depression may affect all functional capabilities. Thus, certain unresolved personal issues may mitigate a parent's ability to respond with his or her potential level of parental awareness when these issues emerge vis-à-vis a specific child. Additionally, certain characteristics of the child, related to the child's temperamental characteristics, or his or her neurological makeup, often impact the experience of parenting by provoking confusion, anxiety, and frustration (Barkley 1990). Such experiences may debilitate the parent's potential reflective capacity through defensive reactions. Moreover, the repeated frustration of the parent's need for recognition by a highly deregulated child may impede the parent's ability to recognize the child (Benjamin 1988) and may be carried forward into a struggle of gaining control or attempts to obliterate difference.

Intervention is therefore effective if it helps either to restore or to enhance mentalizing capacities in the parenting role. Fonagy and Target (1998), although not focusing on parent therapy, have suggested principles for guiding "mentalization-oriented therapy," in which the therapist continually focuses on the mental states of the patient and of the therapist, and thus places a demand on the patient to also do so. I believe that in parent therapy this focus needs to entail the actual encouragement and structuring of new parenting experiences through the therapist's sensitive initiative. These experiences may be presumed to be conductive to internal structural changes in parenting beliefs and reflective ability (Thomas 1996; Peterson et al. 1997) by combining a number of significant therapeutic elements: an empathic, supportive, respectful, and caring relationship; a developing awareness of one's own current conceptions about self, other, and the world; an ongoing examination of the usefulness of current conceptions; and an exposure to alternative conceptions and perspectives. The developing of self-awareness is facilitated both through therapeutic discourse and through observational and behavioral tasks (directives), which the therapist suggests to the parent. The combination of empathy and recognition for the way a parent thinks and feels, together with the gradual exposure to aspects of "otherness" (i.e., the perspectives of other parents, of the child, or of the therapist in a continuous attempt to understand, elaborate, and dialogue) is at the core of possible change.

This process is very evocative of the process of "joining," rooted in the tradition of family therapy and viewed as a fundamental attitude forming the basis for all therapeutic interventions.

In this chapter I suggest that the parental awareness scheme can be a useful tool for joining parents, for understanding the expectations, often voiced as complaints, of parents who seek therapy, and for anticipating the kind of motivation that therapists can recognize in moving toward change, once they have succeeded in joining with the parents. In the family therapy tradition, joining represents the ability to give a family a sense that the therapist understands it; is sensitive, interested, and respectful of the family's perceptions, values, beliefs, as well as its patterns of interaction; and is also working together with and for the family. Yet, joining also entails the concurrent maintenance of a measure of therapeutic flexibility and autonomy allowing a therapist to query the family about its patterns of behavior, to encourage family members to express their disagreements, and to suggest that alternative methods of understanding and interacting do exist (Colapinto 1991).

Thus, the scheme allows sensitive mapping of the extent and direction of the therapist's autonomous queries and reflections. An important guideline to emerge from our clinical experience in employing the parental awareness scheme is that dialoguing with parents to encourage richer and more flexible reflective capacities, and examining avenues for change, should address the parent's current level, and attempt to expand it by addressing no more than one successive stage of parental awareness. This guideline is in line with principles of development according to traditional structural-developmental schemas (Kohlberg 1969) and ideas regarding the promotion of learning and problem-solving skills, such as notions of "zones of proximal development" (Vygotsky 1978) and "scaffolding" (Wood, Brunner, and Ross 1976). These ideas, usually referring to the orchestration of experiences by parents in order to provide maximal support and success to their children in new endeavors, is borrowed here for purposes of planning supportive interventions with parents by the therapist. According to these principles, attempts to progress in a nonsequential manner to address higher levels of awareness may lead to breakdowns in communication or to nonproductive vicious circles in the therapeutic relationship. Frequently, such a failure may be evidenced when a child-centered therapist tries to elicit empathic responses toward a needy child from a parent at the egocentric level. The therapist's attempt, driven by feelings toward the child, is experienced by parents as a nonempathic reaction to their own feelings of neediness. This may lead in turn to an escalation in the intensity of the parent's rejecting complaints about the child and in the therapist's futile insistence to explain to the parent the child's needs.

Parental disagreements about the handling of the "problem" child may often be understood in terms of their different levels of awareness. The therapist's respect for each stance, and challenge to the parents to try to integrate their perspectives, tends to enrich the parental discourse, making it more complex and therefore often resulting in a higher level of awareness and more creative solutions.

WORKING WITH PARENTS AT THE EGOCENTRIC LEVEL

Parents at the egocentric level seek therapy either because of being greatly inconvenienced by the child's actions or often in response to pressure from external agents such as the school, social workers, or the court. They appear unaware and far less troubled about the child's emotional state, in comparison with others who are in contact with the child. In the initial stages of treatment, their cooperation may be motivated by a wish to diminish the pressure and unpleasantness caused by these external agents. They may also attempt to test the therapist, challenging him or her to generate in the child new desired behaviors, that would be rewarding to themselves, or eliminate behaviors that disturb them, and which they frequently perceive as being purposefully directed against them. Their focus often shifts from the child to various changing personal concerns and pressures.

Joining parents at this level is emotionally taxing for therapists, as they are simultaneously witnessing parent-child relationships frequently bordering on, or involving, maltreatment. Often, the added pressures of the referring agent, coupled with the parents' ambivalence about therapy, contribute to the therapist's stress and frustration. Viewing the parents as functioning at a developmentally constricted, immature level, from which they need help to progress, is often more helpful for therapists than labeling them as narcissistic or abusive. By focusing on discerning the structure of the parent's interpretative system, therapists may come to be more empathic toward parents' feelings and needs, even though their behavior toward the child may still be deemed undesirable or harmful.

The therapeutic agreement with the parent must address the fulfillment of the parents' needs as a primary goal. At the same time, however, it must establish that these goals be achieved through the use of better means, that is, means that are socially acceptable and more likely to be effective with children. Increasing the parents' sensitivity to societal expectations of child-rearing practices, and the establishment of culturally and academically accepted expectations of the child, is viewed as advancement from the egocentric toward the conventional level of parental awareness.

An important technique to achieve this challenging end involves encouraging reflection about the parent-child relationship by instigating a discourse on such questions as follow: How does one form expectations from children? How does one determine which expectations and practices are appropriate? and, In what ways can one support the eventual realization of these expectations? Parents may additionally be asked to observe and record various interactions between themselves and their child. They may also be directed to observe other parents as they interact with their children, or the interaction between their child and significant others, who appear to be effective with the child. Parents may also be engaged in a process of examining the origins of their beliefs and child-rearing practices by relating to their experiences in their families of origin. At times, reconnecting and working through repressed painful emotions related to childhood memories, in an empathic and secure context, may be needed in order for the parents to become more empathic toward their own child. When abusive and neglectful practices become evident to the therapists in the course of treatment, they may need at times to serve as the representative of the social convention, contributing to the discourse their knowledge of child development and of the law, and reflecting to the parents the problematic nature of their practices. This needs to be done in a sensitive manner by conveying to the parents the therapist's understanding of their needs and difficulties, and his trust in their joint ability to handle these in better ways. Fraiberg's (1980) work with parents of high-risk youngsters in their homes exemplifies how a therapist may combine the therapeutic tasks of nurturing parents and providing a therapeutically corrective experience with the sensitive communication of child-care expectations.

Creating various alternative sources for gratifying the strong emotional needs of parents at this level may help to decrease their tendency to assign inappropriate roles to the child. A caring and empathic therapist may serve some of these emotional needs, but additional sources of emotional support in the parents' everyday environment are usually needed. This can be achieved by working on strengthening a couple's emotional bond, by recruiting the support of extended family, and by referrals to community organizations.

The most provocative technique to this end is the deliberate reversal of hierarchy (Madanes 1991). When the parent appears depressed, neglecting and too exhausted to assume parental responsibility, the children are asked (if they are not too young) to take steps and reorganize to take care of the parent. The technique has a paradoxical intention: the child's willingness to explicitly reverse roles is expected to gratify and touch the parent, motivating him or her to reverse the hierarchy once again and be nurturing toward the children.

Case Vignette: Working with Parents at the Egocentric and Conventional Level

A sophisticated- and pleasant-appearing couple, both very successful physicians, came to see the therapist, after repeated complaints from the kindergarten teacher about their five-year-old son, and his aggressive and defiant behavior. They reported that at home, too, he was oppositional and out of control. My initial tendency—based on a bias related to their occupations and initial presentation—was to view these parents as child centered and indulgent, thus probably needing help in setting limits. I was mistaken. When meeting the child, I was surprised and shocked to discover many signs of child neglect. The child appeared to be very bright and articulate, yet extremely anxious and preoccupied with his mother's threats to send him away from home "to the gypsies." He had a few bruises and a neglected sore and seemed to be inadequately supervised and cared for. While interacting with him in a play session, the therapist became suspicious that he might suffer from some visual impairments that the parents failed to detect. Indeed, after being referred for an evaluation, he was found to be nearsighted and color blind.

My impressions, following gradual familiarization with the family's lifestyle and with the parents' level of parental awareness, was that the mother saw her child primarily in terms of her own needs, and was functioning at the egocentric level. For example, she seemed completely unaware that both her and her husband's prolonged working hours, and both of them being frequently called away at night, may have any impact on the child. Moreover, she could not see any problem related to the daily after-school child care arrangements that she found to be convenient—a foreign cleaning woman who does not speak the child's language. She argued that this was the best arrangement, as the woman cleaned well, and she could also tend to this child's needs when he pointed to the food that he wanted. It was emotionally difficult for the therapist to see such a bright and educated woman being so limited in her ability to perceive of her child's basic needs.

The father, using a more conventional perspective, was aware that some of their expectations of their child were inappropriate given his age. Nevertheless, he alternated between being silently angry with his wife for neglecting what he perceived as her role as a mother and being openly angry with the child for his "abnormal" oppositional behavior. He devoted some time to teaching the child academic skills, and was irritated by the boy's "lack of seriousness" in this respect. Both parents tried to control him through various punishments and threats to send him away from home, but his behavior only worsened. By the time they came to therapy, he would bark at them like a dog whenever they approached him.

The therapeutic challenge, considering the parents' egocentric and conventional levels of parental awareness, was helping them to become more reflective about the achievement of a better balance between their own needs and culturally accepted parenting responsibilities in relation to their needy five-year-old, thus helping them advance to a more differentiated conventional level, and in some limited respects to the child-centered level of parental awareness.

The first intervention was joining the parents, by listening to them empathically and by explicitly accepting their disappointment and frustration with their son and by validating their wish for a convenient and serene home atmosphere, given their demanding careers. The therapist then offered some strategic interventions designed to provide some immediate relief for the parents, and potentially ease the anger and power struggle between the parents and the child. For example, she suggested that they could adopt a playful stance and respond to their child's barking by barking back. In effect, the planned paradoxical outcome of this intervention was that this behavior ceased immediately, which gave the parents a feeling of satisfaction and control, and established their trust in the therapist.

It was also important to engage the parents in thinking of possible explanations for the problems with the child. In order to advance beyond the parent's initial simplistic explanations (mother: "He enjoys annoying me; he has always been difficult," and father: "Maybe he is bored"), the parents were invited to approach this question in a systematic way, using their diagnostic professional talents. The mother, who was an expert in reading MRI pictures, was challenged to apply her ability to look for what lay beneath the evident surface. The parents undertook to collect observations of their son in different contexts, and also to talk with their colleagues and friends about their children and how they ran their family life. Additionally, a number of conjoint play sessions with the child were introduced in the therapy, as part of the exploration.

The parents discovered that the child was more energetic and probably brighter than most of his peers. They also realized that he had much less structure and stimulation during his after-school hours. From his fantasy play they learned that he had worries related to their work, especially about their contracting their patients' diseases. They were moved by his concern for them. The problem was redefined as arising from a rather unique family situation: an unusually talented and committed dual career couple, having to care for a young, unusually vivacious, sensitive, and bright child, while lacking a good support system. Indeed their conversations with their colleagues had confirmed the uniqueness of their situation: most of their colleagues had much older kids, and had at least one parent more available to tend to the children's needs. Some had the additional support of an extended family. They enviously realized that the other families had more leisure time to spend and enjoy with their children.

Therapy reached an impasse as the need to make for more quality time with their child became self-evident, yet neither parent was willing to change his or her schedule to accommodate the child's needs. When the child became eligible for a special after-school class for gifted children, the parents were very proud but could not work out the time to drive him to it. The father was getting more openly angry with the mother as she tried to rebuff his expectation of her to make a change. This impasse was handled by shifting the focus to the sources of parental needs and motivations. The parents were invited to recount their life stories, and to observe how the past might be impacting the present. The mother achieved an unusual insight following her recall of memories of her own mother, whom she viewed as very talented but frustrated and depressed, as a result of being pressured by her own parents and husband to give up her studies and become a housewife. She reflected on her own career choice, to which her own father had objected, saying: "He had warned me that I would turn out to be either an unsatisfactory mother or an unsatisfactory doctor, and I dismissed him as being old-fashioned and ignorant. Now I know there was much wisdom in his words. It is a complex dilemma." The father's anger at his wife became clearer as he recounted his childhood in an orthodox family, where the roles of each parent were very distinct. In his youth he went through a transformation aspiring to become more liberal. Prior to marrying his wife he agreed to her condition that she be able to pursue a professional career. He had kept his promise to his wife but was only starting to accept its implications in terms of his role as a father.

A period of slow negotiations ensued, in which the parents struggled to achieve a more conventional schedule for the child and themselves. The father offered to devote two time slots a week for quality time with his son. His increased involvement at home made mother feel envious and competitive, and consequently, she managed to achieve more flexibility with her schedule, and to become engaged with the child. Throughout this process, the child's behavior improved considerably, and as the parents felt rewarded, they were able to preserve and reinforce the positive progress in the child's adjustment both inside and outside the family.

The mother requested a consultation two years following the termination of therapy. The boy was doing extremely well in school, and they were enjoying him at home. The reason for the consultation was their planned sabbatical year abroad. She wanted to think ahead and plan for the child's needs. She was considering asking her recently widowed mother to join them for the year as a support system in this new situation. Needless to say, I was delighted by the focus of her concern this time, showing that this mother has indeed developed in her parental awareness. We reflected on the transformation within the evolving transgenerational theme: the possibly depressed grandmother was reoccupied, after being deprived of a career, not finding enough satisfaction and joy in her children, and raising a daughter who felt she could find joy and love only by identifying with and actualizing her mother's career dream—thus repeating with her son the deprivation she had experienced as a child herself. This cycle was interrupted by the symptomatic grandson's successful fight to reclaim his mother, and the mother's subsequent reclaiming of her own mother, in the role of a caring grandmother, in an attempt to achieve a better balance between career and parenting.

WORKING WITH PARENTS AT THE CONVENTIONAL LEVEL

The complaints of parents at this level often pertain to the child's divergence from expected behavioral norms. Their attempts to solve the problem include a number of rigidly implemented, culturally accepted sanctions, which they find difficult to relinquish, even when they prove ineffective. The therapist may be aided in developing respect toward these parents by becoming cognizant of cultural differences, and of his or her own biases. Attempts to guide the parents toward greater flexibility may then be carried out in a more relaxed and nonjudgmental manner. This can be accomplished by a discourse relating to variations within the norm, and outside the norm, and their causes and implications, as well as an examination of the usefulness of currently employed standards and practices. The child's behaviors are discussed and studied as parents are guided to gather new relevant information about the child, while the therapist contributes conventional psychological knowledge about children. Reframing the child's behavior in terms of temperamental characteristics, learning styles, reactivity to stress, developmental stage, and developmental history, for example, become useful ways of making parents aware of differences between individual "normal" children. Expanding parental acceptance of behavioral variation in children, due to identifiable constitutional or environmental conditions, is the prerequisite for their willingness to adopt different expectations and to develop individual patterns of interaction with different children. The reframing of a parent's stigmatic or stereotypic description of the child, or of the problem, must be credible and acceptable to the parents. It needs to be accompanied by information about the specified characteristic or condition, as well as by ideas, resources, or techniques for gradually shaping the child's undesirable behavior.

The use of metaphors, proverbs, and stories drawn from the parents' cultural heritage may best be suited for use with parents at this level. Involvement of spiritual or community leaders may be helpful to these parents as a source of social support and legitimatization of newly adopted parental standards and practices.

A Case Vignette: Working with Parents at the Conventional Level

The parents of a six-year-old girl came to therapy requesting help in stopping a few of their daughter's disturbing habits, especially her hoarding and hiding food and a repetitive head-shaking movement, which seemed to appear in times of stress. The intake revealed that the couple had adopted the daughter less than a year prior to the therapeutic contact. The couple had been childless for many years and had waited for the adoption for a long time, until they could finally feel "like a normal family." A tentative inquiry regarding the circumstances leading to the process of adoption and their related feelings was met with a rigid rebuff by both parents. They did not want to talk about the period prior to the adoption, maintaining they had talked enough about these issues to the social worker at the adoption agency. It was clear to the therapist that they experienced this part of their lives as painful and shameful, and their wish was therefore respected. They seemed proud of the girl's looks but found that they needed to invest a lot of tutoring efforts in advancing her cognitive skills and knowledge base. They were proud of their effectiveness in teaching her manners and in her developing verbal abilities as a result of their tutoring. However, they were extremely upset about their failure to change the disturbing habits that she had acquired at her prior foster home. They were most ashamed of others noticing her head shakes or of their knowing of the food hoarding, and felt these were abnormal behaviors. They had tried to control these behaviors by explanations, reminders, threats, and angry outbursts, and felt ashamed for having reached a rejecting, nearly abusive way of treating the girl. They had difficulty in relating to the therapist's questions focusing on the child's past or present experiences and her feelings, and the impression was that their knowledge of her as an individual was very limited. They continually evaluated her behaviors by rigid adherence to ideas of right and wrong, normal and abnormal. These impressions served as evidence for viewing both parents as functioning at the conventional level of parental awareness. Therefore, therapeutic work needed to establish a way for the parents to accept and appreciate the child's uniqueness, without provoking excess anxiety as to her "normalcy."

Therapy focused initially on validating the parents' investment and achievements in socializing the girl into their family, and on accepting their wish to be more effective in regard to extinguishing her unusual behavior. The possible healthy survival functions of these behaviors in a foster group setting were explored. The parents realized for the first time the soothing function of the head shake, and its importance in situations where the child needs to soothe herself. They could then connect this understanding to the similar functional value of hoarding food, where access to food is not available on demand. The perception of these behaviors was thus somewhat normalized, at least in the context of her previous life circumstances. The parents' wish that she become more like a child in a normal family was dealt with by introducing the idea that this may be related to the progression of her attachment to them. The parents realized that they did not know much about how she experienced their relationship and were puzzled by the therapist's guiding questions, such as if they observe whether she used them as a "secure base." They then agreed that the focus of therapy should be observing and supporting the attachment process. The parents started a period of guided observations of their daughter, bringing this material in for discussion at the therapy meetings. They chose to focus on understanding the circumstances that made her tense, as these were related to the undesired head shakes. They became aware of how they managed to soothe the girl in many circumstances at home. They also discovered that her behavior tended to deteriorate in social situations, when they took her to meet relatives, friends, and colleagues. This caused them much aggravation. While unable to fully access and own their narcissistic vulnerability and heightened emotions in these situations, and admitting only to normal embarrassment, they could nevertheless accept that some of these many new social situations were difficult for the girl to manage. They decided to restrict the extent of these outings, and to spend more time at home with her.

At this stage the parents seemed to be more available emotionally to get close to the girl but still needed encouragement and guidance in starting to be involved in the girl's fantasy play. It seemed to them too childish for a first grader. Information about the many functions of play, especially for a child making a life transition, seemed to ease their acceptance of this activity. The girl came in for a couple of play sessions with them. The girl spent the hours playing a mother taking care of a baby, while the baby called out for her a number of times. To the parents' surprise, in the play, the baby was using the name of the girl's foster mother.

The parents' discovery that the girl was preoccupied with her previous attachment figure had opened a new agenda for exploration and for reflection. Until then whenever the issue of the girl's past was brought up they dismissed the need to talk about it with the girl or with the therapist. The girl's need to make meaning and to build a coherent story of her life and the important people in it slowly became more acceptable to the parents. This acceptance was achieved only after dealing with many of their fears and concerns related to the possible negative impact of remembering the past on her behavior and her development. This work culminated in the parents' decision to ask the social worker to arrange a meeting with the girl's former foster mother. They wanted to learn more about her past, and they wanted to show her that people don't just disappear from one's life.

Much preparation was needed for this meeting, as the parents became much more open about their feelings at this point. The mother in particular shared irrational fears that the girl would want to abandon her and go back to the foster mother. She needed to be empowered by looking at the progress she had made in the attachment process with her daughter. The parents were also supported in preparing the girl for the meeting. This involved the use of conversations, play, and the creation of a photo album with pictures from the foster home, which were not previously included. The successful meeting, in which the child showed happiness in seeing her foster mother, but clear preference for her adoptive parents, was very rewarding to the parents. They learned much about the girl's development and about the group home situation in which their daughter grew up since her first birthday, and delighted in the foster mother's amazement at her development.

Therapy was terminated shortly afterward by the parents, who felt much more comfortable with their daughter's progressive adjustment and their own functioning as parents. They continue to use therapeutic consultations sporadically, at times of difficulty, showing much better attunement to the child's feelings and unique challenges.

WORKING WITH PARENTS AT THE CHILD-CENTERED LEVEL

Parents who function at the child-centered level tend to be the most frequent self-referred consumers of psychological services. Their focus on their children generates numerous anxieties and questions related to the children's adjustment and their own functioning as parents. Often, child-centered parents are unaware of the pitfalls of the excessive focusing on a child's needs, such as parental burnout and impingement on the couple relationship. Moreover, their extreme preoccupation with the child's difficulties often renders them oblivious to their own contribution to the child's problems, that is, how their overprotectiveness and excessive concern may aggravate their child's fears, social difficulties, or insecurity. These parents, being determined not to frustrate their children in any way, may inadvertently deprive them of significant developmental experiences, such as those related to development of capacities for regulating affect and tension states. These may be the kind of parents described by Orenstein (1976) as being particularly attuned to their children's needs for mirroring due to their own narcissistic vulnerabilities, and identifying with them rather than responding to them. The therapist is likely to find it easy to join with these parents but may be unconsciously drawn into the parental pattern of concern and excessive focus on the child.

Such parents can be motivated to change their behaviors through well-documented psychological explanations, relevant to "the best interests of this child," rather than by references to social norms, or to their own needs and welfare. Special care must be taken to implement changes gradually, so as not to arouse parents' anxieties about harming the child. Child-centered parents benefit from a discourse that broadens their previous understanding of their child's needs to include an awareness of such needs as the need to learn to cope with frustration, to test one's abilities, to learn to recover from pain, and to learn to engage in reciprocal relationships. The challenge to the parents is to refrain from engaging in what immediately seems helpful to the child, in the service of long-term goals for the child's development. Evoking the consideration of the child's future needs, and accepting the constraints of natural social environments to which the child must adapt, may help parents to advance from their child-centered perspective to a more relational and systemic one.

WORKING WITH PARENTS AT THE RELATIONAL LEVEL

As parents at this level are capable of coping flexibly and creatively with a wide range of children's problems, they are not often seen in therapy. Nevertheless, such parents may seek help when their competence is undermined by a traumatic event that causes disorganization to the family system. This may occur in the aftermath of a severe loss in the family, an unexpected financial or health crisis, or the discovery of a disability or an unexpected traumatic event or problem with the child.

Parents at this level seem to need support, alleviation of their feelings of anxiety and guilt, and reinforcement of their sense of competence. The therapist may be of help by offering information about children's typical reactions under similar circumstances, by normalizing reactions, and by guiding the family in specific techniques for easing the stressful situation. However, it is most important for the therapist to empower the parents and to bolster their confidence in the capacity of the family to both cope and recover from the current crisis. Through discourse about their past experiences and achievements, and an evaluation of their strengths and internal and external resources, a more balanced and hopeful perspective of the situation can be achieved.

A Case Vignette: Working with Parents at the Child-Centered and Relational Levels

The parents came in for a consultation in regard to their five-year-old son's encopresis. He had been seen in individual psychotherapy for a year by another therapist, but this therapy was recently terminated due to the child's refusal to attend, and the parents' disappointment with the lack of progress in the child's toileting habits. They were quite stressed since he was about to enter a new, demanding school, which would not be tolerant of any accidents. The parents enthusiastically agreed to engage in a number of parent-therapy meetings to see how they could help their son. They came to the sessions together with their newborn baby, as the mother was on maternity leave.

The mother, the dominant parent in the family, was very active in the sessions. She provided a detailed account of the boy's personality, incorporating both enjoyable and disturbing aspects. She described, using many examples, his excellent reasoning ability and verbal skills, his leadership and social skills, his ability to show affection, and acts demonstrating his conscience and good heart. She also pointed out his being extremely demanding, stubborn, argumentative, and manipulative. She painfully recounted his constant state of complaining and unhappiness. This was in a striking contrast to her seven-year-old daughter, who was an easygoing and happy girl.

She invested much energy in trying to make him happy, to be sensitive to his needs and to avoid being in conflict with him. Nevertheless, his demands only increased and became impossible to fulfill ("I want today to be Saturday not Friday"), and he often continued to test her limits, until she lost her patience with him. She felt very guilty for those occasional angry outbursts, feeling that she was not living up to her own image of a good mother, and would consequently try to compensate him. Furthermore, she felt she was aggravating the boys' suffering. She saw the encopresis as a source of shame and suffering for him, and felt additionally guilty for not having been able to help him overcome it. At the beginning of the therapy, she identified with the boy's attitude of despair regarding the possibility of gaining control over his bodily functions. She was anxious to further explore what was bothering the boy, although much work in this area has been done in the previous therapy.

The father sounded less distressed and more optimistic than his wife about the possibility of resolving the child's problem. He was warm and emotionally available to the son when at home but also much firmer and clearer with him. The son behaved in a much more cooperative and mature level when alone with the father. However, the mother was critical of the father's "toughness" and "insensitivity," and since he was spending much less time at home and wanted to avoid conflict with his wife, the father regressed into a marginal, less-involved role with the children. In the sessions he demonstrated a passive, pained, but silently critical, attitude toward his wife's struggles. The therapist needed to use active encouragement to gradually engage him more openly and actively in the therapy and in handling the child's problems at home.

I thought of the mother as functioning on a child-centered level of parental awareness and the father at the relational level. I was therefore focused on helping the mother gradually become less identified and more helpful to her son. This involved recognizing some of the dysfunctional relational patterns that evolved with her son due to her excessive anxiety, high self-expectations, and overidentification with the boy. We were also working to allow more weight to the father's presence and his more balanced perspective, as a support for his wife and as an alternative relational experience, of a less symbiotic nature, with the child.

First, the therapist needed to deal with some of the mother's anxieties. A certain and optimistic view regarding the possibility of overcoming the encopresis was presented by the therapist. This was authentic, as the therapist had much past success in resolving this problem. The boy's cognitive and social competence and the parental investments and motivation were considered assets. The motivation and availability of the parents to take an active role in this project for the next few weeks were insured, and the therapist promised his continuous support, even during nontherapy hours.

When the mother expressed her anxiety while in tears, "But he is stuck; he doesn't know what to do," she was reassured by, "But we know what needs to be done." The mother's feelings of hopelessness and the father's restricted involvement in dealing with the problem needed to be approached gradually while focusing on the attempt to help the boy.

It was stressed that toileting habits constitute socialization demands that may meet with the boy's resistance since, as they described, he was using avoidance and denial in relation to the problem, often expressed in distortions of reality ("I did not make," when he made in his pants). This sounded meaningful to the mother as she could find many more instances, in other areas of his life, of the child's resistance to accept the demands of reality. She was helped to see how she found it difficult to be the one to represent reality demands to him, as she was unable to contain his anger at her. She had a hard time allowing her husband to fulfill that role, experiencing it as abusive, projecting her own unacknowledged anger at him. However, both parents could see, on the conscious level, the damage done to the child's development by their allowing him to bolster his omnipotent fantasies.

The mother's greatest fear that she may have to demand things of him that he could not perform was explored. This reminded the mother of her past feelings, when as a child she was frequently given the big responsibility of caring for her two younger siblings. She felt helpless in managing them and was criticized by her parents for not being more capable.

She was assured that the intervention with the boy will be gradual, and that only reasonable requests will be made of him. The boy was referred for a medical checkup and consultation, since the description of his encopresis suggested that he suffered from constipation and overflow incontinence.

The intervention maintained a double-related focus: The first was reframed as teaching the child "his actual size," namely, helping him accept the demands of reality and authority, and the limitations of his age and capabilities, without losing his sense of self-worth and competence. The second focus had to do with teaching him new regulatory toileting habits.

The change in the mother's way of setting clear limits and handling the boy's problem behaviors was quite striking. She felt supported by her husband and by the therapist, and no longer needed the child's approval in order to feel she was doing this as part of her role of being a good mother. The quick ability of her son to read the new rules of the game further contributed to her ability to disengage from their previous endless arguments and to present clear and effective demands.

However, the toileting intervention was much more complex to plan and to carry out. The doctor had prescribed a mild laxative so better bodily control could be achieved. A gradual program of establishing normal toileting habits needed to be carried out. The child had been in diapers at the time, and for most of his developmental history, and had adopted strange habits like pressing his bottom against a chair or the floor in order to evacuate. He needed to gradually learn new habits involving the use of the toilet, and to adopt the habit of regular and frequent visits to the bathroom. This was to establish control from without, since his reading of inner signs could not be relied on. It was clear that the mother needed the father's active involvement in this venture and the father rearranged his schedule to be more at home for the following two weeks, to encourage and guide the son in learning the new habits.

The learning of the new toileting habits is usually introduced with the aid of behavioral reinforcements for the child. However, the mother strongly objected to their use. She felt she could not deny the child promised things and dreaded the arguments that would be provoked by the child. The father then suggested that the child's reinforcement be the removal of the diaper, which he shamefully wore to his preschool. This was to be done following three days of no accidents, as a result of frequent visits to the toilet. The mother agreed that this was a significant motivator and a reasonable condition.

During the following session the mother proudly recounted how when the child had failed on the third day, and she was tempted to bend the rule and reward him, she remembered our sessions and decided she needed to help the child achieve the required learning, rather than identify with his misery. She received her husband's support on this. The child, to her surprise, agreed to a new start of the counting, and was successful in the following three days in achieving his goal of getting rid of diapers.

The toileting process continued to progress successfully, and the focus of the sessions started to shift to more general questions related to sibling rivalry, to the baby, and then to the mother's big dilemma about returning to work. She requested a few sessions for herself, acknowledging that she needed to work out some historical anxieties as they were affecting her relationships with her husband and children.

CONCLUSION

The presented case vignettes demonstrate how the cognitive-developmental scheme of parental awareness can support therapists with their emotional reactions, as well as with their deliberate choice of strategies for joining parents and utilizing their strengths and motivations for change. The suggested scheme may also help therapists to set their goals and expectations for change at a more realistic level. There is no need for all parents to function at the highest level of parental awareness, or for a single parent to always perform at his or her best ability, in order for children to thrive. It is only when parents reach an impasse in their ability to deal with a child's problem in their habitual manner that a new extended and more complex perspective needs to be introduced. This stance is in accordance with the aims of relational therapists, who attempt in their work with parents, "to retain a notion of sequential development without ignoring context, without devaluing earlier stages, and without assuming that they must be given up in favor of privileged later stages" (Altman et al. 2002, 339). As theory and research relevant to understanding the quality of parental functioning advances, more systematic and comprehensive guides are expected to emerge to assist therapists in mapping out modes of engaging parents and utilizing successful methods of treatment.

REFERENCES

Altman, N., R. Briggs, J. Frankel, D. Gensler, and P. Pantone. 2002. *Relational child psychotherapy.* New York: Other Press.

Barkley, R. A. 1990. *Attention-deficit hyperactivity disorder: A handbook for diagnosis and treatment.* New York: Guilford Press.

Baron-Cohen, S. 1995. *Mindblindness: An essay on autism and theory of mind.* Cambridge, Mass.: MIT Press.

Belsky, J. 1984. The determinants of parenting: A process model. *Child Development* 55:83–96.

———. 1993. Etiology of maltreatment: A developmental ecological analysis. *Psychological Bulletin* 114(3):413–34.

Benjamin, J. 1988. *The bonds of love.* New York: Pantheon Books.

Bornstein, M. H., ed. 1991. *Cultural approaches to parenting.* Hillsdale, N.J.: Lawrence Erlbaum.

Boyd-Franklin, N., and B. H. Bry. 2000. *Reaching out in family therapy.* New York: Guilford Press.

Bromwich, R. 1981. *Working with parents and infants.* Baltimore, Md.: University Park Press.

Carr, A. 1997. *Family therapy and systemic practice.* Lanham, Md.: Rowman & Littlefield.

Celano, M. P., and N. J. Kaslow. 2000. Culturally competent family interventions: Review and case illustrations. *American Journal of Family Therapy* 28:217–28.

Colapinto, J. 1991. Structural family therapy. In *Handbook of family therapy,* ed. A. S. Gurman and D. P. Kniskern, 417–43. New York: Bruner/Mazel.

Cramer, B. 2000. Helping children through treatment of parenting: The mode-mother/infant psychotherapy. In *Work with parents: Psychoanalytic psychotherapy with children and adolescents,* ed. J. Tsiantis, S. B. Boethious, B. Hallerfors, A. Horne, and L. Tischler, 25–45. London: Karnac Books.

Crouch, J. L., and L. E. Behl. 2001. Relationships among parental beliefs in corporal punishment, reported stress, and physical child abuse potential. *Child Abuse and Neglect* 25(3):413–19.

Demick, J., K. Bursik, and R. DiBiase, eds. 1993. *Parental development.* Hillsdale, N.J.: Lawrence Erlbaum.

Diamond, G. M., G. S. Diamond, and H. A. Liddle. 2000. The therapist-parent alliance in family-based therapy for adolescents. *Journal of Clinical Psychology* 56(8):1037–50.

Fonagy, P. 1996. The significance of the development of metacognitive control over representations in parenting and infant development. *Journal of Clinical Psychoanalysis* 5(1):67–86.

Fonagy, P., and M. Target. 1998. Mentalization and the changing aims of child psychoanalysis. *Psychoanalytic Dialogues* 8(1):87–114.

Fonagy, P., M. Target, G. Gergely, J. G. Allen, and A. W. Bateman. 2003. The developmental roots of borderline personality disorder in early attachment relationship: A theory and some evidence. *Psychoanalytic Inquiry* 23(3):412–59.

Fraiberg, S., ed. 1980. *Clinical studies in infant mental health*. New York: Basic Books.

Frick, M. E. 2000. Parental therapy in theory and practice. In *Work with parents: Psychoanalytic psychotherapy with children and adolescents*, ed. J. Tsiantis, S. B. Boethious, B. Hallerfors, A. Horne, and L. Tischler, 47–63. London: Karnac Books.

Gara, M. A., L. A. Allen, E. P. Herzog, and R. L. Woolfolk. 2000. The abused child as a parent: The structure and content of physically abused mothers' perceptions of their babies. *Child Abuse and Neglect* 24(5):627–39.

Garcia Coll, C. T., E. C. Meyer, and L. Brillon. 1995. Ethnic and minority parenting. In *Handbook of parenting, vol.2: Biology and ecology of parenting*, ed. M. H. Bornstein, 189–209. Hillsdale, N.J.: Lawrence Erlbaum.

Green, V. 2000. Therapeutic space for re-creating the child in the mind of the parents. In *Work with parents: Psychoanalytic psychotherapy with children and adolescents*, ed. J. Tsiantis, S. B. Boethious, B. Hallerfors, A. Horne, and L. Tischler, 25–45. London: Karnac Books.

Harrison, C., and K. Sofronoff. 2002. ADHD and parental psychological distress: Role of demographics, child behavioral characteristics, and parental cognitions. *Journal of the American Academy of Child and Adolescent Psychiatry* 41(6):703–11.

Henggeler, S. W., S. K. Schenwald, C. M. Borduin, M. D. Rowland, and P. B. Cunningham. 1998. *Multisystemic treatment of antisocial behavior in children and adolescents*. New York: Guilford Press.

Horne, A. 2000. Keeping the child in mind: Thoughts on work with parents of children in therapy. In *Work with parents: Psychoanalytic psychotherapy with children and adolescents*, ed. J. Tsiantis, S. B. Boethious, B. Hallerfors, A. Horne, and L. Tischler, 47–63. London: Karnac Books.

Hoza, B., J. S. Owens, W. E. J. Pelham, J. M. Swanson, K. C. Conners, S. P. Hinshaw, E. L. Arnold, and H. C. Kraemer. 2000. Parent cognitions as predictors of child treatment response in attention-deficit/hyperactivity disorder. *Journal of Abnormal Child Psychology* 28(6):569–83.

Jacobs, L., and C. Wachs. 2002. *Parent therapy: A relational alternative to working with children*. Northdale, N.J.: Jason Aronson.

Kochanska, G. 1990. Maternal beliefs as long-term predictors of mother-child interaction and report. *Child Development* 61:1934–43.

Kohlberg, L. 1969. Stage and sequence: The cognitive-developmental approach to socialization. In *Handbook of socialization: Theory and research*, ed. D. Goslin, 347–480. New York: Rand McNally.

Madanes, C. 1991. Strategic family therapy. In *Handbook of family therapy*, ed. A. S. Gurman and D. P. Kniskern, 396–416. New York: Bruner/Mazel.

Mass, M. 1995. The need for a paradigm shift in social work: The study of parenting. *Social Work and Social Sciences Review* 5(2):130–45.

McGillicuddy-De-Lisi, A. V., and I. E. Sigel. 1995. Parental beliefs. In *Handbook of parenting, vol. 3: Status and social conditions of parenting*, ed. M. H. Bornstein, 333–58. Hillsdale, N.J.: Lawrence Erlbaum.

Newberger, C. M. 1977. Parental conceptions of children and child rearing: A structural developmental analysis. PhD diss., Harvard University, Cambridge, Mass.

———. 1980. The cognitive structure of parenthood: Designing a descriptive measure. In *New directions for child development: Clinical developmental psychology*, ed. R. L. Selman and R. Yando, 45–67. San Francisco: Jossey Bass.

Newberger, C. M., and S. J. Cook. 1983. Parental awareness and child abuse: A cognitive-developmental analysis of urban and rural samples. *American Journal of Orthopsychiatry* 53:512–24.

Newberger, C. M., and K. M. White. 1989. Cognitive foundations for parental care. In *Child maltreatment: Theory and research*, ed. D. Cicchetti and V. Carlson, 302–16. Cambridge, Mass.: Cambridge University Press.

Orenstein, A. 1976. Making contact with the inner world of the child. *Comprehensive Psychiatry* 17(1):1–36.

Orenstein, A., and P. Orenstein. 1985. Parenting as a function of the adult self: A psychoanalytic developmental perspective. In *Parental influences: In health and disease*, ed. E. J. Anthony and G. H. Pollock, 183–232. Boston: Little Brown.

Pallazoli, Mara. S., L. Boscolo, G. Cecchin, and G. Prata. 1998. The treatment of children via brief therapy of their parents. In *The work of Mara Selvini Palazzoli*, ed. M. S. Pallazoli and M. Selvini, 121–44. Northvale, N.J.: Jason Aronson.

Pantone, P. J. 2000. Treating the parental relationship as the identified patient in child psychotherapy. *Journal of Infant, Child and Adolescent Psychotherapy* 1(1):19–38.

Perozynski, L., and L. Kramer. 1999. Parental beliefs about managing sibling conflict. *Developmental Psychology* 35(2):489–99.

Peterson, L., S. Gable, C. Doyle, and B. Ewingman. 1997. Beyond parenting skills: Battling barriers and building bonds to prevent child abuse and neglect. *Cognitive and Behavioral Practice* 4(1):53–74.

Pianta, R., B. Egeland, and M. F. Erickson. 1985. The antecedents of maltreatment: Results of the mother-child interaction research project. In *Child maltreatment: Theory and research*, ed. D. Cicchetti and V. Carlson, 203–53. Cambridge, Mass.: Cambridge University Press.

Sameroff, A. J., and L. A. Feil. 1985. Parental concepts of development. In *Parental belief systems: The psychological consequences for children*, ed. I. E. Sigel, 84–104. Hillsdale, N.J.: Lawrence Erlbaum.

Shonkoff, J. P., and D. A. Phillips, eds. 2000. *From neurons to neighborhoods*. Washington, D.C.: National Academy Press.

Siegal, D. J. 1999. The developing mind. New York: Guilford Press.

Sigel, I. E. 1998. Socialization of cognition: A family focus. In *Families, risk, and competence*, ed. M. Lewis and C. Feiring, 289–307. Mahwah, N.J.: Lawrence Erlbaum.

Slade, A., J. Belsky, L. J. Aber, J. L. Phelps. 1999. Representations of their relationships with their toddlers: Links to adult attachment and observed mothering. *Developmental Psychology* 35(3):611–19.

Smetana, J. G., ed. 1994. *Beliefs about parenting: Origins and developmental implications.* San Francisco: Jossey-Bass.

Stern, S. B., and S. T. Azar. 1998. Integrating cognitive strategies into behavioral treatment for abusive parents and families with aggressive adolescents. *Clinical Child Psychology and Psychiatry* 3(3):387–403.

Strike, K. A., and G. J. Posner. 1985. A conceptual change view of learning and understanding. In *Cognitive structure and conceptual change,* ed. L. H. T. West and A. L. Pines, 211–31. Orlando, Fla.: Academic Press.

Thomas, R. 1996. Reflective dialogue parent education design: Focus on parent development. *Family Relations: Journal of Applied Family and Child Studies* 45(2):189–200.

Tymchuck, A. J. 1979. *Parent and family therapy.* New York: Spectrum Publishers.

Vygotsky, L. S. 1978. *Mind in society: The development of higher psychological processes.* Cambridge, Mass.: Harvard University Press.

Wachtel, E. F. 1994. *Treating troubled children and their families.* New York: Guilford Press.

Wood, D., J. S. Bruner, and G. Ross. 1976. The role of tutoring in problem-solving. *Journal of Child Psychology and Psychiatry and Allied Disciplines* 17(2):89–100.

Zimmerman, T., and H. Protinsky. 1991. Strategic parenting: The tactics of changing children's behavior. *Journal of Strategic and Systemic Therapies* 9(4):6–13.

II

TRAUMA: PRECURSORS AND AFTERMATH

4

Projective Identification and the Transgenerational Transmission of Trauma

Stephen Seligman

This chapter makes a series of intertwined points. At the theoretical level, it explores the possibilities for integrating Kleinian theory with intersubjectively oriented infant observation research: infant researches' emerging conceptualization of the nonverbal, internal, two-person relationship model as a basic element of psychic structure illuminates the Kleinian concept of "phantasy." I apply this approach specifically to consider the concept of projective identification. This effort seems quite timely. After decades of neglect, Kleinian concepts are attracting avid attention in North American psychoanalytic centers. But there is still considerable uncertainty about them, including the impression that they are inconsistent with the recent relational innovations. I hope to show that this impression is exaggerated and that, instead, attention to the Kleinian concepts along with the intersubjective point of view allows us to think simultaneously in one-person and two-person terms. In this way, the intersubjective models can be extended to capture the density and variety of insights about the inner world in the contemporary Kleinian literature.

KLEINIAN PSYCHOANALYSIS: CORE ASSUMPTIONS AND TWO-PERSON PSYCHOLOGY

Melanie Klein's insistence on the fundamental role of the self-object relationship at the most basic psychic level is among the most crucial of many innovative contributions to psychoanalysis (Klein 1952; Greenberg and Mitchell 1983; Mitchell 1997; Ogden 1994; Grotstein 1994, 1995; Spezzano 1993).

In 1998 a version of this chapter was originally published in *Psychoanalytic Dialogues* 8(1).

The Concept of Projective Identification

Like many of the fundamental Kleinian concepts, the classical account of projective identification rests on Klein's narrative of an infant who, motivated within the internal object world, handles the anxiety of inevitable inner destructiveness by phantasizing its expulsion into the object. Klein located projective identification as a crucial organizer of mental life in the paranoid-schizoid position, the early phase of development, which is characterized by oscillations, from self to object, in the "location" of anxieties and psychic valences such as goodness and badness (see, e.g., Hinshelwood 1991; Ogden 1987; Spillius 1988).

The mental life of this "Kleinian baby" is thus constructed along the lines of primitive, instinctual, bodily based phantasies; this account is consistent with Freud's original idea that very early psychic life is organized around oral configurations as well as the life and death instincts. But Klein's (1952) remarkable elaboration of the overall concept of phantasy transformed psychoanalysis by extending the original Freudian opposition between destructiveness and libido into an implicit psychology of affective bodily states (Isaacs 1948; Spezzano 1993; Stein 1994) and by insisting on the centrality of self and object organizations within the earliest psychic reality. Klein must be credited with conceiving object relations theory; indeed, she supervised many of its most important innovators, including Winnicott and Bowlby.

Much controversy and uncertainty have ensued over the powerful concept of projective identification—both within the Kleinian centers from which it emerged and in the larger psychoanalytic arena. Subsequent theorists, including Bion (1959), Winnicott (1960), Heimann (1950), Racker (1968), and more recently, Ogden (1982), developed the concept of projective identification to include the possibility that actual others, especially analysts and mothers, would be affected by those processes originally occurring within the mind of the infant or the patient.

Despite these problems, the robust and evocative power of the projective identification concept compels us to make efforts to use it as fully and thoughtfully as possible. As a cornerstone of the extraordinary contemporary Kleinian clinical literature (Spillius 1988; Schafer 1997), the concept captures important elements of patient-therapist experience, particularly those vexing moments when the therapist feels pressured, consciously or unconsciously, to take on feelings or entire roles that seem inauthentic, or unacceptable moments when we feel especially unable to find a way to live within the transference-countertransference field and still be true to ourselves. In many respects, this terrain bears more similarity than is sometimes noted to that of the intersubjectively oriented infant observers—a process in the two-body field, articulated in the preverbal background of psychic reality and interpersonal interaction that shapes interactions and individual experiences, often outside of awareness.

It is, then, well worth taking on the problems, and indeed, some of them can be clarified by integrating the Kleinian phantasy-oriented approach with observational perspectives from infant-parent interaction. Rather than relying on a reconstructively inferred theory of phantasy, I approach projective identification as a particular form of constructing intersubjectivity within the psyche and in the interpersonal field.

PERSPECTIVES ON PSYCHIC STRUCTURE FROM PSYCHOANALYTIC INFANT OBSERVATION RESEARCH: INTERNAL MODELS OF RELATIONSHIPS

Contemporary psychoanalytic infant observers have described the processes in which early infant-caregiver interactions may be structured in the individual in order to become fundamental forms of experiencing the world and relating and communicating with it and outside of reflective awareness (e.g., Beebe and Lachmann 1988; Emde 1983; Kumin 1996; Stern 1995). This description has much in common with the Kleinian point that phantasies like projective identification have effects on other psychic phenomena, including other phantasies, and that they are generally unconscious—that is, they are fundamental organizers of psychic life that give it form rather than just imaginative mental contents organized along the primary process lines. But by directly observing the details of infant-parent interactions and then returning to the Kleinian concepts, rather than starting from the concepts and trying to push the observations into them, we can generate approaches that are more precise and immediate without losing explanatory depth and power. To say that these "structures of subjectivity" (Atwood and Stolorow 1984) can be illuminated by paying attention to very early and basic infant-parent interaction patterns is not to say that they are simple representations of such experiences. Any event takes on meaning in relation to the subjective experience of those involved in it, and the processes by which actual events become internalized as stable elements of the psyche remain very complex, many of whose details are only now coming under careful scientific scrutiny (e.g., Schore 1994; Perry et al. 1995; Beebe, Lachman, and Jaffe 1997; Stern 1985). Instead, I apply infant observation research to the Kleinian theory of phantasy to (a) capture many of that theory's most significant elements, including unconsciousness and the idea that there are basic organizers at the "psyche-soma" level (Winnicott 1992) that influence all of psychic life, especially in regard to important people and (b) emphasize that some of the more cumbersome and controversial assumptions of the Kleinian model are not necessary to create such an account. Indeed, when these assumptions are set aside, the most important elements of the powerful Kleinian approach are strengthened and clarified, thus becoming more available to the wider North American audience that they so richly deserve. More broadly, this synthesis advances the much-needed development of clinical-theoretical approaches that integrate the strengths of established one-person psychologies with emerging two-person approaches. Two aspects of the contemporary, intersubjectivist reading of infant observation research are most relevant here: (a) the image of the infant-parent dyad as a two-person, mutual-influence, mutual-regulation system and (b) new understandings of nonverbal patternings in early dyadic interactions that clarify our understanding of the internal structures of meaning that are organized in preverbal, affective, chorographic, and kinesthetic dimensions of self-with-other experience.

Infant-Parent Dyads as Mutual Influence and Mutual Regulation Systems

In the past few decades, the image of the baby as solipsistic and unorganized has been supplanted by that of the infant and parent continuously monitoring, influencing, and determining each other's behavior and meaning. This view parallels contemporary schemes (e.g., the intersubjectivist and social-constructivist positions) that emphasize similar processes in therapeutic relationships. The emerging recognition of the inextricability of transference and countertransference, for example, finds substantial resonance in infant research's concern with the transactional dynamics of mutual regulation in two-person care-taking systems.

Nonverbal Dimensions of the Construction and Contours of Meaning in Dyadic-Interactional Fields

Infant researchers, offering compelling and detailed accounts of the nonverbal, prerepresentational affective bases of infant-parent interaction, call attention to domains of experience and interacting that differ from the more verbally and symbolically articulated modes more commonly described by psychoanalysts. Overall, these researchers have argued that knowledge of the specific details and processes of preverbal interaction will enhance our sensitivity to the dynamics and structure of the creation and expression of meaning—including unconscious meaning—in affective and interactional modalities at all stages of the life cycle. (Alvarez 1992; Beebe and Lachmann 1988; Emde 1983; Stern 1995; Kumin 1996; Seligman 1996).

Using infant researchers' microanalytic concepts to look at both broad contours of psychic structures and the details of therapeutic interactions can specify these terms at the level of the fine details of both psychic structure and clinical process. Specific microinteractive sequences and patterns in dyadic interaction can be highlighted: Stern's (1985) careful description of affect attunements is an example here, as are Beebe's (Beebe and Lachmann

1988) descriptions of both interactive synchronies and sequences of disruption and repair. Other key interactional concepts (e.g., reciprocity, rhythmicity, contingency, affect, arousal, and relational expectancies) have become central in both research and clinical work with infants and their parents and are offered as useful in tracking the moment-to-moment rhythms and tonalities that give both parent-infant and clinical interactions their distinctive feel (see, e.g., Stern 1985, 1995; Emde 1990; Beebe, Lachmann, and Jaffe 1997). This developing synthesis helps us become more aware of broad, nonverbal, and affectively and narratively organized interactional formats in psychic structure and therapeutic interaction, through which intersubjectivity is created and structured. Various conceptual languages and contributions from several disciplines have been used to describe how self-experience and interpersonal interactions are organized according to generalized representations of relationships (Stern 1985), affective patternings (e.g., Demos 1988; Emde 1983), internal working models (Bowlby 1988), and "procedural rules" (Clyman 1992; Lyons-Ruth et al. 1998) that regulate what individuals do with others and what they expect from them.

Example

To illustrate these points, let me describe a few minutes of interaction in which a six-month-old boy, Jamal Jr., and his father, Jamal Sr., play together. I show how direct and evocative images of infants and their parents can illuminate both the overall structure and moment-to-moment details of prerepresentational interactional process.

The overall tone of the interaction is loving and animated, even somewhat hyper, as Jamal Sr. revs Jamal Jr. up a bit. The father and son are obviously quite fond of each other, and there are frequent exchanges of gazes, an affectionate lilt to the father's vocalizations, and the father's readiness to wait for the son to finish whatever he is doing before taking another initiative or picking the son up. For example, the father lets the son carefully look over and finger the rug fibers before engaging the son in play grabbing a candy box. When the father picks up the son, there is a comfortable and shared relaxation.

Yet, there is also some sense that the father is leading the son too fast, revving him up in a somewhat overstimulating manner. For example, when initiating the candy-box play, the father places the box out of his son's reach, and the son has to strain to crawl for it; Jamal Sr. does not help Jamal Jr. here, even though he sees that strain, and some might feel that there is a slight undercurrent of challenging teasing. But when the infant does get to the box, the father applauds. Meanwhile, Jamal Jr.'s mother can be heard saying, with some pride and warmth, that her boy prefers her husband these days and that she is not surprised, as she wished for a girl. After a few moments, Jamal Sr. leaves after letting his son know that he would be going and saying an affectionate good-bye. Jamal Jr. follows his father out of the room with his eyes, looks at the candy box, looks back at the door, and then settles into play with the box.

Many issues can be discussed here—the separation; the mother's comments about wanting a girl; the cultural dimension, inasmuch as this is an African American family; the father's motivations to have his son be like him; and so on. Many of these broad issues can be seen in the particular nonverbal patterning of affection and influence between father and son. This includes, for example, the various emotions, the pacing of the interaction, and the role of bodily effort and bodily contact, as well as their impact on Jamal Jr.'s sense of his own body, including his strain, his sense of accomplishment, and his comfort in his father's presence. Preverbal antecedents of his sense of himself as a boy are also obvious here. Overall, the influence is asymmetrical, with the father taking the lead most of the time, although he does usually notice his son's cues. At times, it seems that the father is pushing too hard, overstimulating his son, and not paying enough attention to the little boy's inner experience. But at the same time, the whole interaction has a very affectionate tone. This is the way that the elder Jamal loves his son: he is proud of his boy and awfully pleased that his son loves him and looks up to him. This joining is supported by the mother, too; she seems to take for granted that Jamal Sr. is grooming Jamal Jr. to take after him. Assuming that this is a typical interaction, young Jamal will continue to become like his father and will be admired for it; he is being encouraged to idealize and identify with his father. (A more extensive discussion of identification as a two-person process appears later.)

This situation involves a particular configuration of the parents' (and especially the father's) internal expectations, ideals, wishes, self-images, and so on—a configuration that interacts with the baby's constitutional givens (e.g., an apparent motor competence), along with what he has already come to enjoy and how he has already come to experience himself. All of this is expressed in an observable form of relating between father and son, with distinctive rhythms, tonalities, and choreography. For young Jamal, being with father also means being like father, including feeling pushed and revved up somewhat; this way of being is also basic to how the elder Jamal feels, both to himself and to others. In another affective atmosphere, this experience might feel uncomfortably imposing and demanding to Jamal Jr., but the cheerfully proud and affectionate cadences of his father lead one to imagine that the boy might come to see being pushed a bit, as well as pushing people a bit, as part of a congenial form of getting along.

However well this ultimately works for little Jamal, this perspective gives us a window into how it feels to be this baby. Looking at this couple, we get a sense of how much these patterns are registered at unspoken levels of how it feels to be oneself in one's body (e.g., in things like how it feels to use one's muscles) and how it feels to be oneself with someone else (e.g., in interpersonal expectancies and patterns of influence—whether others' cues will be followed and at what pace, when one chooses to listen and when to speak, and so on). These experiences ("senses," to use Stern's term), then, are quite likely to be procedural and prereflective (not in awareness but not repressed) and located in physical and affective registers (rather than narratively coherent verbal forms).

Implications for Contemporary Theories of Psychic Structure and "The Unconscious"

The emphasis on nonverbal forms and meanings in psychic life thus has important implications for such essential concepts as phantasy, "the unconscious," and "psychic structure." These concepts are too often taken for granted: they are necessary for psychoanalytic clinical work and, indeed, have extraordinary metaphoric power, but it is all too easy to fall into casual usages that assume consensus and clarity without making crucial theoretical and descriptive assumptions explicit. Similarly, discussions that rely on assumptions about the nature of unconscious thought are often characterized by such a pseudoconsensus.

Along with developments in related fields like neurobiology, affect research, and cognitive science, contemporary infant research links to a new and more panoramic perspective on the unconscious, as it asserts the importance of prereflective nonverbal interaction structures. The concept of procedural knowledge, for example, refers to knowing-in-action forms that have relatively little to do with language or reflection and that, in fact, might be disrupted if we think about them too much—a prereflective unconscious, as it were (Stolorow et al. 1994). Cognitive theorists cite such familiar examples as riding a bicycle or stopping a car at a red light (Clyman 1992). Similarly, neuroscientists, including prominently those interested in the earliest years, are now describing actual anatomical structuralizations of the brain that carry forward the patterns of the first experiences in order to shape the contours of later experience. These structures do not necessarily correspond to or generate mental events but fundamentally influence them (e.g., Perry et al. 1995; Schore 1994).

CLINICAL AND THEORETICAL APPLICATION: PATHOLOGICAL ASYMMETRIES IN TRAUMATIC PARENT-INFANT INTERACTIONS AND THE CONCEPT OF PROJECTIVE IDENTIFICATION

The possibilities for an integration of the overall Kleinian conception of phantasy with the emerging intersubjective models of infant-parent interactions—

and specifically of applying this approach to the concept of projective identification—will now be illustrated in relation to the issue of the intergenerational
transmission of trauma. Both the overall intergenerational transmission
process and psychoanalytic concepts drawn from reconstructions based on
the analysis of adults are clarified and enriched when reviewed in the vivid
and immediate context of direct observation of infants and their parents. In
addition to projective identification, the list of such concepts includes empathy, mirroring, and, even more broadly, internalization (see Seligman 1991).

Case Illustration: Daniel and His Father

A vignette of a father and his three-day-old son, Daniel, drawn from a video-
tape made just before their discharge from the newborn nursery, can now
be approached in order to clarify the concept of projective identification.
This father had been repeatedly physically abused as a child and had abused
his previous children, which finally resulted in their removal from his care.
In this brief episode, he holds his baby very awkwardly, just below his neck,
and forcefully brings the neonate's face close to his own with a look that
seems to convey some tenderness along with much anxiety. Next, the father
tries to force Daniel to drink from a bottle while the baby desperately shows
that he is satiated, first by not sucking and keeping his mouth closed and
then by tensing up and finally going limp; during this sequence, the father
rebuffs efforts by his wife and a therapist-observer to get him to notice
Daniel's resistance to his brutal ministrations, remaining oblivious to his
son's repeated signals. The father again brings his face intrusively close to
his son's, calls him "Chump!" and pugilistically says, "Do you want to tell me
about it?" He hoists the baby high up in the air, as if he were roughhousing
with a much older boy. Finally, as the baby seems to collapse into a droopy,
withdrawn state, the father exclaims, "That's enough of your garbage!"

This is disturbing to watch. In part, this reflects the extent to which we are
prepared to read the infant as a comprehensible signaler, even at three days,
and we are blatantly disturbed when the father overrides these cues with his
own malevolent attributions. This is not to say that the baby is self-conscious
or signaling with a sense of agency. Indeed, to whatever extent this kind of
interaction will become characteristic of his interpersonal experience, this
boy will feel that helplessness and ineffectuality are fundamental modes of
self-experience. In an extended infant-parent psychotherapy, this father
became aware of how helpless he had been as a child, especially when he
was beaten by his own father; how much having his own children reminded
him of this, and how intolerable this feeling was for him. Thus, the father
was inducing a feeling in his son that he was not able to tolerate in himself,
intensified as the infant's presence evoked that feeling in him. In watching
the details of the interaction, we can see how the infant is pressured to feel
helpless, through interactions that are essentially nonverbal and prerepre-

sentational. This also includes an agonizing sense of Daniel's bodily experience—feeling prodded, tossed about, and deprived of any sense of comfort and control of his own body.

Projective Identifications and Coercive Asymmetries in Early Development: Phantasies, Nonverbal Interaction Structures, and the Intergenerational Transmission of Trauma Projection and Identification as Two-Person Phenomena

This vignette, then, presents specific, observable details of interaction processes by which inner states actually come to be expressed and communicated in the intersubjective/interpersonal arena. With this in mind, we can now approach projection and identification as two-person phenomena, which we can describe in detail and in real time (Nachman 1998).

The most obvious element of the infant-parent interaction is the projective-attributive behavior of the father: he coercively overrides his son's cues, he treats him with hostility while feeling that he loves him, he treats him like a thing without agency, and so on. In doing this, he externalizes and actualizes his own helpless, hostile, depleted, "bad" self and object representations, attributing them to his son and putting them into action without any reflective thought.

Identification as a Two-Person Phenomenon

This nonreflective, coercive, asymmetrical attribution could be described as a relationship format, a structure of subjectivity; there could be many other such formats, including the somewhat more reciprocal but still asymmetrical pattern of Jamal Sr. and Jamal Jr. or, alternatively, an even more reciprocal pattern in yet another infant-parent interaction. In each of these situations, when the baby takes on some of the attributes of the parent as an aspect of the sense of self, we might use the term identification, but each identification pattern would have its own distinctive relational dimensions, including the sense of self-with-other, in a way that would not be best described in terms specific to the particular attributes that are involved but rather in terms of the overall contours of the interactional process. In the case of Daniel and his father, there is a particular kind of identification process, agonizingly characterized by controlling projection; this differs from other forms of identification (e.g., Jamal Jr.'s). (This perspective elaborates and is indebted to, but differs somewhat from, that of Sandler and Rosenblatt 1962).

Projective Identification as a Two-Person Phenomenon

Under these conditions, Daniel has no choice but to identify with those relational-emotional states, including the sense of helplessness, that his father keeps out of his own awareness in thoughtlessly inflicting them on his son. And as the boy comes to take on helplessness as a characteristic mode of experience and relating, he might well, also becoming like his father, come to feel that the only way to get through this to a sense of interpersonal contact and effectiveness would be to forcefully, even violently, override the other's attempts to influence and control him, as this would also be the only way to make his wishes felt with his father. In Winnicott's terms, this would be something like the development of a false-self organization. From another perspective, we would see him thus adopt his father's procedural rules or inner working models—organizing his relationships, at the unconscious, preverbal level, along the affective-relational principle that the only way to make a difference in the world is to push as hard as you can, relying on intensity to overcome the unthought sense of pervasive helplessness (see Bollas 1987).

This development would, then, constitute an identification with both sides of the father's internal self and object world: Daniel, like his father, might become the abuser of the father's own dyadic abuser-abused internal role relationship, but he would simultaneously be taking on the abused, helpless self as well. This identification, then, is with a dyadic relationship system rather than with a single role or, to put it another way, as an orientation of one's subjectivity within a self-with-other relationship dyad characterized by oscillation between one position and the other. This perspective applies the contemporary notion that internal object representations are represented dyadically and is also consistent with the Kleinian account of the ubiquity of projection, introjection, and identification in the internal object world.

"Identification with the Aggressor" as an Intersubjective/Interactional Concept

This general approach can be further illustrated in an effort to clarify the specific term, identification with the aggressor, which was proposed by Anna Freud (1936) and was used so eloquently by Fraiberg et al. (1975) and others in regard to the intergenerational transmission of trauma, as well as more generally: under such conditions, identification with the abusive aggressor is a reproduction of a relational process rather than just of an object representation alone. Daniel's identification with his father as aggressor involves this internalization of the entire dyadic projective identificatory process, with its coercive, unconscious character; under such conditions, the particular nature of the identification-with-the-aggressor process is best described in terms of an internal dyadic model defined by its inescapability and coercive dyadic contours rather than in terms of a conceptualization in which the image of the aggressor is psychically relocated in the self. Identification with the aggressor does not do away with the victimized self; it projectively dislocates it.

To the substantial extent that Daniel's experience with his father organized around the two-person relationship of abuser-abused, with its peremptory affective intensity, Daniel would experience the two sides of the two-person interaction as comprising the universe of possible relational patterns. Under such constraint and without the benefit of reflective thinking that can conceive of alternatives, the controlling position might "settle in" to prevent the even more overwhelming sense of helplessness of which an infant like Daniel can hardly become aware. This sense of helpless inevitability without reflection has been vividly described by, for example, Bion (1962) who writes of a sense of "nameless dread" and, more recently, Main (1995), who writes of "fear without thought." It is, of course, one of the essential features of traumatic states, and the process thus described is one of the central mechanisms in the intergenerational transmission of trauma, as has been noted (see Silverman and Lieberman 1999; Fraiberg et al. 1975; Moore and Coates 1997, etc.).

Some Theoretical and Clinical Implications of Integrating Infant-Parent Observation Research and Kleinian Concepts

The concept of projective identification as an inner phantasy is thus recast in intersubjective terms as describing a particular procedural format at the most basic levels of self-object organization—a particular way of organizing the senses of self and intersubjectivity, with particular features—especially the constraining if not coercive assignment of one's own intolerable and unthinkable mental states into one's others and the foregoing of the coherence, vitality, and integrity that comes with the recognition of others' differences, as that recognition is forfeited in such coercion.

In observing Daniel and his father, then, we are observing the earliest details of the construction of a psychic reality that originates in Daniel's experience with his father—or in the father's experiences with his father or even earlier in the intergenerational history—which then becomes part of the infant's psychic functioning in a fundamental way as both content and process, as a basic form of his core relational-affective world. Careful attention to the moment-to-moment details of such asymmetrical patterns of interactional influence in parent-infant dyads thus sheds light on how such patterning can take place very early on, outside of reflective awareness, and at the most basic, preverbal, procedural level.

The projective identification concept here captures a particular form of asymmetrical influence, with both internal-structural and behavioral-communicational aspects, in which one person pressures another to experience as part of herself something that the first person cannot accept within his own self-experience. If this sounds confusing, that is because it is: it reflects an inner state of confusion about boundaries and interpersonal space. This is illustrated in the extreme in Daniel's father's way of constructing the flux of self and other in the interplay of the internal and external worlds, which is, paradoxically but typically, fluid and rigid at the same time. There is constant chaos and agony in his procedures for organizing which feelings and attributes "belong" to himself and which "belong" to his others.

The Kleinian perspective, in turn, adds to the intersubjectivist infant researchers' perspective. The concept of the internal phantasy in an internally driven psychic world captures the repetitive pressure and compulsion that is so obvious here, along with the destructiveness that is so striking in this father's blatant overriding of his son's cues, as well as the crucial dimensions of unconsciousness and the sense of being a fundamental overarching psychic principle. More generally, then, we can begin to move toward a reading of the Kleinian psychology of the internal object world, including as it does a sense of self, as an account of the subject in the vicissitudes of the intersubjective field. But the synthesis with the contemporary infant researchers' emphasis on the social, dialogical nature of the baby's world calls for a more open and varied model of these vicissitudes than is always offered, at least in the more tradition-bound of the Kleinian accounts: contra Klein, it is not all infants who suffer from the absence of intersubjective vitality and the terrors of omnipotent destructiveness and deprivation; the imagery of the desperate world of the instincts is not universal.

The conventional account of projective identification does offer a powerful evocation of the world of those who have been traumatized: in cases in which the parents' influence is especially forceful and one-sided, without regard for the infant's inner experiences or external cues, the controlling projective identification format will become most dominant in the child's personality and likely will be passed on to the next generation in an inflexible way. Indeed, parents are always influencing their infants and attributing meanings to them, and so there will always be a dynamic interplay of parental projection and the infant's attributes. But often, other kinds of identification—at the most basic, unconscious level of dyadic intrapsychic organization—will be more central, from the beginning of development, and projective identification as a peremptory form of ridding oneself of intolerable feelings will not be the central mode of psychic organization, even in earliest infancy.

Psychoanalytic Instinct Theory and the Infant's Bodily Experience

This approach implies that the classical account of infantile projective identification makes too much of retrospective inferences drawn from the analysis of older children and adults. To the extent that the Kleinian account of these processes anchors the theory of unconscious phantasy in general (and projective identification in particular) to the hypothetical world of the basic, irreducible, and "primitive" oral evacuative and incorporative phantasy structure of the psyche, as it is manifested in infancy, it underestimates the importance of actual early experiences at the most basic levels of the psyche and in the earliest moments of development and so diffuses its potential power. This particular "metaphor of the baby" (Mitchell 1988) is an awkward one, widely criticized as inconsistent with the ordinary experience of those who spend time with infants, both clinically and as parents, as well as with empirical data (see Lichtenberg 1983; Stern 1985) and philosophical rigor (see, e.g., Wollheim 1993, for a careful and sympathetic philosophical exploration of this issue). Many believe that psychoanalytic instinct theory's basic postulates have been fundamentally discredited, and infant research has been essential in this critique.

In the light of these criticisms, defenders of the traditional instinct theories argue that they have the special virtue of capturing something about the bedrock importance of the physical-bodily realm for both infants and adults. Integrating the traditional emphasis on phantasy with direct observational approaches to infancy offers a powerful response to these objections, as the direct observation approach is so attentive to concrete and vivid interactional processes that occur at the most basic psychophysical levels: affects; kinesthetic, proprioceptive, and other bodily experiences; rhythms; synchronies and asynchronies; and other details of interaction sequences. Reconfiguring the theory of phantasy with these elements as the "stuff" on which fantasies and various internal representational formats are built clarifies a burdensome ambiguity in the Kleinian concepts and, indeed, in most of the classical models by untethering the questionable assumptions of instinct theory from the essential goal of keeping bodily experience at the center of the analytic discourse. This approach also responds to problems with the evolution of the projective identification concept that have been raised both inside and outside the Kleinian community. In her review of the projective identification concept, Spillius (1988) wrote,

> Klein was punctilious in specifying the exact physical means by which a projection was being effected and into which part of the recipient's body. Even the original definition specifies [that] "together with these harmful excrements, expelled in hatred, split off parts of the ego are also projected onto the mother, or, as I would rather call it, into the mother" (Klein 1952), thus making it clear that the excretory organs are the executive agents of the projection.
>
> Gradually, however, many analysts have come to speak and think of projection by the mind of the projector into the mind of the recipient without specifying the physical basis of the phantasy, unless it is particularly obtrusive. (84–85)

Describing the actual transmission processes in infant-parent interactions can help fill this gap and offer specific applications to transference—counter transference interactions of the sort from which the original concepts were derived. Accounts of bodily experience should indeed be included at the

center of both developmental and clinical theory, but they should emphasize the entire sense of the body rather than configurations centered on particular zones or arbitrarily privileged physical states such as unpleasant
tension. Moving away from the vestiges of the drive-instinct model's carica-
ture of bodily experience would open more space for the direct, empathic
accounts of the crucial role of the body in personal and social experience, as
is illustrated in the extreme in the overall sense of having one's body
become the object of someone else's force, which is so apparent in the way
that Daniel is handled by his father (Seligman 1996). The account of identification as a two-person process that is simultaneously interactional and
intrapsychic is more powerful than those vestigial narratives supported by
oral ingestive metaphors, like incorporation and metabolism.

This direct approach to the body can be used to break through the traditional position that locates bodily experience in the "one-person" realm and
social experience in the "two-person" arena. Instead, attention to the development of such physical senses of self in the course of relationships, especially those of infant-parent relationships, in which bodily experiences are
relatively unmediated by language and other symbolic structures, locates
bodily experience within the "dialectic of interpersonal and intrapsychic
experience" that other writers have described (e.g., Spezzano 1993; Aron
1996; Hoffman 1994).

Recognition and Self-Reflective Thinking in the Developmental and Clinical Process: Integrating Post-Kleinian and Intersubjectivist Models of Early Trauma and Psychopathogenesis

This integrative approach to Kleinian and intersubjectivist models can also
be extended to the contemporary psychoanalytic interest in the role of
reflective thinking in personality and development overall, especially in the
development of psychopathology. Bion, the most important of all Kleinian
innovators, is among the most articulate analytic observers in this area. Many
of Bion's ideas are now echoed in the work of intersubjectively oriented
analytic writers, especially attachment researchers and trauma theorists. The
integration suggested here provides an opportunity to bring Bion's essential
ideas into dialogue with the relational-intersubjectivist thinking about child-
parent interactions in order to enhance each in a way that demonstrates crucial correspondences between approaches that are sometimes thought to be
distinctive, if not irreconcilable.

Bion and the Impediments to Reflective Thinking

Bion's account of development advanced Klein's by giving a more prominent account of how the mother potentiates progressive development by

understanding and thus "modifying" the infant's most primitive projections, in order to enable the infant to reintroject them in a less primitive and thus more manageable and reality-oriented way (e.g., Bion 1959, 1962; see also Ogden 1994; Grotstein 1994, 1995). The mother is thus responding to the infant by reflecting for him about his own raw experience, about which he cannot think; over time, under such positive conditions, the infant gradually develops a capacity to think for himself as a result of the reintrojection of the modified bits of his primitive world. In contrast to this "normal projective identification," Bion described forms of pathological projective identification in which the caregiver fails to respond in order to transform the baby's destructive impulses, and instead re-presents them in their original danger- ous, hateful, and disintegrative form. This leaves the child without any option but to continue to find ways to get rid of these intolerable feelings, but the reprojection onto the parent leads nowhere but to further intensifica- tion of the anxious state. A self-perpetuating, repetitive trap ensues, leading to potentially malignant and unstable psychological organizations (Rosen- feld 1971; Steiner 1987). This description, of course, captures something that is very familiar in an array of clinical situations, especially in certain kinds of transference-countertransference impasses, as well as in situations like those of Daniel and his father.

Bion's Model and Infant Development Research

From the contemporary infant research perspective, the concept of "normal" projective identification is flawed, overstating the extent to which infants are predisposed to experience themselves as having bad parts as well as organ- izing their response to those unpleasant experiences that they do have along the lines of expulsive phantasies. Instead, infants are understood as pre- pared for a variety of affective responses and predisposed to offer adaptive signals that initiate, respond to, and amplify their caregivers' efforts to help them feel better. In "good enough" situations, babies come to experience biopsychosocial organization and agency without having to be extricated from innately potentiated, catastrophic anxiety states. In addition, the partic- ular idea that infants imagine placing their badness into another is regarded as a further reification of their experience along the lines of instinct theory, as I have already discussed. In a sense, this dimension of the Kleinian image of the infant both underestimates and exaggerates the infant's psychic capacities. But in situations like Daniel's, the pathological projective identifi- cation concept remains very useful, with the caveat that it be understood as describing a psychic situation that emerges from the dynamic interaction of infant and environment rather than as a result of the infant's being stranded in the original instinctual state. It also captures crucial aspects of Daniel's father's psychic situation, including the inner compulsion and pressure that drive him and that he communicates to his son. Under the coercive conditions that Daniel's father inflicts on him (as in many traumatizing situations), Daniel is deprived of opportunities for open development. He is permitted only one possible way to interrelate, and there are no "open spaces" (Sander 1988) in which he can get a sense of his own agency and subjectivity: he cannot rest long enough to think that what is happening to him could be otherwise. At three days, he is already deprived of the chance to feel how his own signals can have effects and can be rendered meaningful by a caregiver's contingent, understanding, and appreciative responses; instead, he is forced to become the receptacle-object for his father's most painful unthought experiences—the site of the identification that his father has inflicted on him. In a sense, he will have no self (of his own), or perhaps more exactly, he will have a nonsubjective self without any self-reflective awareness, a self-as-object-to-his-father, where the potential for a vital interchange between self and other has been obviated, if not annihilated, in the collapse of intersubjectivity that follows from the compelled identifying compliance with his father's traumatizing projective identification (e.g., Davies and Frawley 1994; Grotstein 1994, 1995).

Taken in less extreme forms, this description corresponds to an everyday aspect of psychoanalytic work in which analysands push the analyst to behave, feel, and identify in specific ways that feel coercive and alien; this quality is, in some sense, part of every transference situation, especially negative transferences. Following Bion's innovative readings of the projective identification concept, the Kleinian literature is unparalleled in describing such processes (e.g., Britton 1992; Joseph 1988; Spillius 1988).

Commonalities between Bion and Contemporary Innovations

In building a theory of the central role of relationships in the origin of reflective thought (to which I can only allude here), Bion (1959, 1962) embedded the original Kleinian model of infancy in an intersubjective model, although he was not always explicit about this. As one of Bion's most central concepts, "thinking" has special implications similar to those of emerging models linking the discovery of the intersubjective reflective space with an emerging sense of the security of one's own self-continuity and the reliability of the world of objects.

Bion's work converges with many currents emerging in the intersubjectivist, self-psychological, and relational arenas in linking the mothers' responsiveness to infants' awareness of their subjective experiences as distinct from the objective world. This also includes a recognition that others have minds of their own: by seeing themselves as seen in the minds of others, children come to feel affective vitality, inner coherence, and value, and that it is possible to be one's own self as one is understood by and connected to others. Winnicott

parental attributions that can hardly be reflected on; the more pathological the early processes, the more pressured and immune to reflection the transference will be. Simultaneously remembering that the re-presented relationship state is one in which reflection is not possible while paying careful attention to the details of the analytic interaction can help therapists in difficult transference-countertransference situations. In such contexts, observing the specific details of the interaction through which the patient is attempting to control the analyst and the overall setting is usually more useful than the too-common practice of offering general, inferential comments about the patient's unconscious state of mind. Even when correct, such observations about the patient's motivations or difficulties with such broad issues such as trust, anger, hostility, or even anxiety can fall flat or fuel the negative transference to an extent that careful observation of details will not. The following is a not-so-extreme example of this type of interaction:

One analyst found himself stymied by a woman patient who frequently characterized him as cruel and withholding, although he experienced himself as earnestly trying to be supportive. At one point, he was persistent in trying to help her talk about her feelings about his impending vacation and in trying to communicate how her affect went flat when she said that he "was entitled to take some time off" and that she was glad for him. His subsequent efforts to be empathic with her distress about his persistence were generally ineffective, as the patient would take them as condescending, and his interpretations of the projective and defensive aspects of other criticisms were even more provocative for her, as the patient took them as attacks that confirmed her view of the analyst as using pseudotechnique to humiliate her. As she confronted him, he found her comments to have a "grain of truth" but could not empathize with her saying that he was being sadistic (although he usually took his patients' descriptions of him seriously).

In this atmosphere, it was useful for the analyst to describe the details of how such interactions would proceed to leave him feeling that he could not possibly respond to his patient's critiques, because if he agreed that he was being cruel, he would be confessing to a crime that he did not feel that he had committed, whereas if he tried to explain how he saw things differently, he would indeed be leading the patient to feel attacked. As this description corresponded, in more or less specific detail, with the patient's treatment at the hands of a very critical and sometimes unreasonable mother, she became more able to reflect on the situation and make some links to the past.

At the same time that they supported self-reflection for the patient, these links also served an interactional/intersubjective function in the treatment by helping the analyst feel less controlled and giving him a perspective that relieved his own guilt and anger. He was thus better able to think about the patient's attributions and to work to create an atmosphere in which the patient's attributions could be handled differently from how the patient had been able to handle them when similar assaults were inflicted on him as a child. In addition, this process offered a glimmer of enhanced reflectiveness about the prototraumatic situation that was becoming reproduced in the analytic relationship; the analyst and patient were, together, finding a way to extricate themselves from the shared experience of coercive attribution without the perspective that was indeed characteristic of this patient's child-hood relationships.

There are substantial pitfalls in overlooking the subtleties of such processes: the precocious and overgeneralizing interpretation of the patient's inferred inner states (especially of negative motives), without enough attention to the two-person interaction within which that inferred state is given form, over-looks the actual psychic organization of the patient and substitutes an experi-ence-distant formulation. This can, from the point of view of the patient's subjective experience, actually repeat the original trauma of coercive attribu-tion. Such approaches often overestimate the patient's own agency in creating the coercion—without speaking to the desperate and inarticulate sense of being coerced, which is actually at the heart of the patient's experience. For example, premature interpretations might confirm the patient's fear of being dominated by a needed object that has superior power and is also attributing negative motives.

This is further complicated by the way that a patient's coercive behavior may engender frustration and even hostility in the analyst, even when the patient is not feeling hostile or at least not experiencing the hostility. Thera-pists sometimes presume that their own hostile feelings are evidence of the patient's having transferred a feeling onto the analyst—that is, that the patient actually feels such a feeling, if unconsciously. But this position may instead reflect a misconstruction on the part of the analyst, who has added something derived from her own sense of having been offended and mis-recognized and having her own expectations of the analytic situation vio-lated: the analyst, in other words, may be more aware than the patient is of the rough and provocative side of the patient's behavior and may be adding a sense of outrage because she has known better. When the analyst simply attributes the hostile feeling to the patient, rather than seeing it as a newly constructed outcome of an intersubjective situation, the interpretation may indeed not only be premature but may actually be incorrect, and the patient may again experience misattribution. Here again, a less inferential and attributive approach may be more helpful.

Along related lines, such approaches often call insufficient attention to how inarticulate or constrained the patient is in trying to think and speak about the experience in a meaningful way. In other words, analysts sometimes incor-rectly assume that patients have a sense of subjectivity, intersubjectivity, and agency and that talking is a vehicle of meaning for them; that is, analysts sometimes incorrectly assume that patients can "think" in Bion's sense or, to put it another way, that patients have achieved some modicum of the "reflective self-awareness" that Fonagy has recently described, (cf. Peltz 1998). Inasmuch as many patients cannot actually reflect on the reflective language that is offered, there may be an experience of being told that one is actually feeling something that one does not know about—that one does not actually know one's own mind. This parallels another aspect of traumatization, one in which the victim's basic sense of reality is undermined.

When patients with such experiences—and such experiences are more common than may be realized, even in more moderated forms, in "neurotic" patients—treat their analysts as they have been treated, they may still feel (at the same moment) that they are being treated that way themselves; pathological projective identification is an unstable and unsuccessful defense (organized around oscillations of self and object positions) that leads to its own repetition, as already described. At the same time, patients cannot know that they are doing any of this any more than Daniel's father knew what he was actually doing or perhaps any more than Daniel could have been aware of what was happening to him, because such nonawareness is itself part of the psychic state that is being reproduced, and such nonawareness may be protected by a variety of defensive processes, such as splitting, denial, and dissociation.

The patient may be initiating projective identification in the analysis, but this apparent act of illusory agency may be little more than, as has been discussed, a desperate attempt to avoid the even more unbearable psychic possibilities, including loss of the entire relationship and the sense of desperate frustration and isolated and overwhelming helplessness that are at the core of his or her experience, much as they were for Daniel and, ultimately, his father. Patients are always attempting to make their analytic therapist into someone other than who he or she usually is, someone whom they hope for, and someone whom they fear. This is one of the underlying conditions of transference, and it is one of the essential clinical facts that give the projective identification concept its appeal. Indeed, the contemporary Kleinians have made one of their most distinctive contributions in seeing this type of influence process as ubiquitous in analyses rather than as restricted to treatments of more disturbed patients. But, when this perspective is used without subtlety in order to overattribute negative or destructive motivation to such patterns, locating their origins somewhere within the patient, perception can turn into persecution, and therapeutic opportunities may go awry.

CONCLUSION

Overall, this approach is consistent with many of the points emerging in the exceptionally sophisticated Kleinian literature on transference and countertransference, in the emerging contemporary relational-intersubjective theory in general, and in the emerging clinical literature on the treatment of traumatized patients, which has been driven by both clinical experience and percipient feminist critiques of earlier views; this critique is not intended to diminish the importance of the elusive processes that are captured so incisively in the Kleinian emphasis on phantasies and the internal object world.

The contemporary Kleinians are among the most acute analytic observers of the intricate interrelation of the intrapsychic and transference-countertransference fields; thus, there is greater overlap with the emerging intersubjective paradigms than is often realized. The analytic situation is set up to amplify patients' efforts to influence their therapists to feel and act in order to experience and enact their internal worlds. Kleinian analysts have been especially sensitive to the extent to which such pressure is one of the underlying conditions of transference in general and have used the projective identification concept as one of the cornerstones of this realization. When we delink the image of the infant from analogies with psychic primitivity, severe psychopathology, and the like, what remains in the Kleinian lexicon comprises an extraordinarily rich and surprisingly experience-near set of descriptors of dyadic interaction in general and of the special kinds of interactions and peculiar patterns of dyadic influence that take place in analytic relationships in particular.

REFERENCES

Alvarez, A. 1992. *Live company: Psychoanalytic psychotherapy with autistic, borderline, deprived and abused children.* London: Tavistock/Routledge.

Aron, L. 1996. *A meeting of minds: Mutuality in psychoanalysis.* Hillsdale, N.J.: Analytic Press.

Atwood, G. E., and R. D. Stolorow. 1984. *Structures of subjectivity: Explorations in psychoanalytic phenomenology.* Hillsdale, N.J.: Analytic Press.

Beebe, B., J. and F. Lachmann. (1993). A dyadic systems view of communication. In *Relational Perspectives in Psychoanalysis,* ed. N. Skolnick, and S. Warshaw. Hillsdale, N.J.: The Analytic Press, pp. 61–81.

Beebe, B., and F. M. Lachmann. 1988. The contribution of mother-infant mutual influence to the origins of self- and object-representations. *Psychoanalytic Psychology* 5:305–37.

Beebe, B., F. M. Lachmann, and J. Jaffe. 1997. Mother-infant interaction structures and presymbolic self and object representations. *Psychoanalytic Dialogues* 7:133–82.

Benjamin, J. 1988. *The bonds of love: Psychoanalysis, feminism and the problem of domination.* New York: Pantheon.

———. 1995. *Like subjects, love objects.* New Haven, Conn.: Yale University Press.

Bion, W. R. 1959. Attacks on linking. *International Journal of Psychoanalysis* 40:308–15.

————. 1962. A theory of thinking. *International Journal of Psychoanalysis* 43:306–10.

Bollas, C. 1987. *The shadow of the object: Psychoanalysis of the unthought known.* London: Free Association Books.

Bowlby, J. 1988. *A secure base: Parent-child attachment and healthy human development.* New York: Basic Books.

Britton, R. 1992. Keeping things in mind. In *Clinical lectures on Klein and Bion,* ed. R. Anderson. New York: Routledge.

Clyman, R. 1992. The procedural organization of emotions: A contribution from cognitive science to the psychoanalytic theory of therapeutic action. In *Affect: Psychoanalytic Perspectives,* ed. T. Shapiro and R. N. Emde. Madison, Conn.: International Universities Press.

Davies, J. M., and M. G. Frawley. 1994. *Treating the adult survivor of childhood sexual abuse: A psychoanalytic perspective.* New York: Basic Books.

Demos, E. V. 1988. Affect and the development of the self: A new frontier. In *Frontiers in self psychology: Progress in self psychology,* vol. 3, ed. A. Goldberg. Hillsdale, N.J.: Analytic Press.

Emde, R. 1983. The prerepresentational self and its affective core. In *The psychoanalytic study of the child,* vol. 38, 165–92. New Haven, Conn.: Yale University Press.

————. 1990. Mobilizing fundamental modes of development: Empathic availability and therapeutic action. *Journal of American Psychoanalysis Association* 38:881–913.

Fonagy, P., M. Steele, H. Steele, T. Leigh, R. Kennedy, G. Mattoon, and M. Target. 1995. Attachment, the reflective self, and borderline states: The predictive specificity of the adult attachment interview and pathological emotional development. In *Attachment theory: Social, developmental and clinical perspectives,* ed. S. Goldberg, R. Muir, and J. Kerr. Hillsdale, N.J.: Analytic Press.

Fraiberg, S., ed. 1980. Clinical studies in infant mental health: The first year of life. New York: Basic Books.

Fraiberg, S., E. Adelson, and V. Shapiro. 1975. Ghosts in the nursery: A psychoanalytic approach to the problem of impaired infant-mother relationships. *Journal of American Academy of Child Psychiatry* 14:387–422.

Freud, A. 1936. *The ego and the mechanisms of defense.* New York: International Universities Press.

Goldberg, P. 1995. "Successful" disassociation, pseudovitality, and inauthentic use of the senses. *Psychoanalytic Dialogues* 5:493–509.

Greenberg, J., and S. Mitchell. 1983. *Object Relations in Psychoanalytic Theory.* Cambridge, Mass.: Harvard University Press.

Grotstein, J. S. 1994. Projective identification reappraised: Part I. *Contemporary Psychoanalysis* 30:708–46.

————. 1995. Projective identification reappraised: Part II. *Contemporary Psychoanalysis* 31:479–511.

Heimann, P. 1950. On counter-transference. *International Journal of Psychoanalysis* 31:81–84.

Herman, J. L. 1992. *Trauma and recovery,* 479–511. New York: Basic Books.

Hinshelwood, R. D. 1991. *A dictionary of Kleinian psychoanalysis.* Northvale, N.J.: Jason Aronson.

Hoffman, I. Z. 1994. Dialectical thinking and therapeutic action in the psychoanalytic process. *Psychoanalytic Quarterly* 63:187–218.

Isaacs, S. 1948. The nature and function of phantasy. *International Journal of Psychoanalysis* 29:73–97.

Joseph, B. 1983. On understanding and not understanding. *International Journal of Psychoanalysis* 64:291–98.

———. 1988. Transference: The total situation. In *Melanie Klein today: Developments in theory and practice. Vol. 2: Mainly Clinical,* ed. E. B. Spillius. London: Routledge.

Klein, M. 1952. Notes on some schizoid mechanisms. In *Developments in psychoanalysis,* ed. J. Riviere, 292–320. London: Hogarth Press.

Kumin, I. 1996. *Pro-object relatedness: Early attachment and the psychoanalytic situation.* New York: Guilford.

Lichtenberg, J. D. 1983. *Psychoanalysis and infant research.* Hillsdale, N.J.: Analytic Press.

Lyons-Ruth, K., and members of the Change Process Study Group. 1998. Implicit relational knowing: Its role in development and psychoanalytic treatment. *Mental Health Journal* 19:282–89.

Main, M. 1995. Discourse, prediction and studies in attachment: Implications for psychoanalysis. In *Research in psychoanalysis: Process, development, outcome,* ed. T. Shapiro and R. N. Emde. Madison, Conn.: International Universities Press.

Meissner, W. W. 1987. Projection and projective identification. In *Projection, identification, projective identification,* ed. J. Sandler. New York: International Universities Press.

Mitchell, S. 1988. *Relational concepts in psychoanalysis: An integration.* Cambridge, Mass.: Harvard University Press.

———. 1995. Interaction in the Kleinian and interpersonal traditions. *Contemporary Psychoanalysis* 31:65–91.

———. 1997. *Influence and autonomy in psychoanalysis.* Hillsdale, N.J.: Analytic Press.

Moore, M. S., and S. Coates. 1997. The complexity of early trauma, representation and transformation: New psychoanalytic perspectives on the treatment of sexual trauma. *Psychoanalytical Inquiry* 17:286–311.

Nachman, P. 1998. Maternal identification: A description of the process in real time. *Journal of American Psychoanalysis Association* 46:209–28.

Ogden, T. 1982. *Projective identification and psychotherapeutic technique.* New York: Jason Aronson.

———. 1987. The transitional oedipal relationship in female development. *International Journal of Psychoanalysis* 68(4):485–98.

———. 1994. *Subjects of analysis.* Northvale, N.J.: Jason Aronson.

Peltz, R. 1998. The dialectic of presence and absence: Impasses and the retrieval of meaning states. *Psychoanalytic Dialogues* 8:385–410.

Perry, B., et al. 1995. Childhood trauma, the neurobiology of adaptation, and "use-dependent" development of the brain: How "stages" become "traits." *Infant Mental Health Journal* 16:271–91.

Racker, H. 1968. *Transference and countertransference.* New York: International Universities Press.

Rosenfeld, H. 1971. A clinical approach to the psychoanalytic theory of the life and death instincts: An investigation into the aggressive aspects of narcissism. *International Journal of Psychoanalysis*, 52:169–78.

Sander, L. W. 1988. The event-structure of regulation in the neonate-caregiver system as a biological background for early organization of psychic structure. In *Frontiers in self psychology: Progress in self psychology*, vol. 3, pp. 64–77, ed. A. Goldberg. Hillsdale, N.J.: Analytic Press.

Sandler, J. 1987. The concept of projective identification. In *Projection, identification, projective identification*, ed. J. Sandler. New York: International Universities Press.

Sandler, J., and B. Rosenblatt. 1962. The concept of the representational world. *The Psychoanalytic Study of the Child* 17:128–45. New York: International Universities Press.

Schafer, R. 1997. *The contemporary Kleinians of London*. Madison, Conn.: International Universities Press.

Schore, A. 1994. *Affect regulation and origin of the self.* Hillsdale, N.J.: Lawrence Eribaum.

Segal, H. 1997. Phantasy and reality. In *The contemporary Kleinians of London*, ed. R. Schafer. Madison, Conn.: International Universities Press.

Seligman, S. 1991. What is structured in psychic structure? Affects, internal representations and the relational self. Presented at spring meeting, Division of Psychoanalysis (39), American Psychological Association, Chicago.

———. 1996. Commentary on "The irrelevance of infant observation for psychoanalysis" by Peter Wolff. *Journal of American Psychoanalysis Association* 44:430–46.

Seligman, S., and R. S. Shanok. 1996. Erikson, our contemporary: His anticipation of an intersubjective perspective. *Psychoanalytic Contemporary Thought* 19:339–65.

Silverman, R. C., and A. F. Lieberman. 1999. Negative maternal attributions, projective identification, and the intergenerational transmission of violent relational patterns. *Psychoanalytic Dialogues* 9(2):161–203.

Spezzano, C. 1993. *Affect in psychoanalysis: A clinical synthesis.* Hillsdale, N.J.: Analytic Press.

Spillius, E. B. 1988. *Melanie Klein today: Developments in theory and practice. Vol. 1: Mainly theory.* London: Routledge.

Stein, R. 1994. A new look at the theory of Melanie Klein. *International Journal of Psychoanalsis* 71:499–512.

Steiner, J. 1987. The interplay between pathological organizations and the paranoid-schizoid and depressive positions. *International Journal of Psychoanalysis* 63:241–51.

Stern, D. N. 1985. *The interpersonal world of the infant.* New York: Basic Books.

———. 1995. *The motherhood constellation: A unified view of parent-infant psychotherapy.* New York: Basic Books.

Stolorow, R. D., G. E. Atwood, and B. Brandchaft, eds. 1994. *The intersubjective perspective.* Northvale, N.J.: Jason Aronson.

Stolorow, R. D., D. M. Orange, and G. E. Atwood. 1998. Projective identification begone! Commentary on paper by Susan H. Sands. *Psychoanalytic Dialogues* 8:719–25.

Sullivan, H. S. 1953. *The interpersonal theory of psychiatry*. New York: Norton.

Winnicott, D. W. 1960. The theory of parent-infant relationship. In *The maturational processes and the facilitating environment*. New York: International Universities Press.

———. 1992. Mind and its relation to the psyche-soma. In *Through paediatrics to psychoanalysis*. New York: Brunner/Mazel.

Wollheim, R. 1993. *The mind and its depths*. Cambridge, Mass.: Harvard University Press.

5

Preschoolers' Traumatic Stress Post-9/11: Relational and Developmental Perspectives

Susan Coates and Daniel Schechter

September 11 was not only a day of national tragedy but also a shot that was heard around the world (Hoven, Mandell, and Duarte 2003). Over 3,000 children lost a parent, thousands of children attending schools and day-care centers in the blocks around ground zero directly witnessed the attacks, and untold millions of children around the world watched the attacks over and over again on television. Children from far corners of the globe were reported to suffer from nightmares following the events of 9/11 and for weeks had difficulty concentrating in school (Hoven, Mandell, and Duarte 2003).

Historically, one of the most important observations on the effect of political violence on children came from the 1943 study by Anna Freud and Dorothy Burlingham who found the following during the London Blitz of World War II:

> The war acquires comparatively little significance for children so long as it only threatens their lives, disturbs their material comfort, or cuts their food rations. It becomes enormously significant the moment it breaks up family life and uproots the first emotional attachments of the child within the family group. London children, therefore, were on the whole much less upset by bombing than by evacuation to the country as a protection from it. (Freud and Burlingham 1943, 67)

It is hard to recall now how startling the foregoing observation was at the time. Indeed, it was so novel that its full import could not be integrated into the field. What Freud and Burlingham had discovered went beyond the awful facts of the London Blitz: it was the child's separation from the mother that was traumatic.

Reprinted from *Psychiatric Clinics of North America* 27(3): 473–89, 2004, with permission of Elsevier.

93

Two years after A. Freud and Burlingham's observations, David Levy (1945) observed that the impact of hospitalization on children separated from their parents was so devastating that it resembled combat neurosis. This was at a time when public health policy still dictated that the child be dropped off by their parents, who had no further role to play in their treatment. In the United States, Levy was the first person both to recognize the parent's role in moderating the child's experience of trauma and study its impact systematically. Moreover, he was the first person to develop short-term desensitization techniques for treating the traumatized child (Levy 1939).

The full realization that a prolonged separation from the mother was innately traumatic for a child had to wait for the work of Bowlby in England. Bowlby, Robertson, and Rosenbluth's (1952) deeply moving film *A Two-Year-Old Goes to Hospital* helped improve the fate of hospitalized children all over the Western world (Bretherton 1995).

In this review we will focus on young children's posttraumatic stress reactions to specific events such a terrorists attacks, car accidents, or single traumatic medical interventions rather than chronic interpersonal trauma such as physical or sexual abuse or repeated traumatic medical interventions.

This first wave of clinical research on trauma in children established the importance of the mother's physical presence or absence in moderating the impact of trauma on the child. The second wave begun in 1975 focused on the mother's role in mediating the transmission of trauma from one generation to the next. Fraiberg, Adelson, and Shapiro's (1975) famous paper, "Ghosts in the Nursery," remains a classic contribution to the understanding of trauma as it occurs intergenerationally within a relationship.

The third wave of trauma research in children began about ten years ago with a focus on the factors that contributed to individual differences in intensity and pervasiveness of PTSD. Children were once thought to experience only transient stress in the wake of traumatic events (Gurwitch, Sullivan, and Long 1998). Advances in the nosology of psychiatric disorders led to confirmation of clinical observations that PTSD also occurred in children with a similar duration of symptoms and course as found in adults.

POSTTRAUMATIC STRESS IN YOUNG CHILDREN

The classic triad of posttraumatic symptoms, reexperiencing, numbing or avoidance, and hyperarousal, occur in young children just as in adults (Scheeringa et al. 2003; Coates, Schechter, and First 2003; Schechter and Tosyali 2001; Scheeringa and Zeanah 1995). The youngest case of posttraumatic symptoms reported to date is of a three-month-old described by Gaensbauer (1982). As in adults the range of severity is relative both to the type, duration, and frequency of traumatic exposure. Several large studies

(Breslau et al. 1999; Yehuda, Halligan, and Grossman 2001) have demonstrated that traumatic stress in childhood and, even more so, PTSD in childhood are risk factors for PTSD in adulthood. While systematic long-term studies capable of clarifying the significance of the different symptomatic presentations in children and adults are lacking, descriptive studies have been influential in the development of diagnostic criteria for young children (Scheeringa et al. 2003). Increased separation anxiety, exacerbated specific fears (e.g., of the dark, car noises, or other separation-associated or trauma-associated features), regressive behavior (e.g., increased need for pacifier or bottle), somatoform complaints, and analogues of adult PTSD symptoms such as those clustering in the general categories of reexperiencing the event, avoidance, and arousal have all been noted for children one year old and older (Gurwitch, Sullivan, and Long 1998).

In infants and toddlers, increased irritability and disruptive behavior, exacerbation of startle responses and other manifestations of dysregulation of affect, sleep, and feeding, along with transient loss of milestones (such as bowel or bladder control or speech and language competence), and disorganization of attachment behavior have been reported (Scheeringa and Zeanah 1995).

Reexperiencing traumatic events for preschoolers and school-age children may involve repetitive play in which themes of the traumatic event are expressed (Gaensbauer and Siegel 1995; Terr 1987). Automatic-appearing, rigidly repetitive activity that lacks the sense of fun or creative spontaneity and lacks symbolic abstraction inherent in normative play are hallmarks of posttraumatic play (Terr 1987; Coates and Moore 1997). Such compulsive forms of play or reenactment of the trauma may, depending on the child and his or her developmental capacities, concretely resemble the traumatic event or may be displaced in content, yet contain the affective tone, rhythmicity, or other more abstract features of the event or associated details. Posttraumatic reenactment play can lead to disorganization and obfuscation of meaning-making in the absence of a caregiver who is able to tolerate trauma-associated affects and who is able to reflect on the play's potential meanings. The traumatized caregiver's distress around posttraumatic play may lead to initiation of a referral.

It has been noted that avoidance behaviors will depend on the young child's developmental capacities, such as gross motor abilities (Schechter and Tosyali 2001). For an infant up to the age of twelve months, subtle aversion of gaze, or turning of the head, are common responses to trauma (Beebe and Lachmann 1994). Marked anxiety reactions to strange situations in the six-to-twelve-month period may be noted, with more active attempts to get away from traumatic reminders as the child learns to walk and run.

Avoidance behaviors in young children may take on extremes of generalization perhaps due to developmentally based limitations in cognitive capacities. Preschool children who experienced windows being blown out in their day-care center while in the adjacent building to that which was destroyed in the Oklahoma City bombing would go out of their way to avoid walking near windows in their subsequent schools for some time (Gurwitch, Sullivan, and Long 1998). While social withdrawal, numbing, and other dissociative or internalizing symptoms have been observed in very young children, it is thought that children below the age of four may be more likely to exhibit separation-anxious clinging and externalizing behaviors such as tantrums (Gurwitch, Sullivan, and Long 1998; Scheeringa and Zeanah 1995).

Several authors (Levy 1939; Scheeringa et al. 2003; Gaensbauer and Siegel 1995) have noted that observational assessment and treatment of children with PTSD very often requires a structuring of play in order to permit gradual therapeutic exposure within a supportive, controlled setting to the traumatic events that the child will otherwise avoid during free play. The degree to which a child avoids traumatic themes during free play coupled with a detailed history of their peritraumatic response and degree of associated dysregulation may be the most important factors in assessing the severity of the condition (Scheeringa et al. 2003; Pfefferbaum 2001).

In terms of the hyperarousal symptom-cluster of PTSD, in addition to difficulty falling or staying asleep, traumatized children often have difficulties paying attention and have increased hypervigilance and startle responses. Their disturbances of arousal often take the form of increased irritability and temper tantrums over minor events.

Trauma researchers that have studied young children have found that the DSM-IV definition for PTSD (DSM IV, American Psychiatric Association 1994) as involving "actual or threatened death or serious injury, or a threat to the physical integrity of self or other" (424) has considerable limitations if one considers the very young child's perspective. A preschooler who hears his traumatized mother's shrieks after hearing news of her partner's death may hear his own death knell, even when there is no tangible threat to self or other. Analogous to "shared psychotic disorder" or folie à deux, shared or "relational" PTSD has been proposed as an alternative construct for thinking about trauma in young children who are so thoroughly dependent upon their primary caretakers for their feelings of safety (Scheeringa and Zeanah 2001). In their model of relational PTSD, Scheeringa and Zeanah (2001) consider various ways the care-giving relationship mediates and moderates childhood PTSD symptomatology. They hypothesized the following models:

In the *moderating effect model*, the child is traumatized directly by an event, but the "mother's relationship with the child (including her ability to read cues and respond effectively to needs) affects" (808) or moderates the degree to which the child will become symptomatic. The mother's behavior either amplifies or helps contain the child's traumatic reaction. In the *vicarious traumatization model*, or what one could also call the *mediation model*, the mother has experienced a trauma and the child has not. In this situation the impact of the trauma on the mother impinges on her relationship with her child, altering her responsiveness, and thus mediates the child's development of symptoms. In the *compound effect model* the mother and the child are both traumatized, and each exacerbates the symptomatology of the other.

ZERO TO THREE: NATIONAL CENTER FOR INFANTS DIAGNOSTIC CRITERIA FOR TRAUMATIC STRESS DISORDER

In an effort to improve the nosology for infants, toddlers, and preschool-age children, Zero to Three: National Center for Infants, Toddlers, and Families (1994) has developed the following diagnostic criteria for traumatic stress disorder. While the diagnoses in the Zero to Three classification system are currently under reconsideration for revision (Emde et al. 2004), the following criteria for traumatic stress disorder remains more developmentally specific for infants and young children than the DSM-IV.

1. Reexperiencing of the traumatic event as evidenced by posttraumatic play (that is, compulsively driven play that represents a repetitive reenactment of the trauma), recurrent recollections of the traumatic event, repeated nightmares, distress at exposure to reminders of the trauma, and episodes with features of a flashback or dissociation.
2. A numbing of responsiveness in a child or interference with developmental momentum, revealed by increased social withdrawal, restricted range of affect, temporary loss of previously acquired developmental skills, and a decrease or constriction in play.
3. Symptoms of increased arousal, as revealed by night terrors, difficulty going to sleep, repeated night waking, significant attention difficulties, hypervigilance, and exaggerated startle response.
4. Symptoms, especially fears or aggression that were not present before the traumatic event.

What is traumatic for a young child must also be considered from a developmental perspective: for example, falling off a bed will not be traumatic for a healthy teenager; whereas, for an infant or handicapped young child, such an experience may seem life threatening. For any age, however, there are events like being a passenger in a crashing car, being attacked by an animal, or being raped that are likely to be traumatic. Having any of these experiences more than once is more likely to result in sustained PTSD than being traumatized once (Breslau et al. 1999). Terr (1987) puts forth a simple distinction between isolated traumatic exposures or "type I" traumas, such as a traffic accident or natural disaster, and chronic repeated exposures or "type II" traumas, associated with child maltreatment or chronic illness.

RELATIONAL AND DEVELOPMENTAL PERSPECTIVES ON POSTTRAUMATIC STRESS

In an ongoing study involving assessment of parents of preschool-age children, parent interviews about their children, as well as interviews and direct observation of these children, preliminary analyses have shown that as many as 96 percent of the children—all of whom were ages birth to five years on September 11, 2001, and living near or within viewing distance of the Twin Towers, experienced one PTSD symptom, and 35 percent met DSM-IV criteria for PTSD and DC: 0–3 criteria for traumatic stress disorder (Klein, Devoe, and Miranda 2003). While parental data from this latter study are still pending, in several prior studies where the family and child were both evaluated, a significant relationship has been found between "poorer maternal or family functioning" and worse child outcomes (Yehuda, Halligan, and Grossman 2001; Cornely and Bromet 1986; Laor 1997). Koplewicz et al. (2002) found that following the first World Trade Center bombing in 1993, parents who had greater severity of PTSD had children with more PTSD and disaster-related fears than children of parents with less or absent PTSD.

In a study by Laor (1997) of the impact of scud missile attacks on Israeli children, where effects were studied separately for ages three, four, and five, a strong relationship between family functioning and child outcomes was found in children age three and four but not at age five. Thus, younger children appeared to be more effected by the state of their parents.

Scheeringa and Zeanah (1995) attempted to determine which kinds of trauma best predicted severity of PTSD in children under age four and found only one factor, trauma that occurred in connection to threats to the child's caregivers. In a separate study, Pynoos and his colleagues (1995) found that, after a traumatic event, mothers who tried to avoid being confronted with reminders of the trauma and who were in numb emotional states that restricted their capacity for closeness, were unable to help their children process the experience of trauma (87). These studies show that mother's presence is not enough. For mothers and other caregivers to serve as a "protective shield" to their child in the face of trauma, they need to be emotionally present as well (Saltzman et al. 2003).

The importance of the mother's emotional accessibility to her child after the experience of a traumatic event was dramatically underscored by the impressive findings from a survey conducted at the New York Academy of Medicine after September 11 (Stuber et al. 2002). They found that children whose parents did not know how their child responded after September 11 were 11.1 times more likely to have behavior problems at ages six through eleven and 4.0 times more likely at ages twelve through seventeen. Parents who cannot keep their child's experience in mind after a traumatic event have more behaviorally disturbed children, and this effect is nearly three times greater in younger children than in adolescents (Stuber et al. 2002). This important study brought into stark relief the fact that in the wake of a trauma caused by an external catastrophic event, a child's response, especially the young child's response, depends upon the nature of their parent's relatedness to them after the trauma.

GUIDELINES FOR DISASTER INTERVENTION

Based both on the research findings reviewed above and our clinical observations at the Kids Corner of the Family Assistance Center at Pier 94 in the months following September 11 (Coates, Schechter, and First 2003; Schechter, Coates, and First 2001), and consonant with those developed by Robert Pynoos and his colleagues as psychological first aid after traumatic events (Pynoos and Nader 1988), we devised a set of guidelines for clinicians working with young children and their caregivers in the wake of disasters similar to that of the attacks of 9/11. These guidelines are useful as a first response to traumatic events. These guidelines are reproduced here with minor revisions (Coates, Schechter, and First 2003).

The following guidelines apply to children:

Listen. Some children spontaneously want to talk about what they or their parents and other family members are going through with a sensitive listener from outside the family. Here, acknowledging the reality of trauma and loss is implicit in simply listening.

Clarify. Children who wish to talk can be helped to make sense of their feelings and to find words to name emotions. Finding words promotes containment, the development of symbolic representation, and the capacity for self-regulation. Clarification of affects and events helps toward the restoration of a coherent narrative. It is important to follow the child's lead, to avoid probing exploration, responding only to what the child spontaneously introduced, in order to support containment of overwhelming feelings.

Support attachment bonds. In cases of loss of a parent and for children who are ready to do this, one can provide support for the child's identification with or internalization of the attachment to the lost family member by actively facilitating the child's need to remember and talk about their lost loved one.

Facilitate. It is important to facilitate children's symbolic expression in play and in art projects by being supportively interested and available to observe or join play or to talk with them while they use art and crafts materials.

Support the capacity to imagine repair. Bob Pynoos (2001) describes key moments in the crisis intervention after the bombing in Oklahoma City when he helped children to imagine reparative possibilities. When a session ends with a child who has re-lived the trauma by telling about it or representing it in play or drawings, this may retraumatize the child, unless the session ends by helping the child imagine some way of repairing or healing the damage. It is important to help younger children to think about how their family and community will take care of them.

The following guidelines apply to parents:

Contextualize the parents' reactions by helping them to understand that they were not going crazy and that their fears, anxieties, and flash-backs are expectable reactions to a severely traumatizing event.

Support the child's surviving attachment relationships by helping parents to understand the child's feelings and by facilitating communication between them. Help parents recognize how much their children understand about the events all around them. Help parents, family members, and friends to be more accessible by answering children's questions directly and honestly without providing more information than children need.

Clarify. Help parents to make sense of their children's perplexing and disturbing expressions and behavior. For example, help parents understand and make meaning of the feelings being expressed through children's repetitive dramatic play, traumatized drawings, dreams, or nightmares that parents often have difficulty making sense of and find upsetting. Some parents are frightened or became angry with their children for their increased clinginess, tantrums, and aggression. Parents sometimes are afraid that these reactions are signs of lasting damage and future pathology. It can be difficult for parents to see these reactions as expectable responses to a situation of great insecurity. Parents' anxiety or anger in turn makes the child more frightened of losing them and therefore more demanding or aggressive. It is important to help parents answer the questions that children raise both directly and indirectly, while protecting children from exposure to adult conversations. In this way, the adult's reflective function can be reengaged so that they can begin to understand their child's experience.

It is also important to encourage families to try to *return to ordinary daily life* and customary routines as soon as possible. In highly public traumatic events such as occurred on September 11, 2001, we encourage parents to *turn off the TV* and not expose children to endless repetitions of images of the traumatic event (Pfefferbaum 2003).

CASE ILLUSTRATIONS

In the two case vignettes that follow each preschool-age child was suffering from nightmares after the September 11 attack. Maria was seen soon after September 11 in the Kids Corner at Pier 94, and Abbey was seen five months later in a private practice setting.

The case of Maria

Maria had settled at our play table with some crayons and paper while her father, Mr. P, waited to speak to a benefits counselor at an adjacent booth. He had lost his job as a cook because of the WTC attack. Maria, a three-year-old Honduran girl, was left in the kids corner while her father explored available benefits after he lost his job as a cook at the World Trade Center. Her mother was at home with her younger brother. Since 9/11 Maria had had nightmares and slept in the bed with her parents because she was too frightened to sleep by herself.

Maria began to scrawl intently in bright overlapping reds, yellows, and black. She readily told us that she was drawing the buildings that "fell and burned," adding that she had seen this on television. Maria said her father had escaped from the WTC, as the buildings collapsed. She said her father's lungs had been filled with smoke so that he could hardly breathe. While her father was running from the WTC to get home, burning pieces of the building fell on him and burned his arms. She added loudly, "He has marks from the fire on his arms!"

Mr. P. came over to check on his daughter while waiting for some forms to be processed. Dr. Schechter asked the father about the events his daughter had described. He was surprised. "I was not anywhere near the WTC," he said and added incredulously, "She told you I was there?" Mr. P had indeed been employed as a cook at Windows on the World (hence the old burn scars from splattered grease on his arms), but he had exchanged the breakfast shift with a colleague the week prior to the attack. On the morning of 9/11, while his daughter had stayed home with her mother, Mr. P went out to do some errands in Manhattan, but he was nowhere near the WTC.

Dr. Schechter inquired of the father as to how he was doing. The father, a young man, slight and soft spoken, wanted to downplay any troubles of his own. It took two or three further gentle probes for him to reveal that he was profoundly distressed by the loss of his coworkers at Windows on the World. He struggled with feeling responsible for having switched shifts and also because he had found work at the WTC for some of his friends. His agonizing survivor guilt took the form of feeling obliged to vividly imagine how his friends had died: the fire, the smoke, and what they had felt. He also had nightmares from which he awakened several times a night, leaving him to ruminate over their deaths by himself, as he thought, in the dark.

After the father spoke, Dr. Schechter exclaimed, "So your daughter is drawing your dreams!" Indeed, Mr. P appeared shocked that his daughter's drawings and fantasies (perhaps also her nightmares) so closely resembled his own nightmares; he had not discussed them with her. He went on: "Every night when I close my eyes, I see all my coworkers trapped in the smoke and burning up, and there's nothing I can do to save them." His eyes welled with tears as he said: "I guess I'm lucky. It could have been me there. But I miss all of my friends. I am sorry for the guy who took my place. I pray for his family."

This conversation that began in Spanish between Dr. Schechter and Maria's father, continued in English and was carried on within earshot of Maria, sometimes intentionally including her.

After this, Maria turned to drawing a picture of her school, a low rectangle with many windows and doors. She emphasized that there were as many doors as windows, and counted them. A cotherapist from the Parent-Infant Program faculty, Elsa First, remarked that perhaps she meant that there were many openings, many ways to get out of the school so that it would be safe if there were a fire. When asked if she meant her preschool was safe, Maria replied, "Yes."

In sum, both Mr. P and his daughter were confused about what each other had in mind. Mr. P did not expect that his daughter would assume that he was a hero-survivor of the WTC as she had presented him to Dr. Schechter. He was so preoccupied with his job loss and mourning of his coworkers that it had not occurred to him that his daughter would not understand what his actual experience was on 9/11 unless he explained it to her—and in so doing, contain her anxiety. Maria, on the other hand, resonated with his guilty fantasies but lacked connection with her father's actual experience on 9/11. Neither parent had been available to Maria on this day that created such insecurity for her. She had not been helped to what was going on in the mind of the other. Father and daughter were each attempting to make sense of the trauma in relative isolation. This resulted in their regulating their negative affect individually at the expense of mutual regulation and understanding, which they began to recover through interaction with the two Parent-Infant Program cotherapists.

Dr. Schechter gave the family a referral network phone number, and we asked the father for his permission to make a follow-up call. He agreed. As promised, Dr. Schechter called the following week. Dad answered and spoke of how his daughter and infant son were busy at play. Since our meeting, he reported, the little girl's symptoms had subsided though she still needed to sleep in her parents' bed. He also said that his own symptoms were better, he was receiving benefits, and he was hopeful that he might get another job. He had not felt the need to bring his daughter back to the Kids' Corner and had no plans to seek further evaluation or treatment for himself, wife, or children at the time of the follow-up.

The Case of Abbey

Ms. A and her two-year-old daughter were at Ground Zero on September 11 when the first plane attacked the twin tower. Since September 11 Abbey was having difficulty sleeping including having frequent night awakenings and night terrors, and recurrent recollections of the events of September 11. Ms. A, who was severely traumatized, did not get help at first but waited for five months after the terrorist attack to get help for herself and for her daughter. Since September 11 she and Abbey had been suffering from symptoms of PTSD. Ms. A was suffering from flashbacks triggered by the sound of planes, fire engines, and police cars as well as exposure to any images on TV of the Twin Towers burning or falling.

On September 11 Ms. A was in the plaza between the Twin Towers, rolling Abbey in her green stroller to her preschool classroom on the first floor of Tower 1, when the first plane hit. She immediately panicked, grabbed Abbey, and swung her up in the air while she was still strapped into her stroller. Both were exposed to what she said was an indescribably hideous, loud sound followed by debris falling everywhere. Ms. A thought "it was the end of the world," that "we had been hit by a nuclear bomb." She ran to safety in a nearby building. After a massively traumatic day, she retuned home in the evening. Ms. A's experience of terror was so great that she would not open the door to her home for over a week even to get her mail at the front door. Several weeks later after things began to calm down a little bit, she found a new school for Abbey that to Ms. A's relief Abbey took to immediately. She adjusted without apparent anxiety and went off eagerly to join the other children. Despite continuing to have severe PTSD after six weeks, Ms. A went back to work.

At the time of Ms. A's first appointment, she reported that she was so traumatized on September 11 that she had no memory of Abbey's reactions that day. Nor had she noticed whether Abbey's play has been affected since her experience on that day. Some time after September 11, Ms. A bought a new blue stroller to replace the green one that she had abandoned at ground zero. Whenever Abbey saw the new stroller she got very upset and said over and over again, "green stroller, rocks falling, terrible, terrible, terrible."

During Dr. Coates first session with Ms. A, a plane flew overhead and was then followed by the sound of a fire engine. Ms. A was startled, turned white, looked frightened, and began to weep. She said that this was typical of the constant flashbacks that she had had since September 11 and that they were triggered whenever she heard a plane overhead. Hearing a fire engine afterward only made things worse. She said she had tried to put the whole experience behind her but had been unable to.

Dr. Coates met Abbey in a second session. Abbey was an adorable, spunky little girl who easily made herself at home, exploring the play materials and talking to Dr. Coates readily. In about the middle of the session, her mother left the room to take a cell-phone call. After a minute or so Abbey went to the waiting room to check on her mother's whereabouts and finding her there came right back to the playroom to resume her activities. She discovered some small blocks about three inches long by about a quarter of an inch thick. She began to build two towers with the blocks, building them higher and higher until they fell down. She closely monitored Dr. Coates's face and must have registered her uneasiness about what she was doing because she was worried that Abbey might retraumatize herself. Abbey looked startled when the blocks fell down and looked at Dr. Coates to check her reaction. Dr. Coates said, with a little smile on her face, "Boom, they fell down." In a pause in which she seemed to not know what to do, Dr. Coates said, "Shall we build them up again?" With great eagerness Abbey began to build them up again, and Dr. Coates asked her if she would like to push them over or if she might like her to push them over for her. She became animated and asked Dr. Coates to do it. Dr. Coates built another tower, narrating as she did it, asking Abbey whether she wanted Dr. Coates to knock it over or whether she wanted to knock it down herself. Once again, she pointed to Dr. Coates and nodded her head enthusiastically. Then Abbey began to build them by herself over and over again, knocking them down in a very animated way. Dr. Coates picked up a few blocks and gently dropped them on the floor from a height of about two inches. She had in mind the fact that on September 11 Abbey had experienced debris falling from the sky, some of it landing on her head. Abbey immediately imitated Dr. Coates and began picking the blocks up higher and higher into the air dropping them and becoming more animated with squeals of glee.

Dr. Coates looked over at her mother and saw tears in her eyes. She said, "I can't believe that she can remember all this." Dr. Coates asked her how it made her feel. She said, "I can't bear the sound of the noise of the blocks clinking; it makes me think of the crash." Dr. Coates explained to her that this was her daughter's way of working through and mastering her own experience of trauma just the way she was trying to do by talking to her own therapist. Dr. Coates said, "Abbey needs your help," and invited her to come join in and actively help Abbey build towers and knock them down. Dr. Coates asked her to let Abbey take the initiative and let her be the director of her own story: let her decide who would build up the blocks and who will knock them down. She played with her daughter building and knocking down towers until the session was over. At the end of the session, Ms. A asked me where she could buy these small blocks in the neighborhood so that she could take them home to help her daughter.

As they were leaving my apartment, Ms. A heard some very soft footsteps in the apartment above mine and had a startled reaction to it. Abbey then became very anxious about the sound. Ms. A noted that she needed to try to keep her startled reactions in check because she noticed that Abbey was beginning to have anxious reactions in response to her own startle reactions.

Both Maria's and Abbey's reaction to September 11 illustrates the way that young children's reactions to trauma are closely linked to their parents' own reactions. In the case of Abbey and her mother, each traumatized the other, thereby illustrating Scheeringa and Zeanah's relational PTSD model of "compound effect." Given how unbearable Ms. A found it to witness Abbey reenacting her September 11 experience in Dr. Coates's office, it seems likely that she shut out Abbey's ongoing experience since September 11 much in the same way that Maria's father had done in his grief and while experiencing intense survival guilt. During this time of great threat and disorganization, neither Maria's father nor Abbey's mother were able to reflect upon their child's experience and keep their child's experience in mind. Once they were in the presence of a third, who could help them reflect upon and help them contain their own experience, each parent became able to take in their child's experience.

One might ask how the interventions described would lead to such impressive results so rapidly. As has been described elsewhere by the authors (Coates, Schechter, and First 2003; Schechter 2003), the very young child's unmodulated outpouring of negative affect has the power to render accessible in the parent her own repressed, dissociated, or otherwise post-traumatically avoided feeling states. As Daniel Stern (1995) has suggested, especially when her children are young, there is a window of altruism in which the needs of her child far outweigh a mothers' own needs, and in addition, we believe that the mother not only wants to protect her child but oftentimes has a strong wish to repair the wounds of past traumas, and to protect her child from experiencing the traumas that she has known. These are all positive motivators for change within the safety of a reflective therapeutic relationship.

Thus, these two cases clearly illustrate the principle, supported by research findings (Scheeringa and Zeanah 1995; Schechter 2003; Lyons-Ruth and Block 1996), that trauma and its sequelae must be considered, particularly for young children and caregivers in a relational and developmental context. When secure and organized, attachment can be a source of resilience in the face of trauma or, when insecure and disorganized, can be a vehicle for the exacerbation of trauma's effects as well as transmission of those effects across generations.

When a prior relational disturbance exists, it is even more imperative for the clinician to provide support and guidance to the patient's primary caretaker so that they can help the child after dealing with their own reaction to the trauma (Coates, Schechter, and First 2003). This key principle of a relational approach to treating the effects of trauma is analogous to the airline crew's instructions for caregivers to place the oxygen mask over the face of the parent before putting it on the face of the child.

PRINCIPLES OF INTERVENTION WITH INFANTS AND PRESCHOOL CHILDREN AFTER THE INITIAL REACTION TO THE TRAUMATIC EVENTS

For those children whose traumatic reaction does not subside with the first weeks after a traumatic event, psychotherapy that is focused on treatment of the posttraumatic stress reaction is indicated. The time-honored method for treating traumatized children first described by the psychoanalyst David Levy (1939) is controlled exposure to the traumatizing event in structured play situations that are designed to elicit the memory and affective reactions to the traumatic event in a safe environment. Toys such as toy dogs, cars, doctor kits, fire engines, or any item that is associated with the trauma are useful in eliciting the memory of the trauma in the safe environment of the therapist's office.

Particularly for the traumatized young child, meeting a new person, the therapist, in a new environment is likely to initially create anxiety. It is important that the child establishes trust in the therapist and that the therapist moves slowly enough through the controlled exposure so as not to retraumatize the child. This often takes considerable clinical skill and involves ensuring that the treatment provides a safe, secure base from which to explore both external events and intrapsychic experiences of those events. In order to create this prerequisite sturdy foundation for treatment, the therapist must be active in establishing safety in the present life of the child before addressing past trauma. This can involve calling or assisting a caregiver such as day-care workers or a nursery school teacher.

Initial consultations with parents should take place before the child is seen and should focus not only on taking a careful history but, most importantly, should focus on educating the parent about trauma and PTSD, as well as about child development and the importance of the relationship to the care-givers in the wake of trauma. We believe, along with Gaensbauer and Siegel (1995), that when possible it is important to have the parent or parents in the room with the therapist and child so that the parent can begin to understand the child's experience and can develop effective ways of soothing the child. We consider it to be essential that both the child and the parent develop a coherent narrative together about the traumatic event so that it can continue to be processed by the parent and child outside the therapy session. One of the most therapeutic experiences for the child is to know that his or her par-ent not only holds the traumatic experience in mind but also attempts to hold the *child's experience* of the trauma in mind (Schechter forthcoming; Coates 1998). As the child, the therapist, and the parents rework the traumatic event through, time and again, they coconstruct a shared narrative that over time incorporates more and more fragments of the experience that initially was too unbearable to think about, feel, or integrate. In this way the child begins to feel mastery over an experience that was previously overwhelming.

Because children develop so rapidly, their experience of a trauma will be colored by the developmental challenges that they are grappling with at the time, and the trauma will in turn affect their ongoing developmental progress. Each developmental issue that has been affected by the trauma needs to be addressed as it emerges in the child's therapy (see Gaensbauer and Siegel [1995] for an excellent overview).

CONCLUSION

Trauma in the young child is mediated and moderated by the primary care-taker's emotional reactions to the traumatizing event and to the child's emo-tional reactions to the event. Moreover, the child's symptoms in response to a traumatic event and the particular meaning of that event to that child will be, in large part, dependent on the child's developmental capabilities at the time of the trauma and during the subsequent working-through of the trau-matic experience.

In the wake of a disaster, the guidelines for intervention with the child are to listen, clarify, support the child's attachment bonds, facilitate symbolic expression, and support the child's capacity to imagine repair. Simultane-ously, it is essential to help parents contextualize their responses, under-stand their child's reaction, and facilitate communication between the parent and the child.

In treating entrenched PTSD, controlled reexposure to the traumatizing event should occur within the established safety of the treatment situation and, when feasible, with the parents present during these sessions. This will facilitate the development of a shared narrative about the trauma. While desensitization and the coconstruction of a coherent narrative about the trauma are goals for the child, the restoration of the ability of the caregivers to step outside of the trauma-related dysregulation and to attempt to understand the child's emotional experience is the primary goal of intervention with the parents. Only in this way can the healing caregiver sensitively provide for the child's needs, needs such as that of reestablishing a sense of safety in the world, in the family, and in the self.

REFERENCES

American Psychiatric Association. 1994. *Diagnostic and statistical manual of mental disorders—fourth edition (DSM-IV)*. Washington, D.C.: American Psychiatric Association.

Beebe, B., and F. M. Lachmann. 1994. Representation and internalization in infancy: Three principles of salience. *Psychoanalytic Psychology* 11(2):127–65.

Bowlby, J., J. Robertson, and D. Rosenbluth. 1952. A two-year-old goes to the hospital. *Psychoanalytic Study of the Child* 7:82–94.

Breslau, N., H. D. Chilcoat, R. C. Kessler, and G. C. Davis. 1999. Previous exposure to trauma and PTSD effects of subsequent trauma: Results from the Detroit Area Survey of Trauma. *American Journal of Psychiatry* 156(6):902–7.

Bretherton, I. 1995. The origins of attachment theory: John Bowlby and Mary Ainsworth. In *Attachment theory: Social, developmental and clinical perspectives*, ed. S Goldberg, R. Muir, and J. Kerr, 50. Hillsdale, N.J.: Analytic Press.

Coates, S. W. 1998. Having a mind of one's own and holding the other in mind. *Psychoanalytic Dialogues* 8(1):115–48.

Coates, S. W., and M. S. Moore. 1997. The complexity of early trauma: Representation and transformation. *Psychoanalytic Inquiry* 17:286–311.

Coates, S. W., D. S. Schechter, and E. First. 2003. Brief interventions with traumatized children and families after September 11. In *September 11: Trauma and human bonds*, ed. S. W. Coates, J. Rosenthal, and D. S. Schechter, 23–49. Hillsdale, N.J.: Analytic Press.

Cornely, P., and E. Bromet. 1986. Prevalence of behavior problems in three-year-old children living near Three Mile Island: A comparative analysis. *Journal of Child Psychology and Psychiatry* 27:489–98.

Emde, R., A. Guedeney, H. Wright, E. Fenichel, and B. Wise. 2004. Diagnostic classification of 0–3 results of clinical trial, user survey, and a preliminary revision. Paper presented at the World Association of Infant Mental Health, Melbourne, Australia.

Fraiberg, S., E. Adelson, and V. Shapiro. 1975. Ghosts in the nursery. *Journal of the American Academy of Child and Adolescent Psychiatry* 14:387–421.

Freud, A., and D. Burlingham. 1943. *Children in war*. New York: Medical War Books.

Gaensbauer, T. J. 1982. The differentiation of discrete affects: A case report. *Psychoanalytic Study of the Child* 37:29–66.

Gaensbauer, T. J., and C. H. Siegel. 1995. Therapeutic approaches to posttraumatic stress disorder in infants and toddlers. *Infant Mental Health Journal* 16(4):292–305.

Galea, S., J. Ahern, H. Resnick, D. Kilpatrick, M. Bucuvalas, M. J. Gold, and D. Vlahov. 2002. Psychological sequelae of the September 11 terrorist attacks in New York City. *New England Journal of Medicine* 346:982–87.

Gurwitch, R. H., M. A. Sullivan, and P. J. Long. 1998. The impact of trauma and disaster on young children. *Child and Adolescent Psychiatric Clinics of North America* 7(1):19–32.

Hoven, C. W., D. J. Mandell, and C. S. Duarte. 2003. Mental health of New York City public school children after 9/11. In *September 11: Trauma and human bonds*, ed. S. W. Coates, J. Rosenthal, and D. S. Schechter, 51–74. Hillsdale N.J.: Analytic Press.

Klein, T. P., E. Devoe, and C. Miranda. 2003. Impact of the World Trade Center disaster on young children at Ground Zero. Paper presented at the biennial meeting of the Society for Research in Child Development, Tampa, Florida.

Koplewicz, H. S., J. M. Vogel, M. V. Solanto, R. F. Morrissey, C. M. Alonso, H. Abikoff, R. Gallagher, and R. M. Novick. 2002. Child and parent responses to the 1993 World Trade Center bombing. *Journal of Traumatic Stress* 15(1):77–85.

Laor, N., L. Wolmer, L. C. Mayes, and A. Gershon. 1997. Israeli preschool children under scuds: A 30-month follow-up. *American Academy of Child and Adolescent Psychiatry* 36:349–56.

Levy, D. 1939. Release therapy. *American Journal of Orthopsychiatry* 9:713–36.

———. 1945. Psychic trauma of operations in children and a note on combat neurosis. *American Journal of Diseases of Children* 69:7–25.

Lyons-Ruth, K., and D. Block. 1996. The disturbed caregiving system: Relations among childhood trauma, maternal caregiving, and infant affect and attachment. *Infant Mental Health Journal* 17:257–75.

Pfefferbaum, B. 2001. The impact of the Oklahoma City bombing on children in the community. *Military Medicine* 166(12):49–50.

———. 2003. Media exposure in children one hundred miles from a terrorist bombing. *Annals of Clinical Psychiatry* 15(1):1–8.Pynoos, R. S. 2001. Personal communication to S. Coates. November 3, 2001.

Pynoos, R. S., and K. Nader. 1988. Psychological first aid and treatment approach to children exposed to community violence: Research implications. *Journal of Traumatic Stress* 1(4):445–73.

Pynoos, R. S., A. M. Steinberg, and R. Wraith. 1995. A developmental model of childhood traumatic stress. In *Developmental psychopathology. Vol. 2: Risk, disorder and adaptation*, ed. D. Cicchetti and D. J Cohen, 72–95. New York: Wiley.

Saltzman, W.R., C. M. Layne, A. M. Steinberg, B. Arslanagic, and R. S. Pynoos. 2003. Developing a culturally and ecologically sound intervention program for youth exposed to war and terrorism. *Child and Adolescent Psychiatric Clinics of North America* 12(2):319–42.

Schechter, D. S. 2003. Intergenerational communication of maternal violent trauma: Understanding the interplay of reflective functioning and posttraumatic psychopathology. In *September 11: Trauma and human bonds*, ed. S. W. Coates, J. Rosenthal, and D. S. Schechter, 115–42. Hillsdale, N.J.: Analytic Press.

Schechter, D. S., S. W. Coates, and E. First. 2001. Observations from New York on young childrens' and their families' acute reactions to the World Trade Center attacks. *Bulletin Zero to Three* 22(3):9–13.

Schechter, D. S., T. Coots, C. H. Zeanah, S. W. Coates, J. F. Grienenberger, M. Davies, M. Myers, and M. R. Liebowitz. forthcoming. On the interplay of posttraumatic psychopathology and reflective functioning in the wake of interpersonal violence exposure: Understanding determinants of maternal perceptual distortion. *Attachment and Human Development.*

Schechter, D. S., and M. C. Tosyali. 2001. Posttraumatic stress disorder from infancy through adolescence: A review. In *Anxiety disorders in children and adolescents: Epidemiology, risk factors, and treatment,* ed. C. A. Essau and F. Petermann, 285–322. New York: Brunner-Routledge.

Scheeringa, M. S, and C. H. Zeanah. 1995. Symptom expression and trauma variables in children under 48 months of age. *Infant Mental Health Journal* 16:259–70.

———. 2001. A relational perspective on PTSD in early childhood. *Journal of Traumatic Stress* 14:799–815.

Scheeringa, M. S., C. H. Zeanah, L. Myers, and F. W. Putnam. 2003. New findings on alternative criteria for PTSD in preschool children. *Journal of the American Academy of Child and Adolescent Psychiatry* 42:561–70.

Stern, D. N. 1995. *The motherhood constellation: A unified view of parent-infant psychotherapy.* New York: Basic Books.

Stuber, J., G. Fairbrother, S. Galea, B. Pfefferbaum, M. Wilson-Genderson, and D. Vlahov. 2002. Determinants of counseling for children in Manhattan after the September 11 attacks. *Psychiatry Services* 53(7):815–22.

Terr, L. C. 1987. Childhood psychic trauma. In *Basic handbook of child psychiatry. Vol. 5: Advances and new directions,* ed. J. D. Noshpitz, 262–71. New York: Basic Books.

Yehuda, R., S. L. Halligan, and R. Grossman. 2001. Childhood trauma and risk for PTSD: Relationship to intergenerational effects of trauma, parental PTSD, and cortisol excretion. *Developmental Psychopathology* 13:733–53.

Zero to Three: National Center for Infants, Toddlers, and Families. 1994. *Diagnostic classification: 0–3 (DC: 0–3).* Washington, D.C.: Zero to Three: National Center for Infants, Toddlers, and Families.

III

COMMON TREATMENT
SITUATIONS

6

The Initial Meetings

Kerry Kelly Novick and Jack Novick

Editor's Note: This chapter is excerpted with minor revisions from the book *Working with Parents Makes Therapy Work* (2005). The original work included discussions of individual treatment with children. However, in keeping with the theme of this book we have focused here on the work with parents.

EVALUATIONS ASSESS BOTH CHILD AND PARENTS

Evaluations of children, adolescents, and adults are usually done for diagnostic purposes. When they are done by analysts or therapists influenced by psychoanalytic ideas, the goal is to reach beyond description to a sense of the dynamic and historical factors that may be at the root of the difficulty. In our model there are additional goals. The evaluation is not only to assess and diagnose the child but first to assess the parents and to develop a working relationship with them. This turns parents into partners who can work with the therapist to see how far they can go in helping the child. Together, parents and analyst may reach a point where it is clear to all concerned that there are underlying problems—that there is more to the child's story. Then a recommendation for therapy or analysis makes sense, as the purpose of an analytic treatment is to understand what is behind the symptoms.

TREATMENT OF CHILDREN AND ADOLESCENTS HAS DUAL GOALS: RESTORATION OF THE CHILD TO THE PATH OF PROGRESSIVE DEVELOPMENT, AND RESTORATION OF THE PARENT-CHILD RELATIONSHIP TO A LIFELONG POSITIVE RESOURCE FOR BOTH

Anna Freud defined the goal of child analysis as restoration of the child to the path of progressive development. We have extended this idea to include a second goal: helping parents achieve the developmental phase of parenthood, that is, restoring parents to the path of progressive adult development, in which parenthood is one phase.

Our view of the parent-child relationship provides a framework for evolving a technique of parent work that encompasses both the resistances and the developmental aids to therapy. The aim of child analysis can be recast as not only the restoration of the child's progressive development but also as the restoration of the parent-child relationship that has been disrupted from its potential as a lifelong positive resource for both. This idea is not only an implicit assumption but also an active and explicit assertion. We tell parents early in the evaluation that we have these two goals for our endeavors together. We work with this idea until it becomes an intrinsic motivation for continued treatment.

THE THERAPEUTIC ALLIANCE IS A CONCEPTUAL FRAMEWORK FOR ONGOING PARENT WORK

Parents' intense wish to do right by their child, to be the best parents they can be, is a powerful motive force for entering into a therapeutic alliance with the analyst. The framework for parent work that we use is our revised concept of the therapeutic alliance, which includes building and maintaining an alliance between therapist and parents or significant others. There are parental tasks for each phase of treatment. Looking at the therapeutic relationship through the lens of the therapeutic alliance explicates and operationalizes analysis as a developmental experience for both child and parents.

The parental therapeutic-alliance tasks through the different phases of treatment provide a shared arena for working on interferences with aspects of psychological parenting. Each phase of treatment presents parents with new alliance tasks whose accomplishment consolidates progressive development in the parents. Parallel with the child's internalization of the therapeutic alliance is the parents' internalization of ways of functioning that foster and maintain mutual respect, support, love, and continued growth. These transformations begin during the evaluation as parents and therapists work together to change

   guilt to usable concern,
   self-help to joint work,
   circumstantial explanations to internal meanings and motivations,
   externalizations onto the child to attunement with the child,
   parental helplessness to competence,
   despair to hopefulness, and
   idealization or denigration of the child to primary parental love.

The analyst learns a great deal about the parents' personalities and the prospects for a successful working relationship from how parents respond to the task of beginning these transformations. Making a start lays the foundation for a relationship of collaboration and mutuality between therapist and parents. Progress in the transformation tasks during the evaluation can be measured by changes in parental capacity to see the child as a separate person. Only then can they feel genuine empathy with his distress in contrast to angry exasperation, injured vanity, or frustrated control.

PARENTAL ANXIETIES

Within each parental anxiety, at any point in treatment, there may be a corresponding issue for the analyst. For example, a parents' wish and fear to get rid of their child complements analysts' rescue fantasies or rivalry with the parents. A major parental anxiety is that the child's affections or loyalties will be stolen by the analyst (Furman 1997). Guilty and defensive, out of touch with their love for their child, parents come to the situation feeling, consciously or unconsciously, that they may deserve to have their child taken away. To the extent that they are angry and frustrated with the child's lack of response to their efforts to ameliorate the situation, they may also wish to hand the child over, dump the child on the therapist, and get rid of the trouble and pain the child's difficulties have caused.

PARENTAL GUILT AS AN INTERFERENCE

During the evaluation we establish explicitly with parents that one of the treatment goals is restoring their relationship with the child. A tone of respect for their knowledge, perceptions, good intentions, and renewed love toward their child, coupled with genuine collaboration in the process of coming to an understanding of the child's troubles, may provide enough counterbalance to crushing guilt and anxiety for parents.

TRANSFORMING GUILT TO USABLE CONCERN

Parental anxiety is indeed a powerful motivator that fuels most initial contacts with a therapist. We suggest, however, that one task of the evaluation is to transform guilty anxiety into constructive concern. Several assumptions are implicit in this idea. In the evaluation, and over time during extended work with parents, we are also eliciting and fostering primary parental love, which is only possible when the child is seen as a separate, valued person in his own right. In addition, we are assessing the degree of enmeshment between parent and child, which denies autonomy and ties them together through externalizations. Parent work can often successfully dissipate initial parental anxiety and bring real improvement in the situation.

THE IMPORTANCE OF EVALUATION

The evaluation phase has hitherto been somewhat neglected, often dispensed with, and rarely thought about as the crucial foundation for a successful treatment. Parents very frequently initiate contact with a request for therapy for their child, skipping over evaluation entirely. Both Furman and Rosenbaum have emphasized the importance of dealing with the anxieties and resistances of this crucial part of therapy. E. Furman (1995), among other issues, underlines the necessity for addressing parental guilt and harnessing it constructively, while Rosenbaum (1994) has described the long time needed to help parents see their child as a separate person with his or her own problems. We have subsumed all these issues under the rubric of the therapeutic alliance with parents.

Engaging parents in the tasks of transformation is not only vital for the success of a child's treatment but is also the crucial beginning of change in the direction of full functioning in the phase of psychological parenthood.

PARENTAL DENIAL

The paucity of child and adolescent cases reported by most analytic centers is especially pronounced in relation to the preschool population. This is not because preschoolers do not manifest developmental deviation, but rather because parental denial is especially intense at this phase. Those of us who have worked or consulted in typical preschools can confirm what large-scale studies demonstrate, namely, that at least 25 percent of preschoolers have problems that will not be outgrown but will result in impaired functioning in elementary school. Denial seems to be parents' main defense, one colluded with by pediatricians and teachers, and these parents generally do not seek professional help until pressured by schools after obvious developmental failures in midlatency or early adolescence. With pregnancy, or even before, the capacity to conceive and bear an intact, healthy, well-functioning child becomes a major source of parental self-esteem, especially for mothers. This deep involvement with the child's development may eventuate in a need to deny difficulties because facing them causes unbearable psychic pain to the parent, or it may operate as a progressive force, serving the child's growth despite the cost to parental self-esteem. Denial is often a problem with fathers, who can be particularly reluctant to face their children's difficulties.

THE ROLE OF FATHERS

The first child analysis was actually a treatment conducted through the father, the case of Little Hans (S. Freud 1909). Some analysts have emphasized the importance of the father in children's development (Abelin 1975, 1980; Burlingham 1973; Herzog 1982; Pruett 1985, 1992). But in the meager literature on parent work there is almost no specific discussion on the vicissitudes of work with the fathers of child or adolescent patients. To some extent, this reflects a continuing practical reality that many mothers are more flexibly available for appointments than are fathers. Nevertheless, we have found that fathers play a crucial role in all aspects of a child's development, including treatment outcome. Thus, it is very important to include fathers in parent work somehow and examine any particular technical issues in that work.

We have noted two resistances in fathers to treatment of their child and to their involvement in the therapeutic process. One springs from fathers' underestimation of their own importance to the child, which often relates to issues in the marriage over parental primacy. A further contributor is defense against feelings of failure. Another is a denial of the internal nature of the child's difficulties in favor of blaming external circumstances, the mother, or other children, or reacting with moralistic anger over bad behavior. Fathers may feel their masculinity is assailed if their child has emotional difficulties. Despite apparent cultural changes, many men still feel that it is babyish or girlish to be emotional, have troubles, and need help. They expect their children, especially boys, to take control of themselves and "suck it up."

Woven through this chapter are many examples of the variety of parent work, including issues with fathers. Here, however, is an example of a simple intervention with a father that proved crucial for his son's development.

Robert, at the age of three, was a nonspeaker with a diagnosis of autism. He had a congenital deformity of the leg and walked with a noticeable limp. His father, a very nice giant of a man, had been shunted out of care-taking by Robert's mother and grandmother, a position he readily accepted, as he found it very difficult to connect to his damaged son. After the initial interviews, he said that he would support the treatment but that his wife alone would attend parent sessions while he focused on earning a living and taking care of their five-year-old daughter. The analyst suggested separate regular meetings with the father at a convenient time for him and made this a condition of the treatment. Robert's father accepted under pressure from his wife and desperation at his son's predicament.

The father hinted at and the analyst could verbalize the father's pain and aversion to Robert's deformity. The father had been a champion swimmer—the therapist said that he could understand the father's anxiety and focus on Robert's leg, which still required nightly splinting. "But he is more than a leg," said the analyst. "What I see is a tall, strong boy with large shoulders who will probably end up as large and strong as you are." He went on to ask the father which part of the body was more important in swimming. Robert's father smiled broadly, thanked the analyst, and from then on remained connected to Robert through all the emotional vicissitudes of the treatment.

At the outset we have to acknowledge a major technical issue in work with parents. Parents are not the designated patients; they usually come because they or someone else sees the *child* as needing psychological intervention. Parents come to professionals because they feel helpless. If their response to helplessness is the invoking of feelings of hostile omnipotence, they may then feel overwhelming guilt. This in turn can lead to frantic attempts to avoid being traumatized by guilt, which may take the form of blaming others, especially the child, and then eventually the analyst, for their own failures. Given the constellation of failure, omnipotent defenses, overwhelming guilt, and externalization, how can we enlist the parents in an alliance whose aim is not only to help the child but also to help the parents grow? Guilty parents may be apt to hear any suggestion of engaging in a process of personal change as a criticism or, conversely, become enthralled in a relationship with a wished-for omnipotent therapist, co-opting the child's treatment for their own.

Guilty and defensive, parents come to the situation feeling, consciously or unconsciously, that they may deserve to have their child taken away. To the extent that they are angry and frustrated with the child's lack of response to their efforts to ameliorate the situation, they may also wish to hand the child over, dump the child on the therapist, and get rid of the trouble and pain the child's difficulties have caused. This wish can cause further guilt, which may be defended against by clinging to the child and undermining the development of his new relationship with the therapist. In extreme cases, this is one of the determinants of a negative therapeutic motivation (J. Novick 1980).

THE UTILITY OF THE THERAPEUTIC ALLIANCE FRAMEWORK

This constellation of conflicting feelings can leave the analyst feeling overwhelmed. We think this may be one reason for therapists' demonstrable ambivalence about working with parents—it is hard to know where to start. The very parents who most need help often generate helplessness in the therapist, with real dangers to the therapeutic process posed by the mobilization of the analyst's defenses. An adaptive response to helplessness is to seek solutions through competence. For therapists, this means feeling effective in understanding the situation and having a repertoire of appropriate interventions to call upon.

We think that our developmentally informed revision of the concept of the therapeutic alliance expands the repertoire of therapists by suggesting additional ways to approach intense parental resistances. Parents' deep wish to do right by their child, to be the best parents they can be, regardless of degree or type of interfering pathology, is a powerful motive force for the therapeutic alliance. The transformative tasks of the therapeutic alliance, beginning in the evaluation phase, are designed to help parents gain or regain some feeling of competence as parents and love for their child as a separate person.

THE FORMAT OF AN EVALUATION

The traditional format of child or adolescent evaluation has been to have one or two initial interviews with the parents, some meetings with the child, and then a final interview with the parents, in which the therapist presents the results of the evaluation and the treatment recommendations. Our approach is to extend the evaluation in order to do as much as possible through working with the parents. Testing the power and limits of working via the parents is, in our experience, essential to the establishment of a therapeutic alliance with the parents. It reconfirms that parents are active partners in their child's treatment, that parents remain primary, and that therapists are not rival or substitute parents. Rather, the different adults have different functions, each essential to restoring the child to the path of progressive development, whether it is a referral appropriate for a psychotherapist or psychoanalyst, or whether other services might first be indicated.

Treatment of the child via the parent is a technique that was used by Anna Freud and others in the early days of child analysis in Vienna (A. Freud 1966). It was elaborated and established by Anny Katan, first in Holland and then with her colleagues in Cleveland (Furman and Katan 1969). Development of this powerful procedure with preschoolers continues in Cleveland, and clinical illustrations abound in the journal of the Hanna Perkins Center, *Child Analysis*. Modifications and variations are used by others such as Rosenbaum (1994), and we have increasingly found it to be an essential part of the evaluation process for all ages, not only with preschoolers. The value of placing these powerful techniques within the framework of the therapeutic alliance is to allow the inclusion of the additional goal of restoring parents to the path of progressive development.

THE FIRST PHONE CALL

Working via the parent or working with the parent can start as early as the first phone call. We always make sure that we have at least twenty to thirty minutes available for an initial conversation with a parent who has called. We ask the parent if it is convenient to spend some time talking on the phone. Most parents welcome the opportunity to talk a bit right away, as they have called a therapist at a moment of great anxiety or frustration. There are various reasons for taking care and time at this point, and we hope thereby to accomplish a number of things. First of all, it conveys our interest and respect for what the parent is worried about and makes it clear that we want to listen. We ask the parent if they would like to tell us a bit about their concerns, why they are calling just now. This allows for immediate assessment of whether there is a situation so urgent that it demands immediate transfer to an emergency room. There is also the question of whether it is a referral appropriate for a psychotherapist or psychoanalyst, or whether other services might be indicated. For example, a mother who calls with concerns about severe delays in language development may benefit from immediate advice to pursue a hearing, or speech and language, evaluation before continuing with addressing the psychological and emotional dimensions of the difficulties.

When parents describe what is worrying to them about the child's functioning, or what the school has reported, it allows us to respond in terms of taking them seriously and complimenting their effort to take good care of their child by investigating whether there is a problem. This speaks directly to the ambivalence and guilt that are inevitable when parents have reached the point of calling a therapist. We reassure parents that therapy is not a foregone conclusion but rather that an evaluation of the situation will help them determine how best to meet their child's needs. The message is always that parents are in charge.

We describe a stepped process: it begins with parents filling out a developmental history form and returning it to us before the first meeting. With preschool or school-aged children, we ask parents to fill out the form. With adolescents, we ask parents to do it with their child. In divorce situations, each parent is asked to do a form. The request to complete this simple form, which can be faxed, mailed, or e-mailed, has several aims. We note to parents that the information provides us both with a beginning context, starts us thinking about the child, and thus, may save time and money. When we meet for the first time, there is then already a shared knowledge base—analyst and parents are, in a sense, not strangers. It lets parents know that we assume they have the important knowledge about their own child. It conveys that the past is meaningful in understanding what is going on. And it demonstrates that the therapist is interested in the whole child, not just the current difficulties.

The plan for the evaluation is discussed in detail. The first meetings are described as an effort to learn more details about the current concerns, how they arose, and what parents and others have attempted in dealing with them. We note that therapist and parents are bound to begin to pick up patterns as they talk, to formulate questions and hypotheses, and to generate together some ideas for the parents to try out in relation to the issues. The implicit message is one of collaboration.

In some cases working via the parent may continue for some time and may be sufficient to restore progressive development in child and parents. Sometimes we can predict which cases will or will not respond well to initial work via the parents, but often we have been surprised at how much can be accomplished. This may be partly related to the traditional mental set, conveyed in training and in much of the professional literature, which underestimates or even omits the importance of parents in treatment of children of all ages. The gains of attempting to accomplish therapeutic goals by the most conservative and economical means, that is, through first working via the parents, are many.

George's parents called seeking an evaluation because their four-year-old son wanted to dress up in his older sister's clothes. George had been doing this for a year, but his parents had been advised by the pediatrician to ignore the behavior, as he would grow out of it. The telephone call was prompted by the concern expressed at George's nursery school, where the teachers noted that he avoided playing with the boys and was beginning to be teased by classmates. The parents were confused and anxious, not knowing how to respond to the feminine behavior.

The parents had taken George to a number of psychological and medical specialists without any definitive answers. Endocrine specialists had determined that there was no physiological disorder underlying the behavior. George had told his parents that he wanted to be a girl and that he dressed up because it made him feel "so good." George's parents wanted the analyst to evaluate the reasons, to see George, and to tell them whether George was "a boy pretending to be a girl or a girl in a boy's body."

The analyst suggested to the parents that he would like to meet with them first to explore George's history and see if together they could begin to make sense of the mystery. They came to regular sessions, without George, for six months. During this time it emerged first that George said clearly that he knew he was a boy, but that he felt it would be safer to be a girl. As they explored George's development to find out what might feel so dangerous, a serious medical history emerged.

George had undergone a series of three major surgeries to address a cranial/sacral fusion, starting at the age of nine months, with a further operation projected for age nine. In the first few meetings, the analyst provided a space for the parents to express their intense sadness and anxiety. They said they had never been able to talk about these issues with the many medical personnel who had taken care of their son.

The operations themselves had been frightening, and after each one, they had to restrain George and prevent any gross motor activity. Both parents worried about George's future, and his father, who was a former star high school wrestler and football player, said with great sorrow that George would never be able to play contact sports. This work led quickly to the realization that they believed and conveyed the idea to George that being a boy exposed him to serious danger, since boys are drawn to rough sports. As they understood this, they became able to more easily separate this idea from their love for him as the boy he was. They talked to George about how they would work together with the doctors to help him stay safe from injury. They noted that he would be able to do all sorts of things that big boys liked, such as running and swimming. Clarifying the history of the medical interventions and the prognosis with the analyst gave the parents practice in how to talk with George about the scary things that had happened when he was a baby, and to give him appropriate explanations of his condition. George then told them he could remember being held down and restrained. He recalled his frustration, terror, and rage and revealed that he felt he was being punished for being a bad boy. When the analyst wondered if George might be making any additional connections between the surgeries and the dangers of being a boy, the parents remembered that his six-year-old sister, out of her own terror, had told George that girls never needed that kind of operation.

The final piece of work related to George's pleasures in masturbation and his oedipally tinged conclusion that having boy feelings in his penis for his mother and sister would bring further medical trauma upon him. The parents themselves had been traumatized, first by having a damaged child then by unsupported medical experiences. After the initial period of sharing, sorrow, and reliving of their panic and distress, they worked together with each other and the analyst very effectively on George's behalf. George responded within weeks. After six months of working via the parents, George was functioning in an age-appropriate masculine way at home and at school. He played with boys, loved fire trucks, never talked about wanting to be a girl, and still loved ballet.

The case was closed for the time being, with the parents understanding that the medical situation left George vulnerable to finding magical solutions at times of stress. They felt equipped to help him more effectively, and also knew how well they could make use of professional assistance to enhance their parenting in good times and bad. They talked about coming back for help when George reached adolescence.

PARENT WORK ON BEHALF OF OLDER CHILDREN

Working via the parent has traditionally been a method used mostly with parents of preschoolers, but we have found that the principles and techniques involved can sometimes usefully be applied across age groups.

Katrin's parents sought help because they felt their adopted fifteen-year-old daughter was in need of treatment, but she refused any suggestion to see someone, and her parents were afraid that pressure even to have an evaluation would make her run away from home. The analyst agreed to see the parents for a while to clarify their feelings about the situation and to see if it were possible to find some ways to work with their daughter around the difficulties that were causing her to fail in school and disrupt her relationships with adults and peers.

In discussions with Katrin's parents, it became clear that they, particularly the mother, were overly involved in her body and daily care. Both parents were exceptionally anxious about Katrin and about aspects of the outside world—her mother would not drive on the freeway, and her father telephoned home to check on the family's safety several times daily. Many aspects of their own early histories were played out explicitly with their daughter. Issues of separation had become confused with their feelings about their late adoption of Katrin. They had been afraid that they would not be able to truly love her unless they "made her their own" by changing her name at the age of nearly two. Fear of feeling unconnected had led them to stay completely enmeshed in her psychological and practical life.

Over a period of eighteen months, Katrin's parents attended regular sessions to talk about their parenting. They were able to differentiate more from her, to distinguish their feelings from Katrin's, and to begin to delimit areas of responsibility. Katrin's response to the changes in her parents was to grow considerably, giving up much of her rebellious behavior, while continuing to go her own way in pursuing an unconventional academic career.

Treatment via the parent for under-fives seems to work, among other reasons, because of the emotional availability of the young child and the parents' developmentally appropriate emotional closeness at that age. In Katrin's case, her parents' closeness to her represented a developmental arrest in their growth as parents but provided a temporary entrée to the dynamics of their relationships. With insight into their overinvolvement, they returned to the path of progressive development as parents and were able to achieve appropriate separation from their daughter. When Katrin went on to professional training in another city, she was able to ask the analyst, whom she had never seen, for a referral for treatment in her own right.

INITIATING THE TRANSFORMATIONS OF EVALUATION

Although each situation is different, the following story of the evaluation phase with Henry and his parents can be used to illustrate the initiation of a sequence of transformations. Henry's parents began to shift from acute anxiety to realistic concern, then renewed denial, which, when confronted, required the transformation of guilt to concern. Finally, defensive withdrawal gave way to a renewal of primary parental love for the child.

In the first phone conversation, four-year-old Henry's mother talked about his inability to separate from her and the degree of anxiety he seemed to experience at night. The parents were worried that these problems might interfere with his adjustment to school. In the first meeting, the parents' anxiety was acute. The mother felt sure that her son was severely disturbed and feared guiltily that she had damaged him. The father minimized Henry's problems but also blamed his wife for any difficulties.

There was clearly long-standing friction between them about managing their son. They were united in their desire that the therapist provide a definite answer to their question about school adjustment. Like many parents, their conscious model of seeking help was that the therapist had the answer and would somehow generically know what was going on. Henry's parents presented one of the first transformative tasks, that of changing the authoritarian relationship model they carried into the meeting into a more collaborative one as a basis for an ongoing therapeutic alliance. The therapist had to find a way to begin to remodel their idea of the therapist providing all answers in order to formulate together the questions the assessment should address.

The therapist agreed about the importance of their question but suggested that his parents were the people who knew Henry best and they could use both their knowledge and their feelings about him now and in the past to understand what was going on. The answers would emerge from pooling the knowledge from the parents, the therapist, and Henry. By examining all aspects of his development and functioning, joint questions could be formulated and the answers sought together in the assessment process. Thus, the answers would be a shared achievement of the parents, Henry, and the analyst.

As the parents and therapist worked together to formulate the questions, many of the parents' fears and fantasies about Henry came to light. Henry's mother felt very close to her son, had the sense that he was just like her, and that she knew all the distress he was feeling. Yet his very dependence on her for all reality testing made her terrified that he might be psychotic. Her deep fear that she had damaged him in some basic way emerged in relation to this diagnostic question. Henry's father was ambivalent about his son's resemblance to himself as a child; the narcissistic gratification to his vanity of Henry's identification was offset by memories of his own childhood unhappiness and miserable obsessionality. This material allowed the therapist to verbalize these parents' hurt and sorrow, and their pain about Henry's difficulties. They could then begin to share these feelings with each other supportively, rather than deal with them by externalization and blame. This led to their increasing ability to see Henry's feelings as inside him, so starting the crucial transformation of perception of the difficulties from an external battle between parents and child to the internal conflicts Henry was struggling with.

Understanding these worries of the parents not only brought out many additional symptoms and clarified the diagnostic assignment, but there was also a further benefit in relation to the therapeutic alliance. The transformation of understanding Henry's problems as internal to him shifted the focus away from the parents and allowed them to imagine joining the therapist to understand together how to help Henry. The analyst could address directly the responsibility they did carry for some of Henry's problems, and further proceed to help them appreciate their heeding Henry's signals of distress as an indication of their basic devotion to his needs and their own investment in being good parents. The lens of the therapeutic alliance tasks facilitated focus on the strengths these parents brought to the situation and a transformation in their perceptions of Henry's difficulties.

Henry's parents had been surprised by his evident relief and enthusiasm about the evaluation sessions. The analyst felt sure that Henry was not psychotic but indeed had many troubles. When this was conveyed to his parents, they first expressed their enormous relief but then retreated quickly from discussion of Henry's ongoing anxieties. His father expressed continued annoyance over Henry's clinging; his mother seemed to withdraw her concern and sounded airily cynical about how "kids this age sure do seem to give their parents the runaround."

The analyst understood the parents' change in attitude as a defensive retreat from renewed feelings of helplessness and failure, as well as wondering whether there might be a deeper unconscious wish to have him be severely disturbed, which was thwarted by the diagnosis. Because parents and analyst had been working together throughout the weeks of the evaluation, a relationship had been established that at least allowed them to address the defense directly. The analyst took up the effective work the parents had done to recognize Henry's own worries as distinct from theirs, which had already provided them and Henry with some relief. In the context of this shared experience of their positive parenting, direct questioning of their withdrawal was possible. Henry's mother then became curious about her change of attitude, and wondered with the analyst whether Henry had triggered something of her own.

A different set of problems arises when the therapist perceives serious difficulties in the parent's functioning, but the referral has been made for the child, and the parent does not recognize any problems of his or her own.

THE IMPORTANCE OF DUAL GOALS OF TREATMENT

This illustrates one solution to the technical problem of the parents not being the designated patient. The joint work that helped Henry's mother and father function more effectively as parents was also explicitly acknowledged as a goal of the evaluation and any eventual treatment. Henry's mother could see that the way they had worked with the analyst helped her child and made her feel like a better parent. So it was worth it to her in a new way to address some of her own issues. The parents and the analyst agreed to meet regularly once a week for a time to try to better understand what aspects of the parents' functioning might be affecting Henry adversely, particularly his father's anger and his mother's withdrawal.

Henry's father had earlier opened up the topic of his identification of Henry with himself as a child, and the analyst could wonder with him why he did this. Henry's mother, in describing some of Henry's mannerisms, realized that she was using words that better suited her older brother. He had been a deeply disturbed youngster who had terrorized her and her sister, but their parents and the extended family had all denied the problems, until the boy became unmanageable in adolescence and was finally sent to a residential treatment center. As this history unfolded, and the mother became increasingly able to see the differences between Henry and her brother, Henry's father also saw that he was replaying a hostile, argumentative relationship with his younger brother, whom he had always seen as demanding more of his mother's attention.

At this point some major alliance tasks of the evaluation phase were accomplished, in that Henry's parents were seeing him much more as a separate individual, rather than as a transference object. Traumatic guilt, from which they had recoiled, had been transformed into usable concern.

As noted earlier, the evaluation phase has usually been given too little weight. In fact, the evaluation phase could be likened to the overture to an opera, an important section of the work in which all the themes are prefigured, however fleetingly. Transformation is an alliance task that is only begun in the evaluation, and continues throughout each subsequent phase of treatment.

The highly anxious single mother of eight-year-old Thea was referred to the child psychiatric clinic of the local hospital by both teachers and pediatricians because Thea was unable to concentrate. The psychiatric resident who saw them prescribed medication for the child and wanted to refer the mother for therapy, but the mother had made no mention of her own state, focusing the discussion solely on her child's troubles. So the resident recommended parent guidance with the idea that he would use this setting to provide therapy for the mother. This is a fairly common dilemma and solution, which carries many pitfalls.

Thea's mother spent the year of the psychiatrist's rotation yelling at him, saying *she* did not need treatment. She would not be blamed for her child's problems, calling at all hours to harangue the therapist for not helping her child more. The mother became known in the child clinic as "that angry mom," and none of the residents and interns the following year wanted to accept transfer of the case. A staff social worker took it on and sought consultation with one of us.

This seemed a situation where the options of referral to someone else for therapy of the parent, or parental therapy under the guise of parent guidance, were not viable. We suggested a third possibility—that the social worker suggest to the mother that they work together on how her parenting could support Thea as she grew and changed. The social worker could, in effect, start over with this mother, validating her positive wish to help Thea and enhancing her strengths for the child's sake. This alliance provided a holding environment for the mother in which she could use her ego strengths to support Thea's individual treatment. Thea was able to go off medication and showed significant improvement in school, as well as improved friendships and interactions with her mother.

Thea's mother, reassured by her daughter's progress and mindful of her own role in promoting that growth, asked the social worker about how she could deal with her own problems that were less involved with Thea. Then the therapist could make a referral for the mother's individual therapy, while assuring her that they would continue to work together on her parenting.

Thea's mother had been helped to marshal her strengths in the service of her daughter's needs. Through this process of work on her parenting function, she rediscovered genuine internal resources for her own self-esteem, which in turn helped her better appreciate Thea.

CREDITING PARENTS' WISH TO DO A GOOD JOB

Children are readily available and vulnerable to maternal and paternal externalizations. Children who are the objects of parental externalizations may experience conflict rooted in the acceptance of the devalued or idealized self and the inability to integrate real, positive aspects with the conscious self-representation (Novick and Kelly 1970). When we start examining parenting issues during the evaluation of a child, we risk confronting defensive efforts to maintain intact parents' sense of stability and needed narcissistic equilibrium. A long-enough evaluation can give the analyst a sense of what lies ahead in treatment. At the same time, the wish to be a better parent is often the only or best entrée to motivation for change in adults. The efforts of the analyst to generate a therapeutic alliance provide a framework that may allow parents access to their best selves in the context of the child's treatment. It is crucial that hope and positive feelings in the parents be fostered and maintained. The therapist helps parents regain their primary parental love for the child and find something to genuinely respect and admire in the child. But analysts also need a source of hope and conviction to sustain them, and this is best found through contact sustained long enough to discover what is admirable in the parents. As we noted earlier, seeking help is usually a sign that parents have entered into the phase of psychological parenthood and are willing to suffer something for the sake of their child's needs. Therapists can build on this positive fact and credit parents with the wish to be the best parents they can be.

Therapists need to feel at least a glimmering of this initial respect, since child work can bring us into contact with severe adult disturbances. Parents of child patients may be more troubled than adult patients who are sufficiently aware of their own distress to seek help in their own right. For instance, Henry's parents were each very disturbed. His father was a lifelong obsessional neurotic, with gaps in his conscience, superego lacunae, that led him to flout the law habitually in front of his children. His affects were inaccessible except for unpredictable moments of overwhelming rage, and his characteristic tone with his wife and children was demeaning. Henry's mother suffered from psychosomatic symptoms, debilitating fears, and a hysterical need for perfection in her surroundings, her person, and the children.

Also not detailed in our focus on the parent work during Henry's evaluation was his extensive symptomatology and nascent character pathology. Henry's self-representation was not of a human boy but of a part robot with omnipotent powers. His multiple tics, obsessions, and phobias, coupled with the mechanical quality of his functioning and his lack of visible affect, made diagnoses of borderline condition or Aspberger's syndrome plausible. Thus, he was a very difficult prospect for analysis, and his parents' pathology threatened their relationship with him and potentially with the therapist. Without the framework of the therapeutic-alliance tasks in the work with Henry's parents, the pressure of the parents' transference might have made the parent work degenerate into the kind of negative interaction typical of each grouping in the family. Therefore, in order to counteract this possibility in the initial parent work, we emphasize the positive qualities and strengths parents and children bring. This provides a bridge to open-system functioning and the possibility of choosing an alternative way to relate to the child.

FAMILY SECRETS

The destructive impact of family secrets on children's psychological development and functioning is well established. They can have a similarly undermining effect on a treatment, producing confusion and lack of genuine affective contact, negatively affecting the formation and maintenance of the therapeutic alliance.

Sometimes the therapist forms the impression that there is a secret when in reality there is a major event or issue being unconsciously denied by all family members. This was the case, for example, through the evaluation and beginning of treatment with eleven-year-old Johnny, who was referred for anxiety and learning difficulties. Treatment began on the basis of generally good beginning transformations with parents, but the therapist continued to feel that something was being omitted. Because of the good alliance begun during the long evaluation, the therapist could directly ask the parents whether there was something important that was going unsaid. The parents were puzzled at first but then associated to the therapist's use of the word "missing." They realized that they had never talked about Johnny's having an undescended testicle. In this instance the therapist had responded to the operation of a defense, rather than a conscious parental protection of a family secret. A lengthy evaluation gives therapists opportunities to pick up intimations of family secrets—almost all families have some events, family members, or actions that they are reluctant to talk about. There is a whole spectrum of reasons for such material to be omitted during even a long evaluation, with a corresponding range of feelings in the therapist around such gaps. Secrets can play an important role throughout treatment. (In the book from which this chapter is drawn, the Novicks [2005] discuss the impact of secrets at each phase of treatment.) At the time of setting the working conditions for therapy, however, there are three typical scenarios.

One is when the therapist has a distinct and uneasy feeling that something is being suppressed consciously. This can be a time bomb for treatment, but as we noted above, describing the universality of the situation to parents, and making an explicit reminder of the value of candor, are ways to invite parents to be more forthcoming. Describing straightforwardness as a necessary dimension of the collaborative relationship of parent work can be included in the list of working conditions. Another crucial issue can be addressed in the context of family secrets. The therapist works hard to help parents make good judgments about how, when, and whether to share information with their child to avoid usurping the parents' position. Rather than being only a dreadful pitfall and interference to therapy, the existence of family secrets can also be used to stress the primacy of the parent-child relationship and reassure parents that they are the most important people in their children's lives.

A second is a vague sense that something is missing, without the analyst feeling the annoyance inherent in being strung along or excluded. As we described above in terms of the operation of a defense, this may be a signal that parents have either truly repressed something significant or that they are genuinely unaware that an element of family history matters in the etiology of their child's troubles. The solution in this case is to continue working, tolerating the frustration that not all data can be collected before starting treatment.

Third, and most demanding, is the situation when parents disclose something to the therapist but enjoin silence: "We don't want our child to know about this." This is a very difficult situation for the therapist, who has several important judgments to make. The therapist must decide whether it is possible to withhold the knowledge from the child; is it possible to work honestly if one knows the child is adopted when the child does not know? The therapist may need to decide, or advise the parents to decide, whether the information should be kept from the child; is it helpful or harmful to a child to know that a parent has had an affair? The therapist must decide his or her role in relation to bringing reality to the child.

All three of these situations provide opportunities to help parents understand how treatment is going to work. Keeping in mind that improved parent-child communication is part of improved parent-child relationships, and that the nature of the desired relationship is one of open and loving partnership, according to the needs and capacities of all parties, the analyst can stress to the parents that they will be working together to define how to make judgments about what to share with the child, and how and when.

Therapists' concerns about difficulties in handling confidentiality when parents are seen regularly can also be due to our own discomfort at being put in a position of feeling caught between two parties. Loyalty conflicts and internal tensions are hard to bear; they can even interfere with our capacity to listen to the patient. These are important signals of child or parental externalization onto the analyst of impulses, feelings, or ego functions. Sooner or later these defensive externalizations will have to be addressed in treatment in the parent work.

This can be especially true when working with divorcing or divorced parents. The prevalence of divorce, the disproportionate number of children of divorced parents needing therapeutic help, and the fact that many therapists may also be divorced may blunt us to the actuality of divorce as a major disruption that often reaches the level of traumatic and overwhelming. Some divorced parents claim that they have moved on and harbor no ill feelings toward each other. We have never found this to be the whole story; at some point in the work, the therapist and the child are inevitably drawn into a continuing angry battle between the parents. There are many different forms this can take; with Linda, described below, there was a complex background of externalizations intermingled with the history of her parents' marriage.

Linda was the nine-year-old daughter of two professional parents who had each been in analysis and claimed that their divorce had been amicable, with no residual hard feelings. The mother, however, seemed especially hard on Linda, frequently becoming flooded with rage at her little girl. Linda, too, was a very angry child and was well practiced in knowing exactly what would most provoke her mother. In parent work with the mother, the initial focus was on better ways to avoid being provoked, but there was clearly something in the intensity and frequency of the mother's anger that spoke to the presence of more complex dynamics.

The therapist and mother began to track what in particular she found so infuriating in Linda. One day the mother said, "It's obvious—right there in front of my face. I get furious when she acts like her father. I hated him for those characteristics, and now, I hate her for the same reasons. What can I do? I can't divorce her!" In the subsequent work they could unravel the source of her anger as stemming from externalization of hated parts of herself onto her husband. Now, with him out of the picture, she was repeating that dynamic with her daughter. In this instance we can see that hurt and rage between the partners in a problematic marriage can end with divorce but can continue to be played out with the children of divorced parents.

THE NEED FOR PRIMARY PARENTAL LOVE

If we return to the case of Henry, we may see another way in which the element of love was brought into the situation. By remembering the framework of the various transformation tasks of the evaluation phase, the analyst was able to hold off until another crucial element could be discerned. What was the theme not heard? It was the parents' pleasure in and with their child, a primary parental investment, akin to what we, drawing from Winnicott (1949), have called "objective love" (J. Novick and K. K. Novick 2000, 191). Without a note of this positive investment, their commitment to his treatment would not be strong enough to withstand the inevitable negative patches.

The analyst and the parents were in accord about Henry's troubles, anxieties, and obsessional symptoms, but the analyst began to ask them about their perceptions of Henry's strengths, good qualities, and what they enjoyed together with him and about him. Much struck, his mother burst into tears as she realized that it had been a long time since she and Henry had giggled together, as they used to when reading his favorite Dr. Seuss books. His father had been so involved with Henry's fearfulness at the beach that he had forgotten the pleasure of long walks together to the ice cream store, and his pride when Henry had been able to ride his bike with him in the park.

With the remembered and shared good feelings foreshadowing future pleasures, the analyst felt comfortable continuing regular work with his parents. This was a situation where the technical structuring of the evaluation phase accomplished its aims, and the recommendation and beginning of treatment followed naturally from the transformative work. Using the techniques of working via the parent, during an extended evaluation phase, Henry's parents could regain a sense of competence, transform their guilt into usable concern, and see their child as separate from themselves. As they began to separate their transferences to the child from his reality, they could see his own pain and regain their primary love for their son. These initial transformations, begun during the evaluation phase, continued throughout the treatment.

REFERENCES

Abelin, E. 1975. Some further observation and comments on the earliest role of the father. *International Journal of Psychoanalysis* 56:293–300.

———. 1980. Triangulation, the role of the father and the origins of core gender identity during the rapprochement subphase. In *Rapprochement*, ed. R. F. Lax, S. Bach, and J. A. Burland, 151–69. New York: Jason Aronson.

Baruch, G. 1997. The impact of parental interventions on the analysis of a 5-year-old boy. *International Journal of Psychoanalysis* 78:913–26.

Benedek, T. 1959. Parenthood as a developmental phase: A contribution to the libido theory. *Journal of the American Psychoanalytic Association* 7:389–417.

Boelich, W. 1990. *The letters of Sigmund Freud to Eduard Silberstein, 1871–1881*, trans. A. J. Pomerans. Cambridge, Mass.: Harvard University Press.

Brenner, C. 1985. Some contributions of adult analysis to child analysis. *Psychoanalytic Study of the Child* 40:221–34.

Brown, C. 2003. *Good morning midnight: Life and death in the wild*. New York: Riverhead Books.

Burlingham, D. 1973. The pre-oedipal infant-father relationship. *Psychoanalytic Study of the Child* 28:23–42.

Burlingham, D., in cooperation with A. Goldberger and A. Lussier. 1955. Simultaneous analysis of mother and child. *Psychoanalytic Study of the Child* 10:165–86.

Chethik, M. 1989. *Techniques of child therapy*. New York: Guilford Press.

Committee on Child and Adolescent Analysis. 1997. Survey, chaired by Sam Rubin. New York: American Psychoanalytic Association.

Devito, E., J. Novick, and K. K. Novick. 1994. Cultural interferences with listening to adolescents. *Adolescenza* 3:10–14.

Ehrlich, L. 2004. The analyst's reluctance to begin a new analysis. *Journal of the American Psychoanalytical Association* 52(4):1075–93.

Emde, R. 1988a. Development terminable and interminable I. *International Journal of Psychoanalysis* 69:23–42.

———. 1988b. Development terminable and interminable II. *International Journal of Psychoanalysis* 69:283–96.

Freud, A. 1965. Normality and pathology in childhood. In *The writings of Anna Freud*, vol. 6, 3–236. New York: International Universities Press.

———. 1966. A short history of child analysis. In *The writings of Anna Freud*, vol. 7, 48–58. New York: International Universities Press.

———. 1970. Child analysis as a subspecialty of psychoanalysis. In *The writings of Anna Freud*, vol. 7, 204–19. New York: International Universities Press.

———. 1980. Preface. In *The technique of child psychoanalysis: Discussions with Anna Freud*, ed. J. Sandler, H. Kennedy, and R. Tyson. Cambridge, Mass.: Harvard University Press.

Freud, S. 1897. Letter to Fliess, November 14, 1897. In *The complete letters of Sigmund Freud to Wilhelm Fliess: 1887–1904*, ed. and trans. J. M. Masson, 279–81. Cambridge, Mass.: Harvard University Press.

————. 1909. Analysis of a phobia in a five-year-old boy. In *The standard edition of the complete psychological works of Sigmund Freud*, vol. 10, ed. by J. Strachey et al., 3–149. London: Hogart Press, 1953–1974.

————. 1966. Some thoughts on development and regression—aetiology. In *Introductory lectures on psychoanalysis. Part III: General theory of the neuroses*, ed. and trans. J. Strachey, 421–44. New York: Norton.

Furman, E. 1957. Treatment of under-fives by way of parents. *Psychoanalytic Study of the Child* 12:250–62.

————. 1969. Treatment via the mother. In *The therapeutic nursery school*, ed. R. Furman and A. Katan, 64–123. New York: International Universities Press.

————. 1992. Toddlers and their mothers. Madison, Conn.: International Universities Press.

————. 1995. Working with and through the parents. *Child Analysis* 6:21–42.

————. 1996. Parenting the hospitalized child: Consulting with child life workers. *Child Analysis* 7:88–112.

————. 1997. On motherhood. *Child Analysis* 8:126–49.

————. 1999. The impact of parental interventions. *International Journal of Psychoanalysis* 80:172.

Furman, R. A., and A. Katan. 1969. *The therapeutic nursery school*. New York: International Universities Press.

George, C., N. Kaplan, and M. Main. 1996. Adult Attachment Interview protocol. Unpublished manuscript, 3rd ed. University of California at Berkeley.

Glenn, J., L. Sabot, and J. Bornstein. 1992. The role of the parents in child analysis. In *Child analysis and therapy*, ed. J. Glenn, 393–426. New York: Jason Aronson.

Heller, P. 1990. *A child analysis with Anna Freud*. Madison, Conn.: International Universities Press.

Hellman, I. 1960. Simultaneous analysis of mother and child. *Psychoanalytic Study of the Child* 15:359–77.

Herzog, J. M. 1982. On father hunger: The father's role in the modulation of aggressive drive and fantasy. In *Father and child: Developmental and clinical perspectives*, ed. S. Cath et al., 163–74. Boston: Little Brown.

Hirshfeld, L. 2001. Work with parents in child analysis and psychotherapy. PhD diss., Center for Psychological Studies, Albany, California.

Hurry, A. 1998. Psychoanalysis and developmental therapy. In *Psychoanalysis: A developmental therapy*, ed. A. Hurry, 32–76. London: Karnac Books.

Isaacs, S. E. 1988. The Kleinian setting for child analysis. *International Review of Psychoanalysis* 15:5–12.

Kris, A. 1981. On giving advice to parents in analysis. *Psychoanalytic Study of the Child* 36:151–62.

Leon, I. 1997. How parents are made. Paper presented at "Children and the Law." Interdisciplinary Forum for Mental Health and Family Law. New York, November.

————. 1998. The psychology of reproduction: Pregnancy, parenthood, and parental ties. In *Gynecology and obstetrics*, vol. 6, ed. J. Sclarra, chapter 82. Philadelphia: J.P. Lippincott.

Levy, K. 1960. Simultaneous analysis of a mother and her adolescent daughter: The mother's contribution to the loosening of the infantile object tie. With an introduction by Anna Freud. *Psychoanalytic Study of the Child* 15:378–94.

Mahler, M. S., F. Pine, and A. Bergman. 1975. *The psychological birth of the human infant.* New York: Basic Books.

Meissner, W. W. 1996. *The therapeutic alliance.* New Haven, Conn.: Yale University Press.

Novick, J. 1980. Negative therapeutic motivation and negative therapeutic alliance. *Psychoanalytic Study of the Child* 35:299–319.

———. 1982. Termination: Themes and issues. *Psychoanalytic Inquiry* 2:329–65.

———. 1990. Comments on termination in child, adolescent, and adult analysis. *Psychoanalytic Study of the Child* 45:419–36.

———. 1997. Termination conceivable and inconceivable. *Psychoanalytic Psychology* 14:145–62.

Novick, J., and K. Kelly. 1970. Projection and externalization. *Psychoanalytic Study of the Child* 25:69–95.

Novick J., and K. K. Novick. 1994. Externalization as a pathological form of relating: The dynamic underpinnings of abuse. In *Victims of abuse,* ed. A. Sugarman et al., 45–68. Madison, Conn.: International Universities Press.

———. 1996a. A developmental perspective on omnipotence. *Journal of Clinical Psychoanalysis* 5:124–73.

———. 1996b. Fearful symmetry: The development and treatment of sado-masochism. Northvale, N.J.: Jason Aronson.

———. 2000. Love in the therapeutic alliance. *Journal of the American Psychoanalytical Association* 48:189–218.

———. 2001. Parent work in analysis: Children, adolescents, and adults. Part 1: The evaluation phase. *Journal of Infant, Child, and Adolescent Psychotherapy* 1:55–77.

———. 2002a. Two systems of self-regulation: Psychoanalytic approaches to the treatment of children and adolescents. *Journal of Psychoanalytic Social Work* 8:95–122.

———. 2002b. Parent work in analysis: Children, adolescents, and adults. Part 3: Middle and pre-termination phases of treatment. *Journal of Infant, Child, and Adolescent Psychotherapy* 2:17–41.

———. 2003. Two systems of self-regulation and the differential application of psychoanalytic technique. *American Journal of Psychoanalysis* 63:1–19.

———. 2004. The superego and the two-system model. *Psychoanalytic Inquiry* 24(2): 232–36.

Novick, K. K. 1988. Childbearing and child-rearing. *Psychoanalytic Inquiry* 8:252–60.

———. 1997. What am I going to do in a little canoe: The sequestering of sado-masochism in women's lives. Paper presented at annual meeting, Division 39, American Psychological Association, Chicago, August.

Novick, K. K., and J. Novick. 1987. The essence of masochism. *Psychoanalytic Study of the Child* 42:353–84.

———. 1998. An application of the concept of the therapeutic alliance to sado-masochistic pathology. *Journal of the American Psychoanalytic Association* 46:813–46.

————. 2002a. Parent work in analysis: Children, adolescents, and adults. Part 2: Recommendation, beginning and middle phases of treatment. *Journal of Infant, Child, and Adolescent Psychotherapy* 2(1):1–27.

————. 2002b. Parent work in analysis: Children, adolescents, and adults. Part 4: Termination and post-termination phases. *Journal of Infant, Child, and Adolescent Psychotherapy* 2(2):43–55.

————. 2005. *Working with parents makes therapy work.* Lanham, Md.: Jason Aronson.

Pruett, K. D. 1985. Oedipal configurations in young father-raised children. *Psychoanalytic Study of the Child* 40:435–56.

————. 1992. Latency development in children of primary nurturing fathers: Eight year follow-up. *Psychoanalytic Study of the Child* 47:85–101.

Rosenbaum, A. 1994. The assessment of parental functioning: A critical process in the evaluation of children for psychoanalysis. *Psychoanalytic Quarterly* 58:466–90.

Sandler, J., H. Kennedy, and R. L. Tyson. 1980. *The technique of child psychoanalysis: Discussions with Anna Freud.* Cambridge, Mass.: Harvard University Press.

Sprince, M. 1962. The development of a preoedipal partnership between an adolescent girl and her mother. *Psychoanalytic Study of the Child* 17:418–50.

Tahka, V. 1993. *Mind and its treatment: A psychoanalytic approach.* Madison, Conn.: International Universities Press.

Winnicott, D. W. 1949. Hate in the countertransference. Reprinted in *In one's bones: The clinical genius of Winnicott,* ed. D. Goldman, 15–24. Northvale, N.J.: Jason Aronson.

Zetzel, E. R. 1965. The theory of therapy in relation to a developmental model of the psychic apparatus. *International Journal of Psychoanalysis* 46:39–52.

7

The Vulnerable Child: Working with the Parents of Preschoolers

Peter Deri

A common referral for parent consultation is for the temperamentally sensitive preschooler. Parents generally appreciate that the children they are concerned about do not necessarily need to receive direct psychological service. This population thus lends itself to a discussion of direct intervention with parents as an effective approach in helping the very young child.

In the past thirty years of working with preschoolers and their families, I have become convinced that the referred preschooler is not representative of the preschool population at large. In this chapter, I will present data and theory from various fields, as well as clinical vignettes, emphasizing the shifts in our thinking about early development and how these shifts offer a framework for parent therapy with the parents of very young children. Data and theory from psychologists and researchers that emphasize the effects of constitution and neurobiology on the child's attachment to primary caregivers are working their way into mainstream thinking about the etiology of problems and, therefore, treatment of young children.

With children, ages one to four, I find it helpful to look at developmental lines that are frequently observed but sometimes overlooked as clinically meaningful correlates, causes, and predictors of psychological difficulties. There are a number of "child variables" or individual differences that are important to consider when assessing the overall difficulties seen in early childhood. They contribute subtly yet profoundly, through the "effect of the infant on the caregiver" (Lewis and Rosenblum 1974) to the developmental process of projections and introjections interwoven between parent and child.

In child therapy there has been a pronounced shift in etiological emphasis; heretofore, the emphasis has been weighted on the parent end of the parent-child dynamic, and not enough on the child end of the equation. In parent therapy, which I believe is the treatment of choice with this population, there is an opportunity to explore the ways in which the child's own intrinsic sensitivities influence the parent-child relationship, which, in turn, contribute to the child's behavioral life. The notion of the "effect of the infant on the caregiver" is a prominent one in animal studies and has significant implications for our understanding of early childhood development. It is important to explore the ways in which parents respond to the particulars of any given child's development, specifically the ways in which the infant's innate temperamental and constitutional endowments interact with parents' capacities. In other words, the parent-child relationship is unknowingly shaped by unacknowledged yet significant causal factors that reside in the child's neurobiological makeup.

The following two citations from Stern (1985, 1995) help create a framework to explain the shift in clinical emphasis to include the mutual and self-regulatory factors in early childhood development. In *The Motherhood Constellation: A Unified View of Parent-Infant Psychotherapy* (1995), he states, in reference to child therapy,

> At present, this field [child therapy] consists of applications of and borrowings from well known therapeutic concepts (including psychoanalysis, behaviorism, systems theory, social networks, and pediatrics) that have been modified for use with a new population. Most often these approaches try to remain faithful to their intellectual origins. At first glance, therefore, the field resembles a continent, previously unexplored, that has been divided into areas ruled by different colonial therapeutic empires. On closer examination, however, the established therapies are all undergoing modifications in their confrontation with this new setting and are converging. One can begin to see the general outlines of a future unified country, a single coherent field of psychotherapeutics with its own contributions to make to the general ideas of psychotherapy. (1)

In 1985, Stern also stated,

> The capacities that permit the infant to yoke his diverse experiences of the social world are to an enormous extent constitutionally . . . determined. . . . For the immediate future, the study of individual differences of these capacities may prove to be the most fruitful area of clinical research on the development of psychopathology in the very young. (188)

The first passage lends a legitimizing framework to the collection of theory and data I have emphasized in my understanding of the various causes of child psychopathology. The second passage suggests that this approach is consistent with typical psychoanalytic approaches with very young children. Thus, interventions that consider the impact of constitution, sensory apparatus, and neurology on the development of childhood psychopathology may contribute most productively to the efficacy of the parent consultation.

Starting with my definition of the population of preschoolers who end up in our offices, this group is not a random population of preschoolers, who happen to have psychological difficulties. Rather, the group we see, in most cases, has atypical aspects of development that are often overlooked by mental health professionals. It is these atypical aspects of development that necessarily tax parents to a significantly greater degree than expectable phase-specific developmental difficulties. They begin a cycle through which parental anxieties increase and parental effectiveness concomitantly decreases. In such situations, the inclination to focus on intensified parental anxiety as a primary causal variable may obscure, from the clinician's view, the very significant factors emerging from the constitutional irregularities of the child.

We often observe how the natural and benign instincts with which parents and teachers approach preschoolers who are experiencing difficulty can be unproductive, even counterproductive. A certain discernable subset of children is more inclined by nature toward "avoidance" rather than "approach" responses. Efforts to connect, approach, and make contact with them when they are in distress often exacerbate rather than ameliorate their discomfort. They tend to have a disregulated response to "approach" behavior from people in their environments and reject the natural inclinations of adults to sooth. Clinical observation also confirms that a high percentage of these avoidant children have some speech or speech and language difficulty.

The literature on approach and withdrawal and hemispheric asymmetry (Rothbart and Bates 1998) provides a theoretical framework for understanding why there are so many speech-and-language-delayed children who are, by temperament, more avoidant than the average preschooler. The literature on cerebral asymmetries in children, specifically those with lagging left hemisphere functions, convinced me that I was observing a brain-based pattern of behavior in the referred children of my clinical practice. Davidson's (2000) research on emotional correlates of cerebral asymmetry is pertinent to this clinical position; his research suggests that lagging left-hemispheric activity correlates with a propensity to withdraw. In my opinion, the connection between speech and language delays, delays understood as strongly left hemisphere based, and a propensity for withdrawal behavior in very young children should not be minimized in our attempts to understand childhood psychopathology. Rather, it must be incorporated into the clinical understanding of the parents' experience as well. In offering such a formulation to a parent, which posits a possible neurobiological contribution to their child's behavior, behavior for which parents often blame themselves or their child, we have the opportunity to significantly affect the parent-child dyad in a highly mutative fashion. Assisting parents in their ability to cope with their children's behavioral anomalies by postulating a new sequence of events—that is, that parents' anxiety is a response to, rather than a cause of, difficult child behavior— becomes one of the most critical components of effective parent therapy.

The work of Alan Schore (1997, 2000) is helpful in linking the concept of attachment behavior to neuroscientific research and in reframing metapsychological concepts along neurobiological lines. His orientation supports thinking about the presence of biological proclivities that implicate delays in the very same brain areas that Schore feels are the "home of psychic functioning." I am referring to the population of preschoolers who exhibit lags in what are considered right hemispheric or prefrontal functions. An example of this would be a three-and-a-half-year-old with well-developed language who tends to resist any graphomotor activities. The idea that right hemispheric delays, often described in older children as a nonverbal learning disability, are accompanied by significant difficulties in processing social-emotional data is not new. Denkla (1983) labeled this disability of the right hemisphere a "social-emotional learning disability." This idea emphasizes the relationship between cognitive and personality profiles (shared brain-based etiology), which needs to be given greater weight in working with young children and their parents. In summarizing his early work, Schore (1997) states,

> For some time, psychoanalysis has speculated that developmental disorders reflect a defect in an internal psychic structure, but it has been unable to identify this structural system. I believe that the orbital prefrontalimbic system is this psychic structure, and further, that every type of early forming disorder involves, to some extent, altered orbital prefrontal limbic function." (39)

Schore locates what we refer to as self-experience, which includes both self-regulatory and attachment functions, in the prefrontal lobe and suggests that the essential elements of the self are also right hemisphere based. Furthermore, he emphasizes the plasticity of prefrontal functions and maintains that this plasticity in the brain of the developing child lends itself to the influence of ameliorative interpersonal interactions. The implication here is that minor neurological anomalies in this area are amenable to modification through the enhancement of parental awareness of these phenomena.

Schore goes on to state that Bowlby offered a speculation suggesting that the instinctive drive for attachment-seeking behavior is located in the prefrontal cortex, the same general area of the brain that is often implicated in a large class of phonological disorders. It is because of a generic tendency for disregulation in this group of children that we often find both disinhibition and perseveration in play. This, in an observational context, becomes a plausible explanation for what can appear to be aberrant play activity. Clinical theory has previously tended to attribute unconsciously driven affective themes to children's play without sufficient regard for the influences of neurologically based sensitivities. Needless to say, one variable does not necessarily preclude the other. Moreover, the disregulation and disinhibition can have obvious effects on the parent-child relationship and are clearly implicated in the development of dynamic patterns of anxiety and stress. Traditional psychoanalytic clinical theory has tended to attribute unconsciously driven affective themes to children's play without sufficient attention to the influence of neurologically based sensitivities on the content and quality of the play. Though the two are not mutually exclusive, children's play themes are often more determined by a proclivity to react hyperbolically to the stimuli that they are presented with. To reiterate, the failure to give sufficient salience to the effect of the infant on the caregiver can result in a treatment approach that is characterized by premature formulations about parental projections and fantasies that create confusion and anxiety for parents and are discordant with their own experience.

If we also consider the importance of Bowlby's notions about the innate nature of attachment behaviors, comparable to food-seeking behavior (Zeanah and Boris 2000, chapter 22), then it is not surprising that caregivers are likely to experience something odd and atypical in the behavior of the child with certain delayed or disordered aspects of speech and language development. That the caregiver will then respond oddly, particularly if they do not understand what might be happening, is axiomatic.

A somewhat-reconfigured version of Anna Freud's idea about disharmonies in development can be used in conjunction with the concept of the "shadow syndrome." In Ratey and Johnson's (1997) *Shadow Syndromes*, the authors define this subclinical presentation of symptoms as follows: "(The child] may fit every aspect of a syndrome down to the smallest detail and yet be so mildly affected compared to other people [who exhibit a full blown manifestation of a disorder)" (11–12). Although these "shadow" symptoms often go unaddressed, they continue to haunt both the child's experience and the general perceptions of the child. I am referring here to partial presentations of profiles, symptoms, or early precursors of what may become an axis II label. In their description of children with partial presentations of ADD or ADD shadow syndromes, Ratey and Johnson (1997) suggest that there is a tendency to view these children as underachieving or failing to live up to their potential. This type of psychologizing is rife in clinical practice and may often obscure more salient etiological understanding and intervention approaches.

Parents often cherish and value and, therefore, reinforce traits that they call exuberance, outside-of-the-box thinking, and creativity in the very child who has been referred for not being able to sit through circle time, interrupting the class, and controlling peer interactions. Blaming the environment in these situations is a ubiquitous defense among parents of referred children. Referrals by nursery programs are often related to children's inattentiveness, disinhibited behaviors, and impulsivity. The initial hypotheses generated by parents and teachers to explain these behaviors seem invariably to be environmental and dynamic in nature. Taking Schore's thoughts about the centrality of prefrontal function in psychopathology, in conjunction with what developmental psychopathologists (Pennington and Welsh 1995) say about the relationship between prefrontal deficits and executive functioning, it seems reasonable to hypothesize that such children are struggling with brain-based difficulties. Secondarily, parents typically compound their children's difficulties by implicitly relying on dynamically driven reactions. These difficulties, which fall under the rubric of executive functioning, are best understood as difficulties with adaptation to novel situations, inadequate self-regulation in the presence of intense stimuli, and poor ability to inhibit or modify behaviors that are ineffective in achieving intended results (Goldberg 2001).

In the earliest stages of development, I believe one often sees residuals and hints of traits that, if presented in a full-blown form, would be clearly evident to everyone. We can also see that, in the stages of skill acquisition (i.e., early childhood), there are irregularities that become smoothed over, masked, or reduced over the course of development, training, and experience. The disharmonies that Anna Freud wrote about may thus be another way of describing a "shadow" or a situation in which lines of development are more disparate from one another in their rates of growth than is typical. Although the "disequilibrium between developmental processes," of which she spoke (Fonagy and Target 2003), were typically thought to be expressions of internal conflict and the matrix of ego, superego, and id functions. I am suggesting that behavioral disequilibrium in the child, manifested in uneven levels of cognitive development, is often a comorbid presence with emotionally based psychological problems. These behaviors are often considered to be psychodynamic in nature, the more recent contributions of systems and interpersonal theory notwithstanding, which have shifted the focus onto the projections of parental conflict, both internal and interpersonal. However, this focus may obscure the contributions of real, though subtle, neurological and sensory influences on developmental disharmonies that affect both the child's overall functioning and the parent-child relationship.

Again, in this context of mutual influence between parent and child, working directly with parents may be the most effective way to address the presenting problems of the referred preschool population. Beyond the immediate field of psychoanalysis, contributions from the fields of developmental child psychology, language development, and neuroscientific studies of affect and temperament have all enhanced our knowledge of sensory-motor difficulties in the very young. Jacobs and Wachs (2002), in presenting some of their reservations about the efficacy of family and child therapy, also make the point that temperament and internally driven capacities in the child are often given short shrift in psychotherapy with children.

Fonagy (Fonagy and Target 2003) describes the history of the development of psychoanalytic theory, which locates this theoretical position on an explanatory continuum and blends one- and two-person psychologies.. He states that, at different phases or stages in the development of psychoanalytic theory, various ideas have assumed dominance. Describing what he calls the "state of constant evolution" in the field, he refers to the path of theoretical emphasis—from instinct/drive to ego to relationship. What I am suggesting here is an integration of psychogenic and nonpsychogenic, largely biological, variables in early development. Thus, in working with young children and their parents one cannot meaningfully speak of the relationship without understanding the instinct/drive dynamics particular to each child. According to Stern (1985), the infant "yokes in" social data through receptive capacities that process, grade, integrate, and metabolize sensory and affective stimuli. It is possible and also quite important to assess the strength and smoothness with which the child processes incoming information. In this way we can incorporate the one-person psychology of early individual differences and biologically driven aspects of development, that is, the regulatory or yoking-in capacities of the child, and the two-person early parent-child relational matrix.

To some degree, my point is similar to Anna Freud's critique of Melanie Klein's failure to give sufficient weight to the reality of the parents in her work with very young children. (Klein 1975). I am suggesting something analogous, namely, that current trends in the field have minimized the other aspect of the equation: the biological and temperamental realities of the child and their impact on the parent-child relationship. So many referred preschoolers exhibit traits that clearly reflect the early manifestation of individual temperamental differences, that it, is impossible to overlook the influence of these biologically based factors. In other words, different children exposed to the same parental milieu, marital conflict, anxiety, material circumstances, and stressful life events, may nonetheless exhibit markedly different behaviors. Thus, children will vary in their vulnerability to impingement or their receptivity to a facilitating or maladaptive environment.

CASE MATERIAL

Dan, a three-year-old fraternal twin with an easygoing, compliant sister, came to me because his mother was distraught about a host of his behaviors. He would make remarks to his mother such as "I don't want you near me," and he would retreat into a closet for forty-five minutes. At times, he would say things to his mother such as "Dad and I are going to get our own house." Often at breakfast, Daniel would reject the cereal bowl he had and ask for one identical to his sister's. After receiving the requested bowl, he would insist on having maple syrup. The amount mother would pour would never be just right. He would then say he wouldn't eat unless his mother would sit closer to him. He would then instruct her to be quiet. As she sits silently next to him, he would repeatedly ask if she were being quiet.

At school Dan presented with a significantly attenuated version of the same type of behavior with difficult moments triggered by the unexpected, such as a fire drill. His mother had sought therapeutic advice from another clinician prior to seeing me who emphasized the following themes: twin dynamics, such as parental splitting of twins into a good child and a bad child; and the mother-father-son triangle and the exploration of the "unholy alliance" between the father and Daniel. The clinician also explored the mother's experiences with her own mother; the unconscious fantasies she had about having Daniel; any conscious or unconscious preferences for the girl over the boy; and any other sources of possible unconscious projection. The mother had also been referred for a psychopharmacological consultation as a result of which antidepressant medication was prescribed.

These issues, while all potentially meaningful, focused exclusively on the parental influence on the child's behavior. What was left unexplored was the child's subtle, yet clear-cut articulation difficulty, which was generally viewed as "cute" speech. While Dan's speech difficulties were clearly in a "shadow" state, it was plausible to consider immaturities and delays in areas of the left frontal lobe (Rosenzweig, Leiman, and Breedlove 1999). In addition, an assessment of the child indicated that every physical sensory input channel had mild to moderate threshold irregularities. Thus, his thresholds for responses to auditory, tactile, olfactory, light, and temperature input, although not causing significant problems, were atypical. As I elicited this history, I started to adopt a more educative than interpretive approach with the mother. Jacobs and Wachs (2002) also refer to the parallel between parent therapy and clinical supervision and suggest that a supervisor's role is both exploratory and educative. It is interesting to note in this context that Freud, toward the end of his career, called his patients students (Lothan 2003).

The initial work with Dan's mother was comprised of information about the psychological correlates of certain aspects of child development and phase-specific developmental milestones. First, Dan's patterns of misarticulation appeared to be connected to his overall difficult temperament, possibly related to prefrontal cortex difficulties. Articulation, as well as certain other aspects of language, and what are considered "executive functions" or what we used to call ego functions, are located in the same general left prefrontal area of the brain. This information about the link between the infant's sensitive body and the young child's sensitive mind proved to be highly elucidating for this mother.

The pathogenic power of the various relationships among family members, the projections and presumed introjections, were not minimized in our work together, nor was the anxiety with which this mother approached her parenting. However, her newly acquired information about her son's nature profoundly affected her and helped her to recognize that, because of these mild idiosyncratic traits, Dan was "too sensitive for his own good," both physically and psychologically. The alliance that developed between us, based on the new information, allowed an intimacy to enter the work through a reduction in her defensiveness, rage, and endless self-recrimination. In addition, as often happens, the educative component and specific information resonated with something the mother had known intuitively but had not fully allowed into conscious awareness. The therapeutic work, which emphasized a "gathering of information" about her child, created a therapeutic environment in which the mother felt deeply understood about something that had previously gone unspoken. The sensory integration difficulties, emphasized in this vignette, often inform my assessment of these common disruptions in early parent-child relationships.

The diagnostic category of sensory integration difficulties, typically the domain of occupational therapists, is a confusing area; one of the problems is that its name is somewhat of a misnomer. When people refer to sensory integration difficulties, they are usually referring to a subgroup of young children who show threshold irregularities in their reception of sensory stimuli, that is, how they process stimuli through the various somatic-sensory domains. Irritation from a variety of textures, inclination to remove clothing, sensitivity to noises, unduly keen sense of smell, odd thresholds of pain, and peculiar responses to too much or too little light are all examples of what I am calling sensory threshold irregularities, or what are often labeled sensory integration difficulties. The trajectory of sensitive body to sensitive psyche is known by all occupational therapists but is not sufficiently emphasized by psychologists who work with very young children. Since the sensory irregularities will wane, either through treatment, maturation, or both, it is important to take a detailed history of these aspects of early childhood. De Gangi (2000) refers to Greenspan's reference to the link between somatic and affective experience. In my experience, the occupational therapy treatment recommendations she presents in *Pediatric Disorders of Regulation in Affect and Behavior* often fail to deliver the intended neutralizing effect of reducing threshold irregularities. Rather, irregularities in the reception of somatic stimuli seem to wane through maturation. However, the trajectory of "irregular somatic reception to irregular affective reception" unfortunately persists (144). A host of plausible, psychodynamic theories, focusing on both one- and two-person dynamics, have been generated to explain the behavioral anomalies that are more likely the result of these somatic irregularities.

To digress from preschoolers for a moment and to apply the template of this kind of thinking to understanding later forms of psychopathology, consider the following: the progression of a child's feeling considerable physical irritation and complaining about it to irritating the caretakers around him with his complaints, getting attention through reprimands, and negative attention-seeking behavior as a learned generic response all happen under the age of three. When we think of the behaviors that mental health professionals have chosen to call "oppositional-defiant" or "borderline personality disorder" later on, we can see the precursors of those diagnostic categories in these early childhood regulatory difficulties. Explaining to parents that their child's irritability is not primarily psychodynamic in nature can be enormously effective in shifting the direction of the parents' thinking and thereby altering the interaction, and potentially transforming the parent-child relationship itself.

Although speaking of a slightly different progression, Escalona (1963) also spoke of a "body to mind trajectory." Her interest was in tying together Piagetian and Freudian notions regarding early development. She stated: "My data suggest . . . that the emergence of such functions as communication, modulation of affects, control over excitation, delay, and aspects of object relations and hence identifications, all are the result of a developmental sequence in sensorimotor terms, before they can emerge as ego functions in a narrower sense" (189–89).

This presents further support for the interdependence, in young children, between nonpsychological and psychological lines of development. Another nonpsychodynamic developmental line, which, although not ignored, is nonetheless minimized as a significant covariate and clue for recontextualizing psychological difficulties, is the development of speech and language. Shapiro (1995) suggests that, because speech and language development is such a robust and elaborate developmental line, a delay in this area is bound to produce significant effects in other areas of development.

In my capacity as psychological evaluator, I have frequently heard parents, teachers, and psychologists describe the frustration children experience because they could not express their needs and wants. While a small percentage of children fit that description, the vast majority did not. I see children who, when left alone, are fine; yet, often when they are approached by another, become irritable, withdrawn, aggressive, or generally rejecting. Furthermore, this group also seems to have exaggerated, somewhat-hyperbolic responses when their compliance is requested or demands are made on them. As a group, they seem to have relatively little need for interaction, and typically, their interactions are motivated largely by a desire to have their needs met. Their speech is often understood only by their parents, and they need to repeat themselves frequently until they are understood. This raises the question about why, if they are so frustrated, they do not develop gestural language? What people had been labeling as frustration at not being able to communicate may be better described as frustration at being bothered by the "other." The work of Richard Davidson, referred to earlier, on atypical cerebral lateralization (i.e., stronger right hemisphere), seems to be a plausible hypothesized explanation for a subtle manifestation of avoidant temperament, a temperament that then shapes the "motherhood constellation." Stern (1995) considers the parent-child relationship as the identified patient. In his description of his treatment of a parent-child relationship, he suggests that "it is not yet known how much of the infant's psychological nature is a construct of the parent's imagination" (3). He goes on to say that the motherhood constellation is "a unique organization of mental life appropriate for and adapted to the reality of having an infant to care for" (3). It is my hope that the "motherhood constellation" will, with increased research, reflect more reliable perceptions of the child, which will in turn permit more ameliorative interactions between parent and child. Much of my work with parents assists them in making the home the locus of therapeutic activity with the child.

In this regard, the case of Stevie, who was treated by Stern (1985) and Beebe, might have benefited from a greater exploration of some of the nonpsychogenic factors in this child's behavior. Stevie's propensity to withdraw, coupled with his mother's unusual sensitivity to rejection (this mother interprets each infant head aversion as a "microrejection" and attempts to repair and undo it with obvious negative effects on Stevie), seems to warrant further investigation of Stevie's early speech and language development. Although there is no reference to this developmental line in the case material, it seems pertinent to consider whether there was a history of or residual difficulty in language acquisition. The presence of even mild aberrations might have provided data to support an educative stance with Stevie's mother who might, then, have been able to focus on her son's constitutional weakness. She might have thus been helped to understand that her son was not yet capable of responding favorably to her overtures. The following brief treatment illustrates some of these theoretical points with particular reference to the presence of regulatory difficulties.

Ben's mother sought clinical intervention at the suggestion of her son's teacher. The teacher suggested that there were difficulties with peer interactions. It had previously been determined that Ben had delays in fine and gross motor functioning for which he was going to receive occupational therapy. He negotiated stairs in a cautious manner, refused to climb a ladder to use a slide, and pushed rather than pedaled a bicycle. At three years and eight months, he had an extensive vocabulary, an ability to construct long and elaborate sentences, and a fantasy life that was remarkably complex. He arrived at my office with a small plastic container, which held about a dozen rubber animals and talked about them from the moment I greeted him in the waiting room. Instead of responding to my questions about the animals, he told me about them in his own spontaneous fashion. While he did that he became visually distracted by a magazine cover, walked toward it to examine it more closely, and while he lost eye contact as he turned his back to me, he continued to talk animatedly about his animals.

Ben's mother did not feel that there was really a need to see a psychologist; she felt that he was highly intelligent and saw his deficits as both discrete and a consequence of the energies he put into his areas of strength. As we continued to speak, however, she revealed that it was very difficult for her or her husband to gain compliance from Ben, and they often reverted to threats to confiscate props for his imaginative play with his little animals. That seemed to be a certain way to jar him into compliance. His father also tried, playfully, to get him to "fess up" and admit that his imaginary friends were indeed imaginary by asking him how to drive to the houses of the various characters. This, ultimately, resulted in Ben craftily squirming out of these requests.

An informal screening indicated robust measures of verbal functioning; language functioning was at the 98th percentile, while some measures of motor and visual-spatial functioning fell at the 4th percentile. It was interesting to note that he had a facility for reproducing block design patterns but could barely do, and self-selected away from, simple puzzles and graphomotor tasks. He exhibited a subtle but significant lag in graphomotor skills. As a right-handed youngster he drew circles in a clockwise rather than counterclockwise fashion. When I inquired about his mother's perception of his facility with block patterns, a skill which should have been low, along with his overall right hemispheric visual-spatial lags, she reported that his father engages him in building zoos, parks, and houses for his collection of real and imaginary friends.

As Ben's mother spoke more and more about him, she began to acknowledge how rigid, fixed, and unduly sensitive he could be. He quite often made remarks about facial expressions he saw, and misread them in a number of situations. His mother further explained that in the previous year her father had died suddenly, her mother had become seriously ill, and Ben's life had undergone considerable disruption because she traveled each weekend to visit her own mother. She also noted that some portion of Ben's fantasy life revolved around young twin boys, an apparent reference to his own seventeen-month-old twin brothers. His mother maintained the position that Ben had a quirky but engaging personality, and that his behavior was a delayed reaction to the birth of his brothers and the emotional upheaval from the medical crises to which the family had been subjected over the past year. While I did not disagree that these were plausible hypotheses with which to explain her son's behavior, I inquired about whether anyone had connected the cognitive disharmonies demonstrated by Ben with a strong propensity for intense fantasy, obstinacy, and lack of interest in pleasing his caretakers. She looked somewhat vindicated and stated, "I knew it. He's just like his father." Although I gently suggested that she team up with her mother-in-law to help Ben, she revealed that her mother-in-law had lost the battle and that she would have to fight much more effectively to improve Ben's behavior. With this in mind we continued to meet to discuss an effective plan. After only several sessions Ben's mother recognized that, for different reasons, she and her husband were too coercive in their efforts to bring Ben into greater responsiveness, and that their efforts were propelling him further into fantasy. The support she garnered from the consultation decreased her anger at her situation, and she began to see that to connect with Ben, she would first have to join him in his own mental arena. She engaged more in his play with him and was able to alter it in small increments, injecting new themes, characters, and feelings into the play. In effect she was neutralizing some of the intensity from the "movies" in Ben's mind. Despite the fact that the consultation was brief and was conducted exclusively with Ben's mother, I was able to encourage her to assist her husband in grasping the idea that he would never be able to shame his son into relinquishing his fantasy experience. Rather, they would have to form an alliance with which to accept Ben's fantasy experience while engaging him gently in greater attention to his environment. Ben's profile seemed to be an early precursor of the profile labeled "nonverbal learning disability," a profile that developmental psychopathologists are more likely to label a "social-emotional learning disability" (Cicchetti and Cohen 1995).

Let us now consider an example of parent work, with a preschooler, which does not follow an educative approach but which attempts to shift parental perceptions of the child's problems.

Mary, a five-year-old child, carried a devastating diagnosis of a rare right-brain deficit in conjunction with a host of physical conditions making her vulnerable to seizures and cyclical vomiting (continuous vomiting that requires hospitalization) of unknown etiology. Motoric milestones were so delayed that she began to walk only at about age three. The parents sought clinical advice because they sensed that their approach to this child was so stilted and self-conscious that it was becoming a catalyst for greater problems than her physical and intellectual difficulties warranted. I saw the child in order to assess her overall functioning, both cognitive and emotional, and met with the parents biweekly. One of the difficulties they spoke of was the mother's concern that the father minimized the severity of Mary's problems, often trivializing things by suggesting activities that the mother felt were beyond Mary's capacities or that put her at risk for the onset of medical problems. For example, their specialist doctor had said that excitation, whether negative or positive, might be a contributing factor in the vomiting episodes. Thus, when father suggested some new activity that required a "reach," the mother saw this as a reflection of his failure to attend to the child's plight. Having a very young child with difficulties of any sort exacerbates the typical polarization in parents' approaches to child rearing that is so common in cases of early psychopathology. When the father's brother needed psychiatric hospitalization, the father started to speak of the pathogenic manner in which his own mother had raised him and his brother. There was great worry about very small problems that the two brothers might manifest, as well as a tendency by this paternal grandmother to infantilize her children. The father referred to his mother's parenting as Munchhausen by proxy, which he felt afflicted his sick sibling even more than it did him. As the two boys grew older their mother tended to infantalize herself. She was extremely attached to Mary, perversely curious about all the medical details of her condition, and often made remarks about the parents' irresponsible behavior, such as going away for a weekend and using a babysitter. Mary's father and mother simultaneously realized that his mother's tendency to pathologize his brother and him and keep them young and overprotected had resulted in his excessive worry that he would do the same with his daughter, particularly since there were so many real factors to worry about. Somewhat excessively and defensively he committed himself to raising Mary quite differently than he had been raised. The parent consultation helped him to understand that this commitment was not in Mary's best interest and was, moreover, creating too great a polarization in parental approaches to child rearing. He also understood why his mother was so attached to his daughter, something that he had always observed with a certain degree of puzzlement and concern. At the same time Mary's mother reframed her understanding, and subsequently her response, to what she had viewed as her husband's seeming disregard to all the risk factors in Mary's environment. They realized that they were each extremely concerned about their daughter's development, although they approached interventions with quite different styles. Interestingly enough, in one of the few assessment sessions I had with the child, she played out a scene with her grandmother in which her grandmother's strong attachment to her was driven by the secret that the grandmother had the same condition as she, Mary, was diagnosed with.

In summary, consultation with the parents of young children combines apparently divergent clinical concepts, all related to understanding the parent-child dyad. Concepts related to biology, temperament, cognitive patterns and proclivities, unconscious projections and internalizations, as well as sensory and linguistic development are constantly in the mix. In addition, treatment of the very young leads the practitioner to think more about gradations of traits rather than the simple presence or absence of a trait. So many of the children we see, while viewed as precocious, may also be struggling with varying degrees of difficulty, with one perception of the child dominating the self-representations as well as the parents' views. When the clinical intervention is used to enhance, broaden, and deepen the overall picture, parents can guide their children through a smoother developmental experience.

REFERENCES

Cicchetti, D., and D. Cohen. 1995. Perspectives on developmental psychopathology. In *Developmental psychopathology, vol. 1: Theory and methods,* ed. D. Cicchetti and D. Cohen, 3–23. New York: J. Wiley.

Davidson, R. 2000. Affective style. Psychopathology and resilience: Brain mechanisms and plasticity. *American Psychologist* 55(2):1196–1214.

De Gangi, G. 2000. *Pediatric disorders of regulation in affect and behavior.* San Diego, Calif.: Academic Press.

Denkla, M. 1983. The neuropsychology of social-emotional learning disabilities. *Archives of Neurology* 40(2):461–462.

Escalona, S. 1963. Patterns of infantile experience and the developmental process. *Psychoanalytic Study of the Child* 18:189–245.

Fonagy, P. 2001. *Attachment theory and psychoanalysis.* New York: Other Press.

Fonagy, P., and M. Target. 2003. *Psychoanalytic theories: Perspective from developmental psychopathology.* New York: Brunner-Routledge.

Goldberg, E. 2001. *The executive brain: Frontal lobes and the civilized mind.* Oxford, UK: Oxford University Press.

Jacobs, L., and C. Wachs. 2002. *Parent therapy: A relational alternative to working with children.* Northvale, N.J.: Jason Aronson.

Klein, M. 1975. Symposium on child analysis (1927). In *Love, guilt, and reparation and other works 1921–1945,* 139–69. New York: Delacorte Press/S. Lawrence.

Klin, A., and F. Volkmar, F. 1997. Asperger's syndrome. In *Handbook of autism and pervasive developmental disorders,* ed. D. Cohen and F. Volkmar, 94–123. 2nd ed. New York: J. Wiley.

Lewis, M., and L. Rosenblum, eds. 1974. *The effect of the infant on its caregiver.* New York: J. Wiley.

Lothan, Z. 2003. What did Freud say about persons and relationships? *Psychoanalytic Psychology* 20(4):609–18.

McLaughlin, J. 1978. Primary and secondary process in the context of cerebral hemispheric specialization. *Psychoanalytic Quarterly* 18(2):237–67.

Orenstein, R. 1997. *The right mind: Making sense of the hemispheres.* New York: Harcourt.

Pennington, B., and M. Welsh. 1995. Neuropsychology and developmental psychopathology. In *Developmental psychopathology,* vol. 1, ed. D. Cicchetti and D. Cohen, 254–91. New York: J. Wiley.

Ratey, J., and C. Johnson. 1997. *Shadow syndromes.* New York: Pantheon Books.

Rosenzweig, M., A. Leiman, and S. Breedlove. 1999. *Biological psychology: An introduction to behavioral, cognitive, and clinical neuroscience.* 2nd ed. Sunderland, Mass.: Sinauer Associates.

Rothbart, M. K., and J. Bates. 1998. Temperament. In *Handbook of child psychology, fifth edition,* ed. W. Camom and N. Eisenberg, 105–177. New York: J. Wiley.

Schore, A. 1997. Interdisciplinary developmental research as a source of clinical models. In *The neurobiological and developmental basis for psychotherapeutic intervention,* ed. M. Moskowitz, C. Monk, C. Kaye, and S. Ellman, 1–77. Northvale, N.J.: Jason Aronson.

———. 2000. Attachment and the regulation of the right brain. *Attachment & Human Development* 2(1):23–47.

Shapiro, T. 1995. Grand rounds presentation, child and adolescent rounds, Westchester Division, New York Hospital, October.

Springer, S., and G. Deutsch. 1981. *Left brain, right brain: Perspectives from cognitive neuroscience.* 5th ed. New York: W.H. Freeman.

Stern, D. N. 1985. *The interpersonal world of the infant: A view from psychoanalysis and developmental psychology.* New York: Basic Books.

——. 1995. *The motherhood constellation: A unified view of parent-infant psychotherapy.* New York: Basic Books.

Zeanah, C. H., and N. W. Boris. 2000. Disturbances and disorders of attachment in early childhood. In *Handbook of infant mental health*, ed. C. H. Zeanah. 2nd ed. New York: Guilford Press.

8

The Vulnerable Parent: The Case of a Five-Year-Old Boy and His Family

Ionas Sapountzis

The cute little boy with the frozen smile conveyed the feeling, as he walked cautiously into my room, that he expected to be evaluated and to be found lacking, by an unknown doctor whose name his parents could hardly pronounce. It was not an unreasonable expectation. Already, at the age of five and a half, David had experienced a series of failures in the nursery and preschool programs he had attended and had been engaged in incidents that were viewed, depending on the diagnostician, as typical symptoms of a child with perhaps ADHD, sensory integration deficit, frustration intolerance, conduct disorder, or even the first signs of a bipolar condition. The incidents in school had contributed to his reputation of being a difficult child, unpredictable in his reactions, and rather awkward in social situations, perceptions that had affected considerably the attitudes and expectations of everyone around him. His demeanor, as he entered the room, suggested not only a history of failure and fear but also an awareness of how others were viewing him, how unlikable he felt. He had just been expelled from one program for hitting a teacher on her arm as she tried to remove him from the play area. According to the teacher, he was unwilling to make the transition from solitary play to a group activity. He was too involved with the towers he had been building and did not want to leave his construction, lest another child might accidentally destroy it. The teacher described him as a boy who was rigid and volatile, and prone to react aggressively if he did not get his way. He had recently enrolled in a new program, which accepted him only on condition that his parents would pay the cost for an additional teacher assistant who would be monitoring David throughout the day.

The incidents in school and his behavior at home had alarmed his parents and made them very anxious about his upcoming transition to kindergarten. On the phone they had expressed their concern and fears about his future along with their feelings of guilt and exasperation. As they walked in the room behind their son, they impressed me as bright and likable individuals, who were unsure what to expect from our encounter, hopeful and guarded at the same time, feeling themselves as lacking and ineffective as parents as, in all likelihood, their son felt about himself.

As we settled into the room, I realized that I was not prepared for the sight of a polite and cute-looking boy who smiled at me furtively before darting his gaze away. I expected an angry, moody, and volatile child who would be very demanding and self-centered. I certainly did not expect a child who would ask for my permission to use the toys from the toy cabinet, who would express his surprise and affirmation at the selection of the toys that were available, and who would display his astonishment by holding each toy up, showing it to his parents, and naming each one of them. I did not expect to see a boy who, with minimal prompting from his parents, would put the toys back in the cabinet before he picked another container of toys. I certainly did not expect a child who seemed able to engage in symbolic play, whose capacity for fantasy and enthusiasm seemed to offer many entry points of interaction. I was expecting a bully, a rather uncontrolled child who would be difficult to like. Like the teachers at school, my expectations were very negative and, one might say, biased.

What I did not realize at the time was that my expectations were established, not so much by the incidents in school, as his parents had enumerated them over the phone, but by the manner in which the parents had described their son. David was described as a boy who, from very early on, was difficult to soothe and control. He was a very active and strong-willed boy who was quick to become frustrated when his requests were not met. Some developmental tasks were easily achieved while others were the source of very intense conflicts. Thus, his sleeping, eating, and grooming habits were established rather quickly, while others, like toilet training, had been the subject of protracted exchanges. David was still, at the age of five and a half, not completely toilet trained, and thwarted his mother's attempts to train him by refusing to sit on the toilet seat. He was a chronically constipated boy who would refuse to go to the bathroom and would not give any indication when he needed to use it. Left to his own devices, he would become increasingly agitated until his mother, sensing his need, would quickly help him to put on pull-up diapers.

When David was eighteen months old, the parents started, at the advice of their son's pediatrician, to implement prolonged time-outs and physical restraints when he failed to obey them. Two years later David's tantrums and oppositional behavior had increased with such intensity that the parents became concerned that they were harming their son. They expressed their resentment at the advice of the pediatrician along with their guilt for having enforced this futile regimen for such a long time. They seemed to regard it as the sort of advice that they had often received from professionals that was ill conceived and contributed to the difficulties they were experiencing with their son.

By the time they contacted me, the parents had concluded that David's behavior problems were linked to his high sensitivity and intolerance of any physical discomfort. They had become increasingly convinced that the occurrence of almost every incident in school or at home correlated with a physical condition, whether a virus, a cold, a stomachache, or constipation, the physical manifestation becoming manifest a day or two later. The possibility had not been contemplated that many of these somatic complaints might have been linked to David's anxiety over the incidents that caused so much distress to his parents. Although the parents had some awareness that his anxiety and irritability might have correlated with the tension at home and the intense marital conflict, this did not lead to changes in their overall understanding of the behaviors.

The parents' search for an organic etiology was supported by and certainly consistent with the zeitgeist that is prevalent in our culture nowadays, and which places the emphasis on a cluster of symptoms attributable to neurological factors. This position can obviate the need to understand the connection between neurobiological conditions and the ways in which family dynamics may mitigate or exacerbate a child's problems. For these parents it seemed to refute the school personnel, who implicitly suggested that the parents were, in large part, responsible for David's behaviors. The parents and teachers had become involved in an adversarial relationship with each side questioning the other, and each side feeling that the other failed to effectively address David's needs. The antagonistic and accusatory exchanges between the school and the parents had left little room for contemplating David's anxieties, for considering how his sense of ineffectiveness and failure in the world might have contributed to the intensity of his defiant and rigid reactions. David, too, may have had some awareness that all the adults were actually angry with him and each other, which they often were.

David's case is perhaps typical of many children who present a bewildering array of experience: childhood omnipotence, intense fragility, dependence and fearfulness, entitlement, and isolation. His parents' ambivalence and search for an organic explanation was similar to the ambivalence and reactions of other parents who vacillate between their desire to provide for and protect their child and their discomfort with children's developmentally normative impulsivity, aggression, and self-interest. Their confusion and exasperation reflected a common difficulty parents have in establishing a balance between discipline and boundary setting on the one hand and tolerance and encouragement on the other. However, this ambivalence may be more difficult to navigate when parents' past experiences and their own internal self-states interact with the child's temperamental sensitivities and impasses to create a "knot" (Brafman 1997, 776), a knot that prevents them from effectively managing their child's behavior. It is a cycle, Brafman feels, where "the child's knot is kept in place by a parallel knot in one or both parents' psyche, whether the child's problem was originally 'caused' by them or whether they have been unable to help the child sort out a knot of his own creation" (776). Ironically, when they turn to professionals for help, understanding, and guidance, the parents encounter, in the often rigid and rather objectified system, another "knot," in which the child's subjectivity and the parent-child interactive matrices are not adequately explored.

The cycle of failure and inadequacy had taken a toll on the couple. Both parents acknowledged, during the initial phone consultation, having experienced periods of intense marital discord, and felt that the tension between them might have affected David to some degree. Their marital problems, which had been present from the beginning of their relationship, became more pronounced after David's birth. The mother had been very depressed during the first two years of David's life, and the couple had seriously contemplated divorce. Despite the parents' agreement that David's problems were primarily organic in etiology, this explanation did little to reduce the increasing strain on the couple. The mother felt that David's sensory problems and tension were exacerbated by the father's impatience and intense reactions. She felt that he blamed her for being inconsistent and ineffective. She was quick to feel defeated and brushed aside and was likely to respond to his criticisms, irritation, and outbursts by withdrawing and refusing to speak to him. She felt that a great deal of the early tension at home and her depressive state were aggravated by her husband's impatience and intolerance. The father was quick to react intensely when things weren't going as he expected, and responded to his wife's helplessness and depressive episodes with growing irritation and dismissive comments. He attributed David's early failures and difficulties to her immaturity and "flakiness," and felt even more irritated and rageful at her passive dismissal of him and her tendency to withdraw. In an almost symmetrical collusion, the same conflict and cycle of blaming that existed between the school and the parents also existed within the couple.

The knot in the family was compounded by the school's "knot," by the tendency of the school officials and teachers to regard David as a troubled and disturbed child, and not as a small child who was at a loss about how to negotiate the challenges of being in a new environment and engage with his teachers and peers. The frustration intolerance that school officials attributed to David was matched by the intolerance of the school's staff to contain their own frustration and anxiety and to address his developmental needs without resorting to knee-jerk reactions. The failure of the school staff to address David's behavior in the classroom is, in many respects, similar to the failure and inconsistency of professionals in other schools, who are often at a loss about how to approach a child who does not entirely blend in—who does not fit the image of the confident, disciplined, motivated, and socially appropriate child, the type of child who has become the archetype in our culture of what a healthy, normal child should be. In treating David as a troubled and inappropriate child, his teachers inadvertently conveyed to him that he was unlikable and unwanted, experiences and realizations that are very detrimental to a child's (indeed everyone's) development, as Willock (1987) has pointed out. Much like the cases of other symptomatic and emotionally troubled children, David's case was emerging as a case where parents and school officials were failing to contain their own anxieties, just as David's self-regulatory capacities were failing.

In the initial assessment session, David did not seem to pay attention to his parents' descriptions of past incidents and conflicts, and their experiences with the schools. After exploring the toy cabinet, he became absorbed in lining up the soldiers on the carpet and creating two camps: his, which had the best soldiers and all the weaponry he could amass, and the enemy's, which had few soldiers, no tanks or airplanes, and was likely to get trounced. He seemed oblivious to what was being discussed, although the theme of his play captured vividly the underlying tensions his parents were describing. He seemed interested only in preparing his army for the impending battle with the foregone outcome. His play was structured, and his desire for an undefeated army was a telling metaphor of his desire to be strong and to feel victorious and unassailable. His soldiers, which he called "warriors," could not die, and his army had never been defeated. He built a small castle for the enemy and seemed to enjoy the attention his play was generating. Yet, his excitement over his parents' interest in his game was short lived. The parents quickly became alarmed and impatient at David's insistence on adding soldiers to his camp and inventing storylines and conditions that rendered the outcome of the battle a foregone certainty.

Why the alarm? How else would a little boy stage a battle scene if not for the pleasure of feeling victorious and invincible? Why did the mother, as she watched one of his knights destroying all opponents, scaling the walls of the castle, and wreaking havoc without any casualties or the need to mobilize the rest of his formidable army, anxiously seek to curtail his exuberant childhood omnipotence by insisting on introducing rules? His was fantasy play, a make-believe game, and yet, his mother was very uncomfortable with it. Why did the father insist that David fight a "fair" battle and then, after joining him on the carpet, proceed to resurrect the dead enemy soldiers and, much to David's alarm, knock down several of his soldiers? This occurred despite David's visible anxiety and frantic efforts to shield his soldiers with his body while imploring his father to stop. Could it be that the past failures and the tension that had accumulated at home prevented them from enjoying their son's play, from being attuned to his age-appropriate and even gender-appropriate play? Or was it that his play, the theme of invincibility and conquering that he was enacting, mobilized in them their deep anxieties over a child whose narcissism, rigidity, and preoccupation with being victorious were more prominent than in the average child?

As the father stopped, bewildered by the intensity of David's reaction, the mother commented apologetically that David did not know how to play with others and always wanted to win. "Don't we all?" I observed and added that every child, indeed every individual, should have room to feel victorious and invincible in his fantasy, and that for David, who had experienced his share of failures, the themes of his play could be understood as a metaphor of his wishes and, perhaps, a refuge. Both parents seemed intrigued by my comments, but whatever momentary relief they experienced was quickly offset by their anxieties. For them, the line between fantasy and reality was dangerously thin. Neither parent seemed able to see their child independent of his acts. As the father explained, if David were allowed to play like that, he would never learn to tolerate playing with other kids who would also want to win.

Why the rigidity? Why the insistence on a reality that violated the inner reality and the fun of their child's play? Why the intolerance of their child's playful omnipotence by the two parents who, while expressing their concern over their child's intolerance, seemed equally intolerant of his need to feel powerful in his make-believe play? From a systems perspective, the parents never seemed as united and complementary as when they expressed their criticisms and concerns over David's behavior. Sensing his parents' displeasure with his play, David offered his father two of his soldiers and tried to fix the enemy's castle. His touching act of reparation and concern was not, however, grasped by his parents, who insisted in unison that, to make the fight more fair, he would have to let go of more of his soldiers and to also give out some of the tanks and airplanes that he had lined up behind his knights and Indians. Their rigidity, and resultant failure to appreciate their son's inner world, replicated the intolerance displayed by the schoolteachers who perceived David's reactions and his difficulty in "shifting" readily from one activity to the next, as proof of his oppositionalism and defiance.

David impressed me as a bright, intense, and fragile boy, who both desired contact and was also fearful of it. His play represented both a denial and a wish, but even in his play and in his attempts to have his parents join in, he found that he failed their expectations, since his play was treated as inappropriate and selfish. Was it his failure to curtail his omnipotence in his fantasy play, a reflection of what was enacted again and again with his peers and teachers in school, or was it his parents' failure to separate the fantasy from the fact, the play from the reality? What was enacted? What was the failure? Why did so many exchanges in David's life, from his play in school to his play in my room, from his toilet training to his interactions with his peers, end up with everyone involved feeling failure and bitterness? Why did his parents feel so ineffective in addressing his toilet training, in establishing rules and negotiating the challenges any child faces as he or she grows, in a flexible and facilitative manner? Why did they follow, for so long, the time-out plan advised by the pediatrician, when it was evident that the plan was not working? Why didn't they contact a specialist; why were they so passive? The picture that was emerging from the parents' descriptions of their conflicts at home, their background histories, and their reactions to David's behavior was that of two well-meaning but fragile individuals who were very vulnerable to setbacks, to any incident that reminded them of past failures and fears that they had never addressed. My initial reactions, as I listened to their descriptions, was sympathy for them and annoyance over their mistreatment by the world, but as I started to become more familiar with them, I started wondering about their passivity, at their tendency to cast the world as victimizing and themselves as victims, and thereby avoid feeling blamed while holding on to a paranoid view of the world.

The fear of a breakdown is the fear of a breakdown that has already been experienced, wrote Winnicott (1963). Both parents seemed genuinely pleasant and caring, and their intense reactions, their readiness to feel offended and wounded, was difficult to understand without taking the time to understand their lives, the relational matrices in which they grew up and experienced themselves. The mother was adopted at birth by a couple who could not have a child. Only a month after her adoption, her adoptive mother found out that she was pregnant and gave birth to a baby girl, who was only seven months younger than David's mother, leaving her always trying to cope with the ambivalence, rage, and guilt that her younger, not adopted, sister stirred in her. She described a difficult childhood, always feeling frustrated and surpassed by her younger sister, whose relationships to her parents she felt was closer and more real than hers. She felt bypassed and defeated by the presence of her younger sister whose proximity in age was a constant reminder of her adoptive status, of having been given up at birth by her own mother. She experienced a difficult adolescence and admitted that her marriage at a very young age to a man much older than her was an attempt to move out of the house, to start out on her life faster than her sister, and to develop and preserve her own separate identity.

In contrast to his wife's family, the father's family was large and volatile, a family in which he frequently felt criticized harshly for his wrongdoings and his competitiveness with his siblings. In this family, the issue was not who was right or wrong but rather who was the most dominant, who would be able to successfully claim his space. Quick to feel slighted, he admitted that he was prone to intense reactions that he could not control, especially when he felt threatened. For a man who was very intolerant of his failures and very sensitive to the withdrawal and unavailability of the important others, his wife's depression and rejection were narcissistic blows that reawakened his childhood anxieties and triggered his rage. For a woman who had always felt less important and undervalued, the father's dismissiveness, criticisms, and accusations struck a painfully familiar cord triggering a paralysis in her and an intense depression.

Both parents were aware of these dynamics and understood how their upbringing had predisposed them to react to each other's criticisms in a manner that they would often come to regret afterward and which contributed to their marital problems. David's temperamental vulnerabilities, his impatience and intolerance to frustration, his sensory integration difficulties, his anger at his failure to meet expectations, and his tendency to project blame mirrored their own childhood failures, frustration, and regulatory difficulties—frustration and difficulties that were lurking beneath their pleasant appearance and their effort to achieve what they felt had been lacking in their lives. In David's failure they were faced with their own failures, failures that they had not addressed and their own fragilities and bitter experiences that became quickly reawakened when their early expectations and hopes for a blissful marriage and a family that would become their refuge and pride was put into question. Yet, this understanding did little to offset the way they continued to react to each other. Despite their awareness of each other's emotional struggles in life, they were very intolerant with each other when they felt dismissed or attacked. It seemed as if their understanding was used primarily to experience themselves as victims and to deflect blame, and served as the basis from which they could justify their criticisms of each other.

A picture was emerging of a family caught in cycles of failure in their daily exchanges, a series of setbacks that had left little room for tolerance, for contemplating their child's and their own dynamics, and instead, sought refuge in false certainties and rigid reactions. In that system, in that background of frustrations and disappointments that were so readily reactivated, the stage was set for everyone to be deeply vulnerable to each other's reactions. In the transference, the stage was set for them to experience my comments and interpretations as persecutory, as evidence of taking sides, and of either validating or criticizing them. In that matrix of rigid dichotomies, it was hard for them not to feel failure; it was hard not to feel dismissed or lacking.

From the initial phone conversation to our first meeting and follow-up discussion, the father impressed me as an intense and rather rigid individual. In the demanding tone with which he expressed his concern for his son, and in the relentless manner in which he questioned my ideas, my training, my experience, as well as my policies and my fee, I formed the impression of a man who could come across as off-putting and reprimanding. From my first conversation with him, I had the feeling that I was failing him, that my expertise, intentions, and insight were insufficient. He was quick to pinpoint inconsistencies, to demand clarity and precision that felt forced and rigid, that felt less like an exchange and exploration and more like an interrogation that was based on suspicion. He asked for a timetable for the consultation, and though intrigued by my suggestion to schedule a couple of family and individual sessions in order to have a better understanding of the dynamics involved before drawing any diagnostic conclusions and deciding on the course of the treatment, he was already skeptical about the outcome. He wanted more; he wanted assurances that I could not give. He wanted to know if I could visit the school on a regular basis to instruct the staff how to best work with his son, and seemed disappointed, and even insulted, when I said that would not be feasible, but that I would instead talk with David's teachers on the phone. It was easy to feel with that one was not meeting his needs—that one would always come up short. It was also easy to experience him as a very demanding man, whose intensity and self-involvement could feel intrusive and obliterating. He did come across as a caring, anxious, and articulate man who, nonetheless, seemed to demand too much and seemed unaware of how much he demanded or how challenging his requests and reactions were. It was easy to feel lacking with this father, to feel that one offered him less than what one should, and that I was failing him.

Unlike the father, who sounded very critical and demanding, my initial impression of David's mother left me wondering about her intentions and sense of reality. Yet, in my second exchange with her, she impressed me as an astute and reachable person who was more aware than her husband how her behavior had affected David. This impression was diluted, however, by her tendency to become tangential, to ramble on, before finally concluding that David's behavior was due to his sensory difficulties. What did I think of sensory integration? Was I familiar with the literature? One had the sense of a seemingly open woman who would discuss everything but, ultimately, would settle only for her own view. Like her husband, she seemed unaware of how problematic her behavior could be and how much she might leave others wondering about the purpose of the discussion, whether there was any point at all. Her apparent openness and willingness to explore how she had failed David belied her dismissiveness. Over the course of the treatment, I became aware of how I often experienced her in contradictory terms: as a person who was aware and could be reached and as a person who was unaware of other's emotions; as a person who was open to new ideas and as a person who could not contemplate anything but her own view of the world, and would disengage from others who did not share her view; as a sensitive and wounded person who was empty and indifferent to other's emotions and experiences of her.

In the countertransference with these parents I often had contradictory feelings; I felt annoyed and irritated and also caring and patient. I felt put off by the father's rigidity and quite vexed and impatient with the mother's tangentiality and casualness. Yet, I was also moved by the intensity of the father and his struggle to cope with what was happening, and I realized that every time I saw the mother my irritation at her would dissipate. Instead, I would become caring and conscientious and willing to let go of my earlier determination to confront them. Why this duality? Gradually, I came to understand these reactions of mine in terms of Racker's (1968) concordant and complementary identifications. In Racker's view, the therapist identifies or experiences the patient both as an object and as a subject. Experiencing David's parents as objects, I felt irritated by their rigidity, their inefficiency, their inability to be more empathic, and their obliviousness to how they were impacting others. Experiencing the couple from a subjective, concordant point of view, I felt touched by their loneliness and their sense of inefficiency and failure that seemed to be reenacted again and again in every relationship. These emotions of mine were triggered with such proximity and predictability that they became the blueprint of how I experienced my relationship with them, of what was enacted in our relationship, and gave me a sense of what their underlying hope was: I would become irritated with them, and as I was about to confront them in our sessions and to explore with them my reactions, they would become transformed into sympathetic figures for me, two orphans in this world, and I could not be angry with them. It felt like an unconscious desire was triggered to elicit a caring response from me, for me not to give up or leave them on their own. I suspect that, had I been working with the child alone, my negative responses might have been more intense, and the positive feelings might never have emerged at all.

"What does one do with this understanding?" wonders Alvarez (1992); how can this understanding be used to facilitate change, to address the impasses of this couple, which seemed so caught up with experiences and expectations of failure? What does one do with a child and a family for whom the underlying theme, the common background theme (Grotstein 2000), was not only that each member felt failure and isolation but also that each one felt that his or her efforts would not succeed and materialize. It seemed to me that the task in working with David and his family was not different from the task that many therapists face in working with patients so caught up in cycles of frustration and defeat. The bitterness, the frustration, the high reactivity, and the manic search for a quick fix or for an answer that deflects anxiety— all these issues and dynamics that interfere with one's adjustment in life— have to be contained and gradually explored. As Bion (1962) wrote, the fears and impasses have to become thinkable and have to be treated as experiences that deserve exploration in order to link the past with the present, to feel less persecuted, less thwarted, and foreclosed.

Structuralists and system theorists view a child's emotional difficulties and behavior problems as symptoms that serve a role in the family and express the family's pathology. Whitaker (1989) went as far as to state that in his view there is no such thing as an individual in a family system but only the family system. Yet, even though family therapists regard the child's symptoms as emanating from the dynamics in the family, and emphasize the need for the entire family to be involved in therapy, it is a common practice among family therapy practitioners to ignore the child in the room and, indeed, to continue family therapy after the initial sessions without the presence of the child (Wachtel 1994). As Wachtel remarked, even when the child continues to attend the family sessions, he or she often remains essentially unknown, since all the emphasis is placed on how the family members interact with each other and negotiate boundaries. The initial family session with David and his parents did not go well. Both parents seemed too self-conscious, guarded, and circumspect in expressing their views. In retrospect, this was not surprising. After all, in my conversations with the father prior to our first meeting, he had only communicated with "facts" and seemed to be caught off guard every time I tried to gauge his understanding of the issues he was describing. The mother was equally anxious about bringing up issues that she felt might trigger an unpleasant encounter. She had called me, a day or two after her husband had confirmed the date for our first session, to inquire what was I planning to ask and to convey to me that her adoptive mother, who also worked in the mental health field, did not approve of that form of treatment. After the first two sessions, I felt that insisting on continuing to see the entire family would have re-created the theme of placing blame and feeling criticized, and of being regarded as a scapegoat—themes and experiences that were dominant in the lives of each parent and were being re-created and reexperienced with David.

I felt that a psychological assessment would yield a better understanding of David and the ways in which his unconscious fears and yearnings interacted with his overall functioning. Why was he so tense and fearful? Could he engage in a playful exchange where his hopes and fears, yearnings and aspirations, fantasies and creativity would be explored and expressed? Was there a way to reach this boy, to create a playful exchange and establish a mode of communication? These were issues that were never contemplated in the preschool programs that David attended and were too anxiety provoking for his parents to address them in family sessions. I also felt that I needed to schedule additional counseling sessions with the parents to share my observations with them and to explore, with them, how their failure and past experiences kept being reenacted with each other and with David.

In the assessment sessions I discovered that this difficult boy proved not difficult after all, in fact, David proved to be quite a delightful child. In my office, despite his initial reluctance, he was very engaging and creative. He welcomed me in his play and seemed actually thrilled to engage in tasks. He was excited by our activities and freely responded to my comments. His difficulty with transition times or endings also proved not that much of a difficulty. When time was almost up, and it became apparent that his constructions would have to be put away, he became unresponsive to my probes. It seemed as if he was not listening to me and continued to attempt further activity, refusing to accept the end of our meeting. He seemed obstinate, shut down, transfixed on adding pieces to the structures he had already built, and avoided any interactions, even eye contact, with me. It seemed for a moment that we were heading for an unpleasant confrontation. In fact, his attempt to continue took a compulsive aspect. Was he antagonizing me, just being rigid and oppo-sitional, as his teachers and parents had insinuated? Or, was this behavior indicative of a young child who could not negotiate the limits that were placed upon him, could not organize himself, and in an absence of a contain-ing, facilitating environment, was likely to react in uncontrolled ways.

Our impasse, though, proved surprisingly easy to negotiate. When I asked him to come with me in the storage room to show him where I would keep his constructions and how I would ensure that everything would be avail-able for the next time, a transformation occurred. He seemed pleased to watch me make room on the shelves and procure a container for the materi-als he had used; he enthusiastically scribbled his name on the adhesive label I gave him and which he affixed to the container with the precision of a craftsman. David helped me to clean up and even straightened the chairs and the carpet on his way out. This was a surprising, and for me, hopeful, ending by a boy who had been described as difficult, as only accustomed to getting his way. Over the next several assessment sessions, he continued to work productively, was fully aware of the sessions' time constraints, and responded to all of my inquiries. The difficult, rigid boy was proving to be a boy who could be empathic and integrative, who could accept limits and boundaries, and who could be engaging, playful, and creative.

The information from these sessions provided the background for my consultations with the parents. It was easy to explore with them how engag-ing and responsive David could be, how he needed them to value his play and to guide him out of his impasses by creating a more mutual and tolerant environment. It provided the stage for discussing with them ideas on how to prepare him for the transition to kindergarten, how to explore with him and convey to him what was expected of him in kindergarten, and how he could avoid setting himself up for criticism and rejection. The parents were encouraged to become more active in eliciting the school's cooperation and support, and to seek out a meeting with the principal and teachers in order to express their concerns and ask for their help and advice. They were encouraged to advocate for David and for themselves and to ask for a transi-tion plan in order to enable David to have a better school experience. Avoiding to inform the school about their difficulties with their son and avoiding to express their concern and to seek the school's assistance and

cooperation had not helped David's adjustment in the two preschool programs he had attended and had not eased the parents' fears. By remaining
passive and avoidant, fearful of how the school officials might react, and acting as if David was an easy child to handle, they had deprived school officials from a better understanding of David and had set the stage for David to
be seen as a puzzle, as a boy who did not fit. It was also agreed that I would
contact the school after the parents met with the principal to share my
observations with the school psychologist and the new teacher, to offer my
feedback, and to explore with them ideas about how to better approach and
work with David.

The parent consultation sessions offered them an opportunity to understand aspects of their interactions, to find a language to communicate with
David, and to convey what was expected and what was appropriate without
feeling defeated. All too often, when a problem occurred, the parents would
again find themselves unable to explore and discuss the incident and would
either deny its importance or become overly distressed.

The need to find a way to communicate with David without feeling
defeated or stymied in the process was exemplified in an incident that took
place at a neighborhood gathering, during this period. At that party, David
poured a cup of juice over a girl's head and, later on, pinched a woman's
buttocks, much to the alarm of everyone present. Not surprisingly, his
mother became so embarrassed that they had to leave the party. She felt that
everyone must have been wondering what was wrong with her son and
why she had not been able to teach him more appropriate behavior. She
wondered whether her son was more disturbed than she had realized, and
much to her alarm, she became aware as she kept going over the incident
again and again that she had started entertaining thoughts that the incident
with the woman was, perhaps, a forerunner of future sexual misconduct.
This phenomenon of becoming anxious and overwhelmed when a child
misbehaves in such a blatant way is common for most parents, but for
David's parents it was especially painful and humiliating.

The implicit question was "What's wrong with him?" Was he a sexual per-
vert as the mother thought the other women who were present at the party
must have thought, or was he so disturbed that he could not distinguish
right from wrong? As the mother analyzed the incident, she came to the conclusion that the grape juice incidence was probably the result of David
attempting to impress and gain the approval of some older, rather mischie-
vous, boys from the neighborhood who were also at the party. This felt like
an astute observation, which highlighted how empathic and attuned she
could be to her son's needs and misplaced wishes. Yet, when she tried to
understand the incident with the woman, her anxiety took over. She
ascribed it to his constipation and interpreted it as a sign that he "needed to
go," a need that he could not express appropriately. She did scold David but

did not want her husband to talk to David because she feared that this would only heighten his anxiety. In her anxiety and effort to protect David from further embarrassment and from her husband's wrath, and in her wish to downplay the incident, she was unaware of how her reaction deprived them of finding room for exploration and understanding, and denied David and his father access to each other. Father and son were supposed to go on acting and interacting around that incident, as if nothing had happened, as if the incident had not occurred and could not be discussed or brought to anyone's attention. It was to some extent indicative of how the mother would react to David's misbehaviors and challenges. She would scold him, berate him, and then, feeling guilty over her anger and pained by her son's reaction, she would brush it aside. It was "over" she said, failing to see that it was far from over, in fact, it continued the climate of fear, of reacting to incidents as if they could not been handled. She failed to see that in her anxiety over her son's failure and her own ineffectiveness as a good mother, she was failing him and herself again and was preventing both of them from negotiating the incident and from developing a sense of confidence in their ability to negotiate life's challenges.

Two weeks after the incident, and before having a chance to discuss it in our meetings, against his wife's request and despite her irritation, the father had tried to explore the incident by asking his son what happened at the party. He was apparently not satisfied with his wife's contention that he had a rush or was constipated and therefore was irritated. But all he could get from David was some vague responses that he had tripped, that it was an accident. As he kept probing him about the incident, David became increasingly anxious, avoided eye contact, and responded with monosyllables. Feeling frustrated and becoming anxious by David's responses, the father did not pursue this any further. Instead, he simply remarked, rather cryptically, that maybe it was an accident in David's "mind." As for the incident with the woman, the father could not find the strength to bring up the issue. When I asked him whether he was pleased with this exchange, he admitted that not much was accomplished and expressed his frustration at not being able to reach his son.

It was a proxy communication, more a communication of omissions than of exchange, and they both knew it. It was a communication of omission that was emblematic of how the family tried to address impasses, and in the process felt ineffective. The incident with the girl was not an accident, and settling for that was tantamount to denying what had happened while conveying to his son that the issue was too toxic to be contemplated. Likewise, the pinching of the woman's buttocks was not a displaced communication about his constipation, and trying to frame it in such terms was tantamount to reducing the significance of his acts. I ventured that his alleged discussion with his son was not a discussion but a false discussion that left them with little sense of connectedness and more sense of a persecution and lingering aftertaste. What could David say after all? I suggested that though it is important and necessary to try to understand his son's motives, in moments like this, the desire and effort to understand should not detract or prevent him from conveying in a very simple and straightforward manner what David should and should not do, what was expected of him. With regard to the incident with the woman, I urged him not to hesitate to name what David had done and simply to tell him that he should not touch people in their private parts whatever their age. To do otherwise would leave the outcome of the conversation entirely upon David, and he would be relinquishing his role as a father. It created and reinforced the feeling that these topics could not be discussed and that these conversations, much like the mother feared, lead to further impasses and alienation. He understood that he was saying too much, that he was not communicating with his son in a simple, nonconfusing, clear manner. He understood that at these moments he failed being direct in a simple manner and that David would probably respond well to such a simple and straightforward request. He surprised me by adding that in such instances he had not been able to present his views and reactions in a simple and straightforward manner and added that a simple statement would be a relief for his son, and for him, a way of expressing himself and addressing his son's fears and need for guidance without accentuating his shortcomings and weaknesses. One can say that in finding the language with David one had to find the language with the father, who was, after all, a man who either would loose his patience with his son when he tried to negotiate an issue, or experience such anxiety that he could not explore the incident and express himself with clarity.

David's adjustment to kindergarten, much to the surprise of his parents, was quite successful. The teacher reported that though he was a rather tense boy she found him responsive, bright, and eager to please. She found that if told in advance what was expected of him, and if there were efforts to preserve his work and acknowledge his fears, he was surprisingly responsive. This was very consistent with my perceptions of David. One might say that David was a boy who needed a language, as we all do, through which he could feel protected—a language that could structure his thinking and his behavior and could contain his anxiety. In some ways, the parent consultation helped these parents to develop a vocabulary between themselves, for each of them as individuals, and with their son so that David could be guided at home, at school, and in social settings. The work with the parents helped them to appreciate David's thinking and behavior so that they could help him through difficult transitions.

Both parents felt relieved that my assessment of David, and my consultations with them and with his teachers, had helped to recast David from a pathological boy to a confused and rather frightened boy who was quick to

withdraw and isolate himself, who was prone to become rigid when he felt
that he was failing to meet expectations, and who was seen as a nuisance.
The mother expressed her relief that for the first time she felt that her son
was understood and was not seen as a monster, and felt hopeful about the
future.

REFERENCES

Alvarez, A. 1992. *Live company*. London: Routledge.

Bion, W. R. 1962. A theory of thinking. *International Journal of Psychoanalysis*
43:306–10.

Brafman, A. H. 1997. Winnicott's therapeutic consultations revisited. *International
Journal of Psychoanalysis* 78:773–87.

Grotstein, J. S. 2000. The ineffable nature of the dreamer. In *Who is the dreamer who
dreams the dream? A study of psychic presences*, ed. J. S. Grotstein, 1–36. Hillsdale,
N.J.: Analytic Press.

Racker, H. 1968. *Transference and countertransference*. Madison, Conn.: International Universities Press.

Wachtel, E. F. 1994. *Treating troubled children and their families*. New York: Guilford.

Whitaker, C. 1989. I don't believe in people—I just believe in families. In *Carl
Whitaker: Midnight musings of a family therapist*, ed. M. O. Ryan, 115–21. New
York: W. W. Norton.

Willock, B. 1987. The devalued (unloved, repugnant) self: A second facet of narcissistic vulnerability in the aggressive, conduct-disordered child. *Psychoanalytic
Psychology* 4(3):219–40.

Winnicott, D. W. 1963. Fear of breakdown. In *D.W. Winnicott: Psychoanalytic explorations* (1989), ed. C. Winnicott, R. Shepherd, and M. Davis, 87–95. Cambridge,
Mass.: Harvard University Press.

9

Involving Parents in the Care of Children and Adolescents with Eating Disorders

James Lock

For many years, the involvement of parents in the care of their children with anorexia nervosa and bulimia nervosa has been controversial. In 1874, when Sir William Gull (1874) suggested that parents and relatives "were the worst attendants" (p. 28) of their children with anorexia nervosa, Charles Lasegue (1883) in Paris countered with the observation that treatment should always take place "side by side with the preoccupations of her relatives" (p. 266). The debate was effectively stifled by the predominance of psychoanalysis, with its emphasis on individual therapy in the early part of the last century. When Hilda Bruch (1973) discussed family involvement in treating juvenile or adolescent anorexia nervosa, it was primarily to preclude parental undermining of individuation in the patient's individual therapy. At the same time, family therapy was invented with anorexia nervosa as a paradigmatic illness, claiming that the illness results from and is maintained by family dysfunction (Minuchin, Rosman, and Baker 1978). When bulimia nervosa was first described in 1979, it was presumed to be an "ominous variant" of anorexia nervosa, and the same prejudices about families were applied to this disorder as well (Russell 1979). The net result of this has been the presumption that families are either irrelevant or injurious in the process of treating eating disorders, and many clinicians have been trained with this prejudice.

Only in the latter part of the last century did these ideas about the harmful effects of parents and families begin to be challenged. The notion that parents and families might actually be seen as a resource to help with eating disorders in their children began with a revision of traditional family therapy for anorexia nervosa. The novel revision of traditional family therapy was undertaken by Christopher Dare, a child psychiatrist and psychoanalyst, at the Maudsley Hospital in London (Dare and Eisler 1992). Taking as a starting place that parents and siblings could be helpful in changing the behaviors

exhibited by the patient with anorexia nervosa, Dare and colleagues systematically devised a new type of family approach that aimed to empower parents in particular and to energize the family as a whole to defeat the power
of anorexia nervosa on their son or daughter. This approach was used in
several randomized controlled trials that involved adolescents with anorexia
nervosa and have been shown to be an effective approach with long-lasting
benefits (Russell et al. 1987; Eisler et al. 2000; Le Grange et al. 1992a).

Based on the success of Dare and colleagues' work at the Maudsley, we
have been using a treatment approach based on this model for adolescents
with anorexia nervosa and bulimia nervosa in our clinics and studies (Lock
2001, 2002; Lock and Le Grange 2001; Lock et al. 2001). This has provided us
with an opportunity to refine our understanding of how to help parents
become effective in helping their children with eating disorders. Our
approach differs somewhat between adolescents with each of the major disorders, but there are also similar principles that are derived from the initial
work of Dare and his colleagues.

MAIN PRINCIPLES

There are four main principles that underlie the work we do to help parents undertake the arduous task of helping their children with eating disorders.

No blame: Parents have been told they are responsible for their child's
    eating disorder. They are also told that they are likely to be a hin-
    drance to their child's recovery because of this. When we work with
    parents, the first thing we emphasize is that they should not blame
    themselves for causing the eating disorder. The sense of guilt in par-
    ents that follows from this assumption innervates them and makes
    them ineffective as agents of change and support.
Empowerment: Parents have been told to stand back and allow the
    recovery process to be the product of the child's own efforts rather
    than as a result of parental control. Instead, we emphasize the crucial
    role parents must play in deciding on treatment, supporting treatment,
    and participating in their child's recovery. Parents are told that rather
    than being responsible for the illness, they are a resource to help in
    recovery.
Eating disorders are an illness: Adolescents often see themselves as hav-
    ing brought the eating disorder about through their own choice. Eating
    disorders do not arise out of choice but are rather a disease process
    that is maintained by many factors. By separating the adolescent's own
    beliefs and attitudes from those that are essentially those of an eating

disorder, parents can see that they are fighting an illness rather than a willful child; and additionally, adolescents can ultimately understand that their parents are fighting the *illness* rather than them.

Therapists are consultants: Therapists are often seen as having the answers to the dilemmas of their patients. This therapy, in line with parental empowerment, sees that the answers to the dilemmas that the eating disorder is making for the patient and family must be solved with the unique resources of the parents and family. This means that the therapist helps parents think through their choices and advises them about what they might expect, but leaves decision making and carrying out of plans to parents.

WORKING WITH PARENTS WHO HAVE CHILDREN WITH ANOREXIA NERVOSA

Our work with parents who have children with anorexia nervosa follows the four principles described above. In addition, we have refined the approach developed by Dare and colleagues (Lock et al. 2001). We will first describe the overall paradigm and then focus on how parents of children with anorexia nervosa are helped in the process.

The treatment we use takes place over approximately one year and is comprised of approximately twenty family sessions during the period. It is divided into three main parts: parental refeeding, adolescent transition to self-care, and adolescent development.

The first phase is the most radical element of the approach we use and is aimed primarily at motivating and actively encouraging the parents to refeed their starving son or daughter. Parents are told about the medical dangers of not taking action (i.e., bone problems, growth problems, fertility problems, cardiac problems, and death). In a grave but supportive manner, the therapist challenges the inactivity of parents by raising their anxieties about the dire circumstances they find themselves in while, at the same time, helping to contain this anxiety by promising to assist them in finding a solution. In this process, the therapist specifically counters the parental presumption of guilt and states that the cause of anorexia nervosa is unknown. The therapist emphasizes that their skills as parents are vital to recovery and that, in fact, the use of them is the only way their child will likely escape the clutches of anorexia nervosa. Additionally, the therapist is careful to clearly establish that their son or daughter has a disease and is not thinking as they usually would. This is illustrated in several ways. First, by asking the adolescent to describe what having anorexia nervosa has taken from them (i.e., ability to play sports, attend school, free time, parental approval, etc.). Second, other family members, particularly siblings, often eloquently describe how much their sister or brother has changed. This separation of the illness from the patient allows the parents and the patient to better focus on the problem they are trying to manage rather than on interpersonal struggles about control and autonomy. Thus, parents are asked to take charge of the adolescent's eating and the problems resultant from that (not their child's whole adolescent life) and for only the period of time necessary to modify these behaviors sufficiently to restore normal weight and eating. Finally, parents are asked to be as noncritical as possible about this. We ask them to try to be determined and specific about their expectations about eating, while being supportive and understanding of the difficulty their child has in complying with these. The therapist models this in her interactions with the parents and patient, thereby demonstrating the usefulness of this stance.

In addition, the therapist attempts to help the parents understand that anorexia nervosa is not something that they would have expected or necessarily know how to manage based on their usual experiences and expectations. Parents of adolescents may expect many problems and dilemmas, but the severe thought distortions and behavioral preoccupations associated with anorexia nervosa are perplexing and challenging even to experienced clinicians. Nonetheless, the therapist assures the parents that although they may have been temporarily thrown off by the illness, he or she has great confidence in their ultimate ability to help their child. This confidence in parents comes from clinical experience—that is, the therapist has seen many parents be successful in this endeavor starting from the same place the parents are in at this point—and because the therapist is familiar with the scientific literature supporting this approach as helpful.

At this point, the therapist will usually briefly review the scientific literature for the parents. The main points that are stressed are as follows: (1) there is not a great deal of scientific support for any particular treatment for anorexia nervosa (Lock 2001); (2) for adolescents, the randomized controlled studies available support the use of parental refeeding (Lock 2001); and (3) no medications appear to be helpful for the primary symptoms of anorexia nervosa (Attia, Mayer, and Killory 2001). These points help to buoy the parents by providing them with some information that supports their taking on a challenge that they may otherwise feel ambivalent about.

Sometimes parents report that they have tried to refeed their child prior to starting treatment and "it didn't work." Usually parents have indeed made efforts to refeed. However, the efforts when carefully reviewed—which is something the therapist does in the first or second session—are characterized by hesitation, inconsistency, disagreements between the parents, and a lack of persistence. Parents can be reminded that when they have helped this child or other of their children with problems success came only when the interventions they made were planful, consistent, agreed upon, and persistently applied over time. In this way, the therapist normalizes the process of refeeding as similar to addressing other behavioral problems in children, while also underlining the important features of success.

With the family sufficiently motivated, the therapist next asks the parents to bring a picnic meal to be eaten in the office. The therapist uses the opportunity of the family picnic to confront in vivo the behavioral constraint and hesitancy that characterize the struggles parents have in taking control of refeeding their child. The therapist does not eat with the family but rather observes the family process around meal times and interviews them about who is present and how meals are planned, scheduled, and eaten. This session allows the parents to feel that the therapist understands their dilemmas (after all, the therapist sees what they are up against at meal time) and promotes a sense of unobtrusive involvement.

Toward the end of the session, the therapist asks the parents to assist their child to eat a bit more than she or he planned. This is a direct confrontation of the self-starvation resulting from anorexia nervosa and permits an opportunity for the parents to demonstrate their approach with the therapist present to coach them through the process. The usual problems parents have with this are the following: (1) anxiety about making their child angry with them; (2) struggles with both parents agreeing on what needs to be done and how; and (3) turning over control of refeeding over to the patient or even a sibling. The therapist's presence goes some way to help diminish parental anxiety, but in addition, the therapist reminds the parents of the need to take immediate action to prevent further physical, emotional, and intellectual deterioration due to persistent starvation. Furthermore, the therapist reminds the parents that the anger they are afraid of is really evidence of illness, rather than evidence of real dislike or rejection of them. When parents disagree on how to proceed, it is important to point out how children learn to use such disagreements to their self-perceived benefit, but in this instance, it is only the thinking and behaviors associated with anorexia nervosa that are advanced. Parents are therefore asked to be on the same page, same sentence, same word, or even same letter in their efforts to defeat anorexia nervosa. When parents defer control over refeeding to their child with the illness, therapists remind them of the limited evidence they have seen of the ability for the child to actually manage this. Usually, it is abundantly clear that left to their own devices, the children would continue to lose weight regardless of promises to the contrary.

Some parents object to taking control of refeeding their child because they have been told that the illness is about a need for control and to take this away from their child would be harmful. Therapists remind parents that there are many ways adolescents express their need to control their own lives, but some of them would not be allowed. Sometimes we use the example of the difference between the child who has experimented with alcohol versus one who is habitually drinking. In either case, the adolescent may well be anxious and feel that drinking alcohol improves their sense of control, but most parents readily see they would intervene actively themselves with a teenager who was habitually drinking. The therapist stresses that the analogy is one that carries saliency for anorexia nervosa as well. Adolescents who experiment with dieting and weight loss may well be conforming to the norms of their peer group while also managing their anxiety and feeling more in control; however, when their dieting and weight loss reach extreme proportions, it is no longer appropriate to see these behaviors as proper methods for expressing mastery and control. Sometimes we say that the patient is "driving under the influence of anorexia nervosa."

During the entire first phase of treatment, the patient's weight is recorded and graphed. The graph is used at the beginning of each session to illustrate how successful the parents have been at helping their son or daughter gain weight over the previous week. The graph is not meant to be an exact measure of weight but rather a trend line for the family to evaluate how their efforts played. The therapist uses the graph supportively. When their has been no weight gain or even weight loss, the therapist is appropriately concerned but immediately opens the discussion with the parents about their sense of why there has been a lack of progress. Often, the parents will (and should) feel good about no change in weight if this represents a successful effort at ending a steady decline. The therapist will accentuate the positive view. If there is weight loss, the therapist exams in a detailed fashion their attempts to help their son or daughter eat, always looking for any success, even if the success has not yet lead to significant weight change. When there has been weight gain, the therapist encourages the family to identify how they were successful and how they can build on this success.

Most parents learn that there is not real mystery about how to help your child gain weight. It requires eating at regular intervals, with supervision, in amounts necessary for weight gain, and with a range of types of food adequate for good nutrition. We do not encourage parents to seek consultation from a nutritionist. After all, most parents are adequately nourished as are their other children, so the basics of nutrition are usually well known, but more important perhaps is that parents who defer their expertise to others continue to feel inadequate and unempowered. Of course, many parents seek advice from a nutritionist and are able to use the advice to enhance their own skills. Furthermore, through the refeeding process, parents learn a great deal about nutrition and weight gain. For example, parents are sometimes surprised to learn that although their child is eating normal amounts of food, they still are not gaining weight. Therapists remind them that, from experience, people who are underweight (say, as a consequence of abdominal surgery) usually have to eat a great deal more than usual to actually gain that weight back than they would just to maintain their usual weight. This helps to normalize their sense of the quantities of food often necessary to lead to weight gain. Another reason patients with anorexia nervosa do not gain weight despite improved eating is their continued exercise and high activity levels. This sometimes confuses parents because they believe that increased exercise and activity will motivate their child to eat. This perception is undoubtedly true, but the underlying reasoning is often less transparent; that is, patients with anorexia nervosa are expert calculators of calories, fat grams, and the impact of activity on weight. Thus, they appear motivated to eat because they know they will be able to prevent weight gain via these other activities. When parents are helped to understand better the "mind" of anorexia nervosa, they are less apt to be confused by what appears to be motivation but is, in fact, deception.

The therapist in the first phase is always trying to balance keeping the parents anxious enough to keep them active in finding innovative ways to help their son or daughter eat more with a message of patience and persistence, which must also attend the process of refeeding. Part of the process of taking on the challenge of anorexia nervosa is learning what works and does not work. This takes time and requires experiments, miscues, and sometimes, failures. The therapist encourages the parents to view their efforts in this light. The learning curve is steep in phase 1. But, at the same time, parents are helped to be patient with their son or daughter sufficiently enough to keep them from becoming overly frustrated or angry. We use the metaphor of "climbing a sand hill" to describe the process of recovery. Ultimately, progress must be steady and consistent without interruption or gains will slide away. Only at the top of the sand hill is there sufficient traction to rest.

The first phase ends when parents are firmly in control of eating and the patient is making steady progress in terms of weight gain. Usually, the thoughts related to anorexia nervosa have not changed much, but the behaviors are much improved. Parents (and the family as a whole) feel a measure of relief, and the mood of the family is improved. At this point, the therapist starts to work actively with the parents to help them begin to assess what they will be looking for in behavioral terms in order to begin to turn eating back to their son or daughter. Parents have mixed feelings about this transition. They have usually fought hard to gain the control they have over eating and weight and can be reasonably reluctant to risk a return of the most serious symptoms of self-starvation. On the other hand, they are also exhausted by the constant vigilance around eating and welcome at least the idea of a return to normalcy. Thus, parents sometimes have trouble seeing the need to turn control over; or on the other hand, they want to turn it back too quickly. It is the therapist's job to assist the parents in getting between the horns of this dilemma.

Therapists help parents in a variety of ways in making the decision about how to proceed. First, they provide feedback about how the patient is doing in terms of weight, attitude toward eating, preoccupation with thinness based on the weight graph, change in food choices, and acceptance of weight gain. In addition, the therapist asks the parents to consider being deliberate but cautious in the plan they employ in turning eating back to their child. An analogy we use that parents often understand is suggesting to them that their daughter has gotten a speeding ticket. The response to this infraction might be to not allow her to drive for a period, which would be followed by allowing her to drive to school and then if these exercises go well, full driving privileges would be returned because she would have demonstrated sufficient mastery of driving. Using this type of analogy, parents find they can plan a gradual transition to return of food and weight control that assures them that their son or daughter can manage it while not overwhelming the patient with the task too abruptly. Usually parents begin by allowing snacks to be taken without supervision, followed by lunchtimes at school, and finally dinners and breakfasts. The term "without supervision" requires some clarification. Parents normally observe, to a certain extent, the eating behaviors of their children (even older ones), so it would be abnormal not to continue to do this. In addition, because dieting has been severe in the past, it is also reasonable for parents to keep an eye on eating and weight, though in a less intrusive manner, even during the latter part of phase 2.

During phase 2, usually in the latter stages, parents are asked to think through their management of adolescent issues as they relate specifically to eating and weight. There are a number of such issues including (1) eating at school, (2) activities, such as parties, that include eating, (3) school trips, and (4) athletics. Parents need to assess if it is advisable to allow their son or daughter with anorexia nervosa to eat at school. This is challenging for some teenagers with anorexia nervosa because they are ashamed or anxious about eating in front of others, the choices of foods in school are limited, they feel they cannot manage both the social demands of eating with peers while eating sufficiently, and for some there is simply insufficient time during scheduled lunches. Parents can help with this by being available to unobtrusively join their son or daughter for lunch, by discussing the problem with school staff to ensure that food choices and times are sufficient, and sometimes to involve a school counselor in observing or eating with their child. These kinds of adjustments also apply to school trips; however, because these trips also may entail several days away and sometimes-strenuous activity, parents find it useful to go on these trips to make sure that things go as well as possible. It is also helpful to advise parents to avoid long trips, especially abroad or where gastrointestinal illnesses are common that lead to weight loss (e.g., Africa and India), during this period. It is likely too much too soon and such trips may well trigger a relapse.

Adolescent social activities commonly involve eating, and usually eating foods that most patients with anorexia nervosa are ill prepared to consider until fairly far along in their recovery. In order to support the continued social development of their son or daughter, though, parents are encouraged to identify ways to support attending such events. This might be to reduce the overall time spent at the activity so that meals can be taken outside it; to contribute to the food being prepared for the event so that choices that would be tolerable for their son or daughter would be available; and to encourage experimentation with eating at these events, even if only small amounts initially.

Many times, the entry into anorexia nervosa involves some sporting activity. Usually, there is understandably an interest on the part of the patient to return to the sport. Many times parents and coaches are also anxious for the athlete to return. Parents often struggle with this because they clearly perceive that motivation to recover from anorexia nervosa follows in part with the possibility of returning to sports. Clever parents learn to use this but also to temper their expectations about sport as well. In order to make sure that self-starvation does not return, keeping a close eye on the process of returning to athletics is advisable. Parents accomplish this by insisting on regular weight checks, advising and updating the coach about the illness, and having regular visits with the pediatrician to make sure that cardiac and other physical markers of malnutrition remain in check.

Phase 3 begins when the adolescent is eating normally, weight is in the normal range, and among females, menstruation has begun or returned. The main focus of this phase of treatment is to help the parents make sure that any adolescent developmental problems (e.g., physical, social, academic) that are a result of anorexia nervosa are identified, and necessary interventions to address them are set in motion. This is a modest goal. The therapist does not want to convey to the family that now we will begin conventional family therapy, but rather that this phase is designed to get the patient and family on track with usual problems of adolescence without anorexia nervosa clouding the picture. At this point, therapy sessions are usually monthly, and parents feel that they are back in the driver's seat insofar as their family's health is concerned. Many will still want to know what "caused" the anorexia nervosa and will need to be assured that the cause may never be known but that it is now behind them. It is helpful sometimes to show parents this by saying that we do not know the cause of many, if not most, illnesses and that the treatments we use sometimes bare no relation to the cause. Cancer, for example, is caused in many ways, but the treatments are usually chemotherapy, surgery, or radiation, regardless. We must convince parents, even at this point, that knowing the cause (even if we could know it) would not change what we would be doing, that is, focusing on how to get on with life with a teenager.

Our approach to working in this phase is initially psychoeducational. The therapist reviews the three main stages of adolescence: (1) pubertal adjustment, (2) social group identity exploration; and (3) work and intimacy exploration. Parents are asked to discuss their own experiences of each of these stages of adolescence. This is often the first time parents have shared these experiences with their children. They are asked how they felt as their bodies developed (How did they feel about their height, weight, body shape, rate of maturation?); how they developed friendships and peer groups (Who were your best friends? Why did you think you chose those particular people? What social group did you belong to [athletic, academic, etc.]? How did these change over time? When did you first have romantic feelings for someone?); and how they chose a career (When did you get an idea about the kind of work you wanted to pursue?).

Based on these interviews, the therapist asks parents to remember how their own parents helped them with the dilemmas of adolescence. The responses are quite variable. Some parents respond that they experienced highly authoritarian parents, whereas others had highly permissive parents, as well as everything in between. These experiences often vary between each of the parents, of course. We ask parents how their own parents could have assisted them. Based on these questions and the responses, the therapists ask parents to discuss the way they want to parent an adolescent. Of course, sometimes they have already been the parent of an adolescent and have some experience (both good and bad); the therapist also asks them to include this in their thoughts. Sometimes the older sibling is present (if they still live at home) and can enliven this discussion by talking about their own experience.

Next, parents are asked to assess where their child with anorexia nervosa is in the developmental schema and to identify any types of struggles they may see related to this stage at this point in their child's recovery from anorexia nervosa. For the parents of younger adolescents and older children, the main stage may be pubertal adjustment, and the main themes may be related to helping them to adjust to realistic acceptance of their body size and appearance. In most cases, because the problem of anorexia nervosa is directly related to these concerns, pubertal adjustment is often improved as a result of the earlier phases of treatment. In many cases, parents of children and younger adolescents who have disposed of anorexia nervosa have little more to address in this phase except in preparation for other aspects of adolescence.

More commonly, as the adolescent is recovering from anorexia nervosa, issues related to social identity become more evident. Anxieties about social acceptance are evident. Parents are asked to help their child address these anxieties. Parents have approached this remarkably differently. For example, some parents become very proactive initially in helping to find peer activities that will promote confidence. For example, they may coach an athletic team or sponsor some activity at church or school. Other parents simply encourage the adolescent to take more initiative on their own. This can be as simple as reminding them about the need to plan for some activity on the weekend. These types of parental interventions are designed to support the adolescent in taking up the challenge of middle-adolescent social identity development rather than avoiding it.

Another large portion of adolescents who are recovering from anorexia nervosa are in the third stage of adolescence. With recovery from the illness, these adolescents are poised to take on issues related to romance and work. The main challenges for parents here have to do with support for these activities within a reasonably flexible structure. Thus, the rules about dating, curfews, expectations about alcohol and drug use, and participation in planning for the future are all subjects common to this stage. The therapist's goal is to help the parents identify where they have agreements and disagreements about these types of issues and to encourage them to understand the implications of finding common ground so that the support they wish to provide their teenage son or daughter is the best possible.

Termination of treatment takes place when the three phases of treatment are completed. As we noted, sessions are titrated down from weekly, to biweekly, to monthly over an average of a twelve-month period; thus, parents are naturally encouraged to feel increasingly independent of the therapist. It is the therapist's job, in fact, to actively decrease any dependence on them in order to make sure that parents feel the brunt of the responsibility as well as take the lion's share of the credit for the success they have had in helping defeat anorexia nervosa. At the same time, though, the therapist has from the start been a caring and reliable source for advice and support. Furthermore, the therapist has seen the family, and particularly the parents, through a harrowing process that has taken their child from near death to being on a normal trajectory of adolescent development. As a result, parents feel particularly grateful and attached to the therapist, but usually without the sense of overdependence that often accompanies intensive therapies.

In concluding therapy, the therapist reviews with the parents and other family members the progress made. We do this by carefully remembering what the symptoms and behaviors were at the start of treatment and what is happening at the time of the last session. There is usually a marked change in every aspect. Patients have gained weight, they are eating normally, they do not appear anxious or depressed, they are no longer withdrawn or irritable, and they are getting along better with their parents and siblings. Put another way, the struggles they continue to have are usually within the expected range for adolescents and their parents and siblings.

However, sometimes there are other problems that the patient or the parents perceive that might require additional treatment. Obsessive-compulsive disorder, major depression, and abuse all may be common conditions that co-occur with anorexia nervosa. In addition, there may be other family problems, such as marital problems, or other types of conflicts that require treatment that is beyond the focused scope of the treatment program for anorexia nervosa. The therapist may well recommend that the family or parents, or the individual patient, seek additional treatment for these other conditions. However, most often with these younger patients, there is a sense of things being in a good enough place to allow the family to take up its usual functioning without the ongoing guidance, consultation, or intervention of a therapist.

Parents leave this type of therapy feeling that they have improved their skills as parents, feeling more confident in their abilities because they have taken on and mastered a difficult parenting problem, and feeling ready to take on the challenges of the rest of adolescence because of these changes. They also feel better as a couple: the family has improved its communication, and as a whole, they feel closer. Thus, although not the aim of therapy, family process improves in treatment. Of course, this does not imply that there were major problems that caused anorexia nervosa so much as it suggests that by taking on rather than avoiding anorexia nervosa, parents and families can improve any processes that had been undermined by the presence of the illness or benefit from learning to work together to solve the problem.

Does putting parents in charge of refeeding their children with anorexia nervosa work? The dissatisfying answer to this question is a resounding "probably." Certainly most patients who have been treated using this method improve, but the treatment has not been put to the gold standard test of a large randomized clinical trial comparing it to either no treatment or another viable treatment. That said, though, this approach is the one that is the most studied of any treatments for anorexia nervosa. Unfortunately, there are only a few published randomized, controlled trials using psychotherapy in the treatment of anorexia nervosa. Five of these used exclusively adolescent samples (Russell et al. 1987; Eisler et al. 2000; Le Grange et al. 1992a; Eisler et al. 1997; Robin et al. 1999; Lock et al. 2005). And of these, all five used some form of family treatment that employed parental responsibility for refeeding. All of these trials suggested that this technique was successful in helping patients recover from anorexia nervosa (Lock 2001).

HOW CAN PARENTS HELP ADOLESCENTS
WITH BULIMIA NERVOSA?

Our understanding of how to treat bulimia nervosa, at least in adults, is more advanced than in anorexia nervosa. This is ironic, because anorexia nervosa was first described almost a hundred year before bulimia nervosa was characterized as an "ominous variant" of that condition by Russell et al. (1987). However, the timing of the description of bulimia nervosa coincided with an important development in psychological treatment using cognitive-behavioral approaches (CBT). This fortuitous timing allowed the exploration of CBT for bulimia nervosa, where it has proved helpful for adults (Agras et al. 2000; Fairburn 1981). Other treatments, such as medications (particularly antidepressants) and other focused psychological treatment such as interpersonal psychotherapy (IPT), have also been tested and found useful in treating bulimia nervosa (Fairburn 1997; Walsh and Devlin 1995).

Unfortunately, although there are many numbers of studies that support a range of treatments for adults with bulimia nervosa, there are no published treatments of bulimia nervosa in adolescents (Fairburn and Harrison 2003; Le Grange and Lock 2002). This has left clinicians with the difficult task of trying to fit treatment of adolescents with bulimia nervosa into untested models. The most common approach is to use some form of individual psychodynamic therapy that focuses on presumed underlying psychological conflicts. Other approaches have used traditional family therapy with the idea that, similar to anorexia nervosa, family pathology either causes or maintains the symptoms of bulimia nervosa. Others have simply applied adult models of CBT to adolescents. In contrast, in our work, we have used three approaches with adolescents with bulimia nervosa, each productively and substantively involving parents to help their children with the illness: family-based treatment of bulimia nervosa (similar to anorexia nervosa); family-facilitated CBT; and family-supported IPT.

Family-based treatment for adolescent bulimia nervosa (FBT—bulimia nervosa) is identical in its basic formulation as FBT for anorexia nervosa. That is, parents are not blamed for causing bulimia nervosa, bulimia nervosa is thought of as a disease and not the patient's choice, parents are empowered to become agents of change, and therapists are consultative rather than authoritarian in their stance. Similar to anorexia nervosa, when families are approached in this manner, they are less defensive, more creative and motivated, and more supportive of therapy.

It should be noted at the outset that there are some differences between families with a teenager with bulimia nervosa compared to anorexia nervosa (Le Grange and Lock 2002). For example, there are more single parent families, greater ethnic and racial diversity, and broader and more representative ranges of SES in the overall group. There are also differences between patients with anorexia nervosa and bulimia nervosa. Anorexia nervosa patients are usually more comfortable with their symptoms, deny the seriousness of their predicament, are more medically compromised, and tend to be less autonomous than adolescents with bulimia nervosa. Adolescents with bulimia nervosa also tend to have a variety of other problems, including drug use, sexual activity, and school problems, that are less common among adolescents with anorexia nervosa (Le Grange and Lock 2002).

There is an impact of these differences on working in FBT for bulimia nervosa. For example, because there are more single parent families, there are often fewer parental resources to utilize. Further, because the medical aspects of bulimia nervosa are less obvious and less immediately life threatening, it is sometimes harder to raise parental anxiety about bulimia nervosa. In addition, because adolescents with bulimia nervosa have other problems that parents consider to be as serious or more so (e.g., reckless behavior with drugs, alcohol, sexual relations), it is sometimes difficult for parents to focus on bulimia nervosa as a substantive problem. Also, in part because adolescents with bulimia nervosa are more autonomous behaviorally than many adolescents with anorexia nervosa, there is more likelihood that additional "distracting" problems will arise in treatment—conflicts with friends, dating, curfew violations, trouble with grades, and so forth—that also make it difficult to keep a focus on bulimia nervosa. Nonetheless, in the first session, parents are educated about the severe physical and psychological difficulties associated with bulimia nervosa to help them recognize that the disorder is not simply a diet gone awry but rather a serious, potentially life-threatening illness that requires their involvement to redress.

To adjust FBT for bulimia nervosa, we have made several minor adjustments to the treatment. First, and perhaps most significantly, we have asked parents and the adolescent with bulimia nervosa to *collaborate* in the recovery process, rather than parents taking control of all eating behaviors (including binge eating and purging). This departure is made in recognition of the fact that parents of an adolescent with bulimia nervosa are dealing with a developmentally more independent person who is, because of this, more likely to resist exclusive parental control and undermine the support that parents can offer. Thus, early in the first phase of treatment, the adolescent and parents are asked to work out together how parents can be involved and helpful in preventing binge eating and purging. This often involves parents sitting with their adolescent with bulimia nervosa after meals, preventing them from using the bathroom to purge, and finding ways to distract them from the discomfort and anxiety they feel after eating. In order to prevent binge eating, early sessions are devoted to helping the parents identify foods that are likely to initiate binge eating for their child. With this knowledge, they can either keep such foods out of the kitchen or, when necessary, be particularly vigilant when such foods are present or are being consumed.

There is an early focus of parents helping to normalize eating patterns. Parents are helped to understand that a normal eating pattern is likely to help prevent the emergence of binge eating. So, they are encouraged to prepare and support the consumption of breakfast and lunch in order to forestall late afternoon and early evening binge eating. Adolescents with bulimia nervosa are called upon to help educate their parents about their patterns of eating and of binge eating and purging so their parents will be able to better understand the child's predicament as well as intervene more effectively. As is the case with FBT for anorexia nervosa, it is often necessary for parents to be quite active and involved early in treatment—taking time away from work and being more structured around mealtimes than they may have been for some time, or ever. A difference between anorexia nervosa and bulimia nervosa is that bulimia nervosa patients are generally more ashamed of their behaviors—binge eating and purging often represent a failure of their dieting as opposed to the prideful successful maintenance of severe, restrictive eating present in the adolescent with anorexia nervosa. Shame must be addressed early in the first phase and although difficult initially, once adolescents feel accepted and not judged by their parents, they become less shameful and instead can allow their parents to support them. Again, to distinguish this from anorexia nervosa, the prideful stance of the adolescent with anorexia nervosa can prevent the adolescent from allowing her parents to help.

There is also a slight modification in the way the family meal is conducted. Overall, the purpose of the meal—the evaluation of family process around mealtime—is identical. However, parents are asked to identify and bring to the meal one food item that they know is a trigger food for binge eating for their adolescent. When the trigger food is presented, the family is asked to find ways to help their son or daughter to eat, but not over eat, this food item. In this way, a discussion about the feelings, struggles, and types of support needed can be experienced in vivo by the patient and parents with the therapist present to assist. At the end of the session, parents are encouraged to find ways to prevent any purging that might be attempted after the meal.

During the first phase, a binge-and-purge frequency chart is presented at the beginning of every session, along with a weight chart. These frequencies are self-reported by the patients, but parents are asked if they believe the chart is accurate. Weights are used to help illustrate that there is little relationship between decreasing of purging behavior and weight change. The session then focuses on ways parents supported progress or reversed deterioration over the past week.

As with FBT for anorexia nervosa, the focus during the first phase is almost exclusively on bulimic behaviors with the therapist tracking progress with the family. Nonetheless, with bulimia nervosa, it is often necessary to briefly take on a "crisis" even during the early phase of treatment in order for the parents and patient to be able to return effectively to work on the behaviors associated with bulimia nervosa. When the patient and parent feel that binge eating and purging are significantly improved, a discussion of readiness for phase 2 begins.

Phase 2 should begin when the patient and the family are confident that binge eating and purging are in remission. Furthermore, the patient feels ready to eat more independently and to manage trigger foods and situations without parental support as much in evidence. This phase, like in FBT for anorexia nervosa, is really about transitional mastery by the adolescent with less parental involvement. Parents and the patient are helped to understand that they should expect some episodes of binge eating and purging and that if these occur they should be used as opportunities for learning and further mastery.

Phase 3 for FBT for bulimia nervosa is identical in structure and length as FBT for anorexia nervosa; however, it should be said that it sometimes differs dramatically in character. Most of the third phase of FBT for anorexia nervosa is focused on preparing for and initiating various adolescent tasks. In FBT for bulimia nervosa, many of the issues are practical management of adolescent issues—friends, sexual experimentation, dating, and school performance. Parents of adolescents with bulimia nervosa are therefore more likely to experience difficulty with these behaviors. Parents during this phase are asked to see themselves as an important resource for their adolescent children. We discuss the differences among parenting styles—authoritarian, permissive, neglectful, and authoritative—and the benefits of the last approach in supporting adolescent development. We discuss with them recent studies that have suggested an important role for authoritative parenting during adolescence. Permissive parenting is a parenting style where adolescents are essentially left to their own devices to work out problems as they encounter them. Authoritarian parenting is a style of parenting that sets rules and consequences rather rigidly for adolescent behaviors. In contrast to these two parent styles, authoritative parents are available for consultation, provide general guidelines for behaviors, and support their children's explorations while providing consistent expectations and consequences when behaviors fall too far outside guidelines. Thus, phase 3 focuses parents on building on their success of helping with bulimia nervosa by using these same principles in becoming more authoritative parents in general.

There is no database of research that supports the use of FBT for bulimia nervosa in adolescents as we have described it here. One small study suggested it is helpful (Dodge et al. 1995). In addition, patients with anorexia nervosa who also binge eat and purge have also benefited from this model of treatment, suggesting that parents can be helpful with these problems as well as restrictive eating and dieting (Eisler et al. 2000). Thus, though there is no direct empirical data to support, there are indications that this approach is helpful, as has been our clinical experience (Lock 2002; Le Grange and Lock 2002).

In addition to FBT for bulimia nervosa, we also use CBT modified for use in adolescents with bulimia nervosa. We have written in more detail about our approach to this elsewhere (Lock 2002). However, in using CBT with adolescents, there are several key areas where parents are involved. First is in establishing the need for treatment and keeping their adolescent children coming to treatment. Unlike most adults who seek treatment for bulimia nervosa, most adolescents with bulimia nervosa are brought to treatment by their parents. This often makes the initial engagement, motivation, and alignment with the therapist more challenging.

Our experience with using CBT with adolescents with bulimia nervosa has helped us to develop adjustments for this population (Lock 2002; Lock 2005). We learned that, when adolescents were treated with CBT, they were unlikely to keep motivated for treatment without parental support. In addition, we learned that families need to know what occurs in therapy in order to support it. We found that many (though not all) adolescents responded well to parental involvement in meal planning and monitoring as well as parental assistance with efforts to decrease binge eating and purging episodes. Parental involvement in CBT for bulimia nervosa in adolescents is conceptualized to capitalize on parental abilities to alter the behavioral milieu and support behavioral change as well as being developmentally usual for this age group.

CBT for adolescent bulimia nervosa is similarly constructed to that used in adults with bulimia nervosa (Fairburn 1981; Fairburn and Hay 1992). It is divided into three stages. Parents are involved in different ways throughout treatment with adolescents. In the first stage, the emphasis in CBT is on normalizing eating patterns to prevent binge eating and purging. In FBT for bulimia nervosa there is an active collaboration developed between the adolescent and the parents to monitor and assist with this change. This is similar in CBT, however, the emphasis is patients' food records and the changes in behaviors they report as opposed to how the collaboration between the adolescent and her parents is working as is the case in FBT—bulimia nervosa. Treatment in CBT for bulimia nervosa is individually based rather than taken up in a family context, though parents are regularly asked to participate during sessions to register their concerns or observations.

During stage 2 of CBT, the focus of treatment shifts more to distorted cognitions, beliefs, and attitudes that are associated with bulimia nervosa. The emphasis in therapy is on how these factors interact and maintain eating-disordered behaviors. Parents are usually less directly involved in this stage of treatment as its focus is more on the internal world of the adolescent. One of the major differences between CBT for bulimia nervosa and FBT for bulimia nervosa is that during stage 2 there is a focus on these cognitive distortions and active problem solving around them in individual treatment. There is no emphasis on these aspects of bulimia nervosa in FBT. There are many opportunities for parents to be involved in treatment during this stage. Importantly, adolescent reactions to conflicts with parents or with other family members may serve as triggers to initiate bulimic behaviors again. Thus, sessions devoted to familial triggers for bulimia nervosa are common during stage 2 of CBT for bulimia nervosa.

Stage 3 of CBT for bulimia nervosa is a brief stage focused on identifying factors that may interfere with maintaining abstinence for bulimia nervosa. For adolescents, some of these factors are predictable developmental challenges—falling in love, romantic difficulties, friendship problems, stress at school, and conflicts with parents over autonomy. Parents are active in this stage of treatment, focusing on how they can help prevent these potential triggers from leading to relapse. In a sense, this stage operates similar to phase 3 of FBT for bulimia nervosa because it provides an opportunity for parents and adolescents to identify, prepare for, and develop an action plan about how to manage future adolescent issues without the patient having to resort to bulimia nervosa.

CBT has been used in a case series for younger patients with bulimia nervosa and has been found to be acceptable and as effective in this age group as in adults (Lock, 2005; Schapman et al. 2006). However, definitive testing using a RCT is needed to confirm these impressions.

The third form of treatment for adolescent bulimia nervosa we employ is a form of IPT adapted for adolescents (Fairburn 1997; Klerman et al. 1984; Mufson et al. 1993). IPT, unlike either FBT for bulimia nervosa or CBT for bulimia nervosa, is not focused on the management of behavioral symptoms (binge eating, purging, preoccupations with weight and shape). IPT is presumed to operate by changing the nature of key interpersonal relationships that, in the case of bulimia nervosa, are thought to maintain the emotional state necessary for continuing bulimic behaviors. Of course, IPT is predominantly an individual therapy, but in the case of adolescents, and in adolescent bulimia nervosa in particular, it is clear that parental relationships are almost always examined.

IPT for bulimia nervosa has three phases. The initial four sessions (weeks 1–2) are devoted to a detailed analysis of the interpersonal context in which the eating disorder has developed and been maintained. This leads to the formulation of the patient's eating disorder in interpersonal terms and the specification of a limited number of current interpersonal problem areas. Thereafter, the focus of the treatment is on these problem areas (sessions 3–16, weeks 3–14), the two most common being interpersonal disputes and difficulty with "role transitions" (e.g., disengaging from parents). The precise strategies used depend upon the nature of these areas. In the final phase of treatment (sessions 17–19, weeks 15–20), during which sessions are biweekly, feelings about termination are discussed, progress is reviewed, and ways of handling future difficulties are explored. Throughout treatment the patient's independent competence is emphasized. At no stage in treatment are there attempts to directly modify the patient's eating habits or attitudes to shape and weight, nor does the treatment contain any of the behavioral or cognitive procedures that specifically characterize CBT for bulimia nervosa. For example, there are no behavioral instructions or self-monitoring of behavior or cognitions as is the case in CBT.

In the assessment phase of IPT, parents are involved in helping to identify the problem areas that should be targeted, although the final determination is left to the patient and therapist. Parents provide important information for the therapist, which otherwise might not be available, including early childhood functioning and behavior, longer-term perspectives on problematic interpersonal behaviors, and familial processes.

In almost all cases there is a key role for parents during phase 2 of IPT. In particular, several of the key areas of interpersonal difficulties that are the focus of treatment in IPT are particularly relevant for adolescents (e.g., role transitions, interpersonal disputes, and interpersonal deficits). Although working with significant others is sometimes utilized in using IPT with adults, it is rather the norm that parents would attend many of the IPT sessions with adolescents. The therapist works with parents and the adolescent during these sessions to identify the key issues that interfere with interpersonal functioning in relation to the parents and helps to actively problem solve with them to resolve these difficulties. This phase of IPT resembles, in some respects, the third phase of FBT for anorexia nervosa or bulimia nervosa, as well as the third stage of CBT for bulimia nervosa, because it is focused on adolescent developmental struggles; however, the focus in IPT is exclusively on the interpersonal aspects of these dilemmas. There is no focus on symptoms or other behaviors.

In working with parents of adolescents with bulimia nervosa using IPT, it is sometimes difficult to help them see that by working on interpersonal relationships, the behaviors of bulimia nervosa will improve. It is important to make sure they understand how IPT is supposed to work—that is, indirectly, by focusing on the maintaining factors for the behaviors rather than the behaviors themselves. Parents are active and involved in this treatment, albeit in a very different way than with FBT or CBT, and it can be difficult to convey this. Sometimes we use an analogy of fertilizing a plant to help illustrate this idea. By providing nourishment to the roots of the plant, we know that over time this will strengthen the plant and help prevent or limit disease and promote healthy leaves and flowers on the plant. Thus, by providing support for improvement of interpersonal relationships (the fertilizer), we promote a healthier sense of self in relation to others that is both less anxious and less dependent (stronger roots) and allowing them to give up bulimic behaviors that are self-destructive (prevent and limit disease).

The third phase of IPT for bulimia nervosa in adolescents is a brief phase focused on termination. Parents are involved in this phase because they too are terminating treatment. During termination, the role of parents in continuing to promote and maintain healthy interpersonal relationships that support the adolescent's accomplishment during IPT is a central feature. Parents are encouraged to see their relationship with their adolescent as promoting healthy development and independence at this point.

There are no studies that have been done that empirically support the use of IPT for bulimia nervosa in adolescents, though there are good reasons to think it is likely to be helpful. Three clinical trials and two follow-up studies provide empirical support for the use of IPT to treat bulimia nervosa. Fairburn et al. (1986) compared CBT to a short-term focal therapy (a treatment very similar to IPT) aimed at identifying and modifying interpersonal problems accompanying bulimia nervosa rather than the eating disorder itself. Patients in both conditions showed improvements that were maintained over a twelve-month follow-up period. In a subsequent study designed to replicate and extend these initial findings, seventy-five patients were randomly assigned to CBT, behavioral therapy (BT), and IPT (Fairburn et al. 1991; Fairburn, Marcus, and Wilson 1993). End-of-treatment results again indicated that all three treatments had a substantial effect, with results favoring CBT. However, at the twelve-month follow-up, unlike BT, only CBT and IPT showed consistent improvement, and they were equivalent in outcome. At six-year follow-up, patients who received CBT or IPT continued to do well compared to those who received BT (Fairburn et al. 1995). These studies suggested that bulimia nervosa was responsive to IPT as well as CBT, but that the improvements associated with IPT were slower to develop. Recently, CBT was compared to IPT in a large multisite replication of the Oxford trial involving 220 patients with bulimia nervosa (Agras et al. 2000). In this trial CBT was superior to IPT at end of treatment, but on eight- to twelve-month follow-up no differences were found between the two treatments.

Nonetheless, with its focus on interpersonal functioning, IPT may appeal directly to issues most pertinent to adolescents with bulimia nervosa. Adolescents develop shape and weight concerns when worries about social acceptability and roles (related to friendships and dating) are also increased. The role of peers in body dissatisfaction and the development of eating disorders in adolescents is well known. In addition, as we have noted, problems with parental figures about autonomy and independence are another important interpersonal focus for adolescents. Thus, a treatment that focuses on these interpersonal developmental issues may be particularly salient for adolescents with bulimia nervosa as it has been with depressed adolescents.

CONCLUSION

We have described four different types of treatments for children with eating disorders that involve parents. In FBT for anorexia nervosa, parents have the greatest role in directly managing and changing behaviors. This, we have argued, is consistent with the developmental age of most of the patients as well as the severity of the behaviors and thought distortions of this group. FBT for bulimia nervosa includes parents as active collaborators in behavioral change while emphasizing the family as a context for supporting this. CBT for bulimia nervosa in adolescents resembles CBT for adults with bulimia nervosa in that it is symptom focused and primarily individually based treatment. However, when adjusted for this age group, the approach recognizes and supports the parental role in establishing a behavioral milieu that keeps the patient in treatment (even when not motivated) and supports healthy eating patterns and food choices. IPT for bulimia nervosa in adolescents is also similar to IPT as used in adults with bulimia nervosa. However, unlike adult IPT for bulimia nervosa, parents are almost always involved in the exploration of interpersonal difficulties in this age group. Unlike FBT or CBT, parental support is focused on development of increased capacities and improved functioning in the interpersonal domain rather than directly on symptom management or control.

Generally, parents can be extremely useful; in fact, we believe they are vital to any treatment of adolescents with an eating disorder (Lock and LeGrange 2005). It is clear that involvement can take many forms and be more or less directly focused or more diffuse. However, in every case parents should be involved in assessment, be educated by the therapist about the illness and its consequences, be informed about how treatment is supposed to operate, and be updated on how treatment is progressing. With this information, parents are able to support a range of interventions depending on the therapist's theoretical or clinical orientation.

It should be said that parents are not all the same. In extreme cases, abusive or neglectful parents clearly cannot be expected to or supported by therapists in using therapy as an opportunity to continue these practices. It has been noted in a number of psychiatric conditions, including anorexia nervosa, that parental criticism or negatively expressed emotion are predictors of poor outcome in treatment (Le Grange et al. 1992b; Szmukler et al. 1985). The mechanism of this is not well understood, but is likely that the hostility apparent in the interactions serves as a negative and persistent stress that undermines patients' recovery. The origin of these behaviors is unclear, but it is possible that the chronic presence of a severe psychiatric problem leads to a decompensation in usual parental functioning, increasing hostile comments. Therapists working with parents can help ameliorate this hostile and critical atmosphere by directly intervening when such comments are made and by modeling a noncritical stance in their work with parents and families.

Using parents as a resource and a leverage to increase the effectiveness of interventions with children and adolescents is not unique to eating disorders. However, eating disorders has been an area where the focus of treatment has been more hostile and blaming of parents than in many other conditions. It is clear now that parents can contribute to their children's recovery from their eating disorders in a range of ways if therapists recognize the potential and approach them with respect and encouragement.

REFERENCES

Agras, W. S., et al. 2000. A multicenter comparison of cognitive-behavioral therapy and interpersonal psychotherapy for bulimia nervosa. *Archives of General Psychiatry* 57:459–66.

Attia, E., L. Mayer, and E. Killory. 2001. Medication response in the treatment of patients with anorexia nervosa. *Journal of Psychiatric Practice* 7:157–62.

Bruch, H. 1973. *Eating disorders: Obesity, anorexia nervosa, and the person within.* New York: Basic Books.

Dare, C., and I. Eisler. 1992. Family therapy for anorexia nervosa. In *The nature and management of feeding problems in young people,* ed. I. Cooper and A. Stein, 146–60. New York: Harwood Academics.

Dodge, E., et al. 1995. Family therapy for bulimia nervosa in adolescents: An exploratory study. *Journal of Family Therapy* 17:59–77.

Eisler, I., et al. 1997. Family and individual therapy in anorexia nervosa: A five-year follow-up. *Archives of General Psychiatry* 54:1025–30.

Eisler, I., et al. 2000. Family therapy for adolescent anorexia nervosa: The results of a controlled comparison of two family interventions. *Journal of Child Psychology and Psychiatry* 41(6):727–36.

Fairburn, C. G. 1981. A cognitive behavioural approach to the treatment of bulimia. *Psychological Medicine* 11(4):707–11.

———. 1997. Interpersonal psychotherapy for bulimia nervosa. In *Handbook of treatment for eating disorders,* ed. D. M. Garner and P. Garfinkel, 278–94. 2nd ed. New York: Guilford Press.

Fairburn, C. G., and P. J. Harrison. 2003. Eating disorders. *Lancet* 361:407–16.

Fairburn, C. G., and P. J. Hay. 1992. The treatment of bulimia nervosa. *Annals of Medicine* 24(4):297–302.

Fairburn, C. G., M. D. Marcus, and G. T. Wilson. 1993. Cognitive-behavioral therapy for binge eating and bulimia nervosa: A comprehensive treatment manual. In *Binge eating: Nature, assessment, and treatment,* ed. C. G. Fairburn and G. T. Wilson, 361–404. New York: Guildford Press.

Fairburn, C. G., et al. 1986. A comparison of two psychological treatments for bulimia nervosa. *Behaviour Research and Therapy* 24(6):629–43.

Fairburn, C. G., et al. 1991. Three psychological treatments for bulimia nervosa: A comparative trial. *Archives of General Psychiatry* 48(5):463–69.

Fairburn, C. G., et al. 1995. A prospective study of outcome in bulimia nervosa and the long-term effects of three psychological treatments. *Archives of General Psychiatry* 52(4):304–12.

Gull, W. 1874. Anorexia nervosa (apepsia hysterica, anorexia hysterica). *Transactions of the Clinical Society of London* 7:222–28.

Klerman, G., et al. 1984. *Interpersonal psychotherapy for depression.* New York: Basic Books.

Lasegue, C. 1883. De l'anorexie hystérique. *Archives Générales de Médecine* 21:384–403.

Le Grange, D., and J. Lock. 2002. Bulimia nervosa in adolescents: Treatment, eating pathology, and comorbidity. *South African Psychiatry Review* 8:19–23.

Le Grange, D., et al. 1992a. Evaluation of family treatments in adolescent anorexia nervosa: A pilot study. *International Journal of Eating Disorders* 12(4):347–57.

Le Grange, D., et al. 1992b. Family criticism and self-starvation: A study of expressed emotion. *Journal of Family Therapy* 14:177–92.

Lock, J. 2001. What is the best way to treat adolescents with anorexia nervosa? *Eating Disorders* 9:299–302.

———. 2002. Treating adolescents with eating disorders in the family context: Empirical and theoretical considerations. *Child and Adolescent Psychiatric Clinics of North America* 11:331–42.

Lock, J. 2005. Adjusting CBT for adolescent bulimia: Results of a case series. *American Journal of Psychology* 58:268–81.

Lock, J., and D. Le Grange. 2001. Can family-based treatment of anorexia nervosa be manualized? *Journal of Psychotherapy Practice and Research* 10:253–61.

Lock, J., et al. 2001. *Treatment manual for anorexia nervosa: A family-based approach.* New York: Guildford Publications.

Lock, J. et al. 2005. Short versus long-term family treatment of adolescent anorexia nervosa. *Journal of the American Academy of Child & Adolescent Psychiatry* 44:632–39.

Minuchin, S., B. Rosman, and I. Baker. 1978. *Psychosomatic families: Anorexia nervosa in context.* Cambridge, Mass.: Harvard University Press.

Mufson, L., et al. 1993. *Interpersonal psychotherapy for depressed adolescents.* New York: Guilford Press.

Robin, A., et al. 1999. A controlled comparison of family versus individual therapy for adolescents with anorexia nervosa. *Journal of the American Academy of Child and Adolescent Psychiatry* 38(12):1482–89.

Russell, G. 1979. Bulimia nervosa: An ominous variant of anorexia nervosa. *Psychological Medicine* 9:429–48.

Russell, G., G. Szmulker, C. Dare, and I. Eisler. 1987. An evaluation of family therapy in anorexia nervosa and bulimia nervosa. *Archives of General Psychiatry* 44(12):1047–56.

Schapman, A., and J. Lock. 2006. Cognitive behavioral therapy for adolescent bulimia: A case series. *International Journal of Eating Disorders* 39:252–55.

Szmukler, G. I., et al. 1985. Anorexia nervosa, parental "expressed emotion" and dropping out of treatment. *British Journal of Psychiatry* 147:265–71.

Walsh, B. T., and M. J. Devlin. 1995. Pharmacotherapy of bulimia nervosa and binge eating disorder. *Addictive Behaviors* 20(6):757–64.

10

The Parent-Child Mutual Recognition Model: Promoting Responsibility and Cooperativeness in Disturbed Adolescents Who Resist Treatment

Esther Cohen and Etan Lwow

This chapter addresses the problem of disordered youngsters who resist treatment and demonstrate irresponsible and uncooperative regressive behaviors of an oppositional or dependent nature. The dynamics by which parents become involved in overprotective, indulgent, or overcontrolling patterns of interactions with these youngsters are delineated, by integrating theoretical conceptualizations from biopsychosocial systems theory and from relational psychoanalysis. A clinical model of focused work with the parents alone is introduced, designed to increase "mutual recognition" in the parent-child relationship. It involves the use of two lists of parental behaviors: a list of proscribed behaviors, representing growth inhibiting messages to the adolescent, and a list of prescribed behaviors, symbolizing growth-promoting messages targeted at the adolescent. Parents are supported and supervised in using the lists to introduce unilateral changes in their actions and reactions toward their child, thus allowing the adolescent to experience differentiation, reciprocity, and responsibility in caring relationships.

This chapter addresses the problem of disturbed youngsters who refuse to take part in any treatment, pharmacological or psychotherapeutic, and the related problem of lack of improvement in children who acquiesce to treatment merely as a useless formality. While the clinical literature acknowledges the skillfulness required to engage in therapy reluctant adolescents who may be embarrassed, suspicious, anxious, or angry (Loar 2001; Edgette 1999), it

This chapter was originally published in *Journal of Psychotherapy Integration* (2004), 14(3): 307–22. Copyright © 2004 by the Educational Publishing Foundation. Adapted with permission.

rarely addresses instances where the adolescents are completely unavailable to the therapist's attempts to reach out and engage them (Price 1996).

The problem becomes paralyzing to families and therapists when the adolescent appears out of contact with reality and potentially dangerous to himself or to others. This characterizes the teens who are referred to us, usually after being turned down by other therapists for refusing therapy, and at times following unsuccessful hospitalizations. They exhibit symptoms warranting a range of diagnoses such as psychosis, depression, anorexia, school phobia, oppositional-defiant disorder, conduct disorder, bipolar disorder, anxiety disorder, or borderline personality disorder.

In recent years much progress seems to have been achieved in treating young people with such disorders by adopting an integrative approach, involving both the symptomatic individual and the family. This approach is being validated by the research examining family treatments designed for particular disorders. For example, the addition of such treatments for families of schizophrenic children as family psychoeducation (Anderson, Hogarty, and Reiss 1986) and family behavioral management (Falloon et al. 1985) is reported to have produced a marked improvement in relapse rate when combined with the traditional antipsychotic medication for the adolescents (Lam 1991). Similarly, programs designed for individuals suffering from a bipolar-affective disorder or a borderline personality disorder that include their families have been shown to produce a positive effect on symptomatology and relationships (Simoneau, et al. 1999; Hoffman, Fruzzetti, and Swenson 1999; Rosenfarb et al. 2001). However, all these clinical models assume personal contact between the therapist and the adolescent.

Our clinical experience has thus led us to attempt to break through the impasse, and the sense of helplessness that parents often experience, by working intensively with them alone. The viability of working with parents alone has its roots early in the history of child psychotherapy, since Freud's attempt to treat Little Hans via his father, and Winnicott's consultations with mothers. This approach is also consonant with one of the basic assumptions of systems theory, namely, that change in an individual or in a subsystem affects the whole system. Strategic therapy capitalizes on this idea by flexibly adopting creative interventions with different members and dyads in the family, according to their motivational level (Haley 1973). The focus on the parental subsystem is reflected in a number of models of family therapy (Palazzoli et al. 1988; Zimmerman and Protinsky 1990; Garrett et al. 1998; Sells 1998; Diamond, Diamond, and Liddle 2000) as well as in recent psychodynamic approaches (Rustin 1999; Pantone 2000; Tsiantis et al. 2000; Jacobs and Wachs 2002). It is also being integrated into psychiatric hospital settings (Byalin 1990). This chapter espouses Pantone's (2000) suggestion to conceptualize the parental relationship as the "identified patient" in child psychotherapy and his argument that intensive intervention at the parental level is a necessary condition for a successful outcome in child psychotherapy, and that in some cases it is a sufficient treatment alternative. In the case of disturbed adolescents who refuse therapy, it seems to be the only alternative.

The chapter sets forth an innovative intervention, developed by the second author, which engages the parents in a gradual process of unilateral changes. These changes in the parents' ways of acting and reacting toward their child impact not only their interactions but also constitute symbolic messages for the individuals involved, thus creating new relational meanings. The therapeutic work with the parents to be explicated in this chapter involves teaching them how to challenge and enable adolescents to assume responsibility for their problems, by either becoming a motivated consumer of therapy or by improving their level of functioning without therapy. In tandem parents are challenged and enabled to stabilize their own life and state of well-being, regardless of the adolescent's level of functioning.

In exploring the dynamics of the families with troubled and resistant adolescents who have consulted with us, the similar characteristics of a striking subgroup appeared especially puzzling. No child-abuse or neglect issues seemed to be involved. The parents in these cases appeared to be very caring, worried, and devoted to their children. Additionally, the major arena in need of intervention seemed to be the parent-child relationship, rather than the marital relationship, even though the latter was affected by the children's distressing situation. However, the recurrent dynamic to emerge from the parents' reports related to great joint difficulty in accepting differentiation and in expecting mutuality between parents and adolescents. Family interactions appeared to involve anxious parenting practices expressed by either indulgent, overprotective, or overcontrolling acts. The adolescents, in turn, seemed both to act and to react using passive withdrawal, regressive-demanding behavior, or at times, oppositional, provocative, and destructive behavior, directed at the parents or the self. The children's inappropriate behavior seemed to further elicit in the parents anxiety and guilt, which in turn fueled their additional attempts to please and placate or to control them.

THEORETICAL CONCEPTUALIZATIONS

The suggested intervention model is based on an integrative theoretical and clinical approach. The theoretical underpinnings of our conceptualization of the problem manifested in the above-described cycles of interactions draws from the fields of family systems theory, relational and other psychoanalytic schools of thought, biopsychosocial models, and developmental research.

The described family dynamics can be characterized by using Minuchin's (1974) well-known concept of "enmeshment," postulating that relationships become dysfunctional when they impede the separate functioning of the individuals involved. However, in more recent work (Green and Werner 1996) it has been argued that this concept may have been misused in the family therapy literature, mainly by failing to recognize that self-other differentiation is a very different dimension of relationships than the closeness-distance dimension. Green and Werner (1996) suggest using two separate dimensions in clinical work and research: intrusiveness (blurring of boundaries) and closeness–care-giving (warmth and nurturance). They provide data to support the independence of these dimensions in family connectedness (Werner et al. 2001). It seems that the "stuck" families of the resistant adolescents may be characterized by being high both on mutual intrusiveness and on closeness, but their perceptions of these two dimensions are confounded, and all members of the family seem to fear that differentiation might bring about the loss of closeness. A major aim of our intervention with these parents is therefore to minimize reciprocal intrusiveness in the parent-adolescent relationship in order to increase the clarity of personal boundaries, while maintaining the sense of belonging and caring.

Madanes (1990) underscores the complexity of the blurring of boundaries in families with serious problems of adolescents, as parent and child are caught in two incongruous hierarchies that conflict paradoxically. In one the youth is incompetent and dependent on the parents for protection and need fulfillment. In the other he or she dominates the parents by vulnerability, helplessness, and irresponsible behavior. Empowering parents to correct the hierarchy requires, therefore, addressing the issues of guilt, responsibility, and cycles of interpersonal influences.

Benjamin (1988) approaches the issue of self-other differentiation from an intersubjective-developmental perspective. She finds Mahler's formulation of the process of separation-individuation unsatisfactory because of its sole emphasis on the gradual separation and individuation from the initial symbiotic unity with the mother, and its neglect of the child's developing capacity for actively engaging in relationships with significant others. She maintains that through these relationships the child comes to experience "recognition," that is, validation, sharing, and identification with significant others. This experience is meaningful only if children recognize the significant person as separate, distinct, yet like them. Benjamin sees the different levels of achieving mutuality in relationships as involving the repeated handling of the inherent tensions between self-assertion and recognition of the other. Expanding on the work of Winnicott, she delineates universally important tasks both for the child and for the parents in the process of differentiation and mutual recognition. She argues that the child must come to terms with the fact that he or she does not magically control the mother and that what she does for him is subject to her will. At the same time the mother needs to accept herself as entitled to a separate existence and to develop confidence in her child's ability to survive conflict, loss, and imperfection, accepting that she cannot create a perfect world for her child.

Benjamin describes two major kinds of parental failure in this respect, due to anxiety and unresolved needs, which interfere with the child's task. In the first kind of the "anxiously controlling parents," children become dependent on the parents' omnipotence, experiencing themselves as an extension of the parents, with no agency of their own. In the second kind of the "self-effacing, indulgent parents," children experience themselves as omnipotent, but alone, perceiving the parents and others as their extension. These failures and their results seem to characterize well the group of adolescents under discussion in this chapter, whose sense of ownership and agency seems distorted, and whose ability to balance assertion and recognition of another is greatly impaired.

There is growing research evidence to support the idea that earlier developmental weaknesses in children or in their care-taking environment are involved in the adolescents' failure in establishing both a sense of separateness as well as a sense of interdependence in relationships. These weaknesses are exacerbated by stress (Rubin, Stewart, and Chen 1995; Herbert 2000). Special risk factors in the child associated with such future maladaptation involve both biobehavioral reactivity (Wood, Klebba, and Miller 2000), especially being temperamentally deregulated since infancy, and exhibiting low adaptability, impulsivity, and negative emotionality (Sanson and Prior 1999; Greene 2001). The risk associated with anxious, overprotective or overdirective parenting, beginning early in infancy, is also becoming clearer (Parker 1983; Rubin et. al. 1995; Leckman et al. 1999). This pattern may be related to the parents' own attachment history and adult attachment style such as the "compulsive care-giving" (Bowlby 1977; West and Sheldon 1988), parents' personal psychopathology (Parker 1983; Thomasgard 1998), and life events affecting parenting, such as adoption (Smith, Surrey, and Watkins 1998; Derdeyn and Graves 1998), traumas, and unsatisfactory adult significant relationships or accomplishments. These early relational patterns may reemerge, or become aggravated at times of developmental crisis, such as when the child reaches adolescence and experiences the internal and social challenges to marshal new capacities. The adolescent's struggle may then be undermined by the anxious and regressive messages from his parents, causing personal and familial dysfunction. When the picture is further complicated by psychiatric symptomatology, these regressive patterns are likely to be intensified both for the youngster and for the parents.

The therapeutic work with the parents, based on these conceptualizations, is comprised of two main components. The first is a supportive component, introduced to provide parents some relief of their guilt, shame, anxiety, and hopelessness. As parents' emotional, marital, and everyday life are greatly impacted by their adolescent, they need help in managing their own feelings and stabilizing their own life and state of well-being, regardless of the adolescent's level of functioning. This is intended not only to benefit them but is also part of the differentiation process designed to benefit the adolescent and to prevent the aggravation of the situation of the child by the parents' inappropriate handling of the crisis. It is particularly difficult for the parents to handle the strong ambivalent feelings toward the dysfunctional child, worry and love being mingled with anger and rage. This may lead to inadequate parental coping mechanisms such as denial of the problem, secrecy, falseness of reactions (Micucci 1998), intrusiveness, overreactivity, and excessive ineffective criticisms of the adolescent (Keim 2000). Sharing with the parents our integrative understanding of the problem and its biological, psychological, and social components helps them to relinquish their preoccupation with blame and guilt, and to become more reflective, realistic, and task oriented.

The second component is designed to engage the parents in serving as therapeutic change agents for their children's psychological recovery from psychopathology. This is the most innovative part of our model, and the description of the intervention will therefore focus mainly on this component. The changes the parents are asked to introduce in their handling of their children require an abdication of the parental overreaching responsibility for the child in order to enable the building of mutual recognition. Allowing children to experience and exercise appropriate responsibility for themselves validates their need for recognition. Concomitantly, the parents are required to assume responsibility for themselves as distinct, yet caring, significant adults and parents, whom the child needs to recognize. This component may also be applied with some modifications to problems of younger children, involving less severe psychopathology, yet evidencing difficulties in the development of parent-child differentiation and interrelatedness.

THE COURSE OF THERAPEUTIC WORK

Preparatory Stage: Philosophy Sharing and Contracting

This stage follows an extensive intake (to ensure that the family dynamics do not involve such issues as abuse, neglect, or a destructive battle in the couple, which need to be dealt with appropriately first) and the initial building of rapport with the parents, by adopting an accepting, empathic, and reassuring therapeutic stance.

The therapist then shares with the parents the goals, rationale, and process of the proposed intervention, and communicates the expectation that, through focused work on changing parental modes of relating to the child, significant changes may be evidenced rather quickly. Following parents' engagement, the contract then clarifies the roles of both the therapist and the parents. The therapist's role is to provide specific instructions and recommendations related to dealing with the child and to support the parents in applying them. The parents are expected to share accounts of their daily interactions with the child and of their attempts to apply the recommendations. These are to be analyzed in order to promote learning and internalization and to evaluate, tailor, pace, and plan progress.

The Intervention Program

The change process involves three major therapeutic undertakings: helping parents to relinquish current inappropriate ways of relating to the child and to themselves; instructing them about new ways to be practiced in relation to the child; and dealing with and overcoming anxieties and difficulties related to the change. These efforts are constantly repeated and refined to deepen understanding, improve coping, and achieve a more attuned relationship with the child. The first two components are relatively structured and directive, while the third is flexibly adapted to individual needs.

The structured components involve providing the parents with the first list of parental behaviors, which includes behaviors that symbolically reflect failures in perceiving the child as separate, capable, and resilient. These behaviors are considered to be "growth inhibiting" or "regressive" and are clarified to the parents. The parents are initially requested to pay attention to their interactions with the child and to detect the behaviors by which they exercise parenting that is excessive. The parents' observations are thereafter discussed in the sessions in terms of their messages to the child. At the next stage parents are requested to refrain from using these behaviors, and these directives are coined the "list of proscriptions" (don'ts). This list is conceptualized as equivalent to a rehabilitation program or a health diet, providing opportunities for the adolescents to experience differentiation and to develop inner resources. These include experiences of making choices and learning from their results, becoming aware of their need of others, and learning to satisfy this need in a reciprocal, cooperative manner. As parents are encouraged to practice avoiding growth-inhibiting behaviors, they are not yet expected to give up reacting in their habitual manner to situations that they see as critical. The following proscriptions are in the first list presented to parents.

1. Don't deprive children of their need to self-regulate their mood and emotions:

Don't try to please children in the absence of mutual reciprocity.
Don't do things "for their sake" without their explicit request.
Don't protect children from unpleasant age-appropriate consequences of their actions.
Don't attempt to "rescue" children from their unpleasant moods.

2. Don't deprive children of their need to learn through experience:

Don't offer unsolicited advice.
Don't engage in arguing.
Don't preach.
Don't threaten.
Don't coerce.

3. Don't deprive the children's need to be in charge of their self-disclo-
   sure and self-definition:
Don't interpret or define for children their feelings, motivations, or states
   without their request.
Don't interpret or explain to others children's feelings, motivations, or
   states without their request or consent.
Don't tell them who they are.

4. Don't avoid or distort your reactions to children's actions:
Don't ignore children's actions when they affect you.
Don't fake, blur, minimize, or try to conceal your emotional reaction to
   children's acts.

Clinical Vignette

A short vignette may be helpful in demonstrating the use of this first set of
directives. Noa is the fifteen-year-old adopted daughter of a couple who
have indulged her ever since her early infancy, as she was underweight and
fragile looking when adopted. At the time of referral, her relationships with
her peers and family members are all severed, due to her mood swings and
open undifferentiated hostility. She spends most of her time isolated in her
room, repeatedly watching recorded episodes of a fantasy-action TV series.
She is often late for school and truant from classes. She assumes no responsibility for school assignments and refuses to take tests. She vehemently
opposes the school's request for a psychoeducational evaluation or her
parents' offerings of private tutoring or psychotherapy. She is verbally abusive toward her parents and is extremely uncooperative and defiant. After
having been presented with the first list of directives, the mother reported a
frequent occurrence involving her getting up early in the morning to prepare a nutritious sandwich for Noa's lunch, and Noa's neglect to take it with
her. The mother's rationale for her continued effort was her concern about
Noa's health and her worry that her mood and functioning in school might
be affected by being hungry or consuming junk food. Using the directives
list, the mother became aware that she was taking responsibility for her
daughter's mood and functioning. This understanding was deepened in the

therapy session as she realized that she was communicating to her daughter a sense of mistrust in her knowing, or being able to find out, what she needed and how to get it. The mother decided, with much trepidation, to stop preparing the sandwiches for a week. This was done without any lecturing or admonitions. This seemingly small change opened the space for a very new experience in the mother-daughter relationship. For the first time in years, Noa approached her mother after a few days of missed sandwiches and very sweetly asked her to prepare a sandwich for her. She was given a chance to experience a need and to exercise making a request. Mother then received a chance to examine her genuine feelings about this request and to decided whether or not she wanted to accommodate her daughter's wish.

At the next stage parents are introduced to an additional list of behaviors, which are considered to be "progressive" or "growth promoting" for the child. These behaviors are intended to clearly communicate to children the presence of the "other" (the parent), their subjectivity and boundaries and the interrelatedness of their relationship. These behaviors provide opportunities for the child to repair damages to the relationship, to negotiate in a cooperative manner conflicting preferences, and to make informed choices.

Parents are encouraged to examine their interactions with their children and to discover instances of being paralyzed, intimidated, and fearful of their reactions, as the result of their otherwise reasonable expectations and actions toward them. The parents discuss and practice these communications, first in the sessions and subsequently at home. The following is this list coined the "prescriptions" (dos).

1. Take responsibility for recognizing and sharing your emotions:
   Use "I messages" to express in a full and authentic manner your feelings vis-à-vis the child's conduct toward you, or in managing "his or her own affairs."
   Conduct yourself in a way congruent with your emotions.

2. Take responsibility for sharing your own will, values, preferences, and positions:
   Use clear and overt "I messages" to express and clarify your preferences and valued choices, without implying that the child must comply.
   Make clear that these are declaratively subjective and therefore not given to argumentative debates.

3. Take responsibility for formulating clear, expected codes of conduct in the family:
   Clarify for the child your requirements of him or her as a partner in the relationship and as a member of your family.

4. Take responsibility for protecting yourself and what is precious to you:
   Set down the rules by which you protect yourself and what you value.
   Define the consequences of breaking these rules.
   Take measures to protect yourself, your welfare, and your belongings.
   Take measures, when necessary, to protect your child from self-
   destructive acts.

It is important to note that the changes in the parents' ways of relating to the child are implemented in a differentiated and stepwise manner, sensitive to the child's responsiveness, so that unnecessary massive escalations are prevented. The change process is initiated through the introduction of clear and consistent communications from the parents relating to their positive and negative feelings and their wishes for and expectations of the child. Steps involving rules and their consequences are undertaken only at a more advanced stage, and only if the child is unresponsive in recognizing the parents' communications. The rules are an expression of the parents' need to protect their subjectivity, and the related consequences are intended to defend the parents both emotionally and practically. They usually involve the withholding of parental resources from the adolescent and, when necessary, the enlistment of help from others (extended family, friends, relevant agencies). When applied consistently and in a nonattacking way, these rules provide adolescents with an experience of parental resilience, which is beneficial to the adolescent's sense of self.

Clinical Vignette

The following vignette demonstrates a segment of the work accomplished through the use of the list of parental prescriptions in a stepwise manner. Michael's divorced mother came to see the therapist deeply worried about her nineteen-year-old son. Since being dismissed from the army (following his enlistment by compulsory law) because of total inability to function in that setting, he had been unable to get work or to be involved in studying. He showed bizarre and severely disturbed behavior, such as constant restlessness, speaking to himself, physical neglect, social isolation, and obsessive fantasizing about completely unrealistic affairs with some women. He refused to acknowledge having any problems or needing therapy of any kind. At a certain point in our therapy with the mother, she focused on his humiliating and verbally abusive behavior toward her. The mother reacted to these behaviors by ignoring them or by attempts to appease him. She was encouraged to stop these behaviors and instead to apply the prescription regarding expressing her emotional reactions to his behavior fully and directly. She started to repeatedly verbalize her humiliation and hurt whenever appropriate, and this produced a dramatic change in his behavior within a few weeks. In this instance the mother's repeated insistence on sharing her emotional reactions to the adolescent's behaviors was sufficient to make him recognize her and change his behavior. However, when the issue of the cleanliness of his room came up, this did not improve smoothly. The mother expressed a strong wish that he clean the room, or let her or somebody else clean it, since it had not been cleaned for three years. Sharing her feelings of worry and disgust with her son did not seem to produce any effect. The mother was encouraged to assume responsibility for her legitimate wishes. After communicating to him that she really could not stand this situation, she was assisted in framing her wish as a rule and in deciding on a consequence. Because she could not bring herself to have him leave the house as a consequence for breaking the rule, the consequence became her leaving the house. This action was congruent with her feelings and convictions. Once mother began making the preparations for leaving the house, the son suddenly agreed to allow his room to be cleaned. He consequently cooperated with setting up a regular cleaning routine.

Dealing with and Overcoming Difficulties and Anxieties Related to the Change

Parental anxieties and hesitations about introducing new ways of relating to the child are handled by a variety of means aimed at reducing their anxiety and encouraging risk taking. These means include a therapeutic relationship that is consistently supportive and encouraging of the steady availability of the therapist to the parents. In addition, sensitive tailoring of chosen tasks and individual pacing are employed. Specific resistances are dealt with by a variety of experiential, cognitive, and analytic techniques from different schools of psychotherapy.

Much psychoeducation, cognitive clarification, and rational analysis is involved in working with most parents. Some repeating concepts in the parents' discourse about their relationships with their children warrant special attention and may challenge therapists to sharpen their own theoretical clarity. Thus, many parents struggle in sorting out the difference between being distant and being separate (see Green and Werner 1996); between nurturing, indulgence, and spoiling (see Winnicott 1984) and between being empathic and giving in to the child (see Orenstein and Orenstein 1985).

Furthermore, many parents seem to have difficulty with the meaning of saying "no" (see Phillips 1999) and with conceptualizing how responsibility develops in children (see Morrison 1995). A special difficulty involves the integration of warmth and acceptance with maturity demands (see Baumrind 1991) and the possibility of asserting their expectations and demands without becoming hostile and aggressive toward the child (see Winnicott 1971).

Additionally, strategic and narrative techniques are employed, involving the use of metaphors, storytelling, and letter writing. Thus, for example, the metaphor of the desired parental stance in regard to enforcing rules is likened to that of a referee in a football game (as contrasted with that of a coach) as he delivers well-known consequences in a dispassionate manner, without blaming, shaming, or preaching.

Focused psychodynamic explorations are undertaken, when deemed appropriate, to help defuse seemingly irrational and emotionally weighted positions of the parent. Unremitting anger, anxiety, and despair need to be focused on empathically and resolved. This often involves helping parents recognize their need to mourn for the loss of their ideal child, the loss of their capacity for ideal parenting, and the fantasy of ideal self-fulfillment through the creation of one's own desired child. Transgenerational themes relevant to these feelings and ideas need to be pursued at times before they can be altered.

Systemic interventions are also undertaken at times, involving the enlistment of family supports and working through difficulties in the parental alliance. By respecting the differential pace of change and the extent of involvement in the process of each parent, therapeutic work can still progress, so long as the less actively involved parent does not sabotage the other's efforts. When a parent seems invested in his or her overinvolvement with their child because of personal neediness (e.g., feelings of loneliness or incompetence), steps are taken to replace the role of the child with alternative intimate relationships. This may require some focused couple work or dealing with forming new significant relationships for a single parent. The therapeutic relationship seems to replace some of these needs, at least temporarily.

A special systemic intervention needs to be undertaken in cases where, by unspoken collusion between the parents and the adolescent, the latter's situation becomes a family secret. This makes separateness impossible, paralyzes the system, and deprives all family members of outside help and support. Opening the secret gradually and in a sensitive manner (Imber-Black 1998) is therefore crucial.

Feedback

The model described in this chapter has been used with fifteen families of disturbed adolescents, thus far, and has clinically proven to provide relief to the families and to improve the level of functioning of their adolescents. While no systematically controlled study has been undertaken, extensive follow-up interviews are being conducted with the parents, by independent interviewers, focusing on their experiences in dealing with their adolescent and the therapy. While the analysis of their recorded narratives is beyond the scope of this chapter, some preliminary conclusions may already been drawn, based on nine interviews, and clinical impressions.

All parents interviewed report improvements in the adolescents' situation and their relationships, varying in degree from "noticeable" to "very significant." Most notably, the adolescents are perceived as more considerate, cooperative, and self-sufficient. Additionally, all parents report being surprised by their adolescents' new self-initiated undertakings in areas such as self-care, school or work, therapy, and social activities. They all describe the process of change as difficult but fruitful. They testify to a relaxation of the tension in the family system and a great improvement in their own feelings: becoming more accepting, optimistic, secure, and organized, as well as more soberly realistic. One of the interviewed fathers summed up the change in his relationship with his son, Jo, in a metaphoric way: "In our past dealings with him Jo got the message that we saw him as a monster, as a king, or as a helpless baby. In therapy we learned to treat both him and ourselves as worthwhile human beings."

REFERENCES

Anderson, C. M., G. E. Hogarty, and D. J. Reiss. 1986. *Schizophrenia and the family: A practitioner's guide to psychoeducation and management.* New York: Guilford Press.

Baumrind, D. 1991. Parenting style and adolescent development. In *Encyclopedia of adolescence,* ed. M. R. Lerner, A. C. Peterson, and J. Brooks-Gunn, 746–59. New York: Garland.

Benjamin, J. 1988. *The bonds of love: Psychoanalysis, feminism, and the problem of domination.* New York: Pantheon Books.

Bowlby, J. 1977. The making and breaking of affectional bonds. Part 1: Aetiology and psychopathology in light of attachment theory. *British Journal of Psychiatry* 130:201–10.

Byalin, K. 1990. Parent empowerment: A treatment strategy for hospitalized adolescents. *Hospital and Community Psychiatry* 41(1):89–90.

Derdeyn, A. P., and C. L. Graves. 1998. Clinical vicissitudes of adoption. *Child and Adolescent Psychiatric Clinics of North America* 7(2):373–88.

Diamond, G. M., G. S. Diamond, and H. A. Liddle. 2000. The therapist-parent alliance in family-based therapy for adolescents. *Journal of Clinical Psychology* 56(8):1037–50.

Edgette, J. S. 1999. Getting real. *Family Therapy Networker* 23(5):36–41.

Falloon, I. R. H., J. L. Boyd, C. W. McGill, M. Williamson, J. Razani, H. B. Moss, A. M. Gilderman, and G. M. Simpson. 1985. Family management in the prevention of morbidity of schizophrenia: Clinical outcome of a two-year longitudinal study. *Archives of General Psychiatry* 42:887–96.

Garrett, J., J. Landau, R. Shea, M. D. Stanton, G. Baciewicz, and S. D. Brinkman. 1998. The ARISE intervention: Using family and network links to engage addicted persons in treatment. *Journal of Substance Abuse Treatment* 15(4):333–43.

Green, R. J., and P. D. Werner. 1996. Intrusiveness and closeness-caregiving: Rethinking the concept of family "enmeshment." *Family Process* 35(2):115–34.

Greene, R. 2001. *The explosive child.* New York: Quill.

Haley, J. 1973. Strategic therapy when a child is presented as the problem. *Journal of the American Academy of Child Psychiatry* 12(4):641–59.

Herbert, M. 2000. Parenting skills interventions. In *Family matters: Interfaces between child and adult mental health*, ed. P. Reder, M. McClure, and A. Jolley, 237–56. New York: Routledge.

Hoffman, P. D., A. E. Fruzzetti, and C. R. Swenson. 1999. Dialectical behavior therapy—family skills training. *Family Process* 3(4):399–414.

Imber-Black, E. 1998. *The secret life of families.* New York: Bantam Books.

Jacobs, L., and C. Wachs. 2002. *Parent Therapy: A relational alternative to child psychotherapy.* Northvale, N.J.: Jason Aronson.

Keim, J. P. 2000. Oppositional behavior in children. In *Children in therapy: Using the family as a resource*, ed. E. C. Bailey, 278–307. New York: Norton.

Lam, D. 1991. Psychosocial family intervention in schizophrenia: A review of empirical studies. *Psychological Medicine* 21:423–41.

Leckman, J. F., L. C. Mayes, R. Feldman, D. Evans, R. A. King, and D. J. Cohen. 1999. Early parental preoccupations and behaviors and their possible relationship to symptoms of obsessive-compulsive disorder. *Acta Psychiatrica Scandinavica* 396:1–26.

Loar, L. 2001. Eliciting cooperation from teenagers and their parents. *Journal of Systemic Therapies* 20(1):59–77.

Madanes, C. 1990. *Sex, love, and violence.* New York: Norton.

Micucci, J. A. 1998. *The adolescent in family therapy.* New York: Guilford Press.

Minuchin, S. 1974. *Families and family therapy.* Oxford, UK: Harvard University Press.

Morrison, N. C. 1995. Developing responsibility: A balancing act. *Journal of Family Psychotherapy* 6(4):71–75.

Orenstein, A., and P. Orenstein. 1985. Parenting as a function of the adult self: A psychoanalytic developmental perspective. In *Parental influences in health and disease*, ed. J. Anthony and G. Pollack, 183–232. New York: Little, Brown.

Palazzoli, M. S., L. Boscolo, G. Cecchin, and G. Prata. 1988. The treatment of children via brief therapy of their parents. In *The work of Mara Selvini Palazzoli*, ed. M. Selvini, 121–44. Northvale, N.J.: Jason Aronson.

Pantone, P. J. 2000. Treating the parental relationship as the identified patient in child psychotherapy. *Journal of Infant, Child, and Adolescent Psychotherapy* 1(1):19–38.

Parker, G. 1983. *Parental overprotection: A risk factor in psychosocial development.* New York: Grune and Stratton.

Phillips, A. 1999. *Saying no: Why it's important for you and your child.* London: Faber and Faber.

Price, J. 1996. *Power and compassion.* New York: Guilford.

Rosenfarb, I. S., D. Miklowitz, M. J. Goldstein, L. Harmon, K. H. Nuechterlein, and M. Rea. 2001. Family transactions and relapse in bipolar disorder. *Family Process* 40(1):5–14.

Rubin, H. K., S. L. Stewart, and X. Chen. 1995. Parents of aggressive and withdrawn children. In *Handbook of parenting*, vol.1, ed. M. H. Bornstein, 225–84. Hillsdale, N.J.: Lawrence Erlbaum.

Rustin, M. 1999. The child and adolescent psychotherapist and the family: The place of consultation with parents and therapy of parents in child psychotherapy practice. In *The handbook of child and psychotherapy: Psychoanalytic approaches*, ed. M. Lanyado and A. Horne, 87–92. Florence, Ky.: Taylor and Francis/Routledge.

Sanson, A., and M. Prior. 1999. Temperament and behavioral precursors to oppositional defiant disorder and conduct disorder. In *Handbook of disruptive behavior disorders*, ed. H. C. Quay and A. E. Hogan, 397–417. New York: Plenum.

Sells, S. P. 1998. *Treating the tough adolescent: A family-based, step-by-step guide*. New York: Guilford.

Selman, R. 1980. *The growth of interpersonal understanding*. New York: Academic Press.

Simoneau, T. L., D. J. Miklowitz, J. A. Richards, R. Saleem, and E. L. George. 1999. Bipolar disorder and family communication: Effects of a psychoeducational treatment program. *Journal of Abnormal Psychology* 108(4):588–97.

Smith, B., J. L. Surrey, and M. Watkins. 1998. "Real" mothers: Adoptive mothers resisting marginalization and re-creating motherhood. In *Mothering against the odds: Diverse voices of contemporary mothers*, ed. C. G. Coll and J. L. Surrey, 194–214. New York: Guilford.

Thomasgard, M. 1998. Parental perceptions of child vulnerability, overprotection, and parental psychological characteristics. *Child Psychiatry and Human Development* 28(4):223–40.

Tsiantis, J., S. B. Boethious, B. Hallerfors, A. Horne, and L. Tischler, eds. 2000. *Work with parents: Psychoanalytic psychotherapy with children and adolescents*, 47–63. London: Karnac Books.

Werner, P. D., R. J. Green, J. Greenberg, T. L. Browne, and T. E. McKenna. 2001. Beyond enmeshment: Evidence for the independence of intrusiveness and closeness-caregiving in married couples. *Journal of Marital and Family Therapy* 27(4):459–71.

West, M., and A. Sheldon. 1988. Classification of pathological attachment patterns in adults. *Journal of Personality Disorder* 2:153–59.

Winnicott, D. W. 1971. The use of an object and relating through identifications. In *Playing and reality*, 86–94. Baltimore, Md.: Penguin.

———. 1984. *Deprivation and delinquency*. London: Tavistock.

Wood, B. L., K. B. Klebba, and B. D. Miller. 2000. Evolving the biobehavioral family model: The fit of attachment. *Family Process* 39(3):319–44.

Zimmerman, T., and H. Protinsky. 1990. Strategic parenting: The tactics of changing children's behavior. *Journal of Strategic and Systemic Therapies* 9(4):6–13.

11

Therapy with Divorced and Divorcing Parents

Sharon Kozberg

When parents divorce, children respond in unique and personal ways. Children's responses, always related to developmental level, temperament, and prior history, are most effected by their parents' reactions to the stresses of divorce. In particular, children's adjustment to divorce is adversely effected when parental distress and conflict between parents interfere with effective parenting (Hetherington, Bridges, and Insabella 1998). Such findings underscore the importance of working with divorced or separated parents in order to help their children.

Divorce involves many losses. There is a disruption in the continuity of family life, and children lose the safety and predictability afforded by familiar routines. Just when children most need sensitivity and reassurance, mothers and fathers are distraught and least able to be empathic. Wallerstein and Kelly (1979) observed that the children in her study often felt extremely alone because of parents' unavailability and "diminished capacity to parent." Solomon (1996) posited that when parents experience the loss of a spouse as the loss of an attachment figure, they are unable to assume the security-enhancing protective functions of parenthood. She proposed that "the separation and divorce situation can be inherently disorganizing to caregiving because it has the capacity to force the parent to question her ability to protect the child, arouses strongly her own attachment system, and sometimes does both simultaneously" (6). In response, children often become anxious or depressed. They may feel rejected, abandoned, or guilty and are often sad, confused, ashamed, angry, or frightened. The child's experience is of course intimately tied to the experience of the parents, who are struggling with comparable feelings.

Divorce is a process rather than a discrete event, and children's needs change over time. Parents seek assistance from a therapist at all stages of the process; they often feel a particular need during the early phases of a separation. This is an important time for intervention because of the acute need, intense affect, and potential for parental unavailability. Questions regarding how to tell children about a decision to separate and how to structure visitation are usually paramount at this time. Parents may be confused or in disagreement about these decisions, and the therapist can help them address what is in the best interests of the child. When children evidence difficulties at home or school, parents may feel guilty or blame each other. Often, the therapist must help make distinctions between the parents' distress and that of the child's. Parents who are alienated from each other look to a therapist for mediation in their many disputes about their children. These children are caught in the middle between parents who feel enraged and betrayed and are unable to effectively communicate with each other. Some parents are able to meet together to discuss their children's needs while others cannot tolerate joint sessions and need to be seen separately.

ANXIETY AND DEFENSES IN DIVORCING FAMILIES

In all cases, an understanding of the relationship between the child's experience and that of the parents lays the groundwork for therapy. Since loss of security leads to the need to defend against anxiety, it is important to think about the defensive constellations that develop in families as the reactions of parents and children affect each other.

One frequently observed defensive pattern involves regression as an initial reaction to the stress of a separation. Depending upon their age, children are apt to temporarily return to earlier behaviors such as tantrums and sleep difficulties. Adults are often emotionally labile, with impulsive outbursts and abrupt changes in mood. Not surprisingly, regression in one exacerbates comparable defensive reactions in the other, and both parent and child can feel like distressed children in need of a grown-up.

For example, a ten-year-old boy who previously walked home alone from school became afraid to do so after his parents' separation. His mother became overwhelmed by this additional demand upon her already strained resources and repeatedly lost her temper in frustration. The boy was then also scared of his mother's anger and began to cry frequently. This left the mother feeling increasingly ineffective and tearful and less able to meet the challenge of being a single parent.

Another defensive constellation involves splitting and dissociation. In order to survive the wrenching dissolution of the family, some parents must split off aspects of their experience to preserve a sense of goodness in themselves. Unable to experience realistically mixed feelings, they see themselves as the good parent and their ex-spouse as the bad parent. A child sometimes joins this defensive process by identifying with one parent and rejecting the other. Children often struggle to maintain attachment to both parents. If parents' defenses are rigidly maintained, one or both are unable to recognize and support this need. As children begin to travel back and forth between mother and father, they also begin to rely heavily upon dissociative processes and bring to each parent only the parts of themselves that they feel can be recognized. In order to preserve the attachment bond with a parent, the child dissociates particular self states that are threatening to or cannot be validated by that parent (Bromberg 2001).

Six-year-old Robert was alternately misbehaved and clingy with his mother but restrained and obedient with his father. This was understood by his father as evidence of his ex-wife's inconsistency and inability to discipline and by his mother as evidence of Robert's fear of his father's punitive, critical style. Each parent saw the other as bad, and neither could fully see that Robert, increasingly unable to express genuine anger and fear to either parent, was only able to bring parts of himself to each of them.

Children whose parents are most alienated are at risk for "pathologic dissociation" (Bromberg 2001) and the serious relational difficulties associated with this kind of defense. A high degree of alienation is seen in those parents who resort to custody suits. When courts support parents' rights to maintain contact with children, they may unintentionally violate children's rights to grow up in an environment that nurtures secure attachments and allows for the development of a cohesive sense of self.

As the object of a bitter custody dispute, an eleven-month-old girl screamed uncontrollably when transferred from mother to father for court-mandated weekend visits. When she was returned to her mother, she was passive and relatively unresponsive and demonstrated sleep difficulties. This little girl was transported between two very separate worlds because her parents did not speak to each other and could not communicate about their daughter. The pervasive split in her experience was exemplified by her changing hairstyle: her mother always tied her hair in a ponytail while her father always untied her hair and let it hang loose. The intense conflict and starkly different parental needs posed great obstacles to this young child's fledgling attempts to develop secure attachments and an integrated, cohesive sense of self.

A third type of family relies heavily upon denial as a defense against the pain of loss. Unlike children who display obvious suffering, some rise to the occasion and seem to readily adjust to the divorce. Both parent and child deny aspects of the child's vulnerability, and the child's pseudomature and independent behavior is a relief to parents who feel overwhelmed. Sensing their parents' needs, these children are helpful and understanding and assure themselves and their parents that they will all survive.

The need to support the parent often leads to the development of precocious defenses, which can put children at risk for emotional constriction and depression in later years.

A seven-year-old girl whose parents lived in different states regularly flew alone to visit her father. She acknowledged nervousness and asked her mother to fly with her but regularly rose to the occasion and got on the airplane. She said she understood that her parents had limited time and money, and she'd rather fly alone than not see her father. This mature behavior belied intense anxiety, as revealed in a story she told during an evaluation:

> The fighter killer flies are attacking the airplane where there are only children flying by theirselves and there are stewardesses. Fighter flies come in and attack kids and stewardesses and kids call "mommy, mommy" and mommies come and kill the fighter flies because they're allergic to mommies. So the mommies came with them and had a vacation.

Denial of her intense anxiety reflected this child's determination to preserve her relationship with her father and support her parents' need for a competent daughter.

Fostering Parents' Capacity for Reflection

These examples illustrate how defensive reactions can interfere with parental attunement to children's needs. Fonagy (1993) has written extensively about the importance of the "reflective self function" and its central role in parenting. The capacity to observe and reflect upon one's own mental functioning is essential to the ability to reflect upon the psychological state of another. When a parent's reflective self-functioning is defensively limited, the ability to be sensitive to a child's experience is also limited. Fonagy's view is that "shortcomings in mother's responsiveness to child's needs derive from her own defenses against acknowledging and understanding similar negative affects in herself" (974).

Exploration of parents' subjective experience in therapy is understood as a way of increasing awareness of children's needs. "When internal experience is not sufficiently reflected upon it can be projected outward in relatively crude ways, resulting in a wholesale and unmitigated projection of personal anxieties onto one's child" (Jacobs and Wachs 2002, 171). While limitations in reflective self-function are understood to be rooted in a parent's own attachment history, the heightened anxiety and increased defensiveness characteristic of divorcing parents present additional challenges to the capacity to be reflective and maintain an empathic stance. Guilt and feelings of responsibility for children's distress are also intrinsic to divorce and interfere with the capacity to be reflective as well as to tolerate children's sadness and anger. Since children's conflicts about anger are often intensified, both parents and children can feel overwhelmed by the intensity of feeling. Therapy can help contain the experience while offering the opportunity to reflect upon it.

One father, who was in fact quite devastated by the ending of his marriage, felt he had to be upbeat and "emphasize the positive" to his eight-year-old daughter. Hiding his sadness, he talked to his daughter about the benefits of having two homes, two bedrooms, two sets of toys, and so forth. His daughter was becoming increasingly confused and unable to process her painful experience. When this father was able to recognize how vulnerable he felt, and gain some understanding about his characteristic need to deny pain, he was able to be more authentic with his daughter. In therapy he was able to acknowledge his sadness and anger, and recognize how difficult it was to think about his daughter having comparable feelings. As the therapist helped the father become more able to tolerate his own and his daughter's pain, both father and daughter felt less alone.

Telling the Children: A Therapeutic Issue

Another source of misattunement is grounded in misconceptions about the developmental process. Many parents have unrealistic expectations of children's capacities and can benefit from education about what is necessary for children's well-being at particular developmental stages. Knowing that young children are prone to feel responsible and guilty, for example, can alert parents to these issues and help them clarify confusion and offer reassurance. Anticipating regression as a normal response to stress helps parents feel less powerless and prepare for inevitable difficult times. Speaking in language that the child can understand is essential for communication.

This is especially important when children are initially informed about the decision to separate. Wallerstein and Kelly (1979) noted that children are often insufficiently prepared for their parents' divorce. She described hesitancy on the part of parents to discuss the family breakup with young children and found that four-fifths of the youngest children in her study were not provided with either an adequate explanation or assurance of continued care.

It is not unusual for adult children of divorce to remain confused about their parents' reasons for divorcing. For example, one thirty-year-old patient who was generally articulate and able to grasp complexities remembered simply that "Mom wanted to have more fun." Another usually thoughtful twenty-eight-year-old patient explained his parents' divorce without reflection: "It was the times—everybody was getting divorced in the seventies." One might consider that such abbreviated or distorted memories reflect not only defensive styles and attachment histories but also the actual experiences of learning about their parents' separation.

Parents can prepare children by providing them with a narrative of what is happening to the family. With a therapist's help, they can begin to function collaboratively as they construct a "story," which includes preceding events ("You know that mommy and daddy have been fighting a lot lately"), the decision to separate ("We need to live in different places for a while"), and explanations about the changes to come ("Mommy and you will stay in the house and daddy will stay in an apartment nearby"). Retrospective construction of childhood experience into a coherent narrative is often a central component in a person's psychotherapy. Constructing a narrative of the divorce can help children make sense of things and assimilate confusing information. Siegler (1993) proposes the "reparative narrative" as an opportunity to foster healing for children whose experience has been fractured by shock and confusion. While parents may not want to revisit this painful topic, they should be prepared for the fact that children will need to hear the "story" of the divorce repeatedly. Repetition allows the narrative to evolve and become more comprehensive as the child gets older and develops the capacity to take in more complexity.

Before telling their two young children about their decision to separate, Mr. and Mrs. A consulted a therapist. Mrs. A reported years of unhappiness while Mr. A disputed her picture of the marriage and accused his wife of selfishly breaking up the family. Alternately tearful and enraged, Mr. A was particularly aggrieved about Mrs. A's relationship with another man and threatened to tell the kids "the whole story." It was clear to the therapist that this couple was too reactive to be able to adequately focus on their children's needs. They were not ready to inform the children about their decision to separate in a way that could address the inevitable confusion and anxiety. After commending them on seeking professional help in the interests of their children, the therapist advised them to slow down and make use of therapy to discuss their feelings about separating as well as how to tell their children. This was acceptable to both parents because therapy offered a place to contain the intensity of their emotional reactions: Mr. A was relieved because a delay diminished his dread of loss and abandonment, and Mrs. A's anxiety about her husband's threat to vilify her to the children was alleviated.

Such consultations can help couples begin to mourn the loss of long-held roles and relationships as they make practical decisions about the future. The therapist must help parents attend to children's needs for clarification and reassurance, and balance the wish to speak honestly with the need to protect children from confusing and unsettling information. Asking parents to imagine how their children will react to the anticipated changes is a useful stimulus for discussion, which can be used to reinforce an empathic stance.

Following the initial consultation, Mr. and Mrs. A were each seen twice and then jointly for two sessions before telling their children and proceeding with the separation. Therapy allowed for a focused exploration of specific issues in the marriage, which led Mr. A to recognize that he too had been dissatisfied. Acknowledgment of his personal unhappiness shifted the balance so that he felt somewhat less victimized and, therefore, less helpless and enraged. Although he was still quite depressed, therapy (and the time in between sessions) helped him begin to accept his wife's resolve and plan for the future. The focus in therapy could then shift to the children. When asked to imagine how the separation would affect their son and daughter, Mr. and Mrs. A were able to sensitively talk about each child. They (accurately) predicted that eight-year-old Robyn would be angry and concerned about continuation of school activities while six-year-old Daniel would be scared and fairly nonverbal. Their empathy was noted by the therapist and reinforced as part of the preparation for the days ahead.

For this couple, the decision about how much to tell the children was a difficult one and required the therapist's guidance. Mr. A felt it wasn't fair if the children weren't told about their mother's new relationship, while Mrs. A wanted to keep that part of her life private. In the interests of minimizing the inevitable anxiety and confusion, they did not include this information in the narrative of the divorce. Mr. A was helped to put aside his personal needs by the therapist's support and recognition of his attempts to do what was best for the children, as well as by the understanding that the "story" would be repeated and change over time as the children became more able to assimilate complicated information.

VISITATION AND THE NEED FOR CONTINUITY

After learning about a separation, children need to know how their parents will continue to take care of them. A divorcing parent often fears that the relationship with the child is threatened or that the other parent will take the child away. Feeling anxious, many parents have difficulty differentiating their needs from those of their children. Once again, an understanding of the developmental process is clarifying: when making decisions about visitation arrangements, emphasis should be placed upon the importance of continuity to the well-being of children. Therapists should always aim to help parents reestablish a sense of continuity as quickly and as fully as circumstances allow.

Using Winnicott's well-known concepts, Aronson (2000) compared divorce to an impingement on the "holding environment" of the family with resulting disruptions in the "continuity of being" that is necessary for developing and maintaining a secure sense of self. He described a five-year-old boy who alternated nights with each parent. While this plan may have satisfied his parents' need for contact (or parity), the boy was never able to settle into either home and was deprived of any possibility of continuity. During therapy the schedule was changed so that he moved less frequently and spent more continuous periods of time with each parent.

The issue of visitation engenders intense controversy on the part of clinicians and legal professionals as well as parents. Despite the mandate to make decisions based upon children's best interests, the meaning of "best interests of the child" continues to be debated (Rohman, Sales, and Lou 1987), and differing arrangements continue to be endorsed. Current practices such as overnight visitation for young children, joint custody, and joint decision making are at odds with advice from many experts. Some see overnight separations for infants and toddlers as potentially disruptive to development of secure attachment relationships (Dunn 1997) or urge that the authority to determine visitation be held by one parent alone in the interests of "the child's need for continuity of the primary relationship to his custodial parent" (Goldstein, Freud, and Solnit 1979, 119). Despite all best intentions, neither parents nor professionals are always clear about what types of arrangements are best.

Bowlby's (1973) work on attachment theory and subsequent research conceptualizing categories of infant-caregiver attachment as secure, anxious (Ainsworth et al. 1978), or disorganized (Main and Solomon 1990) have begun to offer guidelines for making these complicated decisions. According to attachment theory, early experiences with caregivers generate mental representations that influence the quality of the infant's attachment relationships. The importance of the quality of an infant's attachment to a primary caregiver has been intensively studied and found to influence many aspects of psychological development including social behavior, affect regulation, and psychological disturbance (Fonagy et al. 1993). "Secure attachment" implies representations of attachment figures who are accessible and responsive and is associated with a generalized sense of competence and self-esteem (Fonagy 2001). "Disorganized attachment" implies disorientation and apprehension regarding the parent, has been linked to "frightened or frightening care-giving" (Main and Hesse 1990) and is considered to be a general risk factor for maladaptive behavior and relational difficulties (Lyons-Ruth, Easterbrooks, and Cibelli 1997).

Solomon and George (1999) studied the development of attachment to mother and father in separated and divorced families with twelve- to twenty-month-old children. They investigated the effects of overnight visitation, "psychological protection" (mothers' responsiveness to infants in the context of visits with fathers), and couple communication and conflict. They found that the effects of overnight visitation are "context sensitive." While overnight visitation is not inevitably associated with disorganization of mother-infant attachment, "repeated overnight separations from the primary caregiver are associated with disruption in mother-infant attachment when the conditions of visitation are poor, i.e., when parents are unable to provide adequate psychological support to the child" (2). Among infants with regular overnight visitation, disorganized attachments were seen when parents demonstrated high levels of conflict and were not able to effectively communicate with each other, while secure attachments were found in infants whose parents had good communication and an absence of intense conflict. Mothers who felt helpless to protect their infant from distress about separations (i.e., felt intimidated into acquiescing to visits, believed that infants would have to learn to adjust to visits) were more likely to have infants who demonstrated disorganized attachments, while mothers who were "psychologically protective" (able to actively adjust visitation arrangements to infant's needs, able to be responsive to signs of distress during separations and reunions) were more likely to have securely attached infants. Overnight visitation was found to be neither an advantage nor a disadvantage to father-infant attachment, and secure attachment was possible without overnight visits. Interestingly, the quality of the attachment to father was found to be most affected by the mother's perception of the father's competence and, once again, the quality of the communication between the parents.

Sally was thirteen months old when her parents consulted a therapist before separating, in order to discuss how to proceed with a visitation schedule. Sally's mother was the primary caretaker, although both parents were actively involved in her care and were in agreement about sharing custody. They had originally envisioned a fairly equal timesharing arrangement but were beginning to question such a plan. They described Sally as a "not so great" sleeper whose ability to sleep through the night was easily disrupted by vacations and other changes in routine. They anticipated that going back and forth between two households might complicate her sleep difficulties but felt that she would have to get used to it "sooner or later." Both mother and father felt that they could comfort Sally when she was upset but agreed that she frequently wanted only her mother. Sally's father revealed that he often felt hurt and confused about this since he had always been involved in Sally's care. He was able to acknowledge that he felt angry when this happened and blamed his wife for shutting him out and making Sally so dependent on her. Sally's mother and father were loving parents who, like all couples in the midst of a separation, were tense and less sure of themselves than usual. The therapist was supportive and educative, complimenting them on their ability to communicate with each other, validating their perceptions of Sally's needs, and offering information about the developmental tasks of children her age. In particular, they were reassured that Sally's need for her mother when she was upset was developmentally appropriate and did not reflect upon either parent's competence. The therapist's discussion of this behavior as reflecting Sally's attachment behavior and emerging experience of herself as able to regulate contact with her parents and have an effect on her world offered new understanding of Sally's developmental needs and served to diminish her father's anger. The therapist also addressed the father's fear that his strong connection with Sally would not be maintained unless he had equal time with her.

Sally's parents left this one-session consultation (which lasted about two hours) considering the possibility of delaying regular overnight visits until Sally was older. They were encouraged to think about other ways of functioning as coparents. One possible plan was for the father to take over dinner, bath, and bedtime activities twice a week in the mother's home. While this would maintain a domestic contact between parents and might slow the process of psychological separation, it had the benefit of preventing undue disruption for Sally while maintaining involvement with her father.

The concerns presented by these parents are not at all uncommon. A young child's need for continuity, facilitated by the absence of unduly stressful separations, sometimes conflicts with parents' needs for contact and involvement. Like Sally's father, parents often feel that equal amounts of time and overnight visitation are necessary to maintain a strong relationship. Parents can be helped to understand that this is not true: providing a young child with a secure home base and delaying regular overnight visitation until the child is less in need of a primary caretaker's availability can facilitate, rather than inhibit, secure and strong connections with both parents.

Attachment security can be affected by significant new experiences. Of importance here is the finding that "negative life events," including parental divorce, can lead to a change from a secure attachment in infancy to an insecure attachment in young adulthood (Waters et al. 2000). In order to protect both the development and the stability of secure attachments, parents should be helped to minimize conflict and communicate more effectively, and they should be helped to develop capacities to be protective of their young children. When couple conflict is high and ability to communicate is poor, regular overnight visitation for young children should be avoided. In general, the advisability of overnight visits for infants and toddlers must be determined on a case-by-case basis and should not be considered in high-conflict families.

Structuring visitation plans for older children also requires careful attention to individual needs. Wallerstein and Blakeslee (2000) emphasized that there is no "one size fits all" arrangement, nor is there a plan that will remain viable until age eighteen, as stipulated in many divorce agreements. What works for one child may not work for another, and what works for a young child may not work for the same child as a teenager. Once again, therapists can help parents reflect upon their children's particular developmental and emotional needs and anticipate the need to be flexible and adjust visitation arrangements in the future: school-age children will begin to need more time with peers and less with parents, and adolescents will begin to need more control over their own activities.

Mr. and Mrs. B saw a therapist intermittently after their divorce. On this occasion they reported that twelve-year-old Norma had become extremely upset one night at her mother's house when she wanted her father's help with difficult math homework. Neither the parents nor the child knew what to do when the math schedule and the visitation schedule didn't coincide. The importance of flexibility was discussed, and since both parents were amenable to change, they decided that Mr. B would take Norma out to dinner when she needed math help even if it was not "his" night. Her father was happy to do it, and her mother, who hadn't relished doing math in the first place, was relieved of guilt about relying on her ex-spouse. It also provided eight-year-old David with the chance to be alone with his mother and paved the way for other flexible arrangements. Importantly, the children saw that their parents could be flexible, reason with each other, and continue to take care of their needs, even though they were divorced.

TRANSITIONS

In all cases, careful attention must be paid to the quality of the transition experiences. When children move back and forth between parents, the transitions are filled with their reactions to separations and reunions. Once again, their experience is intrinsically related to that of their parents. Transitions are sometimes the only occasions of interaction between mothers and fathers and are potentially fraught with anxiety for all concerned. Feeling vulnerable and defensive, parents are more likely to impulsively fight with each other and less likely to be responsive to children.

Recently separated, Mrs. C consulted a therapist because of five-year-old Jenny's reactions to overnight visits with her father: Jenny returned home "upset" and didn't want to sleep at daddy's house anymore. Mrs. C was doubtful about Mr. C's ability to adequately care for Jenny and was considering a custody suit. Mrs. C, feeling scared and unsettled, described her husband as "emotionally absent" and feared that Jenny's experience with him paralleled her own. Characteristically, she had not told Mr. C about the consultation but was amenable to including him after the therapist explained the necessity of doing so. Mr. C was a dependent and somewhat-depressed man who had always deferred to his wife in matters of child care. He acknowledged feeling insecure about his ability to be a single parent but cared deeply about being involved in his daughter's life. Therapy sessions took place intermittently for about a year with each parent being seen separately, sometimes alone and sometimes with Jenny. As Mrs. C began to trust the therapist (and feel less alone), she was able to begin to differentiate her anxieties from her daughter's, especially those related to separation. Mr. C benefited from education about Jenny's developmental needs and was able to explore his long history of feeling inadequate. With the therapist's support he began to gain confidence in his capacities as a father. Before therapy, neither parent felt able to protect Jenny. As each began to understand the reasons for this, they both felt less helpless.

The importance of continuity in Jenny's life was emphasized, and the transitions from one parent to the other were given careful consideration. Since Mrs. C had difficulty tolerating Mr. C's presence in her apartment, the hallway became the place of transition where Jenny and her overnight bag were "exchanged." Typically, Mr. C would return Jenny at the doorway and Mrs. C would inspect the contents of the overnight bag, becoming anxious and critical if anything was amiss. Mr. C would then become defensive and angry, while Jenny stood alone between her parents. Maintaining an empathic stance toward each parent, the therapist facilitated discussion about the effects of such transitions on Jenny and the necessity of helping her move more smoothly from one parent to the other. In time, fighting diminished and Mr. C could spend a few minutes saying goodbye to Jenny in her mother's apartment. With the transitions less conflict ridden and the separations less abrupt, Jenny was less upset. Her parents learned to anticipate Jenny's age-appropriate need for reassurance at these times, and a custody suit was avoided.

Transitions are easier for children when the boundaries between mother's world and father's world are permeable enough to allow for a sense of continuity. If one parent can enter the other's house and spend some time in a young child's room before saying goodbye, for example, the child's experience is less disjointed. The ability of one parent to tolerate the presence of the other without anger or retaliation provides the child with a more integrated experience, which supports the development and maintenance of an integrated sense of self.

Some parents, however, need firm boundaries because they cannot tolerate contact with each other without fighting. There is general agreement that "conflicts in which children are caught in the middle while parents denigrate each other, precipitate loyalty conflicts, communicate through the children, or fight about the children are most destructive to children's well-being" (Hetherington et al. 1998, 175). Contact between some parents must therefore be avoided until conflict can be minimized. In such situations, continuity can be enhanced by providing children with transitional objects, rituals, and even people. Carrying a familiar toy back and forth between parents can be comforting. Establishing similar bedtime rituals in different parent's homes can be reassuring (Aronson 2000). For children who have the lonely experience of being the only one who knows and cares about both parents, a "transitional person"—someone who also has contact with and values both parents—can be extremely valuable. When a friend or a grandparent can visit both parents' homes, for example, the child's experience is more integrated and less lonely.

Transitions are times of vulnerability for adults as well as children. Children can be withdrawn or angry at these times, and parents can feel hurt, unappreciated, and rejected. In extreme cases, unconscious projection of such feelings can lead to the severing of a relationship between parent and child. For example, a thirty-year-old woman who stopped seeing her father when she was fourteen could not remember what caused the loss of contact but did recall that a fight occurred when he came to pick her up for the weekend. "Sometimes I think it was my fault because I told him I didn't want to go with him that day, and sometimes I think he walked out on me." Mired in the subjective experience of projected rage and disappointment, both parents and children feel rejected and guilty, and the relationship does not always survive.

To diminish unconscious projection, parents should be helped to explore their own experiences of separations and reunions. Attention should be paid to their personal histories and the potential to become anxious or feel rejected. They can be helped to understand patterns as they emerge, and encouraged to change or avoid those that are destructive.

After almost a year of separation, Mrs. D continued to feel lonely and hurt while Mr. D felt fulfilled by new experiences of independence. The couple had two daughters aged thirteen and four and a son aged seven. They came to therapy because they could neither stop fighting nor finalize a separation agreement. The different paces of the parents' adjustment to separation and the different ages and genders of the children made for disparate needs and complicated relational dynamics. This couple was stuck together in hurt and anger, and the children had to navigate a path between their mother's sadness and depression and their father's newly found sense of self.

There were many painful difficulties confronting this family. Of primary concern to Mrs. D was her relationship with her older daughter. They were unable to talk as they had in the past, and Mrs. D missed the closeness they once had. A recent fight between them occurred shortly after the children returned from a week with their father. Mrs. D noticed that her daughter returned home wearing new earrings and asked about them. When her daughter was not forthcoming, Mrs. D felt rebuffed and lost her temper.

In individual sessions Mrs. D discussed feeling left out of her children's lives and saw the new earrings as a painful reminder of her daughter's life without her. She began to recognize that she felt abandoned and became angry whenever the children left, and was particularly sensitive to being shut out by her older daughter. As she became aware of these dynamics, she apologized to her daughter for her short temper and became better able to empathize with the children's experience of leaving and returning. She no longer expected them to pack by themselves and began to help them get ready for weekends. This increased her involvement and helped the children leave more easily.

In a joint session, both parents expressed concern about their younger daughter, who was clingy and had frequent tantrums. In therapy, her distress was understood as reflecting a need for fewer transitions and more time with the mother. An arrangement where she sometimes stayed home with her mother while the two older children were with their father had benefits for all concerned. Although it took many months for this couple to sign a separation agreement, relationships between parents and children began to improve soon after therapy began.

As the importance of transitions is emphasized, parents will learn to expect that children (as well as adults) often need time before reconnecting. One mother learned to respect her teenage daughter's need to disappear into her room after returning from a weekend with her father. "I used to think it meant she didn't want to come home, or had had a bad time with her dad, but now I wait until she's ready to come out, and I try not to take it personally." This mother's reflective capacities allowed her to understand how these reunions might cause her to feel rejected and enabled her to provide her daughter with time and space for transition.

CONCLUSION

With headlines like "Two Portraits of Children of Divorce: Rosy and Dark" (Duenwald 2002), the popular press has presented a dichotomous picture of recent research. Wallerstein, Lewis, and Blakeslee's (2000) view of pained and overburdened children of divorce has been contrasted with Hetherington and Kelly's (2002) observation of resilient children who developed strengths from the challenges of postdivorce life. But these researchers are in agreement about their findings that parents' responses to the stresses of divorce are critical to children's adjustment. They both note that some children play a significant role in the family's adjustment by offering emotional and practical support to parents and siblings. They also agree that many of these competent children feel overwhelmed and depressed as a result. Hetherington's "resilient" children (who tended to be girls with competent, caring mothers) were able to flourish only with the help of at least one reliable, protective parent.

Anna is a helpful and sensitive child whose parents separated when she was three. She is now thirteen and can recall only two memories from her life before the divorce: "I remember hiding behind a chair, and they are fighting; then I remember putting my little hand under the chair to help carry it downstairs when my father moved out." Anna has always been a sociable child who can "carry" things for her parents and for others.

Her experience may lead her to deny her need for nurturance and feel burdened by her care-taking role. Alternatively, it could lead her to develop new competencies while enhancing her capacities for empathy and caring. The path she takes will depend in no small measure upon whether she can depend upon a consistent and supportive parent along the way.

Divorcing parents often feel as if they have failed as mothers and fathers, and their confidence in their ability to protect their children has been shaken. The therapist's nonjudgmental, collaborative stance is an important contribution to the work of becoming reflective and making decisions in the best interests of the child. The difficult process of healing wounds and creating new forms of family life can be enhanced by working toward the three complementary goals discussed in this chapter: therapists should educate parents about the developmental process and help them understand their child's specific needs; they should aim to increase parents' awareness of the interplay between their own internal experience and that of their child's; and they should help parents facilitate integration of their child's experience by reestablishing a sense of continuity. As mothers and fathers grapple with these issues in therapy, they can help their children survive profound disappointment and difficult change. Their ability to do so can be affirming and, in the midst of dark and negative times, of lasting value.

REFERENCES

Ainsworth, M., M. Blehar, E. Waters, and S. Wall. 1978. *Patterns of attachment: A psychological study of the strange situation.* Hillsdale, N.J.: Lawrence Erlbaum.

Aronson, S. 2000. Re-establishing "holding" in families of divorce. *Journal of Infant, Child, and Adolescent Psychotherapy* 1(1):39–52.

Bowlby, J. 1973. *Attachment and loss. Vol. 2: Separation.* New York: Basic Books.

Bromberg, P. 2001. The gorilla did it: Some thoughts on dissociation, the real and the really real. *Psychoanalytic Dialogue* 11(3):385–404.

Duenwald, M. 2002. Two portraits of children of divorce: Rosy and dark. *New York Times*, March 26, sec. F, 6.

Dunn, M. A. 1997. Visitation and the developmental rights of children. Practicing Law Institute conference, New York.

Fonagy, P. 2001. *Attachment theory and psychoanalysis.* New York: Other Press.

Fonagy, P., et al. 1993. Measuring the ghost in the nursery: An empirical study of the relation between parents' mental representations of childhood experiences and their infant's security of attachment. *Journal of American Psychoanalytic Association* 41:957–98.

Goldstein, J., A. Freud, and A. Solnit. 1979. *Beyond the best interests of the child.* New York: Free Press.

Hetherington, E. M., M. Bridges, and G. Insabella. 1998. What matters? What does not? Five perspectives on the association between marital transitions and children's adjustment. *American Psychologist* 53(2):167–84.

Hetherington, E. M., and J. Kelly. 2002. *For better or for worse: Divorce reconsidered.* New York: Norton.

Jacobs, L., and C. Wachs. 2002. *Parent therapy: A relational alternative to working with children*. Northvale, N.J.: Jason Aronson.

Lyons-Ruth, K., A. Easterbrooks, and C. Cibelli. 1997. Infant attachment strategies, infant mental lag, and maternal depressive symptoms: Predictors of internalizing and externalizing problems at age 7. *Developmental Psychology* 33:681–92.

Main, M., and J. Solomon. 1990. Procedures for identifying infants as disorganized/disoriented during the Ainsworth Strange Situation. In *Attachment during the preschool years: Theory, research, and intervention*, ed. M. Greenberg, D. Cicchetti, and E. M. Cummings, 121–60. Chicago: University of Chicago Press.

Maine, M., and E. Hesse. 1990. Parents' unresolved traumatic experiences are related to infant disorganized attachment status: Is frightened and/or frightening behavior the linking mechanism? In *Attachment during the preschool years: Theory, research, and intervention*, ed. M. Greenberg, D. Cicchetti, and E. M. Cummings, 161–84. Chicago: University of Chicago Press.

Rohman, L. W., B. Sales, and M. Lou. 1987. The best interests of the child in custody disputes. In *Psychology and child custody determinations*, ed. L. Weithorn, 59–105. Lincoln: University of Nebraska Press.

Siegler, A. L. 1993. *What should I tell the kids? A parent's guide to real problems in the real world*. New York: Dutton.

Solomon, J. 1996. Risk and reverberation: Divorce in infants and young children. New York Freudian Society conference, New York.

Solomon, J., and C. George. 1999. The development of attachment in separated and divorced families: Effects of overnight visitation, parent and couple variables. *Attachment and Human Development* 1(1):2–33.

Wallerstein, J., and J. Kelly. 1979. *Surviving the breakup*. New York: Hyperion.

Wallerstein, J., J. Lewis, and S. Blakeslee. 2000. *The unexpected legacy of divorce: A 25 year landmark study*. New York: Hyperion.

Waters, E., et al. 2000. Attachment security in infancy and early adulthood: A twenty-year longitudinal study. *Child Development* 71(3):684–89.

IV

DEVELOPING REFLECTIVE FUNCTIONS

12

Reflective Functioning as a Change-Promoting Factor in Mother-Child and Father-Child Psychotherapy

Judith Harel, Hayuta Kaplan, and Raya Patt

The present chapter should illuminate the specific role of reflective functioning in mother-child and father-child psychotherapy—a dynamic approach to the treatment of relational disturbances in childhood (Ben-Aaron et al. 2001). We will define reflective functioning and describe its normal development in early childhood, emphasizing the parents' role in this process. Possible impediments to the development and use of reflective functioning will be pointed out, and their putative sources in the parent, child, and their relationship will be described. The therapeutic model will be briefly presented, and its special contribution to understanding inhibitions in reflective functioning and in enhancing the reflective functioning of parent and child will be outlined. Clinical examples will illustrate the main points of this chapter. A detailed case description will be presented to demonstrate the changes that occurred in reflective functioning during the therapeutic process.

DEFINING REFLECTIVE FUNCTIONING

Reflective function (RF) is a specific cognitive skill, dependent on task and context, used to understand self and other in terms of internal states—emotions, intentions, memories, wishes, beliefs, and so forth. This function provides the individual with a well-developed capacity to distinguish inner from outer reality, pretend from "real" modes of functioning, intrapersonal mental and emotional processes from interpersonal communications, and understanding of behaviors as motivated by internal states (Fonagy and Target 2003). The development of the reflective function is intimately linked to the development of a healthy self (Winnicott 1971; Stern 1985; Britton 1998; Fonagy et al. 2002). Reflective functioning is also an important determinant of individual differences in self-organization, as it is intimately involved with many defining features of selfhood such as self-consciousness, autonomy, freedom, and responsibility. Once acquired, reflective functioning permits children to respond not only to another person's behavior but also to the others' beliefs, feelings, attitudes, desires, hopes, knowledge, imagination, pretense, deceit, intentions, plans, and so on (Fonagy et al. 1998). RF or mentalization enables children to "read" other people's minds and makes people's behavior meaningful and predictable (Baron-Cohen 1995; Morton and Frith 1995). RF develops in interpersonal relations and is expressed mostly in interpersonal contexts (Fonagy and Target 2003).

THE NORMAL DEVELOPMENT OF RF

According to Fonagy and Target (2003), the RF develops in the everyday transactions between parent and child or older sibling and child. The child's RF develops through his mental states being reflected upon, mainly in affectively charged moments, such as distress (Gergely and Watson 1996) and later on in play situations. Play has a unique place among the contexts important for the development of the RF. We will consider the role of parents and then the contribution of play to the development of RF.

The Role of the Parents in the Development of the RF in Their Children

The parents and, in infancy, mostly the mother, play a crucial role in the development of the child's RF. Wilfred Bion (1962) used the metaphor of container (mother) and contained (baby) and described mother's "alpha function" as the process transforming internal events experienced by the infant as concrete ("beta elements") into tolerable thinkable experiences. Bion also saw the mother-child relationship as the root of the symbolic capacity. Britton (1998) elaborated Bion's conception of maternal containment of the baby's intolerable experiences. He describes two functions of the containing mother: 1) providing sanctuary—a sense of being held in a safe, bounded place and 2) providing meaning to the baby's experience. Mother not only contains the baby's experience but also gives it a name, thus conveying her understanding of it and placing it in a shareable world of meanings. In time the baby internalizes the alpha function of the mother and becomes able to mentally process its own experiences. Winnicott (1965) emphasized the importance of the caregiver's psychological understanding of the infant for the emergence of the true self. Winnicott also recognized that the psychological self develops through perception of oneself in another person's mind as thinking and feeling. In other words, a mother who cannot or would not contain and name the child's experiences deprives the child from developing mental functions for processing experience. She also gives the child a picture of a world that does not want to know him or be known by him (Britton 1998). Thus, a parent who is limited in the capacity to reflect on his or her own mental processes or on those of the child is not supporting the child's developing reflective functioning. Furthermore, Fonagy, following Winnicott, suggests that the child identifies with the parent's representation of the child as a mentalizing person, provided that the parent represents the child as such a person. It follows that if the parent does not represent the child as mentalizing, but only as a "behaving" human being, the child will develop his self-representation as a nonreflective person and behave accordingly.

Stern (1985), integrating psychoanalytic thinking with developmental research, provided a rich description of the process of the child's developing understanding of minds. He described the "subjective self" developing in the context of "intersubjective relatedness." The sense of a subjective self is one of the five "senses" constituting the self. The peak of the development of the subjective self is in the last quarter of the first year of life. In this period, babies are mostly looking for an interface between their mind and their mother's mind, and the main goal of the interaction is to share subjective experiences, such as affects and intentions. Stern described how mothers attune to the child's subjective message, rather than to the observable behavior, and express their understanding and sharing of this message by performing a behavior different from the child's but conveying the same subjective message; he called this process "attunement." Stern suggests that the process of attunement goes on all the time during mother-child interaction, sometimes unconsciously, and creates a sense of mental intimacy between mother and child.

The subjective self and the reflective functioning are intimately linked to a context of a secure parent-child relationship, where both participants regard each other as having an internal world and are looking to share this world. Empirically, this was supported by research showing the connections between the qualities of parent-child relation as measured by attachment on the one hand and reflective functioning on the other. Fonagy et al. (1991) have shown that the most important element in parental representations of attachment for predicting the child's attachment pattern was the parent's reflective functioning, as revealed in the Adult Attachment Interview (AAI; Main and Cassidy 1998). Parents who showed a secure stance regarding attachment with their parents, even before their own child was born, had a higher chance of having a securely attached child than parents showing an insecure stance. Other research, looking at reflective functioning in parental narratives about their own children (rather than at the parent's' view of the

relationship with their parents as in the AAI), has shown that mothers' reflectiveness in relation to the live and ongoing relationship with the child
predicts the child's attachment security (Slade et al. 2001). The child's attachment security is linked with the mother's use of "mental state language"
(Beeghly, Bretherton, and Mervis 1986) when interacting with her infant;
mothers of secure infants more frequently addressed the infant's internal
states such as perceptions and feelings than mothers of resistant infants
(Harel, Gamzon-Kapeller, and Eshel 2002). Furthermore, research shows
that attachment security (Fonagy and Target 1997) and mother's use of mental state language that commented accurately on the infant's mental states
(Meins et al. 2002) predict the child's later reflective functioning, thus
demonstrating the link between qualities of the parent-child relationship
and the child's later reflective capacity.

The Unique Role of Play in the Development of Reflective Functioning

Play is considered a unique opportunity for the development of self (Winnicott 1971; Stern 1985) and specifically for the development of reflective
functioning as described by Fonagy and Target (Fonagy and Target 1996,
2003; Target and Fonagy 1996).

In early childhood, the child employs two modes of relating internal
experiences to external situations:

1. In the *psychic equivalence mode,* the child equates the internal and the
   external and, if needed, distorts inner experience to match the information coming from the outside.
2. In the *pretend mode,* the child knows that internal experience might not
   reflect external reality; moreover, the child behaves as if the internal
   reality has no connection to external reality. The young child functions
   in this mode while playing.

The child becomes able to integrate the two modes around four years of
age and attains mentalization or the *reflective mode.* In this mode, the child
is able to experience mental states as representations of reality, linking the
external and the internal worlds. From now on, the internal and external
worlds can be related but still differentiated and no longer have to be
equated or dissociated from each other. The child shows this attainment in
play; for instance, when he moves freely from the imaginary world, he is
creating outside reality by giving instructions to the other participants about
"how to play the monster."

The child achieves this mode of relating through the experience of having
its mental states being reflected upon, prototypically, through secure play
with a parent or older child. The person playing with the child facilitates the

differentiation and the integration of inner and outer realities. He shows the child that reality can be "played with," and through this playfulness a pretend but also real mental experience can be created. Winnicott taught us that children who cannot play should be taught to play, as a first task in therapy. In clinical work, we also encounter many parents who cannot play, and the attainment of "playfulness" (Moran 1987) is a challenging task for the therapist, given the importance of play with the parent for the child's developing reflective functioning.

FACTORS IMPEDING OR OBSTACLES TO THE DEVELOPMENT OF THE RF IN CHILDREN

Fonagy and Target (2001) distinguish between two groups of children referred for therapy: 1) those showing problems in mental representations (neurotic children) and 2) those showing problems in mental processes generating representations (such as narcissistic, borderline, conduct-disordered children). The latter do not respond too well to classical psychotherapeutic interventions, such as mirroring of the child's affect or interpreting his unconscious wishes. Understanding the problems of these children becomes possible if we assume that defensive operations for them do not simply entail the modification of specific ideas and feelings but rather the inhibition or limitation of mental processes responsible for generating the mental representations (Fonagy et al. 1993). These children call for a somewhat different therapeutic approach, one that intends to influence the mental processes themselves (Bleiberg, Fonagy, Target 1997; Fonagy and Target 1998). But what causes the inhibitions on mental functioning encountered in these children?

From the literature on reflective functioning and from clinical experience, we can describe the following factors as related to difficulties in the child's development of reflective functioning.

Child's Limitations or Characteristics as a Limiting Factor in Reflective Functioning

The impediment to the development of the child's RF may stem from the child's own limitations or characteristics. The degree of the limitation depends among other factors on the child's specific problem; for example, in autistic children the limitation is more pervasive than in children with learning difficulties. Many childhood disorders can be effectively understood as containing a significant element of reflective functioning limitation, such as children with conduct problems, children with ADHD and ADD, children with regulatory disorders, and autistic children for whom the lack of mentalization is a cardinal feature (Baron-Cohen 1995).

David was two years old when referred because of what his parents defined, "He does not love us." They described a baby who did not want to be held, who did not look at them when they looked at him, who always preferred to play by himself. The developmental examination, including observations of David and his parents, revealed his severe overreactivity to sensory stimulation, mainly tactile and visual. The parents reacted to his problems by limiting their interaction with him. Their relationship with David was functional, joyless, and missing the quality of "intersubjectivity," of intimacy between their minds and David's. David seemed oblivious to his own mind and the minds of others, unable to attend to the inner world by being constantly overstimulated by the outer world. Explaining the symptoms to the parents brought both relief and sadness.

Children's limitations affect their development directly and also indirectly through the negative influence on the parent-child relationship, as in the above example. In some cases, we see children who are not necessarily limited in their potential for developing reflective functioning, but one or both parents find it difficult to relate to the child because of a characteristic or feature of the child—such as differences in temperament between parents and child. The parents find it difficult to understand the child's behavior because they cannot use their own feelings or thoughts to guide them in this task because the feelings and thoughts are so different from the child's. It is as if the parents cannot use empathy or projective identification to orient their behavior toward the child. Similar problems may arise for parents who have a child with developmental limitations, with a physical handicap, and so forth.

Orly's mother was having a very difficult time trying to make sense of her congenitally blind child's behavior. The therapist, working with the dyad in the mother-child, father-child model (described below) was translating Orly's behavior to mother, in terms of intentions, feelings, and so on. In the individual sessions she tried to help Mother to understand why Orly's inner world was so inaccessible for her. In one of the sessions, Mother exclaimed, "I can't imagine myself being her. It makes me feel so helpless; it makes me mad!"

Maltreatment and Trauma as a Limiting Factor in Reflective Functioning

Fonagy and Target (2003) and Bleiberg (2000) emphasize maltreatment and, more broadly, trauma as a limiting factor in reflective functioning. They also implicate trauma as a mechanism for the intergenerational transmission of limitations in reflective functioning. The maltreated child defensively avoids reflecting on the parent's mind because the parents hold negative feelings and intentions toward the child. The child's developing reflective function is further limited because the parent does not see the child as having a "mind" of his or her own. Furthermore, the child is deprived of the resilience provided by the capacity to understand interpersonal situations as motivated by intentions, emotions, and so forth; these children are at risk for developing severe personality disorders. As parents, their children will show limitations in reflective functioning as a consequence of the parent's limitations.

Limitations of the Parent as a Limiting Factor in Reflective Functioning

Parents who cannot reflect on their own or the child's mental states because they are anxious and overwhelmed inhibit the development of RF in their child. In Bion's terminology, they cannot contain the child's experiences and process them. Moreover, they tend to project their own anxieties, and these are added to the child's anxieties (Britton 1998; Coates 1998). Empirically, this situation was shown in anxiously attached mother-infant dyads (Crittenden 1992). The close link between attachment and reflective functioning was already described earlier in this chapter.

The limitation in parental reflectivity might be specific to the child as described powerfully in Fraiberg, Adelson, and Shapiro's "Ghosts in the Nursery" (1975). In these cases, the limitation occurs because of the psychological meaning this child has for the parent. The limitation might be confined to certain topics, such as feeding, or certain affects, mostly negative affects. In other cases, it is more pervasive, for example, in some cases of early attachment problems, such as on occasion in adoption where the parent finds it difficult to contemplate the child's mind, which seems strange, unknown, and unfamiliar and may be harboring hard feelings. Parents limit their reflective functioning because of defensive processes that are vital to their own functioning, but nevertheless this impairs the child's capacity to reflect or mentalize even in playful or imaginary ways, as the following vignette shows:

Roy, the eight-year-old son of a single mother, was referred because of elective mutism. The relationship between him and his mother was very close, interfering with Roy's attempts to create any relations with other adults or children. One of the reasons for this closeness and exclusiveness was Mother's feeling of loneliness and her need to have Roy for herself, controlling his mind and behavior. In one of the sessions, Roy told the therapist that he is confused because the teacher had asked the children to write an essay about the caveman's thoughts and feelings. When he told his mother about the assignment she said to him, "What a stupid thing to ask for; you know the caveman is already dead!"

What interventions can be made with parents and children to facilitate the development or use of RF? The relational perspective, influencing psychoanalysis, child psychotherapy (Altman et al. 2002; Warshaw 1992), and developmental- and attachment-based approaches (Stern 1995; Hurry 1998;

Crittenden 1992), contributed to the development of several new models of working with infants and parents (most of them reviewed in Stern 1995). These approaches assume that working with parents and infants together is more direct and more effective than working with parents alone and that the presence of the infant in the session is of special value. These models and the changing aims of child psychoanalytic psychotherapy (Fonagy and Target 1998) toward enhancing mental processes in the context of a secure relationship contributed to the development of the therapy model to be described below as an extension of these approaches beyond infancy to the preschool years.

MOTHER-CHILD AND FATHER-CHILD THERAPY AND RF

According to Mitchell (1988), the relational-intersubjective view stresses the formative impact of parental character: "The emotional life of the child is filled with and shaped by the contours of parental character and is constructed *out of actual interactions*. The parent's issues become the child's issues. The kinds of interaction they make possible determine the metaphors that ultimately are utilized by the child to constitute *the intrapsychic*" (490). In other words, actual parent-child interactions, influenced (among other things) by parental characteristics, shape and build the child's inner, representational world. Furthermore, children develop specific relations with each parent and different representations of these relations (Van Ijzendoorn, Sagi, and Lambermon 1992).

The mother-child and father-child psychotherapy is a psychoanalytic approach to the treatment of relational disturbances in childhood (Ben-Aaron et al. 2001). In this model, the same therapist meets with the mother-child, father-child dyads on a weekly basis, along with regular meetings with the parental dyad.

The model integrates an intrapsychic, object-relational view with an interpersonal perspective to the treatment of relational disturbances in childhood. The links and the mutual influences between representations (the intrapsychic aspect) and behavior (the interpersonal aspect) are well described in theory (Stern 1995) and are empirically supported (Van Ijzendoorn 1995). Stern (1995) describes how the partners' behavior in parent-child interactions is influenced by the participants' representations, and at the same time, the interaction is the opportunity for building representations and for changing and updating the old representations, when needed.

In our approach we address behaviors and help the parents and child reflect upon the meanings and the intentions behind these behaviors. The therapist is constantly attending to the dyad on two levels: the level of the experiences, the behaviors, or the actual interactions and the level of meanings, mental states, and representations. We assume that the problems of the child, presented in behavior, are defensive strategies and symptoms that belong to disturbances in the parent-child relations. Since most of the children and parents treated by this model display difficulties in mental processes (Fonagy 2001), the aim is to help them recover their capacity to regulate, organize, and represent mental states. This aim of psychotherapy—the facilitation of mental processes that generate representations—is accepted in both Freudian and Kleinian schools today (Alvarez 1992). The uniqueness of our model is that we aim to reach this goal through the parent-child relation rather than the therapist-child relation.

The relational view regards the therapeutic encounter as resulting from both the contribution of the therapist and that of the patient. Thus, the process is mutually coconstructed by both participants. Enactments in the treatment situation are considered as important opportunities to learn about unconscious meanings held by the patient that have not been previously expressed (McLaughlin 1991). As stressed by Lyons-Ruth (1999), the primary interest is in aspects of enactments that echo problematic aspects of the patient's interpersonal experience with other important people.

Applying this orientation to children would mean that the most important enactments are considered to be those that echo problems with the child's parents because, developmentally, these same interactions were the formative interactions as far as the child's representations are concerned. What would later become disturbances of relationship and of self and other representations may be effectively addressed in the actual here-and-now parent-child interactions as the shaping force of the child's representations.

In order to explain how the representations are presented in the therapy hour, we will distinguish between implicit and declarative memory systems in the following section, and in the next section we will describe reflective functioning as the curative factor acting between these systems.

Implicit Relational Knowledge

There is growing awareness in the treatment literature of the problem of addressing issues that are not verbalized or symbolized in any form. Cognitive science distinguishes two kinds of memory system. Declarative or explicit memory is the conscious retrieval of information about the past. This information is characterized by content. In procedural or implicit memory, information is recalled without the experience of remembering. It is independent of content and has to do with acquiring processes. Several concepts, such as "the unthought known" (Bollas 1987), "unmentalized experience" (Mitrani 1996), and specifically in the treatment process, the notions of "implicit relational knowledge" (Stern et al. 1998; Lyons-Ruth 1998) and "enactive relational representations" (Lyons-Ruth 1999), are used to describe aspects of relations, self, and self-with-other experiences that "are different from verbalizable knowledge and from the dynamic unconscious" (Lyons-Ruth 1998, 282). Implicit relational knowledge, according to Lyons-Ruth, is likely to be visible in the structure of fantasized interactions as well as in the enactive structure of real interactions. Fonagy (2001) emphasized the importance of this type of memory, specifically for patients showing limitations in mental functioning. Lyons-Ruth (1999) describes the "two person unconscious" as the focus of the therapeutic intervention, based on the assumption that important object relations are represented and remembered in the implicit mode. In the same line, Fonagy (2001) reasons that "what lies at the root of interpersonal problems, the transference relationship and quite possibly all aspects of the personality that we loosely denote by the term 'unconscious' is not a series of episodes of caregiver interactions stored in the explicit memory, but a set of procedures or implicit memories of interactional experience" (18). Following the importance of the implicit memory system in object-relations representation, addressing this system becomes an important focus of therapy. Indeed, Stern et al. (1998), while trying to define the "something more than interpretation" that acts as a curative factor in therapy, wrote about the "non-interpretive mechanisms in psychoanalytic psychotherapy." This addresses processes related to implicit relational knowledge enacted in the therapy session. Fonagy (2001) also stressed that the only way we can know what might have happened to our patients is through their interaction with us in the transference; therefore, change must occur in implicit memory for the procedures people use in living with themselves and others to change. The importance of the procedural memory for therapy implies that change comes by altering ways of "being with" and not by remembering the past.

Our model follows closely the implications of regarding this memory system as the important system in object relations by emphasizing the here-and-now live experience of the child and each parent interaction as the focus of observation and reflection.

We find that implicit relational knowledge is enacted in the therapeutic process by the parent-child dyad or the parental couple and, when focused on, can become observable, can be reflected upon, and can be mentalized. We believe that the therapy format—the actual participation of parents—and the empathic and supportive atmosphere in our model of therapy maximize the emergence of these implicit themes. This enables an approach to these enactments as important curative factors in the process of change. We witness the occurrence of "present moments" raising the opportunity of "moments of meeting" as change-inducing factors. Stern's model implies that enacted ways of "being with" are transformed in the analytic hour into explicit knowledge of relations. In our model, the therapist has a special role in promoting a kind of translation between the enacted, implicit domain and the declarative domain of experience, by activating the reflective function of the dyad and using her or his own reflective function.

Fonagy and Target (in Ben-Aaron et al. 2001) specify the principal elements of our treatment model:

> It gives the therapist the unique opportunity to observe rather than speculate about the nature of the parent-child relations, to observe the transference—that is—the unconscious attributions of the child to the parent or the parent to the child as it happens, rather than infer these processes from the child's reactions to the therapist. This important technical modification makes the treatment more direct, more immediate, and we hope, also more effective. (11)

In the therapy sessions, the parent and the child present the therapist with their specific ways of "being with" (Stern 1985), mainly nonverbalized, implicit relational knowledge (Lyons-Ruth 1998). Usually, the potential access to these important aspects of the parent-child relations is only by their enactment in the sessions, since they are not declarative knowledge that the parents or the child can tell us about. It is to be acknowledged that some of these aspects could be enacted in the transference, and the therapist could learn about the relationship from the transference, but the presence of the child and the parent in the session affords the therapist a direct and uncontaminated (by the therapist's countertransference, for instance) access to the parent-child relationship.

Furthermore, the separate, direct observation of children with fathers and with mothers clearly shows that children have two different relations and are behaving and experiencing themselves differently in the two relational contexts. This was shown empirically, too, by studying mother-child and father-child interactions with the core conflictual relational theme method (Harel et al. 2003).

Enhancing RF in the Dyad

We consider the dyadic sessions as the most suitable context for the child and the parent to enhance their reflective functioning and to understand the links between their representations and between representations and behaviors.

Embedded in the secure therapeutic situation and encouraged to mentalize, the dyads are enabled to coconstruct new behavioral patterns along with additional meanings to intrapsychic and interpersonal experiences.

With children and parents showing limitations in mental processes, the therapist aims to make them feel that it is safe to be reflective on their own and others' minds. The therapist's efforts to explore the child's and the parents' minds and her readiness to express her own mind and the playful context of the setting all contribute to the freeing process of the dyad's inhibited but potentially available reflective functioning.

The intervention strategies are quite simple and include some of those delineated by Bleiberg, Fonagy, and Target (1997) for children with inhibited RF, adapted to our model and applied to the parents as well:

1. Observing and verbalizing the child's and the parents' feelings, intentions, and thoughts.
2. Developing the capacity to play, at first with objects, then with others, and finally with feelings and ideas.
3. Generating interest in the mental state of others, initially by focusing on the parents' perception of the child's mental state.
4. Demonstrating the therapist's capacity for modulation of experience through RF and verbalization. In cases of very limited reflective capacity in the dyad, the reflective capacity could be enhanced by the therapists sharing with parents and children their own reflective processes. For example, Roy, a five-year-old boy, was referred following his teacher's complaints about his destructive and violent behavior in kindergarten. In the sessions with Father, it became clear that both father and child used very little reflection in their interaction, which was filled with anger. Once, when Father shouted at Roy and humiliated him in the session, the therapist thought aloud, "I feel very uncomfortable, and I am wondering how angry you must feel, Father, and I am asking myself, 'How is Roy feeling now that you are shouting at him?'"
5. Demonstrating to the child and the parent multiple ways of seeing reality.

We believe that inhibited mental functions are reactivated through the active involvement of the therapist in the mental functioning of the parent and the child and the reciprocal involvement of the dyad in the mind of the therapist.

The dyadic meeting, in the secure and empathic atmosphere, enables them to playfully explore their inner worlds, with the help and support of the therapist. The therapist interprets the anxieties that originally caused the inhibition of RF in the child or the parent. The exploration and clarification of each other's feelings, intents, wishes, and so forth, bring differentiation between the partners' respective mental worlds, followed by understanding and empathy. This process facilitates an enrichment of the ways the dyad's members perceive each other and themselves, and a process of updating and reorganizing representations is initiated, followed by changes in behavior.

Sometimes the reflection on each other's minds is anxiety provoking and painful. The therapist is sensitive to these problems and anticipates them from knowledge of the dyads' dynamics or from countertransferential feelings.

The therapist is ready to meet these emotionally charged moments, to deal with them in a way that is sensitive to the needs of both participants, and to transform them from painful and avoided moments to "moments of meeting" (Stern et al. 1998).

Maya, a five-year-old adopted child, was struggling with her life narrative in sessions with her mother and father. Although her parents had told her about her adoption at the age of one and about her teenaged mother and her reasons for giving Maya up for adoption, they had not told her about her first year of life in the children's home. This period was very painful for the parents to talk about because they were very much aware of the terrible conditions that prevailed at that home and the suffering that Maya had experienced there. Whenever Maya tried to talk about herself as a baby, the parents talked about or played out episodes from the very brief period of her life with her birth mother and then her life with the adopting parents, ignoring the period between these two phases in her life. Looking at the repetitive nature of these sessions, the therapist began to feel that something was missing, but it was still not clear what Maya was looking for. Then, as it often happens in this model, Maya helped the adults move ahead. In a session with Mother, she declared that she was going to draw a picture of herself as a newborn, and so she did. Then she proceeded to draw a picture of her first birthday, and pointing at the drawings she asked, "But what happened to me from when I was born 'til my first birthday?" There was a moment of silence—Mother and the therapist looked at each other. The therapist suggested, "I see that Maya has an important question. Would you, Mother, like to answer her? Maybe you are hesitating because you are afraid that it will be too difficult for Maya to listen to your answer. I think that she can listen to it now, with your help." Mother took Maya in her arms and began to tell her about the children's home. At first she told about technical and physical features; Maya listened very carefully. Then Mother looked at the therapist as if asking whether to go on. The therapist suggested asking Maya if she wanted to hear more. When Maya asked for more, Mother told her a few details about the children's conditions, comparing them to what Maya had as a baby at their own home, as if to ameliorate the pain by describing the "reparation" process. In following sessions, this story was told again with both parents and enriched with many details, until a rich and emotionally acceptable narrative was constructed. The parents' emotional experiences regarding their memories at the time of adoption and during the construction of the story were addressed in the sessions with the parents as well.

We believe that the parent-child meetings are the best context for the child and for the parent to enhance their RF. This treatment setting enables them to study, to practice, to correct, and to enrich their RF in the empathic and cooperative ambiance of the session.

The setting allows the therapist to encourage the dyad's reflectivity upon the different components of the material appearing in the session—in the immediate experiences of the enactments in play, memories, fantasies, and coconstructed narratives. In this way, the dyadic meetings offer a wide variety of interactions and contexts for understanding the specific limitations in RF that the dyad is experiencing and for the expression and enhancement of the partner's RF.

The setting, by including the parent in the therapy, and the therapist's stance provide the dyad members with a secure base for exploring their inner worlds (Bowlby 1979). This security is achieved through the therapist's validation of the special role the parent has for the specific child. The therapist conveys to the parent her or his respect and acceptance of the specific parenting skills the parent shows.

The parent's competence and sense of security is further enhanced by the role assigned to her or him as an active participant in the process of helping the child. The parent is "the helper," and is assisted by the therapist in helping the child. Being the helper of his or her own child enables the parent to make use of parental capacities and to free those capacities inhibited for different reasons. The therapist uses each and every opportunity to show the parent how much the child needs him or her and remains as much as possible in the background of the parent-child relationship.

In mother-child and father-child therapy, the participants show the therapist and the therapist experiences in a direct mode the dyads' ways of "being together." The therapist makes use of his own, the parents', and the child's reflective functioning in order to clarify, recognize, validate, enrich, and so on, these ways of being together and to transform them into declarative, symbolized knowledge.

Parallel to the enactments and implicit themes between parent and child in the presence of the therapist are themes presented in the transference. We identify two transference processes, which evolve when working according to this model: One transference process occurs between parent and child and also between child and parent. This transference is different from the one described in parent-infant therapies, for example, what Hopkins (1992) and Barrows (1997) describe as the "mother's transference on the baby"—the parent's projection on the infant. We are looking at a two-way process, the parent projects onto the child, and the child also projects onto the parent, along with a projected "relationship format" (Seligman 1999). As mentioned (Fonagy and Target 2001), our setup affords the unique opportunity to observe the transference as it happens, rather then infer it from the therapist-child relation.

The other transference that develops alongside the transference between parent and child is the transference between the therapist and the participants in the dyad. The parent and the child assign various roles to the therapist, to which the therapist responds both consciously and unconsciously (Sandler 1976). This transference between the therapist and the dyads has various nuances. At the beginning of the treatment, we witness some significant difficulties in the establishment of the working alliance, some stemming from the parents' past experiences, or negative expectations regarding the treatment process. These problems are expressed in projections on the therapist, for example, suspicion toward, avoidance, and so forth. An important positive aspect of transference, one that facilitates the therapeutic process, is what Stern (1995) called "good grandmother transference." The parents see the therapist as someone who appreciates their parental role, does not intrude upon it, and makes every effort to help them to help their child. In the sessions with the child as well as in the sessions with the parental couple, the therapist's respect for the parental role is clearly conveyed, and the parents are enabled to mobilize their parenting resources to help their child. This positive transference is not taken for granted but is an attainment of the treatment process.

At present, the efficacy of the model is based on extensive clinical experience. We are conducting several research projects to empirically show the changes in reflective functioning in the therapy process, changes in the child's play, and changes in the parents' representations of the child.

CASE ILLUSTRATION: RON

Ron's case is a fascinating example of the changes in reflective functioning as enabled following mother-child and father-child therapy. A dramatic shift occurred from the parents' perception of the child as strange and alienated and the relationship as meaningless and lacking mutual significance to a deep emotional relationship that facilitates development. In spite of the difficult and discouraging initial impression, the parents did mobilize their parenting capacities to enable this vital shift to occur. Ron's referral process, a brief history, and a description of him and his parents at referral will follow.

Ron was three years and ten months old when he was referred for therapy. The parents initiated the referral because they noticed Ron's language difficulties and were concerned about his cognitive development.

Ron is his parents' eldest son and has a brother one year and seven months younger than he. Ron was born in a normal delivery following a normal pregnancy. He was described as a baby who cried a lot and was difficult to calm down. He had a hard time consolidating his sleep and arousal cycles. Mother had decided not to breast-feed him, and his bottle feeding was described by his mother as "mutual suffering." When he was one year old, his mother went back to work, and he was taken care of by a hired caregiver. At one and a half years of age, he began to speak a few words, pronouncing them clearly. About a month after that, his brother was born. On the day of his mother's return from the hospital, Ron was hospitalized for one month with severe colitis. During this period, his language development stopped. When he was two years old, he started attending nursery school or preschool, without noticeable separation difficulties. His vocabulary gradually expanded, but he spoke little, slowly, and with faults. Pronunciation problems were most apparent in moments of frustration. The parents described him as an incomprehensible child but, nevertheless, easy "to manage," not interfering, and able to calm down by himself. At home, he spent a lot of time by himself and did not initiate contact with his family members. Ron occupied himself for many hours with puzzles and construction games.

Ron's preschool teacher also described him as a lonely child who rarely participated in the classroom activities. Ron avoided answering questions and did not initiate contact with the other children. At times he suddenly burst into screams with no apparent reason. The teacher perceived his screams as meaningless. In these situations, he also tended to calm by himself and was reluctant to receive comfort from the school staff. The teacher, like his parents, described him as a "strange and incomprehensible child," unpredictable and rejecting contact. But in spite of her description of his difficult behavior, it was apparent that the teacher liked him.

The parents were in their early thirties with academic educations in the field of engineering. Mother was an only child. She looked stiff and frozen and had a nondefined appearance, without any feminine characteristics. She spoke fluently and decisively about herself and her past. She described her own childhood as good but in the same breath mentioned that, following her birth, her mother became ill with an unidentified illness, was confined to bed for two years, and therefore did not take care of her daughter. All her life, Ron's mother was a high achiever and an excellent student. Father dressed sloppily, was silent during most of the sessions, and on the rare occasions when he did speak, he expressed himself aggressively and bluntly. He was the youngest son of parents who divorced when he was a child. He described his childhood as a saga of rejection, deprivation, and abuse by his parents. He remembered himself as an "unusual" child. Both parents described a limited social life in both their youth and today. They both refused to elaborate about their pasts and especially did not find any meaning in discussing them with the therapist.

The Assessment Phase

At the child development center, Ron was initially diagnosed as suffering from a pervasive developmental disorder (PDD). To enrich the information available on Ron and his parents, the therapist invited the parents to an introductory meeting. In this session, the parents expressed their doubts and suspicions toward the medical institute that made the diagnosis. They stated that they were not interested in an "overall treatment" and all they wished for was that "they [the staff] take Ron, fix him, and return him in good order." Noticeable was their difficulty in describing Ron, their thinking of him, and their giving any kind of meaning to his behavior. They both expressed their inability to see themselves as meaningful to him. Father exhibited an almost total lack of involvement, stating that his wife was responsible for the rearing of the children. Mother described her mothering role only in functional terms, finding it difficult to see herself as connected to or having any influence on Ron's functioning and development. At this initial stage, it was not possible to further examine and understand the meaning of the disconnection and estrangement of the parents from their son. The impression was that his inner world was unknown and alien to them.

Ron and his parents were invited for a dyadic assessment process. Generally, the purpose of these sessions is to get a preliminary picture of the relationship in the dyads in terms of characteristic themes, role relations, conflicts, and so forth, as well as of the parental resources available for the therapeutic work. Following this assessment, a decision is made regarding the most efficient therapeutic format. Ron's parents agreed to the assessment process.

Ron and his mother came to the first session. Ron was a good-looking, very tall, and gentle boy. He had bright hair and big green eyes. He had a somewhat-mystical expression of dreamy naivety on his face. His walk gave a feeling as if there were no solid ground beneath his feet. In the session with mother, Ron and she were very distant from one another. Most of the time Ron sat silently, passively staring into space, occasionally mumbling meaningless things to himself, and at times occupying himself by moving a toy car back and forth while making car sounds. At the same time, the mother spoke continuously. She did not pay attention to Ron on her own initiative. As a response to the therapist's attempts to draw her attention to him, she responded with detailed explanations that he had difficulties only in language development, which are affecting his cognitive development, and "as soon as he will know how to speak, everything will be all right." In the room, the dyad was disconnected and sad, with each of its members protecting their self with a private verbal envelope that sustained and strengthened the loneliness. In the supervision process, the therapist mentioned that in these initial sessions the experience of loneliness and sadness was shared by her, too.

Since father failed to keep his sessions, and the situation looked grave, the therapist decided on a session with the parents, after the first session with the mother only. In this session with the parents, the therapist set several goals for herself. She was to share her impressions with the parents regarding Ron's language development—the only subject distressing the parents at

a conscious level—and to share with them her impression of the relationships in the mother-child dyad as they were revealed in the therapy room.
Most importantly, she set a goal to recruit them as partners in the required
dyadic therapeutic work. Knowing their harsh criticism toward the medical
establishment, she was cautious not to create an atmosphere of dispute or
criticism toward them but did find it appropriate to repeatedly emphasize
their importance and centrality in Ron's life and their influence on him in all
areas of development. This claim was very surprising to the parents. In the
therapist's supervisory session, she reported how difficult it was to recruit
her own empathy toward the parents, who repeatedly expressed a cynical
and alienated attitude toward her, especially regarding contents relating to
their own and to Ron's inner worlds. The parents talked mainly in terms of
functioning and achievements, disregarding their own or their child's mental
life. Themes of dependency, regression, and need seemed to arouse anxiety
wrapped up in a distancing and rejecting affect. Nevertheless, the parents
agreed to engage in a mother-child and father-child therapy process of alter-
nating parent-child sessions, with the same therapist-and-parents therapist
sessions once every two to three weeks.

The First Period

The first sessions repeatedly demonstrated the degree of the parents'
detachment—each in his or her own way—from their son.

Again, Mother and Ron arrived at the first session. When entering the
room, Mother stood silently while Ron moved restlessly in the room. The
therapist thought that he was probably trying to express what happened on
the way to therapy or his wariness in the unfamiliar room and with a strange
lady. He was excited, his sentences were fragmented, and his anxiety was
mounting. Mother looked anxious as well, withdrawn into herself and silent.
The more Ron's anxiety signals escalated, the more sealed off Mother
became. Suddenly, without saying a word, she left the room for a few minutes. It became clear to the therapist that it was crucial to give words to the
threatening atmosphere and the overwhelming anxiety. When Mother
returned, the therapist referred to the apprehensions and emotions Ron and
Mother probably had about coming to the session and to Ron's need for his
mother's presence in the room. To the therapist's own surprise, it seemed
liked her comments calmed the dyad for a while. Then Mother said, "Ron
usually does not mind whether I am with him or not. I did not think he
would care if I leave."

In this period, the initial impression that the relationship between Mother
and Ron was based on practical functioning was clearly supported. Ron and
Mother were "doing things" together and were even skilled at that, and the
"doing" was formulated in terms of success or failure and knowing and not

knowing. They were not familiar with communication about feelings, which were unavailable for them as symbolized and distinctive representations and were amazingly absent from their verbal dictionary. In one of the sessions with the mother, during a "memory" game, the therapist remarked that it was probably pleasant for Ron to successfully trace the matching card. To that, Ron reacted, "Pleasant? What is pleasant?" and turning to his mother, he said, "Mother, she says it is pleasant for me. Yes, it is pleasant for me."

The sessions with Mother and her willingness to be in the room soon began to bear fruit. Ron began to look furtively toward the dolls and then to withdraw immediately. In one of the sessions, he finally dared to ask to play with the dolls. He arranged them for play, and Mother leaned toward him. The alignment was arranged; the play "waits," but Ron and Mother did not seem to know how to proceed. Ron and Mother looked unable to express fantasy and were stuck. Ron began to move restlessly, and it was apparent that his frustration was leading to anxiety and that he felt alone in the process. In a matter of seconds, Ron very impulsively dismantled the whole "awaiting" alignment of the game. Ron detached and went back to uttering fragmented and unclear sentences, indicating his mounting anxiety. Mother looked at the therapist helplessly, while ignoring Ron's plea. For a moment, she resembled a frightened and detached child, mainly looking helpless and lost. Her maternal stance dissolved, leaving behind a terrified child. The therapist considered whom to address first in order to channel this difficult experience into more reflective modes. It was clear to her that she should not usurp Mother from her maternal position, although she gave it up at these moments; at the same time, it was obvious that it was necessary to comfort Ron and to give meaning to what had occurred in the dyad. The therapist chose to validate Mother's feelings and to give clear words to Ron's experience. She suggested that "Mother looks confused, but nevertheless Ron needs Mother to help him, to hold him, because it is hard for him to help himself alone." It seemed that Mother needed what was occurring to be deciphered and translated into words. They both needed the meaning that the therapist gave to the child's and to mother's behavior (from a noncritical or intrusive position). As a reaction to the intervention, Mother approached Ron and held him warmly. Ron calmed down, and the two of them started a different, safer, and joint "doing" in the room.

Ron's father eventually engaged in the therapeutic process; nonetheless, the alienation and loneliness in their relationship were strong and very prominent. It looked as if the sessions were very difficult for Father; the forced intimacy with his son (and possibly also with the therapist) aroused unbearable anxiety. As a detaching defense, very often he would doze off on the couch. Ron reacted to Father's sleep with noticeable physical restlessness, while the therapist was also embarrassed, not knowing how to behave in these situations. In one of the sessions in which Father fell asleep, Ron rolled up the carpet in the room and wandered agitatedly while shouting indistinct syllables. It was evident that Ron was very anxious and unable to regulate his emotions and that Father was detaching himself from the session because of his own anxiety. Father was awakened by Ron's screams and said to the therapist, "You see, he plays like that all the time; he cannot play with anything." This was Father's typical position when confronted with the helplessness that Ron's "meaningless" behavior aroused or provoked in him. The therapist chose to refer to Father's having the capability to help Ron. She directly and concretely suggested, "Maybe you will help him find something to play with." Father was surprised and hesitant, but Ron seized the moment and offered the opportunity for him and Father to draw together. Father took a sheet of paper for himself and drew his computer room at home. Ron scribbled without any planning on his own paper. When he was done, he moved to draw on his father's paper. Father sighed, desperate, and said, "Enough, we finished drawing." The detachment was immediate and unpredictable and left Ron surprised and frightened. The therapist chose to focus on translating what occurred between them and suggested, "Maybe Ron wants to get close to Father and that is why he chose to draw on his paper, and Father thought that Ron wanted to spoil the drawing." Ron and Father listened, the tension waned, and the father suggested drawing a house on a shared sheet of paper. Ron happily consented to his father's suggestion, and they worked together. Father watched Ron drawing and remarked that he did not know that Ron drew so nicely. "You do not know anything," said Ron angrily to his father. "You see, he is angry all the time; one cannot be with him," said Father. The therapist tried to mediate between the hurt father and the angry child, saying that maybe it is Ron's way of saying to him that he wants his father to know him better and that maybe he simply wants "more Father." It seems that Father is finding it difficult to remain available for his son; every sign of rejection or aggression from Ron's side leads Father to detach, and in this way maybe to sustain his own representation as a rejected child. Ron also remains helpless, with mounting anxiety. He is not receiving from the father approval or validation for his wishes or intensions; his inner world remains alienated and bad, and he reacts like his father with withdrawal and detachment.

These relationship patterns again found their expression in another session that took place during the first period of therapy: Ron entered the room with his father and sat on one of the couches; his father sat on the other. They were both silent. Father turned to Ron and said, "Come on, tell something; don't you see, we arrived." Ron sang quietly to himself, "Don't see, don't see," laughed a strange laugh, repeated what he said, and wrapped himself in a stream of mumbling. Father, in his characteristic way, closed his eyes and detached. Ron approached the toy basket and noisily and impulsively emptied its content. At this point the therapist remarked, "Maybe Ron wants to say something to Father and to me. Maybe it is not pleasant for him that Father does not see him and that he feels that he also does not see and that is why he wants to be heard."

In reaction to what she said, Father opened his eyes and asked the therapist, "Do you really think so?" The therapist replied, "It is possible that Ron feels uncomfortable alone, without adults that see him, and he has his special ways of showing it." Thus, the therapist emphasized a segment from the behavioral pattern of the dyad and translated the interaction into feelings, wishes, and intentions. Father, who, as usual, reacted with detachment in the face of his son's regressive and incomprehensible behavior, was recruited with the therapist's mediation to try to understand Ron as a subject in his own right. Ron, who listened to what was said and experienced himself as existing and understandable in the mind of the therapist, was quiet for a moment. He then approached her and looked straight into her eyes while turning his head toward her. The therapist reacted, "You look at me surprised that I am saying things about you and trying to understand what you want and feel in your own special way." This way, the therapist translated for both Ron and Father Ron's behavior as a reaction to her previous sayings. Father, with wide-open eyes, said to the therapist, "I do not know how you understand all that so well, but it works." He turned to Ron and asked him if he would like to do what they did two weeks before.

Ron asked to play with the dolls. He chose the role of the child for himself. Father chose to be the neighbor. Ron looked as if he were not pleased with Father's choice and said, "I am at home alone," and while speaking, ruined what he had prepared to play. The therapist interpreted Ron's furious reaction as Ron's wish that Father would choose to be one of the closer family members and his behavior as showing his disappointment that this wish was not being fulfilled. Father insisted on remaining the neighbor. Ron, rejected, reacted in screams that he did not want neighbors and continued furiously, destroying the rest of the house. In reaction, the father said to the therapist, "You see, you cannot play with him."

In this first phase of therapy, the parents and Ron learned in the dyadic sessions the character of the special therapeutic framework. They were exposed to the possibility of meeting each other and of communicating with one another in the interpersonal situations that arise in the room. The therapist is actively creating connections, clarifying and translating behaviors and mental states for each one of the dyads, and trying to give them meanings in the interpersonal and intrapersonal levels.

This is a new and difficult experience for the parents, who are "forced" to meet Ron and to observe themselves as people and as his parents. These experiences, at this point of the therapy, aroused anxiety, guilt, and embarrassment in facing the unpredictable and mainly incomprehensible elements in Ron's behavior. In this period, a special emphasis was put on the sessions with the parents in order to process the experiences brought up in the dyadic sessions with Ron.

In the initial sessions with the parents, Mother repeatedly expressed an accumulating sense of failure as a mother and especially helplessness in facing her son's deficiency. For her, something deterministic in his behavior existed that she, as a mother, could not influence, and therefore she gave up and withdrew. Nevertheless, the sessions with Ron and their processing in the parents' sessions gradually enabled within her a significant shift from practical and concrete functioning that ignored emotional content to an available, more competent parenting and to a growing ability to address in herself and in her son feelings of anxiety, guilt, and helplessness.

Father went through a different process in this period. His difficulties in asserting his presence as a parent, as a father, to his son were prominent. He perceived himself as useless and rejected and withdrew quite quickly to a position of detachment and renouncement. To every hint of rejection, lack of enthusiasm, or even welcoming from Ron's side, he reacted with rage and vengeful withdrawal.

In this period, the parents still found it difficult to give their own meaning to Ron's behavior. Nevertheless, they both asked the therapist for, in their words, "translation" for Ron's affective states of anger, frustration, anxiety, and so forth. This process of constructing new meanings inside the relations was beginning to bear fruit, and the sense of ambiguity and meaninglessness that Ron's behavior arose in them gave way to more clarity. Most importantly, Ron responded rather quickly to his parents' new position of not giving up on him, as well as to the efforts being made to understand him and to give meaning to his behavior. His speech became more fluent, and he took much initiative in searching for contact and closeness with them. In one of the sessions, Ron fell and hurt his knee. Mother, still captured in an old pattern of responsiveness, did not respond; Ron did not even cry. The therapist remarked that maybe the bruise hurt Ron. After a short silence (as if "expecting" permission), Ron started crying, turned to his mother, and asked her to wash it with water. It appeared that the dyad needed to be given meaning and confirmation to the emotional state Ron was in, which then allowed in each one of them an appropriate communication and behavior.

The Second Phase

The second period of therapy, which lasted about four months, was characterized by an active coconstruction of narratives. Ron would come to a session upset, trying to convey his experiences from outside the room. He was expressing himself excitedly, and his speech was fragmented and incomprehensible. The therapist's attempts to gather and process what was said were unhelpful.

In one of the first sessions in this period, upon entering the room, Ron happily began telling about a trip the schoolchildren took to an orange orchard. Ron, as usual, expressed himself in a fragmented way, repeated words, omitted letters, stuttered, and turned around the order of words. Father reacted with ridicule and impatience. This was his typical reaction, but this time Ron reacted with frustration and rage, which quickly turned into a wild temper tantrum. The therapist felt that this was a place to help Ron calm down and give a coherent meaning to what he was trying to express. She suggested that Father and Ron write down what Ron said and then read aloud what was written. Ron accepted the proposal and calmed down. Father did not object or dismiss. From this point on a pattern was formed. At the beginning of every session, the therapist wrote Ron's "story" and read what was written, organizing the experience. Ron very much enjoyed hearing his accumulating stories and asked her to read them to him again and again. The writing created a sense of continuity among the world outside of therapy, and the inside of therapy, and the time between the sessions. Naturally, it also gave Ron and each parent a sense that what is said has importance, is worthy of giving meaning to, and should be shared.

The parents, with time, became active partners in the process. What started as Ron's stories became coconstructions of shared narratives describing the relations inside the family. And so the therapist's idea, the result of creativity and resourcefulness in face of the father's helplessness and being sealed off, turned her into an "active container" for each dyad. This enabled the processing of the chaotic and raw experiences into narratives with coherence and meaning for the partners. Ron was gradually forming a sense of continuity and constancy in the experience of the self. This was apparent in the decrease in anxiety and in his growing ability to bring up, in a more structured way, the developmental themes related to himself and to his relationship with his parents. At the same time, themes from his parents' world were being revealed, giving a clearer meaning to the characteristic relationship patterns in the family.

The sessions with the parent dyad took a significant turn with the consolidation of the therapeutic alliance, as well as with the parents' growing confidence in the therapeutic process and in the relationship with the therapist. These enabled the raising and processing of aspects of the parents' past. Mother brought up, with a lot of sadness, memories from her childhood home, a home in which the dominant experience was of silence, without playfulness, expression of emotions, or spontaneous expressions. She revealed feelings of a lonely, helpless child who finds comfort in reading. She raised doubts regarding her maternal ability. In these sessions she also expressed hard feelings of disappointment and guilt toward herself and toward Ron. The processing of these themes and relating them to her past allowed Mother to give up her defensive judgmental position, which "measure" her son on the basis of intellectual achievements, and to meet him as a subject, more distinctive and loved despite his difficulties.

In these sessions Father also told the story of his past. Quietly and hesitantly, he told about a hard childhood, with continuous physical and emotional abuse, as well as repeated abandonment by his father and mother. It seems that this childhood experience of abandonment and rejection did not permit Father to form a stable relationship with Ron and led him to renouncement or even flight from his parental role. At this phase of the therapy, the therapist's efforts to connect the father's past and his difficulty in asserting his place in relation to his son were rejected. Nevertheless, the changes that took place in Ron's and Father's dyadic sessions, Ron's stubborn and active position not to give his father up, and the stable therapeutic alliance with the therapist enabled him to access strengths and to continue his involvement in the process and in the relationship with his son despite the actual meaninglessness he experienced.

Parallel to the therapeutic work, a new picture emerged about Ron's functioning outside of therapy. The parents reported that Ron tended to withdraw less and was initiating more verbal interactions at home. Father proudly mentioned that Ron invited a friend from school. Mother said the preschool teacher reported a greater involvement in activities with the other children and the beginning of cooperative play with them. It looked as if the push in Ron's language development calmed the parents down and enabled them to deepen their trust in the therapeutic process and in the therapist as well.

In the following months of therapy, the dominant theme characterizing the sessions was of "destruction and reparation" on the intrapersonal level as well as on the interpersonal one. It seems that on the basis of the security and stability obtained in the room, Ron was enabled with a more coherent expression of difficult emotions, without the terror of disintegration previously hovering upon the wholeness of the self. He increasingly dealt with issues of destruction out of a growing sense of security that he had "surviving" partners in the process. The activity was characterized by the joint creation of Ron and his parents. They were engaged in building airplanes, kites, and creatures from paper. Each dyad in its own way was getting used to the idea that in the relationship exists a possibility of repair instead of "throwing to the garbage," on the concrete as well as in the more symbolic level. Opportunities of temporality, relativity, partiality, and reparation substituted the total and hermetic stance.

In this period of therapy, the therapist was in advanced stages of pregnancy, and Ron was in transition from nursery to school. The pregnancy's imposed interruption of therapy and the move to school aroused a sense of anxiety in Ron and his parents. In one of the dyadic sessions with Mother, Ron reacted to the therapist's big stomach. He asked to touch it and was curious about the baby, its condition, its ability to breathe and eat, and so on. This example, like many others, indicated that Ron was more open to dealing with external reality, which enabled learning and enrichment of his inner world, as well as concern for others. Nevertheless, in the room there was no direct expression of the anxieties aroused by the pregnancy and the expected interruption. These anxieties could also be related to the birth of Ron's brother and the traumatic events following it. In one of the sessions, Ron asked to play with dolls, and he chose a child doll while Mother chose a baby. Ron reacted to his mother's choice with withdrawal to idiosyncratic speech and said, "The child Maki walks on the head, doesn't know anything—angry—crying—doesn't want." There is no doubt that the mother's choice aroused anxiety in Ron. It was not clear what motivated the mother in her choice, possibly she unconsciously expressed her wish to be small and held in light of the coming separation. Maybe it was identification with the fetus in the therapist's stomach, along with her anxiety and her difficulty with holding her son in the coming absence of the therapist. At this point the therapist interpreted for them the situation as follows: "Maybe Ron, like the child, Maki, is afraid and confused and feels all kinds of new things will happen; maybe he needs a big mother and not a baby mother." Mother reacted with relief and said to Ron, "I will take a mother doll and not a baby doll. I will be confused Maki's mother, and we will be confused together." This example reflects a meaningful change in Mother's emotional position as well as her growing ability for reflection and empathy in her relationship with Ron. This example also points out Ron's regressive potential despite the apparent improvement in his functioning. There was no doubt that the dyads still needed the holding, mediation, and interpretation of the therapist in confronting emotionally charged situations, both in the sessions and in reality. Similar issues were repeatedly brought up in the sessions with the parental dyad. They experienced a close, stable, and much clearer relationship with their son; at the same time, they brought dilemmas from outside the therapy room. They both expressed a lot of concern about the therapist's maternity leave and claimed that they need her "as a connecting link" between them and Ron. They were worried that an absence, even temporary, would interrupt what had been achieved and "everybody will get lost." Their feelings accurately reflected the therapist's own doubts regarding the stability of the achieved changes and raised her sense of guilt about her "abandonment" of the family.

Following a two-month intermission of maternity leave, the sessions were renewed, and the parents explicitly expressed their happiness about returning to therapy. Ron came with Mother to the first session. He looked troubled and tense and was busy scanning the room, like someone taking inventory. The therapist noted her impression verbally, and the mother remarked that she missed therapy and was happy to return. As a reaction to what Mother said, Ron said, "I am big; I will never come here anymore." He reverted to his wild behavior, throwing things and trying to hit the therapist. His sudden tantrum raised a lot of embarrassment and guilt in the therapist, while Mother reacted with paralysis and sat helplessly. The therapist tried to put into words Ron's feelings of anger because of her absence and Ron's anxiety that nothing would be as it was. Ron continued behaving wildly, as though he were not listening. Every additional verbal attempt from the therapist faced a renewed opposition. The session ended with a door slam and a statement by Ron that he does not intend to return. Ron's behavior raised in the therapist a sense of guilt and anxiety concerning the separation; she assumed that his attempts at the beginning of the session to restore what was lost, perhaps never to return, fell apart in front of the mother's remark that did not meet his own feelings and strengthened his sense of loneliness. The anxiety that overwhelmed Ron led him to recruit the known mechanisms of rage, solitude, and detachment.

The pattern of behavior described was repeated in the following eight sessions with each one of his parents. Ron was not able to organize himself for continued activity in the room; he moved restlessly, screaming, trying to break, tear, and ruin objects. It seemed he was in a terrible overwhelming rage and a state of anxiety that threatened to ruin what had been built. At the same time, the therapist tried to keep the room whole and to give meaning to what was incomprehensible to Ron. She repeatedly said that Father or Mother and she would try to understand what was happening to Ron and what he wanted to say in his behavior, would not give up, and would keep being with him despite his stubborn attempts to interrupt and disrupt every attempt for contact. In one of the sessions with Father, during temperamental wild behavior while hiding behind a couch, Ron said to the therapist, "You will go to your baby and leave me." Father, on his own initiative remarked, "It has nothing to do with it; the baby is not here and she [the therapist] will not leave us because of him." In this session, a crack opened for the first time through which a deeper understanding of the meaning of Ron's anxiety and rage could be achieved. Only later it became clear that Ron's harsh reactions were indeed related to the separation and the birth and that they were a painful repetition of the traumatic experience related to the birth of his young brother.

In the sessions with the parents, the period of the birth of Ron's brother was becoming clearer. Mother described her great joy with the birth of the brother and how she found it difficult to remember her motherhood toward Ron. With excitement and pain she said, "Actually I think I behaved as though I had only one baby." In addition she recalled that immediately after the birth Ron became ill and was hospitalized for a month; Father remembered that it was during this period that Ron stopped talking. In these conversations, Mother understood the meaning of the wish for another baby and the need to be a meaningful and competent mother for a baby, what she had not experienced in her motherhood to Ron. And thus the birth of another child led to her total dedication to his rearing at the price of Ron's abandonment. It was now clear that the therapy room became a symbolic space to the reconstructed occurrence of abandonment and renouncement. This insight led the mother to "struggle" for the relationship with Ron despite the great difficulty roused in the joint sessions with him. The therapist, in her supervision sessions, also reported difficulty in deciding the appropriate way to help Ron. She needed to help him with a very early traumatic experience and also enable a special opportunity to meet an object who does not give up on him, is not ruined, and with that, renouncing a representation of a bad, ruined, and abandoned self. The therapist's repeated mirroring and reconstructing his difficulties as an angry and helpless baby (with the cooperation of the parents) turned out to be useful. Ron calmed down, and the sessions in the room had a new quality.

The joint activity with Mother in this period was characterized by symbolic play in which Ron was a baby, toddler, or child. In the play, Mother succeeded in the role of a competent mother in the face of "challenges" that Ron sets to her in the play, such as expression of wishes, conflict formation, limit checking, and so forth.

With Father, themes of competition, rivalry, and identification were brought up in the dyadic sessions. In the varied activity, it appeared as if Ron was expressing a wish for a strong, present, and attuned father. Father, on his part, managed to stay with Ron in these activities without being hurt, withdrawing, and giving up.

Ron's emotional repertoire is expanding; he is more able to remain in contact even when it is hard and frustrating, he trusts others, and he now can express feelings of anger and disappointment and transfer his experiences into clear words. The therapist feels that her role in the room is narrowing. The parents and Ron need her less as a mediator and translator of their relations. The child is clearer to them, and they perceived themselves as more competent and understanding parents. Ron is starting to show interest in activities outside the family home, such as visiting friends and taking part in recreational activities. In the intellectual area, there is also a sense of development.

In the ending session, Ron said to the therapist, "Now we do not need you anymore to speak, but if there will ever be things we will not know to say, we can come again, right?" In this manner, Ron expressed his own and his parents sense of competence to cope with future dilemmas and conflicts, as well as the security that relations continue to exist. He felt able now and will be able in the future to act, to get help when needed, and ensure that his voice will be heard.

After termination of the dyadic sessions, the parents continued their sessions with the therapist for a number of months. They asked to continue therapy on their own initiative, wishing to deepen their understanding of Ron.

Discussion

In this family, the therapist felt that there was an urgent need for hope. The therapist's focus on the wish for relatedness and understanding in the dyads, which she believed all of the partners latently shared, introduced the needed hope that was missing in the family. The supporting matrix for the parents in the secure therapeutic environment enhanced and validated their parental roles so they were enabled to consolidate the "motherhood constellation" (Stern 1995), which was weak and unstable. This was an essential step enabling the process of Ron's recovery.

The main task of the therapist in the first phase of therapy was to establish a therapeutic alliance with the parents in order to maintain the setting and the process. The therapist shared with the dyads the helplessness, the silences, the avoidance of relatedness, and the anxiety in the sessions' ambiance. She, like each of the other partners, experienced a threatening and silent chaos, which had characterized this family's life since Ron's birth. This chaos evolved due to Ron's sensitivity expressed by regulatory problems and his difficulty in achieving normal functional rhythms, in addition to the parents' difficulties in giving him the "holding" and the sense of "going on being" (Winnicott 1965) he needed so much.

In order to "hold" the dyads and to give meaning to what was emerging in the therapy room, the therapist worked hard to preserve her ability to be "the doorkeeper of mentalization" (Watillon 1993), a stance the parents failed to maintain in their parenthood with Ron. By attributing meaning to what was happening at the behavioral and experiential levels, she helped them be held together, in the context of the shared meanings that were evolving.

Most of the interventions were meant to focus, emphasize, and make clear both Ron's and each of his parents' mental states (Bleiberg et al. 1997). Behaviors and verbalization were repeatedly translated in terms of wishes, feelings, and attitudes. Ron's restlessness, fragmented speech, and high anxiety, which led his parents to withdraw in silence at the beginning of therapy, received meaning and organization.

Ron, who had been only vaguely perceived by his parents, has gradually begun to exist in the sessions as a subject, initially in the mind of the therapist only (which seemed to the parents at the beginning as mysterious and fantastic) and only later in his mother's and father's minds as well.

For many months it was only the therapist who was responsible for the translation, mediation, and making sense of the mental states of each partner for the self and for the other. These interventions have brought Ron and each of his parents to a gradual acknowledgment of the fact that beyond the observable interactions, which were conceived and experienced as detached and meaningless, are also wishes and hope they can share.

Simultaneously, in the regular joint sessions with the parents' dyad, an understanding of their inner worlds, their childhood experiences, and relationships and the connections between these and their parenting patterns were emerging. The reactions of both parents to Ron's difficulties were contaminated by the hurt and pain they had experienced as children and later on as adults. The mother, brought up as a lonely and sad child by a depressed mother, reacted to her son in the same way she behaved with her mother as a child. She used defense mechanisms of detachment, intellectualization, and doing, which helped isolate herself from the pain and the helplessness that parenting Ron aroused in her. There was no pain in her referral to therapy, and there was no identification with her child's distress. There was only a wish to repair his language functioning. In the sessions, her dismissing behavior (Fonagy and Target 1998) was marked by denial of Ron's pain when he hurt his knee or when she suddenly left the room, saying on her return, "I didn't think he would care if I leave." Ron couldn't have found himself in the mind of his mother as a thinking, feeling, and believing entity (Fonagy and Target 1998), so only after hearing what the therapist had been thinking of him was he able to begin to have a reflective self-representation.

The father, who was physically abused and rejected as a child, was also using detachment and isolation as a way of coping with stressful emotional situations. He was uninvolved in the raising of his children, and during the first phase of therapy, he was overwhelmed by helplessness and pain, which led him sometimes to sleep in the session or at other times to outbursts of frustration.

It is important to emphasize that despite this difficult emotional picture, the parents had a positive and trusting attitude that they were able to enlist on behalf of the work for their son. This was the ground on which the secure relationship with the therapist was built and which allowed the working through of the evoked intersubjective themes. Thus, the therapeutic stance of focusing verbally on mental and affective or physical states of both the parent and the child enabled with time the beginning of communication and mutual coconstruction of intersubjective situations. The therapist's continual translation of intrapsychic and dyadic intersubjective experiences and the use of herself as a subject have set meaningful processes in motion.

A beginning sense of continuity and control, necessary for the emergent sense of self and a stronger sense of being an agent for himself (Stern 1985), have become apparent in Ron's experience. Gradually, the parents were able to see Ron in a more realistic way and to reflect upon his and their own subjectivity. Most important was their emergent ability to perceive themselves as more meaningful to him.

A mutative process occurred through the creation of personal stories. Therapy served as a "container" in which personal and familial experiences were collected and kept. The written experiences were processed and consolidated into a stable and coherent narrative, which enabled the gradual construction of Ron's sense of self-history (Stern 1985), as well as a rehabilitation of his sense of existential continuity (Winnicott 1965). The story writing modeled for the parents a useful way of reflecting upon various mental contents that would have been left meaningless unless written and collected. The therapist acted as if repeatedly saying, "There is meaning; there is a sense, and I see that Ron and each of his parents are acting as thinking and feeling people." This therapeutic stance acted as a parallel process to other interventions that were validating the existence of a mind.

Gradually, the chaos was replaced by organization. Mental functions such as memory and symbolization became more available and more stable. Ron's sense of self and his relations to others were more stably organized. The anxieties that were still evoked in stressful situations did not lead to his disintegration or to his parents' detachment from him as before. Ron has become able to express his fantasy world more spontaneously, in the presence of his parents. His impulses, which were processed emotionally and translated in the context of the relationships, did not end in a sense of destruction or to a feeling of abandonment and loss as before. His reenactment in therapy of the traumatic experience of his brother's birth was met now by the new, acquired reflective stance of the parents, which enabled him to cope emotionally instead of reacting somatically as he had done originally.

The meaningful change in Ron's functioning was paralleled by the changes that his parents experienced in their awareness and perception of him, as well as in their perception of themselves as people in general and as parents in particular. From being helpless parents and emotionally "mute" people, they could now see him not as a "strange" child anymore but rather as a child who needs them as parents and to experience themselves as having more competent parental resources. They managed to survive Ron's attacks, allowing him to use them as developmental objects (Winnicott 1971).

The working through of their painful childhood relational experiences with a trustful and empathic therapist, whom they delegated the role of the "connecting thread"—as they put it—connecting them and their son and connecting them to their inner world, to their childhood experiences, and to their independence as parents, enabled Ron to be gradually released from their projections and distortions, liberated to begin his journey as an autonomous agent of himself.

The unique characteristics of this model of mother-child and father-child psychotherapy played a crucial role in the dramatic change of Ron's functioning. In this therapy setting they could experience the mutual and sustained mental involvement of Ron, his parents, and the therapist, without the threat of overwhelming mental pain and destructiveness. We believe this experience enabled the freedom of Ron's inhibited mental functioning.

REFERENCES

Altman, N., R. Briggs, J. Frankel, D. Gensler, and P. Pantone. 2002. *Relational child psychotherapy*. New York: Other Press.

Alvarez, A. 1992. *Live company: Psychoanalytic psychotherapy with autistic, border-line, deprived and abused children*. London: Routledge.

Baron-Cohen, S. 1995. *Mindblindness: An essay on autism and theory of mind*. Cambridge, Mass.: MIT Press.

Barrows, P. 1997. Parent-infant psychotherapy: A review article. *Journal of Child Psychotherapy* 23:255–64.

Beeghly, M., I. Bretherton, and C. B. Mervis. 1986. Mother's internal state language to toddlers. *British Journal of Developmental Psychology* 4:247–61.

Ben-Aaron, M., J. Harel, H. Kaplan, and R. Patt. 2001. *Mother-child and father-child psychotherapy: A manual for the treatment of relational disturbances in childhood*. London: Whurr Publishers.

Bion, W. R. 1962. A theory of thinking. *International Journal of Psychoanalysis* 43:306–10.

Bleiberg, E. 2000. Borderline personality disorder in children and adolescents. In *The borderline psychotic child: A selective integration*, ed. T. Lubbe, 39–68. London: Routledge.

Bleiberg, E., P. Fonagy, and M. Target 1997. Child psychoanalysis: Critical overview and a proposed reconsideration. *Child and Adolescent Psychiatric Clinics of North America* 6:1–38.

Bollas, C. 1987. *The shadow of the object*. New York: Columbia University Press.

Bowlby, J. 1979. *The making and breaking of affectional bonds*. London: Tavistock.

Britton, R. 1998. Naming and containing. In *Belief and imagination: Explorations in psychoanalysis*, ed. E. B. Sphillius, chapter 2. New Library of Psychoanalysis. London: Routledge.

Coates, S. W. 1998. Having a mind of one's own and holding the other in mind. Commentary on paper by P. Fonagy and M. Target. *Psychoanalytic Dialogues* 8:115–48.

Crittenden, P. M. 1992. Treatment of anxious attachment in infancy and early childhood. *Development and Psychopathology* 4:575–602.

Fonagy, P. 2001. Changing ideas of change: The dual components of therapeutic action. In *Being alive: Building on the work of Anne Alvarez*, ed. J. Edwards, 14–31. Hove, UK: Brunner-Routledge.

Fonagy, P., R. Edgcumbe, G. S. Moran, H. Kennedy, and M. Target. 1993. The roles of mental representations and mental processes in therapeutic action. *Psychoanalytic Study of the Child* 48:9–48.

Fonagy, P., G. Gergely, E. Jurist, and M. Target. 2002. *Affect regulation and mentalization: Developmental, clinical, and theoretical perspectives*. New York: Other Press.

Fonagy, P., H. Steele, M. Steele, G. Moran, and A. Higgit. 1991. The capacity for understanding mental states: The reflective self in parent and child and its significance for security of attachment. *Infant Mental Health Journal* 12:201–17.

Fonagy, P., and M. Target. 1996. Playing with reality. Part I: Theory of mind and the normal development of psychic reality. *International Journal of Psychoanalysis* 77:217–33.

———. 1997. Attachment and reflective function: Their role in self-organization. *Development and Psychopathology* 9:679–900.

———. 1998. Mentalization and the changing aims of child psychoanalysis. *Psychoanalytic Dialogues* 8:87–114.

———. 2001. The historical background of psychoanalytic psychotherapy for children. In *Mother-child and father-child psychotherapy: A manual for the treatment of relational disturbances in childhood*, ed. M. Ben-Aaron, J. Harel, H. Kaplan, and R. Pratt. London: Whurr Publishers.

———. 2003. *Psychoanalytic theories: Perspectives from developmental psychopathology.* London: Whurr Publishers.

Fonagy, P., M. Target, H. Steele, and M. Steele. 1998. *Reflective-functioning manual* (version 5). London: University College.

Fraiberg, S., E. Adelson, and V. Shapiro. 1975. Ghosts in the nursery: A psychoanalytic approach to the problem of impaired infant-mother relationships. *Journal of the American Academy of Child Psychiatry* 14:387–422.

Gergely, G., and J. Watson. 1996. The social biofeedback theory of parental affect mirroring: The development of emotional self-awareness and self-control in infancy. *International Journal of Psychoanalysis* 77:1181–1212.

Harel, J. G., Y. Eshel, A. Penso, D. Muchtar, and M. Ben-Aaron. 2003. Relational themes in mother-child and father-child dyads of 5-year-old children: Contextual aspects. Presentation at the Fourth Joseph Sandler Research Conference, University College, London, March 7–9.

Harel, J., G. Gamzon-Kapeller, and Y. Eshel. 2002. Mothers of secure infants use more internal state language. Poster presented at the International Conference on Infant Studies, Toronto, April 18–21.

Hopkins, J. 1992. Infant-parent psychotherapy. *Journal of Child Psychotherapy* 18:5–18.

Hurry, A. 1998. *Psychoanalysis and developmental therapy.* London: Karnac Books.

Lyons-Ruth, K. 1998. Implicit relational knowing: Its role in development and psychoanalytic treatment. *Infant Mental Health Journal* 19:282–89.

———. 1999. The two person unconscious: Intersubjective dialogue, enactive relational representation and the emergence of new forms of relational organization. *Psychoanalytic Inquiry* 19(4):576–617.

Main, M., and J. Cassidy. 1998. Adult attachment scoring and classification system. Unpublished manuscript. University of California at Berkley.

McLaughlin, J. 1991. Clinical and theoretical aspects of enactment. *Journal of the American Psychoanalytic Association* 39:595–614.

Meins, E., C. Fernyhough, R. Wainwright, M. Gupta, E. Fradley, and M. Tuckey. 2002. Maternal mind-mindedness and attachment security as predictors of theory of mind understanding. *Child Development* 73:1715–26.

Mitchell, S. A. 1988. *Relational concepts in psychoanalysis*. Cambridge, Mass.: Harvard University Press.

Mitrani, J. 1996. *A framework for the imaginary*. Northvale, N.J.: Jason Aronson.

Moran, G. S. 1987. Some functions of play and playfulness: A developmental perspective. *Psychoanalytic Study of the Child* 42:11–29.

Morton, J., and U. Frith. 1995. Causal modeling: A structural approach to developmental psychology. In *Developmental psychopathology. Vol. I: Theory and methods*, ed. D. Cichetti and D. J. Cohen, 357–90. New York: John Wiley.

Sandler, J. 1976. Countertransference and role responsiveness. *International Review of Psychoanalysis* 3:7–43.

Seligman, S. 1999. Integrating Kleinian theory and intersubjective infant research: Observing projective identification. *Psychoanalytic Dialogues* 9:129–59.

Slade, A., J. Grienenberger, E. Bernbach, D. Levy, and A. Locker. 2001. Maternal reflective functioning and attachment: Considering the attachment gap. Paper presented at the Biennial Meetings of the Society for Research in Child Development, Minneapolis, April 22.

Stern, D. 1985. *The interpersonal world of the infant*. New York: Basic Books.

———. 1995. *The motherhood constellation: A unified view of parent-infant psychotherapy*. New York: Basic Books.

Stern, D., L. Sander, J. Nahum, A. Harrison, K. Lyons-Ruth, A. Morgan, N. Bruschweiler-Stern, and E. Tronick. 1998. Non-interpretive mechanisms in psychoanalytic therapy: The "something more" than interpretation. *International Journal of Psychoanalysis* 79(5):903–21.

Target, M., and P. Fonagy. 1996. Playing with reality. Part II: The development of psychic reality from a theoretical perspective. *International Journal of Psychoanalysis* 77:459–79.

Van IJzendoorn, M. H. 1995. Adult attachment representations, parental responsiveness, and infant attachment: A meta-analysis of the predictive validity of the AAI. *Psychological Bulletin* 117:387–403.

Van IJzendoorn, M. H., A. Sagi, and M. W. Lambermon. 1992. The multiple caretaker paradox: Some data from Holland and Israel. In *Relationships between children and nonparental adults (New directions in child development 57)*, ed. R. C. Pianta, 5–24. San Francisco: Jossey-Bass.

Warshaw, S. 1992. Mutative factors in child psychoanalysis: A comparison of diverse relational perspectives. In *Relational perspectives in psychoanalysis*, ed. N. Skolnick and S. Warshaw, 147–73. Hillsdale, N.J.: Analytic Press.

Watillon, A. 1993. The dynamics of psychoanalytic therapies of the early parent-child relationship. *International Journal of Psychoanalysis* 74:1037–48.

Winnicott, D. W. 1965. *The maturational processes and the facilitating environment*. New York: International Universities Press.

———. 1971. *Playing and reality*. New York: Basic Books.

13

Representation, Symbolization, and Affect Regulation in the Concomitant Treatment of a Mother and Child

Arietta Slade

Editor's Note: This chapter originally contained material on the concomitant treatment of mother and child in which the mother and the child were seen individually. However, in keeping with the theme of this book, we have focused on Dr. Slade's work with the parent.

REPRESENTATIONAL PROCESSES IN ATTACHMENT THEORY AND RESEARCH: ADULT ATTACHMENT REPRESENTATIONS

The story of attachment theory begins with John Bowlby (1969, 1973, 1980, 1988); the story of attachment research begins with Mary Ainsworth (Ainsworth et al. 1978), who described three major patterns of infant attachment: the secure, insecure-avoidant, and insecure-resistant patterns. These three modes of responding to separation and reunion were seen by Ainsworth as organized and motivated patterns of attachment that emerged as a function of the history of the mother-child relationship. When mothers were responsive to children's needs for comfort and security, able to provide the child with what Ainsworth referred to as a "secure base," such needs were expressed easily and openly; when mothers ignored, rejected, or somehow distorted their children's needs, children developed less functional and adaptive means of communicating their needs to their parents when distressed and seeking comfort (see also Belsky and Cassidy 1994;

This chapter was originally published in *Psychoanalytic Inquiry* 19(1999):797–830. Copyright of The Analytic Press and adapted with permission.

Karen 1997). In the decades since Ainsworth published her original research, secure attachment in infancy has been found by scores of researchers to provide a kind of "protective factor" in later development and has been linked to a wide range of social skills and positive socioemotional development (Belsky and Cassidy 1994). From a clinical perspective, secure children have established resilient and flexible emotional relationships with their primary love objects; preoedipal development proceeds smoothly from a core sense of self and of security in basic relationships (Slade 1996).

Mary Main (Main, Kaplan, and Cassidy 1985) set the stage for the next revolution in attachment research by introducing the theoretical constructs and measures that have become central to the "representational era" in attachment research. On the basis of mothers' and fathers' narrative descriptions of their experience of early relationships (George, Kaplan, and Main 1985), Main was able to discern three patterns of adult attachment: the secure-autonomous pattern, the dismissing pattern, and the preoccupied pattern (Main, Kaplan, and Cassidy 1985). She described a fourth pattern several years later, which she labeled unresolved in relation to loss or trauma (Main and Hesse 1990). Attachment classification was based on the quality of parental narratives, which were distinguished not by their content or by specific childhood events (loss, rejection, or trauma) but rather by patterns of thinking, remembering, and talking about past relationships. Some parents were able to discuss their childhood experiences openly and to remember in a coherent and affectively vivid way the central emotional events and relationships in their lives, whereas others were either unable to remember early relationships and unable to describe their emotional effects or were quite overwhelmed and preoccupied with the negative effects of early family relationships.

Main discovered that the quality of a mother's narrative description of her own early attachment experiences was strongly associated with her infant's attachment classification (Main, Kaplan, and Cassidy 1985); this was later replicated by a number of researchers (Fonagy, Steele, and Steele 1991; Zeanah et al. 1993; Benoit and Parker 1994; Ward and Carlson 1995). Meta-analytic studies have also confirmed this link (Van IJzendoorn 1995; Van IJzendoorn and Bakermans-Kranenburg 1996). Mothers who were flexible and balanced in their capacity to remember and describe early attachment experiences and the feelings attendant to these experiences were likely to have children who were freely able to express their needs for comfort and nurture following separation and to seek proximity upon reunion. Mothers who were either guarded against the memory and power of early childhood experience (the dismissing pattern) or who had remained overwhelmed by such memories and feelings (the preoccupied pattern) had children who disguised their needs for comfort or became so overcome by their distress that they were unable to separate or explore.

REPRESENTATIONAL PROCESSES IN ATTACHMENT THEORY AND RESEARCH: PARENTAL REPRESENTATIONS OF THE CHILD

Thus, the first wave of research in the "representational era" emphasized the powerful relationship between the quality of a mother's representation of her own early attachment experiences and the quality or security of her own child's attachment. Recent research suggests that a second emergent representational system may well play an equally important role in determining the parent's response to the child and the child's subsequent security, namely, the mother's representation of her relationship with her child (Zeanah et al. 1995; Stern 1995; George and Solomon 1996; Slade and Lieberman 1997). As has been well described by psychoanalysts, especially Benedek (1959), Bibring (Bibring et al. 1961), Stern (1995), and Winnicott (1965), mothers (and fathers) begin developing representations of their children early in pregnancy. These representations become increasingly complex and textured over the course of development and reflect an amalgam of parents' perceptions and fantasies about who the children are, how they function, and what they feel. Naturally, such representations include conscious, preconscious, and unconscious aspects and are powerfully affected by the parent's own early object relationships and attachment experiences. These representations of the child and complementary representations of the self as parent are a critical and fundamental aspect of the parent-child relationship and, indeed, may function as a means of regulating his or her response to the child (Lieberman 1997; Slade and Cohen 1996; Solomon and George 1996).

During pregnancy, such representations are based almost entirely upon fantasy because little is actually known about the baby (except, perhaps, the gender and the parents' own interpretations of the child's activity level). Here, perhaps more than at any time during the child's life, the parent's representations of past relationships are creating a template of expectations. However, once babies are born, their actual characteristics, as well as the feelings they actually generate, are increasingly incorporated into the parents' representation of the child and into their representation of themselves as parents. Recent research suggests that parental representations of the child are linked to the parents' own attachment representations; thus, a secure mother is most likely to have a balanced, coherent, and flexible representation of the child and to conceive of herself as providing a secure base for the child, whereas insecure mothers see their children in either limited or distorted ways and represent themselves as detached from their children or as helpless to engage with and contain them (Zeanah et al. 1995; George and Solomon 1996). Security and balance in the parents' representation of the child have also been found to predict the quality of infant attachment

(Zeanah et al. 1995; George and Solomon 1996). Preliminary research evidence indicates that the mother's representation of her relationship with her child may be as important a factor in determining maternal sensitivity as is her representation of her relationship with her own parents (Slade et al. 1999). These findings provide empirical support for analytic notions regarding the importance of understanding the impact of maternal fantasies and projections upon the relationship with the individual child; as much as these may be tied to an individual woman's early history, the way in which these are transformed and reborn in relation to the child are of vital clinical significance (Lieberman 1997).

METACOGNITION, MENTALIZATION, AND THE MOTHER-CHILD RELATIONSHIP

Taken together, the research findings described above make evident the link between the quality and coherence of parental narratives and the child's capacities for affect regulation and symbolization. The clinical ramifications of this link are extensive and will be addressed below. First, however, let us turn to an examination of the mechanisms believed by attachment theorists to account for the relationship between adult and child representational processes, namely, metacognitive monitoring, reflective functioning, and mentalization. Mary Main (1991) was the first attachment theorist to consider attachment processes in light of the capacity for what she termed "metacognitive monitoring." This refers to the individual's capacity to "step back and consider his or her own cognitive processes as objects of thought or reflection" (35). In Main's view, the clarity and coherence of an adult's attachment representations reflect the capacity to think about one's thinking and to—as a consequence—represent the complexity of emotion and memory without distortion. A "secure" representation, in Main's terms, is based upon a "singular" model of attachment; in such a model, both negative and positive aspects of current or past attachment relationships are integrated into an internally consistent, believable, succinct, emotionally real, and coherent representation of attachment (Main 1991). Narrative clarity and emotional "truth" reflect the relative absence of defensive attempts to keep intolerable affects and memories at bay; attachment memories and thoughts, along with naturally occurring inconsistencies and contradictions, can be considered and reflected upon (Main 1995a, 1995b).

Bowlby (1988) suggested that, when children are traumatized, neglected, or in some way hurt by their parents, they form multiple and inherently contradictory models of *the same reality*. Main (1991) suggests that such multiple models are typical of the "insecure" models of adult attachment and stem from early failures to integrate contradictory and painful information into attachment representations. Thus, unintegrated and sometimes unacknowledged "knowledge" remains unmetabolized and distinct in consciousness from more idealized or banal descriptions of the relationship. These are evidenced linguistically in disruptions in the narrative and other linguistic inconsistencies such as logical and factual contradictions, losing track of the narrative, slips of the tongue, anomalous intrusions into the narrative, and so on (Main 1991). Insecure models also compromise parents' ability to respond to their children's attachment needs in a sensitive way. Children's longing for comfort, their need to be held and safe, and their fears and anger are intolerably evocative and painful to a parent who has had to deny such feelings in her own early relationships, for they threaten to make the parent feel what they struggle not to feel and remember what they struggle to forget. The affect evoked by children's needs and demands will lead insecure parents to respond to manifestations of their children's need by either turning away from and minimizing their children's emotional expression or by heightening or maximizing them to diminish their own fears of loss and abandonment (Cassidy 1994; Cassidy and Berlin 1994; Main 1995a, 1995b). In either case, basic emotional reactions, thoughts, and memories must be denied in order for the child to maintain his connection to the caregiver; this begins the cycle of multiple models and insecure attachment representations in the child.

Peter Fonagy and his colleagues (Fonagy, Steele, and Steele 1991; Fonagy et al. 1995; Fonagy and Target 1998) suggest that above and beyond signaling the adult's capacity to think about her thinking, metacognitive monitoring indicates the capacity to reflect on internal, particularly affective, experience in a complex and dynamic fashion. He describes this as the "reflective function," the capacity to *reflect* on internal experience; to know, imagine, and represent inner life and mental states in the self; and to recognize and represent these same states in others. For Fonagy, reflective functioning is vital to making sense of the personal and interpersonal universe: making sense of one's own feelings and behavior and making sense of others' behavior and motivations. It is how we come to label and regulate our own affective experience and how we come to know what goes on in others' minds. As such, it may well provide protection against the damaging effects of abuse and trauma (Fonagy et al. 1995).

Fonagy views the reflective function as an "intrapsychic and interpersonal achievement that emerges fully only in the context of a secure attachment relationship." In insecure relationships, it is, along with other high-level cognitive processes, "subject to the vicissitudes of conflict and anxiety and consequent defensive disruption" (Fonagy et al. 1995, 251). A secure mother will be able to make sense of and make known her child's internal experience, *as a function* of her capacity to reflect upon her own affective experience. The child is thus able to "find himself in the other as a mentalizing individual" (257). Mothers' recognition of children's desires, feelings, and intentions allows children to see themselves as thinking, feeling, and believing. Indeed, Fonagy reports that mothers and fathers rated high in reflective functioning were more likely to have children who were secure.

A mother's capacity for reflective functioning and metacognitive monitoring is necessarily linked to her capacity to regulate, modulate, and ultimately symbolize affective experience, which will in turn allow her to contain and bind her infant's affect expression. Because emotions and their exigencies are familiar and known to her, she can recognize and respond to them as coherent, organized, and meaningful communications. By contrast, mothers who are insecure may well have more difficulty symbolizing experience for their children and making sense of their children's communications, both because they have found it difficult to make sense of and integrate their own emotional experience and because they are disregulated by their child's emotions. Dismissive parents appear to be unable to symbolize or acknowledge their children's dependency needs, desire for comfort, or anger; these feelings are thus not represented or known to the self and therefore cannot be represented in the relationship with the child. Preoccupied mothers seem to acknowledge and symbolize their own negative affects in the extreme, although such acknowledgment is highly enactive (Diamond and Blatt 1994) in that it stimulates feeling and memory, rather than creating a bounded symbolic context for such feeling and memory. Maternal failures to bind or contain the infant's affective experience thus lead to infant failures of regulation and integration.

Taken together, the research findings presented in the preceding sections, coupled with the theoretical advances in understanding metacognitive monitoring and reflective functioning described above, make it evident that mothers who are able to reflect on their own attachment experiences and on their developing relationship with the child (to tolerate and regulate their own affective experience and to express their experience in ways that are at once coherent and verbally mediated) are more likely to have children who have begun to regulate and contain their own affective experience, who can express the range of their needs and feelings in clear and meaningful ways, who have begun to be aware of their own and others' mental states, and who rely upon increasingly symbolic forms of self-expression as they enter middle childhood.

These findings have a direct bearing on a conceptualization of the aims of child psychoanalysis. Fonagy and Target (1998) suggest that child analysis, and particularly the activity of playing with a therapist or analyst who provides a secure base for the child's mind, implicitly affirms and recognizes the child as a "mentalizing" being, and leads to shifts in the capacity to use awareness of his or her own and other people's thoughts and feelings. In children, the mentalizing capacity is "crucially linked with children's ability to label and find meaningful their own psychic experiences, an ability which underlies the capacities for affect regulation, impulse control, self-monitoring, and the experience of self-agency" (92). However, as will be described in the sections that follow, because children's representations of themselves and of their inner experiences must be seen as a direct function of their parents' capacity to represent and imagine their minds, and thus provide a secure base for them as "mentalizing beings," understanding the interface of children's minds with the minds of their attachment figures is necessarily a central focus to the therapeutic or analytic process. And in many instances, understanding and ultimately transforming the parent's conception of the child and of the child's mind and separating such awareness from projections and distortions will be central to the child's progress (see also Stern 1995).

It is this conception of a link between the mother's capacity to recognize and represent her child and the child's recognition of himself or herself as a thinking and feeling person that is at the heart of this chapter and that guided the "concomitant" work described in this chapter, which began as dyadic, mother-infant psychotherapy. From its inception in the late 1960s, when first introduced by Margaret Mahler (1968) in her work with psychotic children and their mothers, and its later development by Selma Fraiberg (1980), dyadic or (with infants and toddlers) infant-parent psychotherapy (Stern-Bruschweiler and Stern 1989; Lieberman 1992; Lieberman and Pawl 1993; Stern 1995) has assumed that change in the child depends upon change in the mother's representation of the child, as well as her representation of their relationship. In the work that is described here, that notion is expanded to encompass what becomes an individual child treatment, concomitant with ongoing individual work with the mother, focused specifically upon the mother's representation of the child and of herself in relation to attachment. Since Anna Freud (1965) and her colleagues introduced what was to become the "child guidance" model of child psychotherapy, virtually all child treatments have included ancillary work with parents. Indeed, Bowlby himself suggested in 1940 that a "weekly interview in which . . . problems are approached analytically and traced back to childhood has sometimes been remarkably effective" for mothers who are struggling in relationship to their children (23). However, the aims of such ancillary work were usually loosely, if not poorly, defined and often included "education" of parents, keeping the therapist abreast of events in the child's life, developing in the parents a better understanding of the child, and—occasionally—working toward developing the parents' capacity to understand the genesis of their own neurotic and distorting responses to the child. Typically, however, the latter kinds of interpretive and insight-oriented work have been relegated to a separate venue, namely, the parents' own individual and, hence, separate psychotherapy. As will be described here, the work with Michael and Julie reflected my attempt to adapt the principles of infant-parent psychotherapy and attachment theory to the treatment of an older child, for whom dyadic work was no longer appropriate. (See also Oram 2000.)

This work is best described in terms of three phases: the consultation and evaluation phase (two months), the dyadic phase (four months), and the phase of concomitant individual work with Michael and Julie (ongoing, over two years).

REPRESENTATION, SYMBOLIZATION, AND PSYCHOTHERAPY: MICHAEL AND JULIE

The Evaluation Phase

Michael had just turned three when his parents came to see me in consultation. They were referred for evaluation by the child's pediatrician because of excessive and unremitting temper tantrums, extreme demandingness, and separation anxiety. The developmental history suggested that, from the beginning, Michael had few resources for regulating his affective experiences; his mother reported that, from his first days in the hospital, he was awake for long periods of time and was soothed only by nursing. His unremitting crying, wakefulness, and irritability did not diminish over time; by the time he was a year old, he was having full-blown temper tantrums that would last for an hour or two. He was a very poor sleeper, often waking up as many as seven or eight times a night during his infancy. He was also hypersensitive to smells, tastes, and sounds and would react very negatively to any that seemed unpleasant to him. At the time of the evaluation, his regulatory upsets were quite extreme: his anger and anxiety would escalate rapidly and intensely and would last for a very long time. These tantrums were very difficult to curtail, and even Michael himself would sometimes cry, "I can't stop! I can't stop!" When his mother would try to hold or physically contain him, he would scream at her, "Don't touch me! You're not fair! You're mean! You're going to hurt me!" Michael's emerging sense of his own "badness" and differentness was already beginning to crystallize: he knew there was something wrong; he knew he had a problem that made his and others' lives very painful, and he didn't know why or what it was. Too young to understand the trouble as anything but the totality of who he was, he incorporated the badness into his sense of himself.

Michael lived with his mother, Julie, his father, Andy, and his sister, Lucy, who was twenty-five months his junior. Andy worked long hours as an engineer, and Julie—who herself had professional training as a respiratory therapist—stayed home with the children full time. She worked one day a week at a local hospital and went out one evening a week for choir practice. During these times, Michael and Lucy were cared for by her mother, who lived nearby, or by Andy. Michael found these infrequent separations nearly intolerable; he would anticipate them anxiously for days and would beg her not to leave. When home with his father, he would cry bitterly as he awaited his mother's return. His efforts to control Julie naturally extended beyond separation; he worked to command her attention and do his bidding throughout the day, especially when she was involved in caring for Lucy. If she resisted any of his efforts to control her or refused any of his wishes, his tantrums were unrelenting. Unsurprisingly, he was unable to tolerate playdates or family gatherings and would rapidly spiral out of control in these situations.

When I met him, Michael was an adorable, compact, and extremely neat little boy who assiduously avoided eye contact with me and who moved from the waiting room to the playroom in such a wide arc as to avoid any physical proximity to me. In the playroom, he shrank away and looked furtively to his mother if I spoke to him; I had to keep a distance of at least five feet, or he would immediately become anxious and move to his mother's side. His tremendous dependency upon her manifested itself in other ways as well: he was extremely reticent to explore the room and asked his mother to take the toys that interested him out of the cabinet. When I asked a question of him, he would direct her to answer it and avoid looking at me. He initiated games in a weak and tentative way and needed her active involvement and initiation to carry the game forward. His play was fairly ritualistic; for the most part he simply lined up figures and animals and was intensely interested in their clothes and other accessories. He would become fixed on details, such as the Playmobil® catalog, the number and placement of weapons on a figure, and so on. At this point, he had no words for his play. His affect was somber, and only rarely did he smile, except in occasional moments of playful exchange with his mother.

In describing Michael diagnostically, it is important to address the various substrates of his functioning. Basic to any discussion of his diagnosis is a severe regulatory disturbance; Michael's capacity for affect regulation and containment were remarkably limited, even for a three-year-old (Zero to Three 1994). Like many hypersensitive (Greenspan 1995) or difficult children (Turecki and Tonner 1989; Lieberman 1994), he was tremendously reactive to shifts in both external and internal stimulation. Concomitant to this biological vulnerability (and likely as a consequence of it), he manifested symptoms of a severe anxiety disorder; this included separation and other forms of generalized anxiety. From the perspective of psychoanalytic developmental theory (Freud 1965; Mahler, Pine, and Bergman 1975), Michael would be seen as a child whose progress along any number of developmental lines was severely impeded: he was functioning like a tormented rapprochement-age child, with no friends, constricted affect, poorly developed symbolic play, and few resources for coping with his emotions; there was little evidence of more mature oedipal development.

From the perspective of attachment theory, Michael would be character-ized as insecure in his attachment to his mother; because of his inability to derive comfort from the soothing and contact he so desperately and contin-uously sought, he would be classified as insecure/resistant in his attach-ment. Michael's attachment to his father was less tormented, certainly, but it nevertheless felt rather tenuous and unsatisfying; his mother was the center of his universe, and his father was a temporary and disappointing substitute. In terms of conceptualizing the relation between his underlying biological disturbance and his attachment security, I saw Michael as a child who had particular difficulties feeling safe and deriving comfort from his caregivers because of the extent of his biologically driven anxiety and disregulation. That is, his capacity to develop a secure attachment to his mother might well have been compromised even under the best of circumstances by his hyper-sensitivity and overarousal. Of course, it is also possible that his biological vulnerabilities had the long-lasting effects they did because his mother found it so difficult to regulate his affective experience or provide both a sense of security and a bridge to autonomy and separateness (Schore 1994; Van den Boom 1994; Belsky, Hsieh, and Crnic 1998).

When I met Julie during the evaluation phase, she was the consummate "historian," providing clear and highly detailed descriptions of Michael's early years, of his disregulation, and her inability to regulate him. An attrac-tive, athletic, and lively woman with a direct and somewhat prickly demeanor, Julie tried hard to minimize the sense of desperation and loss of control that lay beneath her every word. Contained and highly organized in her everyday life, the situation with Michael was quite intolerable to her. She described herself as frustrated and despairing, unable to calm him, unable to understand him, and unable to come to grips with what she realized was a very serious problem. And she was very worried and pained for Michael, whose suffering was quite tangible for her.

Andy, a quiet, passive, and gentle man, provided a vivid contrast to Julie. Although clearly worried about Michael and quite able to talk and think about the situation in an intelligent and thoughtful way, it was evident that he kept himself emotionally and physically detached from the situation. His affect was constricted, and he seemed fairly withdrawn from the emotional exigencies of his life; he found dealing with Michael taxing and difficult and often avoided helping Julie in the evenings, despite realizing that this would be very helpful for both her and Michael. As might be expected, this was a constant source of conflict between them: Julie felt abandoned and unsupported, and Andy felt criticized and unappreciated for what he did do. Although both Julie and Andy participated in the evaluation process, it quickly became clear that I would be working most directly with Julie; this was reinforced numerous times over the course of the treatment when I tried—for the most part unsuc-cessfully—to engage Andy in the work we were doing.

In relation to Michael, Julie seemed most comfortable with the idea that he had a "biological" problem, that he had been born with difficulties in regulation and modulation that left him prone to the kinds of upheavals and tantrums that were disrupting their lives. But she seemed to have little sense of—at a psychological level—what made him tick. She was very sad for him, but she did not understand him. She did not understand why he became disregulated, how her efforts at control made him feel, why he was angry, or why he had so much difficulty with separation: as an emotional being, he was a mystery to her. She had equally little sense of her own feelings; she did not recognize her anger nor could she appreciate the extent of her own rigidity and need to control Michael. She had little understanding of or even interest in her own childhood history: she described her childhood as "fine" and "normal," despite multiple moves, separations, and upheavals. And it was nearly impossible for her to think about the meaning Michael had for her, why she had reacted to him in some of the ways she had, how her history had informed some of her reactions, and so on. Like many parents of disturbed children, Julie harbored the fear that she was somehow responsible for his condition and felt enormous guilt at what she imagined she must have caused. Any exploration of her role in his psychology came too close to these feelings and had to be curtailed. From an attachment perspective, Julie's limited capacity to remember or reflect upon her own childhood attachment experiences, her affective experience, or her current relationships would lead to a classification of "dismissing of attachment." Clearly, her capacity for reflective functioning was also extremely low.

Diagnostically speaking, there was no evidence in Julie of major psychiatric or biological disturbance; however, Andy was diagnosed with a depressive disorder following Michael's evaluation and was placed on Zoloft. In addition, there was a history of severe obsessive-compulsive disorder in his family and evidence of compulsive behavior in his clinical picture. Unfortunately, he declined psychotherapy, despite the fact that both the treating psychiatrist and I strongly encouraged it.

My first meetings with Julie and Andy served as consultation as well as evaluation; I confirmed their sense that this was a biologically disregulated child and emphasized that they had not "created" this level of difficulty by mishandling him. On the other hand, I made it clear that his difficulties could be much better contained if they were able to be more attuned to his needs and feelings and so made a number of concrete suggestions about managing his behavior while remaining sensitive to his feelings. I tried to describe to them what I imagined it felt like to be Michael and what it felt like to live in his skin (a first step in helping mentalize his, as well as their own, experience of him). Julie and Andy were eager to enroll Michael in nursery school, which I discouraged. Nevertheless, Julie was so stressed by the difficulties of caring for him full time and by managing his jealousy of

Lucy that she was determined to give it a try. We agreed that they would try my suggestions, try nursery school, and be back in touch if the need arose.

Dyadic Treatment Phase

About six months later, I received a call from Julie. The nursery school experiment had been a dismal failure—largely because of Michael's separation anxiety—and she was about to withdraw him. Because Michael was unable to separate from his mother and come comfortably to the playroom, I began by treating them dyadically and saw Julie for intermittent individual sessions. Individual sessions with Julie focused on Michael and the upheavals that continued to dominate their daily life. It soon became clear that Julie needed these sessions on a regular basis because we were hampered in the fullness of our discussions by Michael's presence in dyadic sessions. I began meeting with Julie twice a month, in addition to weekly dyadic sessions.

Dyadic sessions began with Michael turned away from me and toward his Mom, as if ignoring me would make me disappear. As long as he could ignore my presence, Michael seemed comfortable and happy with his mother; he giggled, his eyes twinkled, and he molded to her easily. Indeed, given the level of both of their difficulties, it was surprising to see how sensitive and responsive she was in these sessions. They seemed to enjoy each other, and she picked up on cues readily and comfortably. Her voice betrayed little of the anger that she was beginning to openly acknowledge in individual sessions, and she seemed physically comfortable with him and readily available. The only clue to her anger in these sessions was the subtle aggression that would sometimes emerge in her play, when she would playfully wipe out his army. But he seemed to enjoy this and retaliated in kind. He was also enormously sensitive to her attempts to get him to take initiative; as soon as she pushed him to do something on his own, he would move toward her and cling to her. Michael's play was evidently symbolic or imaginary, although he used absolutely no language to set the stage or give voice to the figures he had chosen; occasionally, he would have his characters speak in a kind of modulated gibberish, but otherwise, his play was, for the most part, silent exploration and enactment. Stories and voices, so typical in children his age, were notably absent.

Because of Julie's remarkably limited capacity to reflect on her inner life or on her relationships, I had very little clear sense at the outset of what had gone so wrong between them (other than to speculate on the obvious effects of her emotional distance). So, in our individual sessions, I began by first trying to make Michael's experience meaningful to her—identifying the cycles of regulation and disregulation, the link between his symptomatology and his anxiety, and the cues to his becoming overwhelmed and frightened.

And as he began to make sense to her and she began to be able to represent and understand his experience, she became more sensitive to his affective experience and to the nuances of his biological disregulation. She became more containing and empathic and less abandoning and rigid during his tantrums; she began to recognize the situations that would trigger his distress and try to modify them or at least help him anticipate them. She became, in essence, more of a secure base. During this phase, it was simply not possible to explore the deeper levels of her own feelings about Michael; she could not yet imagine that his difficulties had any connection to her feelings toward him or were in any sense a response to aspects of her inner life that were unconscious or unacknowledged.

It was now a year since Michael had left nursery school, and the child psychiatrist and I felt it was time to try again. Michael had calmed down a great deal at home and was tolerating separation much more easily. As a function of treatment and medication, he was also considerably less angry and controlling, although he and his mother still had their moments of great conflict. Plans were made to begin Michael in a preschool classroom in local private school, where the teachers and staff had been apprised of Michael's difficulties and were willing to work him into the school program at his own pace. Up to this point, my work with Julie had been limited to helping her think about and understand Michael's experience, with the result that she was increasingly sensitive to his fears and the triggers to his becoming overaroused. Nevertheless, the work had not progressed to the deeper level that seemed so very essential to her understanding of why she responded the way she did and why Michael continued to struggle with anger and anxiety; she was still closed and defensive whenever I probed about her own history of separation anxiety and the reasons for her emotional distance and anger.

Finally, nearly two years into my work with this family, as Michael began school and approached his fifth birthday, a remarkable shift occurred in a session with Julie. She had shown signs of increasingly overt anxiety as the date for his beginning school approached. She worried that his classmates would be mean to him, that the teachers wouldn't understand him, that they'd force her to leave the class before Michael was ready, and so on. But none of these fears were being realized: Michael loved school. And Julie was allowed to stay in the classroom. But soon it would be time for her to leave, to let him cope without her, and this was what frightened her. What would happen if he were to fall apart and she were not there to help him? Would he go crazy? Would the teachers know what to do? Would he recover? As he began outlining her many fears of his decompensating should she leave, I said to her, "Now, we are about to encounter your separation anxiety!" The tears began to flow, and finally, after so many months, Julie was able to tell me how, from the day of Michael's birth, she had been afraid of losing him. He was too special to her. From his first moments in the hospital, she felt the nurses took him away from her too quickly and for too long; she was the only one who could care for him. She was exquisitely concerned for his physical well-being, even before his temperamental difficulties became apparent. Once they did, her anger and disappointment became viciously entangled with her fear of losing him. As she told me this, I could finally begin to understand how her fear of losing him, coupled with her anger at his biological vulnerability, made it very difficult for her to regulate his affective experience or facilitate his autonomy. Instead, she and Michael remained enmeshed in an angry dependency.

This began a slow and painstaking process of Julie tentatively beginning to explore her own history and particularly her relationship with her own mother. At each milestone in Michael's emerging autonomy—his first class session without her in the classroom, his first "meltdown" in class while she was absent, his first day of a full classroom program—Julie was beset with fear and anxiety. And she slowly began to understand that his growing away from her made her anxious about his survival and that this somehow had to do with her early fears and her mother's unavailability to soothe and comfort her. When Julie was three, she and her two brothers and parents moved to rural Austria, where her father was to run a small business. Her father's company was an hour away, and Julie was herself enrolled in a local preschool. A year later, she was enrolled in a school that was an hour's bus ride away. Julie has no conscious memory of anxiety during this period or during any of the other multiple moves and upheavals that characterized her childhood. But we have reconstructed a situation in which her mother, put in full charge of relocating her family and coping with her husband's long absences in a foreign culture, simply "coped" and expected her children to do the same. There was no room for distress.

One day, Julie came into a session and plopped down into her chair. She was on the verge of tears as she recounted an incident with her mother that spoke volumes to both of us. Michael was now attending school on a regular basis, and Lucy had started school, too. Julie was beset with anxiety, as she had been every morning since the children began school. On the morning of our session, Julie had been unburdening herself to her mother, recounting her anxiety and fear for the children. To her surprise and profound upset, her mother told her simply to "just deal with it, and get on with your life." Up until that moment, Julie had never realized how little tolerance her mother had for her feelings, particularly her anger and her anxiety. Only now could she begin to understand why she had had to bury her own feelings and worries time and time again. Until Michael was born, she had been the ultimate "coper." Only in her representations of his emotional experience could she allow herself to feel the anxiety she had not been allowed to feel and to respond to him in the way she had never been responded to by her own mother. His difficult temperament undoubtedly set the stage for this reenactment, because it made it easy for Julie to see him as vulnerable and in desperate need of her comfort. Unfortunately, because these representations and feelings were unconscious, her projections severely limited and distorted Michael's autonomy and likely worsened his biological vulnerabilities.

As Julie began to reflect on the complexities of her relationship with her parents and her capacity to tolerate and understand her own emotional experience, there were fascinating shifts in Michael's play and in his understanding of the world. Despite his obvious intelligence and evidence within our sessions of his rich and vivid imagination, Michael—even at five—had remained somewhat confused by the distinction between what Fonagy and Target (1996) term the appearance-reality distinction. In his interactions with playmates and with his parents, he would become frightened and upset by the boundary transgressions and violations that are part of normal social intercourse. He would often take his playmates' "tall tales" as truths (Colin's house really burned down last night) and had difficulty, particularly in the absence of visual cues, recognizing humor and teasing. Unless there was a smile or linguistic marker to indicate humor or teasing, he would remain lost to the subtle and less evident meanings of the exchange. To him, what was was. However, as his and his mother's treatment progressed, he began actively grappling with the distinction between reality and pretend. This manifested itself at both a verbal and a symbolic level.

At home with his mother, he asked numerous questions about the difference between real and pretend. "Is that real? Is that pretend?" When his mother took him to a performance of the musical *Oliver*, he was both agitated and fascinated. He had to work very hard to keep the awareness that this was fiction and a play and, throughout the play, asked his mother whether these were actors, whether this was really happening. A fascinating corolary to his struggling to distinguish between real and pretend was his attention to others' subjective experience. Often, he had imaginary squirrels "watch" an episode of particularly violent play; their role was to comment, observe, and reflect on what was going on. In all of his interactions, he became more attuned to the connection between affect displays and internal experience. He began to understand and appreciate that his parents and other children had emotional experiences that were both similar to and different from his. He would ask his mother, "Did that happen to you too, Mommy?" and took close note of his playmates' emotional reactions and upsets. Seeing that they, too, got upset during a routine school day, had fights, lost control, and so on, he became more confident and more social. It seemed as if he felt less and less "different," more a part of the human world.

Michael is now about to enter first grade and seems happy and comfortable at school. He is a full and appreciated member of his class, with friends, playdates, and a range of interests and enthusiasms. He has begun learning to write, spell, and read and is a voracious consumer of facts and information.

His obsessional symptoms as well as his anxiety have diminished considerably and tend to emerge primarily when he is stressed or upset. And, although holidays and other times of great excitement can disregulate him, he is usually even and content. He still has flare-ups with his sister, along with areas of rigidity and fragility that get in his way. And, although his oedipal development will necessarily be limited by his father's passivity and inaccessibility, he has developed a stronger and more resilient connection to his father. He is no longer "different" in the way he once was, and even his biological vulnerabilities are contained and less disruptive. Most striking, however, is the change in the relationship between Michael and his mother. The anger, disappointment, and anxiety that had infiltrated their closeness are greatly diminished and in its place is a growing delight and understanding.

DISCUSSION

What emerged over the course of my work with Michael and his mother was a kind of hybrid treatment that combined aspects of infant-parent psychotherapy (Fraiberg 1980; Stern-Bruschweiler and Stern 1989; Lieberman 1992, 1997; Lieberman and Pawl 1993; Stern 1995), play therapy for Michael, and insight-oriented supportive psychotherapy for Julie. These kinds of flexible and evolving treatments are not unusual in day-to-day psychoanalytically oriented work with young children. Indeed, I am hardly suggesting that I happened upon a "new" approach to child treatment; rather, I am trying to understand what often happens naturally in child work in light of current developments in the study of attachment and related processes. Concomitant work with mother and child allowed me to address intertwined and interacting representational worlds simultaneously: Julie's representation of Michael and of their relationship, Julie's representation of herself in relation to attachment, and Michael's representation of himself and others. Changes in both the mother's capacity for self-reflection and in the child's capacity for symbolic expression were linked to changes in both the quality of their relationship and of their attachment, as well as to changes in Michael's overall functioning, despite ongoing biological disruptions to his adaptation. As Julie's treatment progressed, Michael's way of being began to make emotional sense to her, and her understanding made it possible for her to "recognize" him and thus contain and regulate his emotional experience. Michael began to be able to reflect on, organize, and play about his inner experience: slowly, it became possible for him to describe and reflect on his own feelings, as well as on the feelings of others; to contain and symbolize what had been overwhelming experiences of disregulation and distress; and to distinguish between pretend and real in increasingly complex and differentiated ways. Indeed, differentiation proceeded on all fronts. As

Stern (1995) points out in his recent discussion of the interdependent, dynamic, and mutually influencing nature of the parent-child relationship and of infant-parent psychotherapy, "a successful therapeutic action that changes any one element will end up changing all the separate elements" (16).

Shifts in reflective functioning, which Fonagy would attribute to Michael's developing "theory of mind," were linked directly and explicitly to diminution in his separation anxiety, obsessional symptoms, and temper tantrums, and to his developing increasing spheres of competence and mastery. However, what I believe was equally—if not more—central to his improvement and to the improvement in his relationship with his mother were the changes in Julie's representation of herself and of Michael that emerged as a function of my concomitant work with her.

The child's mentalizing abilities emerge most fully within the context of a secure relationship; however, secure communication between Michael and Julie was severely limited not only by his biological vulnerabilities but also by Julie's inability to recognize and be sensitive to his needs. Although she could be quite sensitive to him when he was calm and playful, she withdrew from him and became controlling and angry when he was anxious or angry. It seems likely that even as early as the neonatal period, Michael's naturally occurring distress—which may or may not have been extreme—was profoundly disregulating for Julie. And just as her mother withdrew emotionally and abandoned her when she was frightened and angry as a child, Julie's only recourse was to withdraw from Michael and his distress; by the time of the family's initial consultation, Julie clearly felt helpless and in its grip. When he was born, she consciously feared losing him, and she feared that harm would befall him. But in a sense, her fears for his safety reflected her awareness that she could not meet his needs or contain him because the anxiety elicited by his distress and need for her was intolerable; she was losing him because she found closeness to him terrifying and impossible. And so she withdrew from him; she did not have the resources to do otherwise.

Coming to "know" Michael through the course of treatment allowed Julie to begin to master and contain the anxiety she felt in the face of his distress and needs for intimacy. Seeing him more clearly and in a more differentiated fashion allowed her to experience his needs—not as terrifying and overwhelming but rather as comprehensible and containable—was intrinsic to her beginning to provide a secure base for his emotional experience. And it was intrinsic to Michael's emergent security, his sense of separateness, and his beginning ability to imagine, understand, and regulate his own inner experience. Julie's ability to make meaning of Michael and their relationship allowed her to meet his needs and make them meaningful for him; her coming to know and recognize him led to his becoming known to himself. These changes were at the center of his being able to become a more differentiated, coherent, and representational person and were at the heart of their developing a healthy and joyful intimacy.

In many ways, these formulations are reminiscent of Winnicott's (1965) thinking about the true and false self. In his view, the infant's sense of the self as real and separate arises from the mother's recognition of the infant as real and separate; it is this capacity to know the self as separate that leads to the development of the symbol. "It is an essential part of my theory that the True Self does not become a living reality except as a result of the mother's repeated success in meeting the infant's spontaneous gesture. . . . It is the infant's gesture . . . that is made real, and the capacity of the infant to use a symbol is the result" (145). For Winnicott, the mother's capacity to know, represent, and reflect the infant's experience back to him is intrinsic to the infant's capacity to represent and symbolize his inner life. The mother provides the means of the child coming to know and represent his own experience; the child's sense of subjective reality, as well as his capacity to symbolize, is linked to the "mediating" (Mitchell, 1988) effects of the mother's consciousness.

The work with Julie moved from disentangling and making sense of the aspects of Michael and her relationship with him that were least threatening and disorganizing to those that were deeply upsetting and quite unconscious. I began by making sense of Michael's biological disregulation, imagining with her what it was like for Michael to be emotionally disregulated and fly out of control and what it was like for him to experience such profound sensitivity to change and to environmental stimulation. I suggested ways that she might describe Michael's experience to him in words, so that he could begin to make sense of what was happening to him and between them. His arousal cycles, his episodes of disregulation and consequent obsessions, his rages, and his panics began to make sense to her, and she could clearly understand them as a reaction to his biological difficulties. The chaos of his temperament and emotional reactivity began to take on a shape and a reason to her, and began to be differentiated from the complexity of her response to his biological difficulties. She began to understand what set him off; at long last, she had words to describe it, to herself as well as to him. This allowed her to mirror and "mark" Michael's affective experience (Gergely and Watson, 1996).

This led directly to our trying to make sense of his emotional experience, as distinct and differentiated from her own. Children who are biologically vulnerable, which he clearly was, live in an emotional universe that is fraught with the fear of disregulation and anger at its effects. For the hypersensitive child who reacts to every touch, sound, or change as if it were an earthquake, life and maintaining a sense of internal regulation are continual challenges. These children, more than most, are enormously reliant upon their "self-regulating others" (Stern 1985) for containment, modulation, and organization. Julie was too angry, disappointed, and separation anxious to recognize Michael's separate experience; as a consequence, his biological and emotional needs remained mysterious to her, and she was an erratic and poor self-regulating other. Once she began to recognize these needs, it was possible for her to remain both emotionally available and emotionally containing for him. And, at long last, it became possible for her to experience real pleasure and delight in their relationship.

Intrinsic to realizing how Michael felt was realizing how her feelings affected him. It took Julie a long time to acknowledge that her feelings, rage, sadness, separation anxiety, and so on had an effect on Michael. Acknowledging such feelings meant acknowledging the tremendous guilt she felt about his condition (which she had few resources to handle), and it meant acknowledging that she too had had feelings to which her mother had been unresponsive. In a sense, our work proceeded from reworking aspects of her conscious representation of Michael (i.e., her conscious recognition of his biological difficulties) to her less-articulated representation of his inner life and to her even lesser conscious awareness of his response to her affective experience. Finally, we began to address the relationship between her representations of her own parents and those of Michael and their relationship.

The shift in their relationship that resulted from changes in her capacity to understand and make sense of his emotional experience was, from my perspective, probably the most important catalyst to change in the dyad and likely most healing for Michael. Had Julie been in treatment with a separate therapist, she might have changed considerably, and Michael might have benefited considerably from his own psychotherapy, but it is very unlikely that their relationship would have changed the way it did or that either of them would have changed as much or as fully as they did. By becoming the intermediary between them, I had access to two profoundly complementary and interacting representational systems and emotional worlds. This made the potential for individual and dyadic therapeutic change and growth all the greater.

Whereas the articulation of Michael's and Julie's feelings, intentions, and motivations enhanced mentalization for both, it was the creation of shared illusions through play within the context of the therapeutic relationship that enhanced Michael's symbolic capacity (D. Diamond, personal communication, June 24, 1997). When Michael began treatment, he had little capacity to play. However, coincident with his mother's emerging capacity to imagine and contain his experience, his developing relationship with me, and my specific efforts to imagine and represent his experience, both in play and in words, he began to play, to symbolize, and to distinguish between pretense and reality. He began by telling stories in his play, enacting the panoply of his anxiety and rage; over time, he shifted to drawing and to words. As his play came gradually to express his anger and his fear, his anger and fear came under his control for the first time in his life. His play and his words richly expressed his emerging understanding of the world, of pretense and reality, and his wish to make sense of the content of others' minds. As he began to make sense of himself and the contents of his mind could be imagined by his mother, it became possible for him to imagine the contents of others' minds, as well as his own. He began to experience himself as "known" and, thus, separate. These changes in consolidation and regulation were accompanied by dramatic shifts in affect expression. His somber mood gradually gave way to exuberance, delight, and true pleasure in the world around him.

Before closing, I would like to briefly consider the role of what I have been calling Michael's "biological vulnerabilities" in derailing or complicating the early mother-child relationship. Certainly by the time I met him, Michael would have been described as a "difficult" child. But to what extent were these qualities intrinsic to Michael, and to what extent did they emerge as a function of the mother-child relationship? Given Julie's description of her early relationship with Michael, it seems possible, if not likely, that whatever temperamental difficulties he brought to their relationship, they were greatly exacerbated by the extent to which she felt overwhelmed, fearful, and angry in her earliest relationship to him. Negative temperament does not—in and of itself—predict either insecure attachment or later emotional disturbance; however, insensitive parenting in combination with difficult temperament does (Van den Boom 1994; Belsky, Hsieh, and Crnic 1998). These children may be particularly susceptible to rearing influence. Julie's likely inability to respond sensitively to Michael in his earliest months may well have left him susceptible to extremes of emotional disregulation that had she been able to regulate his affective experience and remain emotionally available to him would have rapidly been integrated and contained, leading to a more normal developmental course.

Recent evidence from the domain of neuroscience suggests that the structures of the brain and of regulatory systems are profoundly influenced by the quality of the early relationship (Schore 1994; Hofer, 1995, 1996), and by the mother's presence as regulator of basic physiological systems. Most fascinating is Hofer's (1995) recent report that when two-week-old infant rat pups are separated from their mothers, there is widespread evidence of disregulation across a number of physiological systems, suggesting the profound import of maternal regulatory functions in the formation of attachment, even in earliest infancy. In particular, infant rats manifest an increase in attachment behaviors, specifically rates of "separation crying" and proximity seeking. These same behaviors, which Hofer suggests are the most evident manifestation of the first anxiety state, are powerfully reduced by a number of antianxiety drugs, including serotonin reuptake inhibitors such as Prozac. Thus, we can speculate that Julie's withdrawal from Michael and her inability to regulate and contain the earliest and what might well have been normally occurring manifestations of attachment and, specifically, the need for proximity, led to a failure of regulation at a biological, systemic level. The neural systems responsible for down regulating his anxiety and regulating the production of certain neurotransmitters functioned poorly, if at all. As a result of Julie's inability to regulate his earliest anxiety, he was stuck, both behaviorally and neuroanatomically, in a perpetual "separation cry." Medication, specifically a serotonin reuptake inhibitor, biologically reduced the extremity of Michael's disregulation and made it possible for Julie to approach him and ultimately understand him.

For children like Michael, more flexible approaches to individual therapy, as well as more direct work with parents, are vital to promoting change in the attachment system, as well as in the individual mother and child, even though—as Stern (1995) points out—such situations often seem theoretically and technically complex, if not messy and certainly "impure." However, as Selma Fraiberg once described so brilliantly, the child's presence in infant-parent psychotherapy brings the mother's inner experience alive in a way that simply cannot be reproduced in individual psychotherapy. The same was true in this work. As successful as a therapist may be in "meeting" the child's mind, the parents' capacity to imagine the child's experience will provide healing and intimacy of yet another order. Representing the child's experience in a way that makes sense to the parent invariably enhances and strengthens the attachment between them because the parents' emergent and differentiated representation increases sensitivity and genuine attunement and thus makes it possible for the child to trust the parent and express himself in an open and clear way.

REFERENCES

Ainsworth, M. D. S., M. C. Blehar, E. Waters, and S. Wall. 1978. *Patterns of attachment: A psychological study of the strange situation.* Hillsdale, N.J.: Lawrence Erlbaum.

Belsky, J., and J. Cassidy. 1994. Attachment: Theory and evidence. In *Development through life,* ed. M. Rutter and D. Hay, 373–402. Oxford, UK: Blackwell.

Belsky, J., K. Hsieh, and K. Crnic. 1998. Mothering, fathering, and infant negativity as antecedents of boys' externalizing problems and inhibition at age 3: Differential susceptibility to rearing influence. *Development and Psychopathology* 10:301–19.

Benedek, T. 1959. Parenthood as a developmental stage. *Journal of the American Psychoanalytic Association* 65:389–417.

Benoit, D., and K. Parker. 1994. Stability and transmission of attachment across three generations. *Child Development* 65:1444–56.

Bibring, G. L., T. F. Dwyer, D. S. Huntington, and A. F. Valenstein. 1961. A study of the psychological processes in pregnancy and of the earliest mother-child relationship. Part I: Some propositions and comments. *Psychoanalytic Study of the Child* 16:9–24.

Bowlby, J. 1940. The influence of early environment in the development of neurosis and neurotic character. *International Journal of Psychoanalysis* 21:1–25.

———. 1969. *Attachment and loss: Attachment.* New York: Basic Books.

———. 1973. *Attachment and loss: Separation.* New York: Basic Books.

———. 1980. *Attachment and loss: Loss.* New York: Basic Books.

———. 1988. *A secure base: Parent-child attachment and healthy human development.* New York: Basic Books.

Cassidy, J. 1994. Emotion regulation: Influences of attachment relationships. In *Biological and behavioral foundations of emotion regulation*, ed. N. Fox, 228–50. Monographs of the Society for Research in Child Development 59.

Cassidy, J., and L. J. Berlin. 1994. The insecure/ambivalent pattern of attachment: Theory and research. *Child Development* 65:971–92.

Diamond, D., and S. Blatt. 1994. Internal working models and the representational world in attachment and psychoanalytic theories. In *Attachment in adults: Clinical and developmental perspectives*, ed. M. Sperling and W. Berman, 72–98. New York: Guilford.

Fonagy, P., M. Steele, G. Moran, H. Steele, and A. Higgitt. 1993. Measuring the ghost in the nursery: An empirical study of the relation between parents' mental representations of childhood experiences and their infants' security of attachment. *Journal of the American Psychoanalytic Association* 41:957–89.

Fonagy, P., M. Steele, and H. Steele. 1991. Maternal representations of attachment during pregnancy predict the organization of infant-mother attachment at one year. *Child Development* 62:880–93.

Fonagy, P., M. Steele, H. Steele, T. Leigh, R. Kennedy, G. Mattoon, and M. Target. 1995. Attachment, the reflective self, and borderline states: The predictive specificity of the adult attachment interview and pathological emotional development. In *Attachment theory: Social, developmental, and clinical perspectives*, ed. S. Goldberg, R. Muir, and J. Kerr, 233–79. Hillsdale, N.J.: Analytic Press.

Fonagy, P., and M. Target. 1996. Playing with reality. Part I: Theory of mind and the normal development of psychic reality. *International Journal of Psychoanalysis* 77:217–33.

———. 1998. Mentalization and the changing aims of child psychoanalysis. *Psychoanalytic Dialogue* 8:87–114.

Fraiberg, S., ed. 1980. *Clinical studies in infant mental health.* New York: Basic Books.

Freud, A. 1965. *Normality and pathology in childhood: Assessments of development.* Madison, Conn.: International Universities Press.

George, C., N. Kaplan, and M. Main. 1985. The Berkeley adult attachment interview. Unpublished manuscript, Department of Psychology, University of California, Berkeley.

George, C., and J. Solomon. 1996. Representational models of relationships: Links between caregiving and attachment. *Infant Mental Health Journal* 17:198–217.

Gergely, G., and J. S. Watson. 1996. The social biofeedback theory of parental affect-mirroring. *International Journal of Psychoanalysis* 77:1181–1212.

Greenspan, S. 1995. *The challenging child: Understanding, raising, and enjoying the five "difficult" types of children*. Reading, Mass.: Addison-Wesley.

Hofer, M. 1995. Hidden regulators: Implications for a new understanding of attachment, separation, and loss. In *Attachment theory: Social, developmental, and clinical perspectives*, ed. S. Goldberg, R. Muir, and J. Kerr, 203–30. Hillsdale, N.J.: Analytic Press.

———. 1996. On the nature and consequences of early loss. *Psychosomatic Medicine* 58:570–81.

Karen, R. 1997. *Becoming attached: First relationships and how they impact our capacity to love*. New York: Oxford University Press.

Lieberman, A. F. 1992. Infant-parent psychotherapy with toddlers. *Development and Psychopathology* 4:559–74.

———. 1994. *The emotional life of the toddler*. New York: Free Press.

———. 1997. Toddlers' internalizations of material attributions as a factor in quality of attachment. In *Attachment and psychopathology*, ed. L. Atkinson and K. Zucker, 277–91. New York: Guilford Press.

Lieberman, A. F., and J. H. Pawl. 1993. Infant-parent psychotherapy. In *Handbook of infant mental health*, ed. C. H. Zeanah, 427–41. New York: Guilford Press.

Mahler, M. 1968. *On human symbiosis and the vicissitudes of individuation*. Madison, Conn.: International Universities Press.

Mahler, M., F. Pine, and A. Bergman. 1975. *The psychological birth of the human infant*. New York: Basic Books.

Main, M. 1990. Cross-cultural studies of attachment organization: Recent studies, changing methodologies, and the concept of conditional strategies. *Human Development* 33:48–61.

———. 1991. Metacognitive knowledge, metacognitive monitoring, and singular (coherent) vs. multiple (incoherent) model of attachment: Findings and directions for future research. In *Attachment across the life cycle*, ed. C. Parkes, J. Stevenson-Hinde, and P. Marris, 127–60. London: Routledge.

———. 1995a. Attachment: Overview, with implications for clinical work. In *Attachment theory: Social, developmental, and clinical perspectives*, ed. S. Goldberg, R. Muir, and J. Kerr, 407–75. Hillsdale, N.J.: Analytic Press.

———. 1995b. Discourse, prediction, and studies in attachment: Implications for psychoanalysis. In *Research in psychoanalysis: Process, development, outcome*, ed. T. Shapiro and R. N. Emde, 209–45. Madison, Conn.: International Universities Press.

Main, M., and E. Hesse. 1990. Parents' unresolved traumatic experiences are related to infant disorganized status: Is frightened and/or frightening parental behavior the linking mechanism? In *Attachment in the preschool years: Theory, research, and intervention*, ed. M. T. Greenberg, D. Cicchetti, and E. M. Cummings, 161–82. Chicago: University of Chicago Press.

Main, M., N. Kaplan, and J. Cassidy. 1985. Security in infancy, childhood, and adulthood: A move to the level of representation. In *Growing points of attachment theory and research*, ed. I. Bretherton and E. Waters, 66–104. Monographs of the Society for Research in Child Development 50.

Mitchell, S. 1988. *Relational concepts in psychoanalysis: An integration*. Cambridge, Mass.: Harvard University Press.

Oram, K. 2000. A transitional space: Involving parents in the play therapy of their children. *Journal of Infant, Child, and Adolescent Psychotherapy* 1:79–98.

Osofsky, J. D. 1995. Perspectives on attachment and psychoanalysis. *Psychoanalytic Psychology* 12:347–62.

Schimek, J. G. 1975. A critical re-examination of Freud's concept of unconscious mental representation. *International Journal of Psychoanalysis* 2:171–87.

Schore, A. 1994. *Affect regulation and the origins of the self.* Hillsdale, N.J.: Analytic Press.

Slade, A. 1994. Making meaning and making believe: Their role in the clinical process. In *Children at play: Clinical and developmental approaches to meaning and representation,* ed. A. Slade and D. Wolf, 81–110. New York: Oxford University Press.

———. 1996. Longitudinal studies and clinical psychoanalysis: A view from attachment theory and research. *Journal of Clinical Psychoanalysis* 6:112–23.

———. 1999. Attachment theory and research: Implications for the theory and practice of individual psychotherapy. In *Handbook of attachment: Theory, research, and clinical applications,* ed. J. Cassidy and P. R. Shaver, 575–94. New York: Guilford.

Slade, A., and J. L. Aber. 1992. Attachments, drives and development: Conflicts and convergences in theory. In *Interface of psychoanalysis and psychology,* ed. J. Barron, M. Eagle, and D. Wolitzky, 154–86. Washington, D.C.: APA Publications.

Slade, A., J. Belsky, J. L. Aber, and J. L. Phelps. 1999. Maternal representations of their relationships with their toddlers: Links to adult attachment and observed mothering. *Developmental Psychology* 35:611–19.

Slade, A., and L. J. Cohen. 1996. Processes of parenting and the remembrance of things past. *Infant Mental Health Journal* 17:217–39.

Slade, A., and A. F. Lieberman. 1997. Affective development during the third year of life. In *Handbook of child and adolescent psychiatry, vol. 1,* ed. J. Noshpitz, S. Greenspan, S. Wieder, and J. Osofsky, 89–99. New York: Wiley.

Solomon, J., and C. George. 1996. Defining the caregiving system: Toward a theory of caregiving. *Infant Mental Health Journal* 17:183–98.

Stern, D. N. 1985. *The interpersonal world of the infant.* New York: Basic Books.

———. 1995. *The motherhood constellation.* New York: Basic Books.

Stern-Bruschweiler, N., and D. N. Stern. 1989. A model for conceptualizing the role of mother's representational role in various mother-infant therapies. *Infant Mental Health Journal* 10:142–56.

Target, M., and P. Fonagy. 1996. Playing with reality. Part II: The development of psychic reality from a theoretical perspective. *International Journal of Psychoanalysis* 77:459–79.

Turecki, S., and L. Tonner. 1989. *The difficult child: A guide for parents.* Rev. ed. New York: Bantam.

Van den Boom, D. 1994. The influence of temperament and mothering on attachment and explorations: An experimental manipulation of sensitive responsiveness among lower-class mothers and irritable infants. *Child Development* 65:1457–77.

Van IJzendoorn, M. H. 1995. Adult attachment representations, parental responsiveness, and infant attachment: A meta-analysis on the predictive validity of the adult attachment interview. *Psychological Bulletin* 117:387–403.

Van IJzendoorn, M. H., and M. J. Bakermans-Kranenburg. 1996. Attachment representations in mothers, fathers, adolescents, and clinical groups: A meta-analytic search for normative data. *Journal of Consulting and Clinical Psychology* 64:8–21.

Ward, M. J., and E. A. Carlson. 1995. Associations among adult attachment representations, maternal sensitivity, and infant-mother attachment in a sample of adolescent mothers. *Child Development* 66:69–80.

Winnicott, D. W. 1965. *Maturational processes and the facilitating environment.* New York: International Universities Press.

———. 1971. *Playing and reality.* London: Tavistock Publications.

Zeanah, C. H., D. Benoit, M. Barton, C. Regan, L. Hirshberg, and L. P. Lipsitt. 1993. Representations of attachment in mothers and their one-year-old infants. *Journal of the American Academy of Child and Adolescent Psychiatry* 32:278–86.

Zeanah, C. H., D. Benoit, L. Hirschberg, M. Barton, and C. Regan. 1995. Mothers' representations of their infants are concordant with infant attachment classifications. *Developmental Issues in Psychiatry and Psychology* 1:1–14.

Zero to Three. 1994. *Diagnostic classification of mental health and developmental disorders of infancy and early childhood.* Arlington, Va.: Zero to Three National Center for Clinical Infant Programs.

14

From Conflict to Cooperation: Hadarim, a School-Based Adlerian Parenting Program in Israel

Joseph Prinz

Editor's Note: This consultative program has been developed for parents and teachers in Israel. Although the theoretical assumptions and approach is extremely useful for a parent-focused treatment model, the literary exercises in the manual have not yet been adapted for an American audience.

Developing cooperation and ownership of responsibility where conflict and blaming once held sway is the goal of Hadarim, a brief, economical, practical, and effective parental guidance course. The most unique feature of the program is that it is taught by the classroom teachers of the children whose parents are taking the course. The teachers are doubly qualified as, not only do they know the children who are the concern of parents in their classes, but they have also been through the course they are teaching, having been trained by the counselor in their school. As the program innovator, I trained the counselors. Having been through the course from the perspective of parents, the teachers are able to empathize and establish immediate rapport with the parents in their class. Teachers and parents quickly become allies, instead of adversaries, in educating the children in their charge.

LITERATURE REVIEW

Research suggests that parent training has a major impact on diverse aspects of child development (Halberg and Hakansson 2003; Roberts et al. 1999; Nicholson et al. 1998; Weissner 2001). Alfred Adler (1958) was one of the first authors who wrote on the need for parent guidance. Rudolf Dreikurs, his follower and the developer of his educational path, continued this direction and founded the Adler Institute in Chicago. He believed that people who follow the Adlerian method are capable of guiding parent groups for effective parenting. He prepared many instructors who taught the method and provided tangible tools to help parents cope with their children. Dreikurs believed that his method, approach, and tools improved the relationship between parents, teachers, and children (Dreikurs 1967).

Most parenting classes in Israel are held at counseling centers, community meeting rooms, and other public places and draw participants from many different neighborhoods. The instructor may be a mental health professional or a trained counselor but, typically, is unacquainted with the children of her class participants. Parents taking the course may change their interactions with their children at home, but these changed behaviors will not be reinforced at school nor, in most cases, practiced by the parents of their children's classmates.

In contrast, the Hadarim program is designed to change the culture of an entire school by offering ten-session Adlerian-based classes to all the parents of children in that school. Each class is taught by its classroom teacher, who has completed the course, with class participation limited to the parents of children in the class. Participating parents are exposed to a common set of principles and goals and develop a shared vocabulary and arsenal of new behaviors, which are reinforced by their fellow classmates and the teacher. By focusing on and encouraging positive behaviors, a supportive and democratic environment is created, and teachers and parents become allies instead of adversaries in the education and training of their children.

The implementation of parenting education has encountered several obstacles. Parenthood is one facet of life for which no training is required. However, the need for such training is widely acknowledged. Even if it is acknowledged that parenting may be improved by parent guidance, it is often feared by school administrators due to the belief that informed parents may have demands that cannot be fulfilled and that they will apply undue pressure on schools.

The Hadarim program, established under the auspices of the Israeli Ministry of Education, has overcome those limitations by initiating a structured, economical, and time-efficient parent guidance program that operates within schools and teaches techniques to improve the relationship between teachers, parents, and children in a feasible and structured way.

THEORETICAL ASPECTS

The program combines elements from various theories and applies a variety of psychological approaches including neo-Freudian, Adlerian, cognitive, and behaviorist theories.

The Adlerian teleological approach (Adler 1951) is applied to help the parent to understand and support the child's goals and focus on solutions, rather than finding and assessing the reasons behind the problems. The child's social interest (Adler 1964, 1979) is developed by teaching parents to watch for and reinforce positive social behaviors. The program transforms basic Adlerian philosophical and theoretical principles, self-determination, holism, and phenomenology into operational methods that can be applied easily by the teacher in the classroom and by the parent at home.

The focus is on helping teachers and parents strengthen their ability to develop an optimistic perspective and a tendency for internal locus of control in the school setting. Understanding and applying Erik Erikson's psychosocial approach (Erikson 1963) strengthens the students' self-confidence.

The program tries to increase the children's basic confidence, autonomy, initiative, and diligence. Albert Bandura's social approach (Bandura 1997) emphasizes the importance of the social influence on children's behavior patterns and stresses the need to strengthen their self-efficacy. According to Bandura, those who "believe in the fulfillment of their expectations increase their efforts and, if necessary, will try to change their environment" (Bandura 1997, 141). People who believe in their own ability have a better chance of coping with difficulties.

THE COURSE STRUCTURE

The Hadarim program operates according to the "pyramid system." Schools interested in applying the program send their counselors to a 112-hour training course, which I teach, as the developer and chief trainer. This earns the counselors the credentials to be program leaders. After they return to their respective schools, they convey the program to the teachers through a school in-service training course of eighty-four hours. The homeroom teachers of each class then invite the parents of their students to participate in a parents' training course and deliver the program to them in ten weekly meetings. During all its stages, staff members of Hadarim supervise the program leaders. This includes visits to the schools, observations of sessions, and feedback meetings with the staff. As a key work tool, every instructor (counselors and teachers) receives a structured guidance kit, which includes an instructional manual and visual accessories, handouts, and props developed uniquely for this program (Prinz 2004).

HOW DOES IT WORK?

The classroom structure of the course, that is, having a course taught within the natural setting of the child's class, enables the parents to act as a supportive and sharing group that also extends beyond the school framework.

The program is oriented toward the participants' experiences, as related to their own parental experience and not as related to a theoretical description of parenting. Teachers and parents alike share their own experiences and submit their own personal material. The principles of the program are demonstrated in concrete ways through role plays, interactive activities, and peer and teacher feedback on techniques practiced at home. The parents are invited to take an active role in the demonstrations. The participants' children are invited to several of the workshops, and the program leaders use them to demonstrate the topics explored.

Each of the ten sessions includes warm-up exercises, a sharing and learning discussion related to the previous session, role playing, the study of specific topics, experiential exercises, poem readings (related to the workshop topic), and homework. At the end of every workshop, each parent receives a leaflet containing the homework.

The uniqueness of the program lies in its attempt to encourage the education system, the school, and the parents to take responsibility for their relationship with each other and with the children. The school profits from this program by becoming an institution that not only teaches children but also teaches parents. This is personally enriching for teachers, improving both their parenting skills and their professional skills, and permitting them a better understanding of how to motivate children and how to teach parents to motivate them.

The parents received clear guidelines for increasing their children's good behavior and were grateful to the teachers who came to the sessions for ten weeks to teach them how to develop positive communications with their children. Coming to their children's classroom reconnected them to the institution from which they had frequently felt alienated (often since childhood) and against which they often felt they had to protect their children, improved the relationship between parents and teachers, increased tolerance and mutual respect, and improved behavior in the corridors and the schoolyard as well as in the parent-school committees. Through this program, the involved communities now enjoy not only a school but also a "house of education" that teaches values as well as knowledge.

"It all begins at home." —D. W. Winnicott

THE OBJECTIVE

The Hadarim Program was designed for parents. Throughout the course, parents will adopt a new, positive angle of vision on their children. The parents will learn to use *encouraging and meaningful verbalization* and will practice the techniques so that they can convey verbal messages of validation and encouragement to reinforce their children's self-confidence and their faith in their own ability. The program may also affect the parent's attitude to other members of the family.

THE PROGRAM'S GROUP LEADERS

The agents who will convey the program to the parents are the educators of the children, namely, the kindergarten or school teacher. The teachers undergo an eighty-four-hour training course (in fourteen sessions) where they learn the principles of the method and acquire skills as leaders of parents' groups. As part of their training, the group leaders get practical experience in leading a group. The contribution of the Hadarim Program to the teachers and kindergarten teachers who undergo this training is reflected in several areas:

- On the personal level: The program improves the educator's personal and professional image by giving skills as a leader of parents' group in the Hadarim Program.
- On the family level: Over the course of the training, the educators experience the course themselves in a parents' group, and going through the course with their own individual children and family members. Many educators report positive changes in their relations with their children and even with their spouses following participation in the Hadarim Program.
- On the professional level: Teaching the Hadarim material leads educators to a new evaluation of their pedagogic theory and adds new dimensions to their work with children during activity in the kindergarten or school. Internalizing the content material and positive attitude of the Hadarim Program also contributes to strengthening the relationship between the teachers and their pupils and between the pupils and their parents, improving the atmosphere between them, and adding a new, positive personal flavor to them.

SELF-EFFICACY

The importance in building confidence in an "I can" attitude ("I can persevere, be responsible, help, find my role in the family and in the group") is also supported by the idea that there is a connection between a sense of the ability to cope with challenges and the ability to realize expectations. A person who believes in his or her own ability has better chances of coping with difficulties: "People who believe in the fulfillment of their expectations increase their efforts, and if necessary, will try to change their environment" (Bandura 1977, 141).

THE BASIC APPROACH OF THE HADARIM PROGRAM

The program is unique for its six principles. These principles were designed to ensure that the program will succeed in reaching the parents and spur them on to apply what they have learned:

1. The program combines elements from different theories, and it is the intersection of a variety of psychological theories: Neo-Freudian, Adlerian, cognitive, and behaviorist.
2. The participants in any group are drawn from the parents of one kindergarten or one class. Recruiting parents from one kindergarten or one class allows them to consolidate into a learning group whose members are able to support each other.
3. The program is held in the educational institution itself (kindergarten or school) and is implemented by the kindergarten or school teacher after they have been trained to lead parents' groups according to the Hadarim Program.
4. The group's treatment of the child is not of a theoretical child, one that exists in the literature, or of the group leader's child ("From my experience as a parent . . .") but rather the individual children of all of the participants in the course.
5. For the tenth session, the kindergarten or school psychologist is invited, and he answers the questions presented by the participants. We believe that the participation of a psychologist reduces the teachers' fears of questions that they do not know how to answer or do not feel comfortable answering.
6. The principles of the program are demonstrated concretely using structured and active firsthand experience. The parents are invited to take an active part in the demonstrations. For some of the seminars, the children of those parents will also be invited, and the kindergarten/ school teacher will use them to demonstrate the subjects that he or she wishes to teach. The teacher will try to invite children who can benefit specifically from the subjects being taught in the group.

RECRUITING PARENTS

As part of the preliminary activities of the program, the kindergarten/school teacher must plan the actions to be taken to recruit the optimal number of parents to the program (twelve to fourteen families). The following activities may help in marketing the program and increasing parent response:

Invitation

We suggest sending an invitation to all of the parents of the children approximately one month before the first meeting. This invitation should notify the parents of the course, the number and dates of the sessions, and the topics that are offered for discussion in the workshops. The invitations should be attractive and include an up-to-date picture of every boy and girl (see sample invitation in appendix A).

Reminder

It is a good idea to send out reminders periodically, using fliers and other means, reminding people about the beginning of the course, and also reminders before the first meetings (see appendix B).

Payment

It is recommended that a nominal fee be charged for each workshop to be collected in advance of the course to help guarantee parental commitment.

STRUCTURE OF THE WORKSHOPS

Each workshop will last two hours. Light refreshments are served during the first twenty minutes when there will also be private conversations between parents and the kindergarten/school teacher and among the parents themselves.

Preworkshop: Individual Conversations

In advance of each session (including the first one), the kindergarten/school teacher will prepare a list of positive things that were said or done by each of the children over the week. Recording positive events and reporting them to the parents will be carried out throughout the course and will serve as the basis for the first conversation with the parents before each workshop.

The Course of Each Workshop

Each workshop is divided into three parts:

Personal conversation: The twenty minutes before group activity begins are devoted to personal conversations between the parents and teacher. During this time, the parents will receive an individual report about the positive things that their child did or said over the past week (and which were recorded during the individual observation). This informal meeting will also accommodate the parents who wish to raise subjects that they are nervous about raising in front of the whole group.

The report (45 minutes): During this part of the meeting, members of the group (in turn) will give their feedback to their experiences over the preceding week, including to the assignment that they were given to do at home. This part begins with a "gimmick"—some entertaining group activity that indicates what the workshop will deal with and also to compensate those who come to the meeting on time.

The instructional part (55 minutes): This part takes place after a ten-minute break. In every workshop the teacher will teach one of the subjects of the course. She will use the theoretical material and exercises offered in the pamphlet under the title "Activities": the teacher will activate the parents and sometimes will also use the children who come to the workshop with their parents in order to demonstrate the subject being taught at that session. In most workshops this part will end with the reading aloud of a relevant children's poem on the subject of the workshop taken from appropriate poetry selections.

CONTENTS

WORKSHOP 1: SEEKING OUT THE POSITIVE IN THE CHILD

Preparations for the Workshop

Recommended: Arrange the chairs in a circle.

Prepare a poster with a list of subjects that will be discussed in the course (use the table of contents).

Bring a puzzle to put together (between forty and sixty pieces).

Straighten up the classroom and prepare refreshments.

Prepare a personal card for each child whose parents are participating in the course where the teacher records positive things that the child has said and done all week and get ready to show samples of work the child has done over the past week.

Prepare empty cards to pass out to the parents where they can list both their expectations of the meetings and their assignments for home.

Photocopy selected poems to hand out to the parents.

Photocopy the first "Page for parents" to hand out to the parents at the end of the meeting.

Conduct individual conversations (20 minutes before the group session): The teacher will hold a personal conversation with each parent before the group session. At this time the teacher will recount the positive things the child has said or done based on the report in the personal card. Examples of positive comments include the following: "See what a nice color combination he made"; "He gave good answers in . . ."; "I had never thought of that idea"; and "She helped her friends on the school trip."

The First Part (approximately 45 minutes)

The first part of the workshop will be devoted to the participants getting acquainted and giving general information about the course program:

Opener

It is a good idea to start the workshop with a short game whose object is to help the participants get acquainted with each other and to create a pleasant atmosphere. Try to choose a game that demonstrates the principles of the course. An example of an opener is "1–10": The group leader announces "one," and the rest of the participants have to continue spontaneously counting until to ten, without having two people call out the same number, at which point they have to start the count all over again.

Contract

The kindergarten/school teacher reads and explains the clauses in the contract that the participants must adhere to throughout the course (see appendix D).

Round 1: Getting Acquainted

The teacher gives every participant a chance to introduce himself or herself. All participants must be given the opportunity to present themselves as they wish (they may describe their profession, family, areas of interest, number and ages of children, etc.).

Round 2: Look for the Positive

At the end of the first round, the second round will begin, where each parent will be asked to say positive things about his child in the class. The teacher will intervene when the parents get "carried away" and begin to describe negative things about the child or where they undercut the positive things they are saying with "but . . . ."

Content Matter of the Workshops

The kindergarten/school teacher will show the parents the poster that has been prepared, hand out a page with a detailed description of the material in the course, and briefly explain each of the subjects.

  Coffee Break (10 minutes)

The Second Part: Instructional Activities (approximately 55 minutes)

Activity No. 1: Looking for the Positive—The Goal: Identifying Children's Behavior While Putting Together a Puzzle

  Divide the participants into teams of three to four each.
  The teams will prepare a list of "What positive behavior can be identified in the child who is putting together a puzzle?" Examples: "knows how to concentrate"; "cooperates with others"; "shows good organizational ability"; "has good spatial sense"; "can identify shades of color"; "shows leadership ability"; or "creates a pleasant atmosphere."
  At the plenary session, each of the teams presents a summary of the discussion in each team and the list they have put together.

The list will be used by the participants for the next activity—putting together the puzzle.

Activity No. 2: Putting Together a Puzzle—The Goal: Practice in Looking for the Positive and Giving Positive Feedback

The participating parents are divided into pairs of parents and children.
The children's group puts together a jigsaw puzzle.
The parents group watches the children putting together the puzzle.
  While observing, each parent records positive things on the card about the specific child that she or he has been observing.

It is important to ask the parents to point out what they are basing their generalizations on. In order to make the job of the parents more challenging and closer to reality, we suggest discreetly selecting one participant from each children's group and instructing her or him to deliberately cause a disturbance during the puzzle exercise.

In order to give everyone a chance to try out both roles, the two groups switch over after the puzzle is assembled; the parents become the children and the children become the parents, writing down positive remarks.

Mutual feedback: After completing the puzzle, the parents sit opposite their children and tell them, according to what is written on their card, the positive aspects that they noticed while the children were putting together the puzzle. It is important that the parents mention what they are basing their positive statements on, and that they are as concrete as possible.

At the end of this feedback, the children should say how they feel about what they just heard, and if they discovered anything new about the parents (as adults) following this experience. Afterward, the parents and children exchange roles in giving feedback. At the end of the feedback session, one or two couples (as time permits) should present the feedback that they gave each other. (It is best if one of the couples includes the participant who was instructed to misbehave, to demonstrate to parents that one can find the positive in every child, even in those who are disruptive.)

At Home

Look for positive things that your child did or said during the week and write them down on the cards.

Before the following home assignment, parents should be instructed as follows: when they come home, they must immediately begin to write down positive things about the child. This should be done openly (but not by making a statement) in order to stimulate the child into asking questions like, "Why are you watching me and writing things down?" The parent's answer in this case should be, "I'm in a parents' group now, and I have homework to prepare. I have to write positive things about you, that you say or do." If children ask about what would happen if they do negative things, they should be answered that writing down negative things is not part of the homework.

If children say that they do not want to be written about, their wishes should be respected. Explain to the parents that if they do their homework properly, and teach themselves to identify the positive, they will sense changes in the child and perhaps even in the entire system of family relationships.

WORKSHOP 2: REINFORCING THE POSITIVE IN THE CHILD

Seize the moment.

Preparations for the Workshop

Write on each child's personal card the positive things that the child has said and done all week in school/kindergarten and prepare samples of work the child has done over the past week.

Send reminders to parents (see appendix B).

Get organized for the workshop: arrange the kindergarten or classroom and prepare props—strips of paper and pins (for attaching to clothing)—for each participant.

Photocopy the poems to be selected to hand out to the parents.

Photocopy the second "Page for parents" to hand out to the parents at the end of the meeting.

Conduct individual Conversations (20 minutes before the group session)

The First Part (approximately 45 minutes)

Opener: Finger Game

The group pairs off. A looks at his partner, B, and raises a finger. B looks at A and after a few seconds must think, "I like him." When A senses this from B's expression, A must bend the finger. Then they exchange roles, and finally, they discuss the conclusions.

The Report

The kindergarten/school teacher asks the parents, each in turn, to read the cards or tell about the positive things that they have recorded over the preceding week about their children.

Coffee Break (10 minutes)

The Second Part: Instructional—Detailing, Explaining, and Demonstrating the Four Stages of Positive Reinforcement

The correct use of the four stages of positive reinforcement is one of the building blocks of the Hadarim Program. The purpose in using the four stages is dual: to reinforce positive behavior or qualities and to reduce negative behavior ("I believe that there is no child who is messy, unsociable, or inattentive in an absolute sense"). We all move on a continuum: "There are among us those who are more or less attentive, neat to a larger or lesser extent," and so forth. In the child, too, who is considered by his parents, teachers, and so on, to be messy, inattentive, or unsociable, one can find the moment when the child is attentive (even for a short span), plays with a friend (even for the briefest time), or neatly arranges his or her possessions or straightens his or her room. That is why it is important to catch that moment and encourage the child using the four stages as outlined here:

Stage 1: General

At this stage, one should say to the child some positive statement about his or her behavior that emphasizes a quality (attentive, neat, etc.) or ability (understands, draws well, etc.). This statement must be made about behavior that is taking place at that moment in reality. For example:

Concentration: "You have the ability to concentrate."
Consideration: "You are a considerate boy."
Orderliness: "You are a girl who likes to neaten things up."
Sociability: "You are a sociable boy."

Stage 2: Specific

At this stage, relate to the specific action that the child has done and which have caused her or him to be encouraged. For example (following up the earlier stage):

Concentration: "I saw how you sat there for ten minutes and put the puzzle together."

Consideration: "I noticed how you let your little sister play with your favorite car."

Orderliness: "I saw you put your schoolbag in your room when you came home today."

Sociability: "I noticed that your friend Eran came to visit and you got along very well with him."

Stage 3: Elaboration

At this stage, we elaborate on the behavior that we wish to reinforce. It is important to stress that this stage should open with the words "I am sure that . . . ." Experience has shown that this kind of address gives the children confidence and improves their chances of achieving a change.

One must stay with the quality or behavior that has been reinforced until then and not elaborate beyond that, to avoid creating a feeling of overload or overly high expectations. For example (following up the earlier stage):

Concentration: "I am sure that in class you are also very attentive."

Consideration: "I am confident that your considerate nature will be very useful to you in many situations."

Orderliness: "I am sure that your love of order will help you in many other areas."

Sociability: "I have no doubt that you know how to make friends at school, too."

Stage 4: Emotional/Personal

The purpose of this stage is to reinforce the connection between the parent and child by adding the emotional/personal dimension. At this stage, a connection is also made with the first, general stage, and thus, the cycle is completed. For example (following up the three earlier stages):

Concentration: "I'm proud that you have the ability to concentrate."

Consideration: "I'm touched by what a considerate girl you are."

Orderliness: "I'm happy that you like things to be neat."

Sociability: "Daddy will also be happy to hear how well you get along with your friends."

Following is a chart of the goals, the key words for the four stages, and a demonstration of how they are used.

Table 14.1. Reinforcing the positive using the four stages

Stage	Examples	Key words	Goals
General	You have the ability to concentrate. You are a positive child.	**You have . . .** **You are . . .**	A general positive statement about the child's behavior or a quality he or she has.
Specific	I saw you sitting for ten minutes doing the puzzle. I noticed that your friend Eran came and that you got along well.	**I saw that . . .** **I noticed that . . .** **I detected . . .**	Relating to a specific (true) action that the child has performed.
Elaboration	I am sure that at school, too, you participate nicely. I am convinced that you make friends at school, too.	**I am sure that . . .** **I am convinced that . . .** **I am sure that also . . .** **I have no doubt that . . .**	Elaborating about the action that we want to encourage and reinforce.
Emotional-personal	I am proud that you know how to persevere. Dad will also be happy to hear that you get along so well with the kids in the class.	**I am proud that . . .** **I am happy when . . .** **I am excited that . . .** **Your mom (dad) also . . .**	To let the child hear positive things from someone who is meaningful to him or her—the parent.

Activity: Learning and Practicing the Use of the Four Stages of Encouragement—The Goal: Getting Firsthand Experience in Giving Meaningful, Positive Feedback

The participants pair off and decide who will be the "parent" and who will be the "child." Each pair will alternately practice using the four stages of encouragement. It is a good idea for each participant to choose a topic that bothers her or him about the kindergarten or school child (for example, a child who is not attentive, orderly, or sociable). During the exercise, the teacher will move from pair to pair, giving them directions and making comments (positive, of course). The teacher will ask each parent to demonstrate the exercise in front of the class.

In order to demonstrate to the parents how important it is to receive positive reinforcement, I suggest that each parent attach a strip of paper to his shirt that states the first stage of the positive statements that he or she has tried out. For example, "I am able to be attentive. I like order."

Afterward, the parents will walk around the room while demonstrating in pantomime, and afterward with words, what is written on their shirts. It is recommended that this experience end with the parents giving their reactions to how they felt during the activity. Idea: Photograph the group with all the parents wearing the statements that they prepared.

At Home

Write positive things about your child according to the four stages.

WORKSHOP 3: THE FAMILY AS A MOBILE AND CONDUCTING NEGOTIATIONS

When you come to speak to your child, mainly listen.

Preparations for the Workshop

Write on each child's personal card the positive things that the child has said and done all week in school/kindergarten and prepare samples of work and products made by the child over the past week.
Send reminders to parents about the meeting.
Arrange the kindergarten or classroom and prepare refreshments and props: a mobile and a twelve-meter-long rope.
Prepare strips of paper and clips.
Photocopy the poems to be selected to hand out to the parents.
Photocopy the third "Page for parents" to hand out to the parents at the end of the meeting.

The First Part (approximately 45 minutes)

Opener: The Persuasion Game

The participants stand in two lines, the first one in line A convinces the first one in line B to move over to his or her side, and then sits down. The one who was convinced (and moved to the other side) must convince the one opposite to move to the other side, and so on. Afterward, the results are discussed.

The Report

Parents all report in turn to the group on positive things that they observed in their children over the previous week and how they were able to reinforce them using the four stages.

Coffee Break (10 minutes)

The Second Part—Instructional (approximately 55 minutes)

The mobile helps us demonstrate these subjects:

The importance of the family hierarchy: The mobile is built of two levels, the parent level and the child level. In the family, too, it is important to preserve this kind of structure and to clarify the difference between the levels. The hierarchical structure may be blurred and challenged when one of the parents joins one of the children against the other parent or when a small child controls both parents. Undermining this structure may harm parental authority and the functioning of the family as a whole.

The influence of the absent parent: It is important to convey the message that even in families where one parent is missing (due to divorce, death, unknown parentage, etc.), this parent still exists in the child's consciousness. Using the mobile, one may demonstrate how the family structure changes when one of the parents is missing (the weight of each parent now rests on the shoulders of the other parent) and how the role of the children changes: the eldest child, for example, takes on a more central and responsible role.

The influence of the relationship between the parents on the children: By increasing and decreasing the distance between the figures of the father and the mother on the mobile, one may demonstrate the relations of intimacy and distance between the parents and their effect on the entire family. When we move the parents in the mobile far apart from each other, we are playing out a situation where the parents are in a state of tension that is reflected in long silences and ignoring each other (in such a situation we see that the children in the mobile appear tense and "pulled" between them both). When the parents are pushed together so that they bump, we see where we can demonstrate a situation of fighting and clashes between the parents (in such a situation we see the children in the mobile getting jostled and jolted helplessly between the parents).

The significance of the order of the children in the family: The child's placement in the family is known to be very significant; the first child gets exclusive and undivided attention—everyone is amazed by her or him and they are always taking pictures. The second child is often more competitive and interested in catching up with the first but generally chooses to excel in his or her own field. The second child frequently seeks and obtains the parents' help in struggles against the older sibling. The third or fourth child enjoys attention by virtue of being little and creates coalitions with one of the siblings.

Conducting Negotiations: Demonstrating the Situations That Arise When There Is a Need for Negotiations (Using the Rope)

It is recommended that the simulation include the following figures: father, mother, sixteen-year-old daughter, and four-year-old boy. The situations:

> The father pulls the family without talking to them about it.
> The family does not take the small boy into account.
> The small boy is recommended for a special education class.
> The mother and father disagree, and the children are in the middle.
> The father and mother do not take into account the teenage daughter's wishes.

Note: At this stage it is a good idea to teach the group the principles of conducting negotiations (see later on in the workshop). The kindergarten/school teacher will ask the family members to negotiate with the teenage daughter according to the principles they have learned.

Activity No. 1: Preparing a Mobile to Learn Principles of Negotiating

The participants draw a mobile of their extended family (both on the mother's side and on the father's). The participants sit in couples and involve their partner in preparing the mobile.

Activity No. 2: Practice in Conducting Negotiations in Pairs

Members of the group will divide up into groups of "parent" and "child." The "parents" will prepare crowns for their "children" from strips of paper and write on them "good relations." The object is to remind the parent that the first principle is good relations with the child. The parents will raise a subject that preoccupies them with their real children and discuss it with their partner, with the crown "good relations" facing them. Then the participants switch roles. The discussion will make it possible to actively practice the principles of negotiations that were taught in the workshop. Each of the couples will present the process and the outcome to the plenary group.

At Home

Give positive reinforcement according to the four stages. Use the principles of negotiations within the family as learned in the workshop.

WORKSHOP 4: FAMILY DISCUSSION—THEORY AND PRACTICE

You cannot change the air outside, but you can change the atmosphere inside the house.

Preparations for the Workshop

Write on each child's personal card.
Send reminders to parents about the meeting.
Photocopy the poems to read with the parents.
Photocopy the fourth "Page for parents" to hand out to the parents at the end of the meeting.
Conduct individual conversations (20 minutes before the group session).

The First Part (approximately 45 minutes)

Opener: *The Balloon Game*

Divide the group into "families," with four to five participants in each group. Each group forms a circle. A balloon is thrown into the circle, and the participants are asked to make sure the balloon does not touch the floor. A new balloon is constantly being added, and the game continues until one of the balloons touches the floor. No one is allowed to touch the balloon more than once consecutively. Afterward, the results are discussed.

The Report

There is a review of what was learned in the previous session. The parents report on conducting a family negotiation.

The Second Part—Instructional (approximately 55 minutes)

When is it important to hold a family discussion? Principles and rules for a family discussion follow:

Principles

It is important to take pains to create an encouraging atmosphere. This meeting must not be turned into a "kangaroo court" where the parents preach to their children, judge them, and use the opportunity to settle accounts with each other. The decisions reached in the family discussion are the result of thoughtful consideration and require general consent, not parental coercion. It is very desirable to include a pleasant subject of discussion in the list of topics for family discussion (like a family outing, a

Table 14.2. Agenda for a family discussion

Number	Subject	Suggested by
1.	Trip to Mt. Hermon	Mom
2.	Giving out chores in the house	Dad
3.	Yoav hits me	Yael
4.	A new computer	Yoav
5.		
6.		

birthday celebration, etc.) in order to create a feeling of pleasant anticipation before the family discussion.

Thus, for example, rules accepted by the family such as, "We do not travel on the Sabbath," "We do not lift a hand against each other," and so forth, are not subjects for discussion, and upholding them obligates everyone. In contrast, family rules such as deciding meal times, who helps out with the chores, allowances, and so on, are subjects that can be discussed. On subjects like moving, the parent's place of work, or the like, the children should be informed, but it must be made clear that the decisions made about them are solely the parent's field of responsibility.

Rules for a Family Discussion

Below are a number of rules that can help in managing a family discussion:

Every discussion will begin with encouraging words and positive feedback. The positive feedback will be given by everyone in turn, so that everyone will get positive feedback from everyone in the family.

The family discussion will be run by a chairperson and a secretary. These roles will be rotated among all of the members of the family. Appointing the people to these roles will be done at the end of each discussion.

Everyone must give respect and support to the secretary and chairperson on duty.

The job of the chairperson is to run the discussion while maintaining the rules: the chairperson must insist on promptness in beginning and ending the meeting (recommended time: 30 minutes). The chairperson must make sure that the meeting is run out of a feeling of mutual respect: listening to each other, giving encouragement, making sure everyone has an equal opportunity to express themselves, being considerate of each other's opinion, and maintaining a pleasant atmosphere.

The job of the secretary: To remind everyone of the subjects that were postponed from previous meetings, to report on the implementation of decisions that were made in previous discussions, and to write down the decisions made by the family in its discussion.

Note: It is important to prepare refreshments that the children and other family members like, to treat the participants.

Activity for Practicing the Family Discussion: The Simulation Game

The participating parents are divided up into "families." Every family chooses a chairperson and a secretary. The families practice having a family discussion in accordance with the principles and rules that were learned.

The kindergarten/school teacher moves from family to family and offers guidance to the participants as needed. When the discussion in each family is over, some kind of refreshments are served.

After the drill, a discussion is held where everyone, in turn, tells what difficulties arose, what questions came up, and the like.

At Home

Prepare a page with an agenda for a family discussion and hang it up in a prominent place (for example, on the refrigerator). Encourage the members of the family to write down subjects for a family discussion. Bring the list with you to the next workshop (do not run a family discussion yet this week).

WORKSHOP 5: MODERATING SIBLING DISPUTES

Win-win situations

Preparations for the Workshop

Photocopy appropriate poems to read with the parents.

Photocopy the fifth "Page for parents" to hand out to the parents at the
end of the meeting.

Conduct individual conversations (20 minutes before the group session).

The First Part (approximately 45 minutes)

Opener: Siblings

The participants are divided into oldest, middle, and youngest children.
Each group holds a discussion of "siblings." Then they discuss the results.

The Report

The parents present the chart of "Agenda for a family discussion" and tell
about the reactions of each member of the family. This is the time to encourage the parents to hold the family discussion.

Coffee Break (10 minutes)

The Second Part—Instructional (approximately 55 minutes)

How to Relate to Sibling Squabbles

Major factors in sibling fighting: jealousy, struggle over emotional (parental
love) and material (possessions) and turf (Jealousy: The feeling that the
other sibling is preferred or possesses a quality that you wish you had). Sibling fighting is not a new invention. We find many accounts of brothers
fighting way back in the stories in the Bible (Cain and Abel, Jacob and Esau,
Joseph and his brothers, etc.). Sibling rivalry is normal and healthy, and it
happens in every family where there is more than one child.

In order to understand the background to the rivalry between siblings, it is
necessary to go back to the moment when the parents come home from the
hospital with a new baby. In many cases this period is attended by the older
sibling's feeling that the mother does not love him or her the same way she
loves the new baby. Parents have an important role in preventing arguments
and moderating them. One can help the older child to cope in the following
ways:

It is important that the parent be aware of the older sibling's feeling. Parents must allow the child to express his or her feelings and give legitimacy to the feelings of jealousy.

One can show the older siblings the advantages in their new situation:
they become a big brother or sister, there are things they can do that
the baby cannot do yet, and they can help the parents take care of the

baby and, at the same time, teach the baby new things and play with him or her.

The father can have a very important role when the second child is born: when the first child was born, it is often the mother who fulfills the major parental role and the father who helps her and learned his new job. When the second child is born, the father should deepen his relationship with the first child, spend more time with her or him, and help the child get through this period safely.

Sibling rivalry also has advantages; the children learn life skills:

To protect their own rights and possessions
To develop effective ways to convince figures of authority of their position
To develop the ability to work under pressure
To learn to be flexible and to compromise

How Can Parents Learn to Help Prevent Rivalry and Fighting between Siblings?

Many times children develop characteristics that are typical of the order of birth. Frequently, oldest children try to be first, the leader. Second children develop a sensitivity to injustice and are preoccupied with their attempts to catch up with the big sibling, while youngest children generally believe that they are entitled to more attention. The parents can help prevent rivalry in the following ways:

The parents can convey the message to their children that each one of them is special in his or her own unique way, and that they recognize the special abilities and qualities of each of their children. This message can be conveyed among others by the four stages in encouragement that we learned in workshop 2: it is important that each child receive positive reinforcement for the things about her or him that are unique and special.

Parents should refrain from making comparisons on the style of, "See how nicely your big sister behaved and did not make a fuss, and you don't stop teasing" or, "Why can't you sit down and do homework like your brother?" Comparisons of this kind do not contribute to improving motivation and may even cause sibling rivalry and tension.

In a similar vein, parents should avoid creating a competitive atmosphere in the home, and they should convey the message that effort, progress, and using one's ability are even more important than success.

Parents can present to their children the advantages of their placement in the family: "The oldest child can enjoy privileges because she or he is the oldest (and can do things that the younger ones are not allowed to do, go to bed later, etc.), and the younger siblings can learn from the older ones, play with them, get their help, and enjoy their protection.

Parents can ask the child who is complaining about a sibling to write his complaint on the agenda sheet for a family discussion (see workshop 4).

The Damage Caused by Intervention

Parents cannot judge fairly since they are not aware of all of the details of the argument. Frequently, parents tend to see the older sibling as the agitator and the younger one as the victim, but that is not always the case.

Parental intervention prevents children from learning to conduct their own negotiations and solve problems. Intervention shows the children that the parent does not rely on them. Often, intervention of a parent inflames the situation and exacerbates the fight.

. . . Many parents are surprised by the recommendation not to intervene in children's fights. Below are some examples of questions that we encounter frequently and the answers to these questions:

Q. What do you do when your child calls to you and asks for your intervention?

A. You should tell the children consistently and explicitly that you trust them to solve the dispute by themselves. It is very important to adhere to this approach and to do it in cooperation with your spouse. If you demonstrate a lack of consistency in your response, your children will continue to try to drag you into their fights in the future, too. Still you should avoid expressions such as, "I don't care if you break each other's head," which may escalate the fight.

Q. What do you do if during a children's fight they curse each other or do other things that are in violation of the family's rules and values?

A. It is important to differentiate between "intervention in children's quarrels" and "education." Nonintervention in a sibling squabble is not a contradiction of the need to educate the child to behave in accordance with the family's rules and values. For example, if during a quarrel the children curse, we recommend ignoring the curses during the fight itself but later, when tempers die down, act as you normally act when the children curse.

Q. And what happens when they hit each other?

A. If there is a danger that the children will hit each other, the parent should pass by the room periodically using various excuses (to take something, to clean, etc.) and to demonstrate a presence and make sure that everything is all right. If this behavior does not put an end to the violence, you may simply remove one child from the room (without expressing anger either verbally or nonverbally). This action need not be accompanied by words. Frequently, deeds speak louder than words.

Parent's Response in the Event of a Sibling Quarrel

Despite the parents' attempts to create an atmosphere of cooperation and enjoyment in the home, it is important to stress that it is impossible to totally avoid quarrels between siblings. The attitude the parents take toward these quarrels are of utmost importance. When they intervene, they reinforce certain kinds of behavior and eliminate other kinds.

Experience has shown that the less parents intervene in sibling quarrels, and the more they make an effort to transfer the responsibility for their relationships to the children, the better children will learn to get along and solve their problems by themselves. Putting out fires:

Postponement without scheduling a time: "We'll talk about it later."
Distraction: "There's nothing to fight about. We're going out to see a movie/get a pizza."
Compensation: "We'll buy another Coke."

Below is a suggestion for two activities that will demonstrate to parents the importance of nonintervention in sibling quarrels and the need to convey the message that they trust their children to resolve the quarrel themselves, by negotiation.

Activity No. 1: Conversation in Discussion Groups

The school teacher will divide the parents into groups of three each. Each participant will tell the other two comrades about a sibling quarrel that took place between the children in her or his family and the successful resolution. The three of them will decide which case to present to the entire group.

From a summary of the cases described in the plenary group, the following conclusions may arise:

1. It happens to all of us.
2. You don't need any special reason for it to happen.
3. Parents have a share in the quarrel.
4. It is possible to moderate sibling squabbles.

Table 14.3.   Developing dynamic in sibling quarrels

The child wants something and thinks how to get it.	The child does something (to get what he wants).	The parent senses it and thinks . . .	The parent reacts.	How the child understands the parent's reaction and what he does	Alternative: I am counting on you to manage.

Activity No. 2: A Description of the Dynamic

The school teacher presents the parents with a chart that describes the developing dynamic in sibling quarrels. The chart demonstrates what happens to a child who wants to have his or her way and encounters resistance form a sibling, and then turns to the parent for support and protection. The last part of the chart (the alternative) should be left blank to allow the parents to suggest their own solutions. Afterward, you can also present the solution that appears in the chart.

Simulation: There is a possibility of presenting the chart as a role play; the teacher and two parents play the role of the parent and the two siblings who are in conflict, in accordance with the stages listed in the chart.

Activity No. 3

We recommend making a role play from the passage brought in the book by Penelope Leach: the oldest child, the parents, and the second child (in the group leader's handbook).

At Home

Hold a family discussion according to the guidelines in the fourth workshop. Identify the developing dynamic in the quarrel between siblings, if you encounter it this week. Imagine yourself telling the children a sentence such as, "Sit together, discuss what happened, and let me know (within an hour) what solution you arrived at."

WORKSHOP 6: THE CHILD AS SCIENTIST AND THE PARENT AS FACILITATOR

Your child cannot know how deep the puddle is until he steps into it. (Murphy's Law)

Preparations for the Workshop

Invite one of the mothers to come early in order to get a briefing from the teacher before the exercise with the egg or cup of water.

Prepare a carton of eggs or cups full of water.

Prepare the props required: candies, balloons.

Photocopy appropriately selected poems to read with the parents.

Photocopy the sixth "Page for parents" to hand out to the parents at the end of the meeting.

Conduct individual conversations (20 minutes before the group session).

The First Part (approximately 45 minutes)

Opener: The Tangle Game

People stand in a circle, and each participant holds the hands of two people who are not standing next to her or him (also not holding both hands of the same person); that is how the "tangle" is created. Afterward, the participants try to undo the tangle without letting go of each other's hands. At the end of the game, they discuss the conclusions.

The Report

As soon as the workshop begins, the teacher moves among the parents and suggests to half of them, "One balloon now or three at the end of the workshop," and to the second half offers, "One candy now or three at the end of the workshop." An explanation of this will be given later on. The parents talk about their home assignment—identifying the developing dynamic in a quarrel between siblings.

Coffee Break (10 minutes)

The Second Part—Instructional (approximately 55 minutes)

The Child as Scientist or How to Relate to the Child's Experimentation

Already in infancy children acquire characteristics and skills that will help them learn about the world that in which they have arrived and understand physical, emotional, and social process that are going on around: they examine the world around them—grab things, feel them, identify the various textures, feel the different weights, notice differences in size, shape, and color, and so forth. When they begin to walk, they are able to move away and their field of research expands. As a scientist they begin to conduct experiments: they pour water from hand to hand and marvel at how it disappears; they build a tower and test what happens when they pull out the bottom blocks, they pour liquid from cup to cup; and the like. Experiments are not restricted only to the physical world. The experiments of the infant and, later on, the child are also directed at emotional and social spheres. Think about babies who are testing how many times their father will be willing to pick up the ball they have thrown, children who ask the same question again and again to test the adult's reaction, or toddlers who test their parents' limits when they forbid them to do something.

We believe that a parent who is aware of the qualities of investigation and experimentation as developing the child's cognitive, emotional, and social skills will accept paying the "tuition" it entails with more understanding. Puddles of water, smeared food, or "works of art" scattered through the house will no longer be seen only as dirt and disorder but also as a long-term investment. This kind of understanding can turn parents into partners to their child's investigation and experimentation and lead to many hours of mutual enjoyment.

The Parent as Mediator or How a Parent Can Help the Child Investigate the World

The parent acts as a mediator between the child and the world. It is important that the mediator (the parent) recognize the child's natural quick ability to absorb new material. It is important to remember that the parent is not a teacher. Giving children enrichment and reinforcing their ability to learn must be done in a pleasant atmosphere. Take advantage of the fact that you are not bound to a classroom, a table and chair, and make use of varied and different opportunities to enrich the child's world: baking a cake together can teach the child about quantities and calculations; a visit to the supermarket together will expose the child to the possibility of selecting and teach a lesson in budgeting; an outing in nature will expose the child to a range of geographical and botanical phenomena, and so forth.

Below is a list of the ways parents can help reinforce the child's learning ability and a description:

Ensuring a proper learning environment
Helping develop the ability to concentrate, to persevere, and finish things
Training the child to delay gratification (in peacetime)
Helping the child to cope with accidents and mistakes
Exposing the child to a wide range of stimuli and experiences, and
    encouraging him or her to use senses to the maximum
Using play, creativity, humor, and surprise

Environmental Conditions

At a young age, one must ensure the child has a safe environment for playing and expose the child to varied stimuli, both at home and outside. At the school stage, parents can help their children learn more effectively by ensuring proper conditions: creating a friendly learning atmosphere as well as making sure they have a proper table and chair, proper lighting, quiet, dictionaries, and writing equipment.

Developing the Ability to Concentrate, Persevere, and Complete Things

The ability to persevere and concentrate are among the most important skills in the learner's repertoire. Children have the ability to concentrate and persist, and parents can help reinforce this through practice and verbalization. The Hadarim Program recommends that parents "catch" children when they are intent on putting together a puzzle, drawing, or any other activity and, using the four stages of encouragement described in the second workshop, convey the message that they have the ability to concentrate and that this ability will stand them in good stead in whatever assignments they get in the future. It should be noted that many parents tend to concentrate on their own activities (housework, reading the newspaper—"I finally have a few minutes of quiet to myself") when children are involved in their own activities. This is precisely the best time to find some time to comment to children on their ability to concentrate on their task. Another important subject to emphasize to parents is perseverance in carrying out an assignment. Below is an example of encouragement for persevering to complete an assignment using the four stages:

It is important to encourage children to complete assignments, even "small assignments," like wiping off the table. (It is important to restrain yourself and not clean it after them if their performance is less than perfect.)

Developing the Ability to Delay Gratification

Another component that helps the young learner is the ability to delay immediate gratification. If children know that there are advantages in delaying gratification and there is a reasonable chance that, at the end of the long road, they will be compensated for their willingness to forego the immediate reward, their ability to delay gratification will increase. In order to train children in delaying gratification, we recommend an exercise: when children ask for a candy, the mother should offer, "One candy now or two in another hour (after the meal)." Training the children's ability to delay gratification should be done in "peacetime"; that is, it doesn't pay to start to teach them to

Table 14.4. Encouragement for completing an assignment

General	Specific	Elaboration	Personal-Emotional
"You know how to undertake a job and finish it."	"I saw you didn't leave the puzzle until you finished it."	"I'm sure your persistence will help in other areas, too."	"I'm proud that you are able to see a thing through until the end."

delay gratification at a time when they are insisting on getting some specific thing.

Dealing with Accidents and Mistakes

To rely on children also means to allow them to experiment and even to fail. Parents frequently tend to protect their children and prevent them from experimenting, not allowing them a chance to try things for themselves, lest they fail. We believe that this approach develops dependency in children and prevents them from cultivating autonomy and learning to rely on themselves, and also the chance to learn from the consequences of their own actions. Children learn that parents trust them and believe in them also by the way the parent reacts to their accidents and mistakes. Children try to do things by experimenting, and sometimes they fail. Parents find it hard to accept these failures as the "tuition" they must pay. Parent can use a children's mistakes to show them that the parents trusts them and believe that the next time, they will do better. It is important to convey the message to the child that accidents and mistakes are natural (they happen to parents, too) and that one can learn from them and accumulate experience for the future. This message can be taught using the four stages of encouragement. An example of encouraging a child who wanted to bake a cake and scattered the flour all over by accident follows:

General: You are a child who likes to help.
Specific: I saw how anxious you were to help me bake a cake.
Elaboration: I'm sure that you can help me in many things.
Personal: It makes me feel good to know that I have a child who loves so much to help.

The job of parenting can seem to be a bother and a torment, but one can also enjoy one's children: a parent who employs creativity, invents games, uses a sense of humor, surprises by reacting differently than expected, and consults with the child will enjoy cooperation. Above all, it is important that the interaction with one's child bring pleasure, to both the parent and the child. For that reason we recommend making lavish use of

Play,

Humor,

Creativity,

and Surprises (be unexpected)

Unfortunately, these principles, which are taken for granted in interactions with babies, become less common as the children grow up.

Activity No. 1: Delayed Gratification

It is recommended that there is a discussion of the exercise that was conducted at the beginning of the session about choosing candies or balloons. In the course of the discussion, stress the importance of keeping promises in order to guarantee the child's trust. It is also important for parents to realize that there are types of gratification that are easier to delay than others, which may be more difficult.

Activity No. 2: The Participants as Scientists in Their Childhood

The participants will recount incidents from their childhood where they tried to be scientists.

Activity No. 3: Humor, Play, and Creativity

The participants will tell of a situation where they employed play, humor, or creativity in an interaction with their child.

Activity No. 4: Practice Coping with Accidents and Mistakes

The object of this exercise is to teach the parents how we recommend reacting to an accident by a child. The suggested reaction contributes to children's self-confidence and conveys the message that the parent trusts them. The mother who was briefed before the workshop will enact the role of "mother" and the kindergarten/school teacher will play the role of the boy or girl. The mother will hand the girl an egg to be taken into the kitchen, the girl will drop the egg, and it will break on the floor, to the parents' surprise. The girl will react in panic: "Oh no, what did I do?" Her expression of anxiety and body movements suggesting that she is protecting herself physically may remind parents of similar situations from their own childhood. The mother will react: "Don't worry. It happens to everyone. Just last week I dropped the whole carton. Let me help you clean it up." Both of them clean the floor with materials that have been prepared in advance, and the mother, who was given prior instructions by the teacher, adds, "The egg broke but you are a responsible girl, and I can rely on you. Please take this other egg and bring it into the kitchen." Many group leaders prefer to use a cup of water instead of an egg. You should take into account the conditions of the locale. Group leaders who are not willing to forego the breaking of the egg can bring a sheet of nylon and make sure that the egg breaks on top of it.

It is important to remember at this stage to hand out the candies or balloons to the participants who chose to delay gratification.

At Home

In the event of a sibling quarrel, act according to what we learned.

Check to see if the child's learning environment satisfies you.

Try to apply what we learned about delayed gratification (in peacetime).

Make lavish use of humor, play, and creativity in interacting with your child.

Check if your perspective has changed over the week regarding your child's behavior (does any of your child's behavior, which had previously seemed like a nuisance, now seem like experimentation and investigation?).

WORKSHOP 7: THE PARENT AND THE SCHOOL (OR MAKING THE CHILD RESPONSIBLE)

Parent: Don't go back to school—this is your child's homework!

Preparations for the Workshop

Photocopy selected poems to read with the parents.

Photocopy the seventh "Page for parents" to hand out to the parents at the end of the meeting.

Conduct individual conversations (20 minutes before the group session).

The First Part (approximately 45 minutes)

Opener: The Jumping Game

The participants are asked to write down the number of times they can jump on one foot in half a minute (you can switch feet in the middle). Then the group leader asks the participants to stand around him or her, and after the signal, they must start jumping, as they count. There is generally a discrepancy between their estimation of their ability and their actual performance. At the end, they discuss the conclusions.

The Report

The parents report on their home assignment: examining the child's learning environment, practicing delaying gratification, encouraging the child's ability to concentrate and persist, and the use of play, humor, and creativity in their interactions.

Coffee Break (10 minutes)

The Second Part—Instructional (approximately 55 minutes)

The Parents and the Child's Homework

It is our view that preparation of homework is the child's responsibility. The parent is not the teacher, and the house is not the school. There is no need to get into confrontations with your child about doing homework. Leave this task to the teachers and the school. Parents who express confidence that children are capable of preparing homework by themselves will bring about a situation where eventually children accept responsibility for themselves. Children whose parents regularly help with homework, and sometimes do it for them, learn to rely on their parents instead of on themselves and are less likely to write down the homework assignments from the blackboard and to listen to the teacher's explanations. In order to succeed, it is important to act according to the following steps:

Both parents have to agree on noninterference in homework.

They must confide in the teacher about their decision not to interfere in the homework area. They may tell the teacher about the reasons that led them to make this decision: parent-child struggles, tension between the parents, failure to achieve their goal, and losing quality time with their child. They should also mention the strong influence the teacher has on the child in all matters related to studies.

The child should be told, "I am confident that you are capable of doing your homework by yourself. Between four and five o'clock (or whenever it is convenient), I will be in the kitchen/living room/my room, etc., and I will be reading/listening to music, etc. If you ask me for help at that time with your homework, I will be happy to help you if I can."

Accepting Failure (Dealing with Failing a Test or Getting a Bad Report Card)

Sometime the child's failure generates very difficult feelings for the parent: a sense of disappointment with the child, frustration, or even a sense of the parent's own failure. These feelings often lead to a difficult reaction in the parents as well. This kind of reaction not only does not contribute to changing things or improving the child's feelings, but it also damages the child's self-evaluation and may harm the connection with the parent.

The Hadarim Program Recommendation for an Alternative Reaction

We recommend breaking down the parent's reactions into several stages, and not being content with one general statement (like "It's not that bad," Try to do better next time," "I'm terribly disappointed," "Just wait until Dad sees this," etc.). In the spirit of the Hadarim Program, we recommend that the response to failure be given in a positive and constructive spirit, with a forward-looking attitude, rather than judgmental and critical. In other words, parents should not convey a response that deals with the question of "why?" but, instead, a response that focuses on "how to change things." This kind of reaction can also be a model for children to imitate when they have to deal with failures and will improve their feelings of self-confidence and self-image. The approach that "returns the ball to the child's court" also encourages them to think about solving the problem, gain maturity, and accept personal responsibility.

Getting Up in the Morning

In many homes, getting up in the morning and getting ready for school become a battleground at the end of which both parents and children leave for school exhausted and irritable. In many cases, the mother feels that getting the child up and ready for school is her responsibility, and she spends the morning in futile attempts to rouse and move the child along. This situation does not allow the mother enough time to get ready herself, and she is often late for work. This manner of handling things turns the mother into a policewoman and clouds her relationship with her child. In other words, it is a no-win situation.

In this area, too, we recommend that you transfer responsibility to the child. In order to succeed in this, we suggest acting in accordance with the following:

You have to decide together with your spouse that you must change the situation and that you are willing to bear the interim consequences, which are not convenient.

Notify your children that you are confident of their ability to wake up by themselves. You should go out together to buy an alarm clock and teach them how to use it.

Notify the teachers of the change in the parents' approach to the children's getting up in the morning, and enlist their help and support in making the change.

It is most important to be consistent and not to "break." You have to be able to cope with the children being late on the first days and the fact that they are going to bear the consequences of being late at school. If they are late the first days, you should see it as practice where your children are trying to adjust to the change. Do not be angry at them, for they might interpret it as a struggle that they will win in the end.

Awareness of the Child's Learning Style

Learning style is an individual matter and is influenced by several factors: ability to concentrate, ability to divide attention, personal convenience, a tendency to neatness, and so forth. There are people, among them children, who achieve their potential precisely when they study against a background of loud music, or when their desk is overloaded with papers and stimuli, while there are also those who need total silence and a well-organized environment in order to concentrate. We believe that there is no one system that is better than the next. Over the years we all discover the optimal conditions for us to learn.

Activity No. 1

In order to demonstrate the differences in learning style, we propose the following exercise: The parents are asked to fill out the chart with the characteristics of their learning style and that of their child, as in the sample below. Later, the parents will read their charts, or parts of it, to the group. The goal of the exercise is to show the parents in the group how different the various learning styles are and that there are differences in learning style, even within the adults' group and within the children's group (and not only between adults and children, as some people may think).

Activity No. 2

The participants divide up into two groups: parents and teachers. Each group holds a short discussion (10 minutes) on the subject of preparing

Table 14.5.   Learning style of parent and learning style of child

Conditions	The parent	The child
Location	At the kitchen table	On the bed/floor
Timing	Tries to postpone as much as possible	Tries to finish quickly
How long can I sit	For a long time, without a break	For short periods, with many breaks
Organization of working environment	All reference books, papers, and writing equipment prepared in advance on the table	Gets up every so often to get what is needed
Noise, quiet	Prefers to have the radio on	Needs total silence
Presence of other people	Prefers to study alone	Prefers to study with a friend/friends

homework from its own perspective (as a parent in a parent's group, as a teacher in a teacher's group). At the end of the discussion, the group sits one opposite the other and each presents its position.

At Home

We recommend devoting some time at home to thinking over the recommendations that were given in the workshop (in other words, we suggest that you do not take action yet). You may choose one of the subjects (homework, getting up in the morning, etc.) and build an imaginary scenario of how to apply the recommendations, of the child's anticipated reactions, and how the parent will cope. At the beginning of the next workshop, the parents will present their scenario, and there will be a discussion of the subject. Remember, the key to success is the belief that you are doing the right thing. Be consistent!

WORKSHOP 8: EMPHASIZING THE IMPORTANCE OF LIMITS FOR THE CHILD

Without limits, you're out of range.

Preparations for the Workshop

Prepare a rope twelve meters long.

Invite the children to demonstrate the activities described below.

Photocopy poems to read with the parents.

Photocopy the eighth "Page for parents" to hand out to the parents at the end of the meeting.

Conduct individual conversations (20 minutes before the group session).

The First Part (approximately 45 minutes)

Opener

Stand in two lines, with a large distance between the two lines. Each participant talks from a distance to the person who is opposite. The group leader claps hands, and with every hand clap, the sides move one step closer together, until each pair decides what is the distance that best suits them. At the end, they discuss the conclusions.

The Report

The parents report on their home assignment from the previous meeting—planning to make a change in one of the following areas: getting up in the morning, the child's preparation of homework, or coping with failure.

Coffee Break (10 minutes)

The Second Part—Instructional Activities (approximately 55 minutes)

We will demonstrate limits to the parents by using the rope.

Demonstrating the Security That Limits and Rules Give Us

Participants from the group are asked to walk toward the teacher with their eyes closed. They are asked to describe to the group the sensation of moving in space without any limits. The teacher will ask two parents to stand on either side of the room and tie the rope around themselves. The parents who were asked to move across the room with their eyes closed in the previous exercise will be asked to do it again but, this time, between the ropes that they can hold onto. Additional parents are asked to move between the ropes with their eyes closed. A discussion will be held about the feeling of security that the limits offered them.

Demonstrating the Individual Style of the Participants in Walking within the Limits

One of the parents is asked to move between the limits of the rope that were tied around the two parents standing on two sides of the room, and receives instructions that he or she is allowed to change the positioning of the ropes—to pull them to the sides, to bring them closer together, to pull them farther apart, and so on—according to his or her convenience and needs.

The teacher will suggest that every participant in the group move between the two ropes, each according to her or his own individual style. During the exercise, the participants will explain how they are walking between the ropes and what it means for them.

Demonstrating the Individual Style of Children Walking within the Limits

Participants will demonstrate their individual style and, afterward, will be asked to demonstrate how they imagine their child would walk between the ropes, that is, their child's personal style. It is interesting to note the differences between the parent's style and the child's style as the parent sees it.

If you invite some of the participants' children to the workshop, you can also do the following activity: A child is asked to leave the room, and the parent is asked to demonstrate the child's style (as she or he imagines it). When the child returns to the room, the child is asked to demonstrate his or her style in walking between the ropes. The parent may also be asked to leave the room; the child will demonstrate, and then the parent will return and demonstrate what he or she supposes is the child's style.

Important conversation and discussion: Setting and defining limits should be done together with children. Conducting negotiations that take into account their needs, personality, and age may help children internalize in their behavior the need to have rules and limits and understand that the purpose is to help them.

How Do We React When the Limits Are Stifling Us?

A parent who is invited to walk between the ropes (which are tied around two parents who are standing on two sides of the room) will be asked to move toward the teacher who will block the parent's passage by crossing the rope and make it hard for the parent to advance. In order to sharpen the idea, one may add a frame story taken from the world of adults (restriction in the workplace, in studies, etc.).

Other parents will be invited to walk between the ropes and experience the sensation of being confined within narrow limits with their progress blocked. Parents who are demonstrating will describe to the group their feeling when the path is blocked and will explain how they tend to respond in such circumstances.

How Do Our Children React When the Limits Stifle Them?

After the parents finish demonstrating their reaction, they will have to show how their child would react to a restricting of the limits. In this case, too, one may add a frame story, for example, the teacher will portray being a mother restricting her daughter about her curfew. The "mother" and the "daughter" can conduct negotiations as to the limits (while the mother is constantly blocking her daughter's way, using the rope).

Conversation and discussion on the different behavior of each of the participants who walked between the ropes will illustrate to the parents the possible reactions of children in a situation where the limits are stifling them and not allowing them to express their personality and propensities.

What Happens When the Parents Broadcast Inconsistency in Setting Limits?

The two parents, who are standing at different sides of the rope, will raise and lower the rope alternately, without any coordination between the hands that are holding the ropes (once the right hand and once the left).

A parent who is invited to walk between the ropes, while holding on to them with both hands, will find it hard to do so and feel confused and helpless at the unexpected changes, especially when the "parents" holding the rope shower contradictory messages (Walk . . . Don't walk). Additional parents will be invited to walk between the ropes and experience the difficulty and lack of security in such a situation.

Conversation and discussion: The limits that we set for our children must be consistent. Thus, the child will receive clear, consistent messages and can act according to them with a sense of security.

What Happens When the Mother and Father Disagree over the Limits?

The two parents who are standing on the two sides of the room will lower one side of the rope and raise the other, so that difference in height between both ends of the rope is maximal. This position of the ropes represents the different attitudes of each of the parents.

A parent who is invited to walk between the ropes when they are in this position will find it hard to hold onto them and to walk between them. This parent represents the child who is trying to walk (to function) where there are contradictory rules and limits. Additional parents will be invited to walk between the ropes and to experience the difficulty and the insecurity this situation contains. A child who tries to walk between taut ropes will feel a physical pain in the palms of his hands. This will be a demonstration of the interparent conflict and its impact on the child.

Conversation and discussion: The limits that we set for our children must be agreed upon by both parents so that the child gets clear messages and can act accordingly with a sense of security.

At Home

Have you agreed between yourselves on the limits that you are setting for your child? Plan what you will do in the event of a disagreement and be consistent. It is recommended that you review the material learned in the workshops on family discussion and conducting negotiations in order to refresh your memory on the ways of setting limits effectively.

Tell of an instance when you set a limit for your child and describe: did you conduct negotiations with him where you explained why you set those limits? Tell the other participants if you took into account your child's personality, wishes, and constraints (What will my friends say?).

WORKSHOP 9: LEARNING ALTERNATIVES (ALSO TO VIOLENCE) AND REINFORCING MUTUAL TRUST

Make your choice—accept responsibility.

Preparations for the Workshop

Invite two families, parents and children (it is important that at least one of the children know how to read).

Scatter the chairs around the room so that they are obstacles to movement.

Photocopy poems to read with the parents.

Photocopy the ninth "Page for parents" to hand out to the parents at the end of the meeting.

Conduct individual conversations (20 minutes before the group session).

The First Part (approximately 45 minutes)

The Report

The parents report on their home assignment from the previous meeting: setting limits for their children based on the recommendations of the program.

Coffee Break (10 minutes)

The Second Part—Instructional Activities (approximately 55 minutes)

The exercise proposed here was designed to demonstrate to parents how to teach their child that there are several alternatives to violent behavior. The exercise is based on the premise that we learn best when we are teaching:

A child who knows how to read will act as "teacher" to another child.

The second child will be asked to remain with his mother or father in a room nearby and to come in only after the child is asked to do so (this child will be the "pupil"). The first child, the "teacher," is asked to sit on the chair near the teacher.

At the request of the teacher, the child gets up from the chair and takes a turn around the room, and while the child is doing that, another parent comes and "grabs" this child's chair and sits on it.

The child who discovers that his chair has been "grabbed" will be asked to suggest several ways to solve the problem of, "What can you do when another child sits down in the chair that you had been sitting on?"

The schoolteacher asks the child to suggest more and more ways to solve the problem, and writes them on the blackboard. Examples of suggestions:

- You can negotiate with the "usurper" and convince her or him to give up the chair.
- You can ask for the intervention of the kindergarten/school teacher (or other adult).
- You can bring another chair.
- You can stand.

The teacher will ask the parents to suggest other alternate ideas to the child.

The child waiting in the room nearby will be asked to come into the room, and the child who practiced thinking of alternatives will explain the situation. The "teacher" child will tell about the alternatives suggested for getting the chair back. The teacher must also check and make sure that the "pupil" has understood the idea of alternatives.

It may be assumed that the child who is teaching will internalize what has been learned a short time before, throughout the exercise and instruction.

Reinforcing Mutual Trust

The following is a suggestion for an exercise designed to demonstrate to parents how to convey positive verbal messages to their child that express mutual trust. The exercise has two parts: the schoolteacher is led and the child leads. Chairs are scattered around the classroom so that it looks like an obstacle course. The teacher, in the role of the mother, closes his or her eyes and asks the child called upon to lead him or her between the chairs scattered throughout the room. The teacher who is being led by the child says aloud sentences that express confidence and trust in the child who will know how to lead safely: "I know that I can count on you," "You are leading me safely," and the like.

The teacher leads and the child is led. The teacher asks the child to close her or his eyes and leads the child through the obstacle course. The teacher who is leading says sentences that express support of the child and an intention to keep the child safe, like "You can count on me" and, "I'll take care of you, but I'll still allow you to explore the world, to make mistakes so that you can learn from them."

The parents in the group are asked to divide up into pairs and do both parts of the exercise. Parents can do the verbalization about the subject that bothers them. Thus, for example, a mother who is troubled by the fact that her son crosses the street alone will say, "I trust you and know that you are a responsible child"; "I have no doubt that you are being careful about your safety and welfare"; "I trust you to cross the street safely, only at the crosswalk"; "I am sure that you look both ways before you cross the street"; and the like. The teacher will accompany the parents and help them phrase sentences that express confidence that the child can be trusted.

Conversation and discussion: What did we feel when we said and when we were told positive verbal messages?

At Home

Prepare a description of an incident that you can present to the group where you offered your child several alternatives. Tell of cases where you gave your child the feeling that he or she has someone to rely on, and you used positive statements based on the four stages of encouragement (itemized in the second workshop); and you gave your child the feeling that you rely on him or her, and you expressed this in positive statements based on the four stages of encouragement.

WORKSHOP 10: MEETING WITH THE SCHOOL PSYCHOLOGIST, THE GRADUATION CEREMONY AND AWARDING OF CERTIFICATES

Everything that you wanted to know . . .

APPENDIX A: INVITATION TO THE COURSE

Date: _____
To:
Parents of _____

Greetings! I am happy to inform you that a course for parents will be opened on the subject of "How to become more effective parents" based on the program by Dr. Joseph Prinz, clinical psychologist and director of the Department of Education and Welfare Services (Shahar) in the Ministry of Education in Jerusalem. In this course we will study, among other subjects,

How to reinforce your child's self-confidence;
How to cut down on the children's quarrels at home; and
How to improve communication between members of the family.

The course will consist of ten weekly sessions on _____ (day of week) at _____ (hour). Each session lasts two hours.

The cost of participation is one dollar per session. Please pay the whole amount in advance, ten dollars, for all the sessions.

Parents who wish to enroll should contact me. I will be happy to see you participate in a course that will contribute to our children.

Yours truly,

APPENDIX B: ROSE-COLORED GLASSES—GUIDANCE FOR PARENTS

It's worthwhile investing twenty hours to be better parents to our children:

Two hours—To learn how good children are, to see the goodness
Two hours—To learn how to reinforce the good in our children
Two hours—To learn how much we, as a family, are dependent on each other
Two hours—To learn what to do when children quarrel

Two hours—To learn that the child wonders and experiments, makes mistakes, and that it's all right

Two hours—To learn how to be only the child's parent and not another volunteer doing the teacher's job

Two hours—To learn the importance of setting limits for the child

Two hours—To learn how to act consistently even when the parents disagree

Two hours—To learn how things can be done differently

Two hours—For "Everything you wanted to know but didn't dare to ask"—meeting the psychologist.

All of this in a course to be held at _____

Length of course—ten weekly meetings

Days and hours of activity _____

The first meeting will be on _____ (day) on _____ (date) at _____ (hour).

The group leader _____ (graduate of the Hadarim Program)

APPENDIX C: WEEKLY REMINDER

Date: _____

To:

The parents of _____

Our next meeting of the Hadarim Program—Guidance for Parents will take place on _____ (day) on _____ (date) at _____ (hour).

Parents who are interested in hearing positive things from me about their child should arrive at _____ (approximately twenty minutes before the beginning).

Looking forward to seeing you!

APPENDIX D: THE CONTRACT

Registration for the course obligates the participant to come to all ten sessions. The fee must be paid in advance for all ten sessions.

We are a group learning how to improve family connections.

The program will consist of short lectures, demonstrations, exercises, and simulations.

During the course we will concentrate on subjects related to raising children.

We will respect each other and show respect for the problems of others.

We will not raise subjects for discussion that we fear will harm us if spoken about outside of the course.

The discussions in the program will be held in rounds, in turn. Every member of the group will be given a chance to express himself or herself.

No smoking!

Please turn off your cellular phones at the beginning.

BIBLIOGRAPHY

Adler, A. 1957. *The practice and theory of individual psychology.* Trans. By P. Radin. New York: Humanities Press.

———. 1958. *What life should mean to you.* New York: Capricorn Books.

———. 1964. *Social interest: A challenge to mankind.* New York: Capricorn Books

———. 1979. *Superiority and social interest.* New York: Norton.

Bandura, A. 1977. Self-efficacy: Towards a unifying theory of behavioral change. *Psychological Review* 84:191–215.

———. 1997. *Self-efficacy: The exercise of control.* New York: W.H. Freeman.

Dinkmeyer, D., G. D. McKay, and J. S. Dinkmeyer. 1989. *Parenting young children.* Circle Pines, Minn.: AGS.

Dreikurs, R. 1967. *Psychodynamics, psychotherapy, and counseling.* Chicago: Adler Institute.

Erikson, E. 1963. *Childhood and society.* 2nd ed. New York: Norton.

Halberg, A. C. and A. Hakansson. 2003. Training program for parents of teenagers: Active parental participation in development and implementation. *Journal of Health Care* 7:7–16.

Nicholson, B. C., P. C. Janz, and R. A. Fox. 1998. Evaluating a brief parental education program for parents of young children. *Psychological Reports* 82:1107—end.

Prinz, Y. 2004. *Hadarim: Parental guidance.* Jerusalem: Ministry of Education.

Roberts, E., M. H. Bornstein, A. M. Slater, and J. Barrett. 1999. Early cognitive development and parental education. *Infant and child development* 8:49–62.

Weisner, T. S. 2001. The American dependency conflict: Continuities and discontinuities in behavior and values of countercultural parents and their children. *Ethos* 29:271–95.

Index

About the Editors and Contributors

Carol Wachs is a psychoanalyst and child psychologist in private practice in New York City. Dr. Wachs is coauthor, with Linda Jacobs, of *Parent Therapy: A Relational Alternative to Working with Children*. She sees individuals, couples, and parents and also consults with physicians on parenting issues.

Linda Jacobs is associate professor, Department of Human Development and Leadership, Long Island University. Dr. Jacobs is a psychoanalyst and professor of graduate studies in school psychology. She is the coauthor of the book *Parent Therapy: A Relational Alternative to Working with Children* with Carol Wachs (Jason Aronson, 2002) and is in private practice in New York City.

Elizabeth Berger, M.D., is a board certified child and adolescent psychiatrist and the author of *Raising Kids with Character: Developing Trust and Personal Integrity in Children* (Rowman & Littlefield, 2006). Dr. Berger has thirty years of experience treating children and families in community settings, hospitals, and private practice. She is a member of the American Academy of Child and Adolescent Psychiatry and has been on the faculty of the Columbia University College of Physicians and Surgeons, Northwestern University Medical School and University of Cincinnati College of Medicine.

Susan Coates, Ph.D., is associate clinical professor of psychology in psychiatry, Columbia University College of Physicians and Surgeons, and director of The Parent-Infant Program at Columbia University Center for Psychoanalytic Training and Research.

Esther Cohen, Ph.D., is a professor and the former head of the graduate program for child-clinical and school psychology at the Hebrew University of Jerusalem, Israel. She is a licensed supervisor in clinical psychology and family therapy. Her main research and clinical interests focus on parenthood and its development and change, and on the effects of exposure to terrorism on parents and children and preventive and posttraumatic interventions. Her latest book, *School-based Multi-systemic Interventions for Mass Trauma*, with Avigdor Klingman, was published in 2004.

Peter Deri is a graduate of the New York University postdoctoral program in psychoanalysis and psychotherapy and has a practice with children and adults in New York and White Plains, NY. Dr. Deri is a consultant to a number of preschool special education programs.

Judith Harel is senior clinical and developmental psychologist and a professor at the graduate program in clinical-educational psychology in the Department of Psychology, Haifa University, Haifa, Israel.

Hayuta Kaplan is senior clinical and developmental psychologist and teaches in the graduate program in clinical-educational psychology in the Department of Psychology, Haifa University, Haifa, Israel.

Sharon Kozberg has a private practice in psychotherapy, psychoanalysis, and couple therapy. Dr. Kozberg teaches in the postdoctoral program in marriage and couple therapy at Adelphi University and in the advanced specialization in couple and family therapy at the New York University postdoctoral program in psychotherapy and psychoanalysis.

James Lock, M.D., Ph.D., is associate professor of child psychiatry and pediatrics in the department of psychology and behavioral sciences at Stanford University School of Medicine where he has taught since 1993. He is board certified in adult as well as child and adolescent psychiatry. In the division of child psychiatry and child development, he is currently director of the eating disorders program that consists of both inpatient and outpatient treatment facilities. His major research and clinical interests are in psychotherapy research for children and adolescents, specifically for those with eating disorders, and in the psychosexual development of children and adolescents and related risks for psychopathology. Dr. Lock has published more than one hundred articles, abstracts, and book chapters. He is the author of *Help Your Teenager Beat an Eating Disorder* and coauthor, with Doctors le Grange, Agras, and Dare, of *Treatment Manual for Anorexia Nervosa: A Family-Based Approach*, the only evidence-based treatment manual for anorexia nervosa. He serves on the editorial panel of many scientific journals, has lectured widely in the United States, Europe, and Australia, and is the principal investigator (at Stanford) on an NIH-funded multi-site trial comparing individual family approaches to anorexia nervosa in adolescents.

Etan Lwow, M.D., is from the Israel Institute of Psychoanalysis and he is a psychiatrist who treats the parents of children and adolescents in private practice in Jerusalem, Israel.

Kerry Kelly Novick and **Jack Novick** are child, adolescent, and adult psychoanalysts on the faculty of the Michigan Psychoanalytic Institute and the Michigan Psychoanalytic Council. They trained with Anna Freud in London and have been working with children and families for thirty-five years. They joined other colleagues to found a nonprofit psychoanalytic school, Allen Creek Preschool, in Ann Arbor.

Raya Patt is senior clinical and developmental psychologist and teaches in the graduate program in clinical-educational psychology in the Department of Psychology, Haifa University, Haifa, Israel. She is also a senior psychologist at the Psychological-Developmental Clinic, Ministry of Health, Haifa, Israel.

Joseph Prinz is a clinical psychologist and educator from Jerusalem, Israel, who earned his doctorate at the Adler School of Professional Psychology in Chicago. He developed the Hadarim parent guidance program while working as administrator of educational welfare and neighborhood rehabilitation programs for the district of Jerusalem. Dr. Prinz has trained kindergarten and elementary school teachers in Israel to teach Adlerian parenting techniques to the parents of their pupils. He is one of the founders of the Adlerian Society of Jerusalem and is currently adapting the Hadarim program for use with at-risk youth.

Ionas Sapountzis, Ph.D., is associate professor at the School Psychology Program of Long Island University, Brooklyn Campus. He is also faculty and supervisor at the post-doctoral program in psychoanalysis and psychotherapy of the Derner Institute, Adelphi University, and at the post-doctoral program in child, adolescent, and family psychotherapy of the Derner Institute, Adelphi University. Dr. Sapountzis maintains a private practice in Garden City, New York.

Daniel Schechter, M.D., is assistant professor of clinical psychiatry (in pediatrics), Columbia University College of Physicians and Surgeons, medical director at the Infant-Family Service, New York-Presbyterian Hospital, and director of research at The Parent-Infant Program, Columbia University Center for Psychoanalytic Training and Research.

Stephen Seligman, a psychoanalyst and clinical psychologist, is clinical professor of psychiatry at the Infant-Parent Program, University of California, San Francisco. He is coeditor in chief of *Psychoanalytic Dialogues*, associate editor of *Studies in Gender and Sexuality*, and a member of the founding executive board of the *Journal of Infant, Child and Adolescent Psychotherapy*. He is a member of the faculty of the San Francisco Psychoanalytic Institute, the NYU Postdoctoral Program in Psychoanalysis, and the Infant Studies Program of the Jewish Board of Family and Children's Services in New York City. He is a personal and supervising analyst at the Psychoanalytic Institute of Northern California.

Arietta Slade, Ph.D., is professor of clinical and developmental psychology at the City University of New York and associate research scientist at the Yale Child Study Center. She has also been in private practice for more than twenty years, working with both children and adults. She has published widely in a number of areas including the clinical implications of attachment theory and research, the interface between psychoanalysis and attachment theory, the development of the parent-child relationship and parental representations of the child, the relational contexts of play and early symbolization, and—most recently—the development of parental reflective functioning. She is editor, with Dennie Wolf, of *Children at Play: Developmental and Clinical Approaches to Meaning and Representation*. She is on the editorial board of *Attachment and Human Development* and reviews regularly for a number of scholarly journals.